Two-Spirit People

Two-Spirit People

Native American Gender Identity,
Sexuality, and Spirituality

Edited by Sue-Ellen Jacobs, Wesley Thomas,
and Sabine Lang

University of Illinois Press
Urbana and Chicago

Illini Books edition, 1997

© 1997 by the Board of Trustees of the
University of Illinois
The copyright to "Reflections on a Mescalero Apache
Singer of Ceremonies" is retained by Claire R. Farrer due
to a prior agreement with the Mescalero Apache Tribal
Council.
Manufactured in the United States of America.
I 2 3 4 5 C P 5 4 3 2
This book is printed on acid-free paper.

Library of Congress Cataloging-in-Publication Data
Two-spirit people : Native American gender identity,
sexuality, and spirituality / edited by Sue-Ellen Jacobs,
Wesley Thomas, and Sabine Lang.
p. cm.
Includes bibliographical references (p.   ) and index.
ISBN 0-252-02344-7 (acid-free paper). —
ISBN 0-252-06645-6 (pbk. : acid-free paper)
1. Indians of North America—Sexual behavior.
2. Indian women—North America—Sexual behavior.
3. Gays—North America—Identity. 4. Lesbians—North
America—Identity. 5. Gay men—North America—
Social conditions. 6. Lesbians—North America—Social
conditions.
I. Jacobs, Sue-Ellen, 1936– . II. Thomas, Wesley, 1954– .
III. Lang, Sabine, 1958– .
E98.S48T86   1997
306.7'089'97—dc21   96-51214
CIP

★ ★

This book is dedicated to the memory of
Arnold R. Pilling in gratitude for his monetary
and spiritual support of this project
and to the memory of those Native Americans
who have died as a result of homophobia,
HIV/AIDS, and racism.

May this publication assist in decreasing
the death and destruction caused by these
social ills.

Contents

Acknowledgments

Our collective expression of gratitude goes to Sydel Silverman for believing in this project from the outset, to Laurie Obbink for working with us once the funding was awarded by the Wenner-Gren Foundation, and to the Wenner-Gren Foundation for Anthropological Research for generously supporting conferences in Washington, D.C., in 1993 and Chicago in 1994. We also thank all of the participants of the first and second conferences as well as those who participated in or attended the 1993 American Anthropological Association session entitled "Revisiting the 'North American Berdache' Empirically and Theoretically." We appreciate David Aberle's encouragement and support and are grateful to Lucille Horn, conference director of the American Anthropological Association, and Deborah Gewertz, program editor for the ninety-second annual AAA meeting, for assuring that our session in Washington, D.C., would run smoothly on the day immediately after the first Wenner-Gren Conference. Our appreciation also goes to the Women Studies Program at the University of Washington for providing assistance with telephone, copying, and mailing costs as well as serving as the institutional conduit for securing the funding necessary to hold both conferences and prepare the manuscript for this volume. Susan Jeffords made doing so possible. The University of Washington Graduate School provided $100 to facilitate manuscript preparation.

We also thank those from the Seattle Native gay/lesbian/two-spirit community who gathered at Sue-Ellen Jacobs's house in January 1994 to write the proposal for the second conference in Chicago and Doyle

Robertson and Greg Jeresek for their input as well as for videotaping "the anthropologists at work" that day and evening. Tim Haye of the Chicago Indian Center, Anawin, arranged the honoring dinner for the Native participants and two evenings of entertainment during the second conference, which helped lighten our spirits while working on heavy topics. We thank all who prepared the dinner, greeted us, and made us feel welcome at the Anawin Center.

Paul Adams worked untold hours above those required for his job at Chicago's Field Museum, literally risking his life and health in order to assure that the Wenner-Gren Foundation Conference in Chicago would be successful. He arranged housing for participants, obtained space in the museum, arranged for a reception there, and provided equipment and access to specific collections.

Our enduring gratitude also goes to Randy Burns, Bill Gibson, Erna Pahe, and other members of Gay American Indians in San Francisco for their work with us in 1992 and for the work they have been doing to "meet the needs of [gay American Indians], to foster group interaction and solidarity, and to provide a support system to meet the specialized needs of an ethnic group" (Medicine 1979 and in this volume). Even though not everyone who met in San Francisco in 1992 was able to be together for the last conference, those not with us in person were so in spirit because we were frequently drawn back to the ideas and concerns expressed in the remarkable meeting at GAI in November 1992. We were also inspired by their writings from 1988 (Gay American Indians, comps., ed. Roscoe 1988).

William L. Leap of American University offered detailed suggestions for improving the volume's content and structure after careful readings of two versions of the manuscript. Elizabeth G. Dulany, our editor at University of Illinois Press, successfully argued that her press should get this work for publication, and she negotiated skillfully through frequent telephone conversations and faxes. We are sincerely grateful for their strong, earnest, and unwavering support from the outset. We also appreciate those anonymous reviewers who gave important, supportive suggestions for revisions to all contributors. On behalf of all contributors, we extend appreciation to our copy editor, Mary Giles, for her attention to details.

On October 27, 1994, our dear colleague Arnold Pilling died from complications associated with AIDS. We acknowledge posthumously that which he would not let us do before his death: generous financial support to our project that allowed us to prepare the second Wenner-

Gren Foundation grant application and support specific aspects of the second conference. In spite of suffering from conditions related to AIDS, he finished his chapter (chapter 3), assuring that details were in order, two months before his death. His generosity of spirit, his intellectual support, and his genuine interest in Native American cultures were inspirationally consistent.

Finally, we wish to acknowledge the leadership provided by Beatrice Medicine. Our success is due in large part to her determination from the outset that there should be a true dialogue between Native and non-Native people who have dealt with, or want to do so, the topic of Native American gender diversity and sexuality. Without her support this entire enterprise (from the conferences to the book publication) would have failed in its overall objective: to engage two-spirit Native Americans in direct conversation with those non-Native scholars who have written about them in order to bring to light the differences between "'lived life' and the way it is characterized in anthropological and historical writings" (Introduction). We extend our heartfelt thanks for attending the meeting with GAI in San Francisco, for being at each session, for reading all the papers and essays, for keeping us focused and on track at both Wenner-Gren conferences, and for giving us all courage to continue our work.

References Cited

Medicine, Bea. 1979. "Changing Native American Sex Roles in an Urban Context." Unpublished ms.

Roscoe, Will, ed. 1988. *Living the Spirit: A Gay American Indian Anthology.* Compiled by Gay American Indians. New York: St. Martin's Press.

Two-Spirit People

Introduction

*Sue-Ellen Jacobs, Wesley Thomas (Navajo),
and Sabine Lang*

In U.S. popular culture of the 1990s, gender bending, gender blending, gender changing, and more have become increasingly a part of the public landscape, with performances and presentations of self by people of diverse ages, races, ethnic groups, and classes. Through the media, in stories ranging from those about *The Adventures of Priscilla Queen of the Desert* (a film depicting the adventures of a male-to-female transgender person who travels the Outback with two male professional drag queens or transvestites) to those about gay rights and antihomosexual movements, the general public watches and engages in discussions of this experimental moment as people stretch and push the boundaries of gender markers and categories. In academic circles since the early 1980s, studies of gender and sexuality have led to a proliferation of new professional organizations (e.g., the Society of Lesbian and Gay Anthropologists), journals (e.g., *GLQ: The Journal of Lesbian and Gay Studies*), and books (see the references cited for each chapter in this volume) as well as new specialties within old departments and the creation of interdisciplinary departments—or at least degree-granting programs in lesbian and gay studies, gender studies, and queer theory. Thus there is a body of literature, in large part stimulated by the politics of location that lesbian, gay, bisexual, transgender, and other scholars have brought to their search for scientific understanding of sexual and gender diversity.

In our work, we use the term *gender* to refer specifically to cultural rules, ideologies, and expected behaviors for individuals of diverse phenotypes and psychosocial characteristics. *Gender identities* refers to people's own locations within a range of gender identity possibilities within their cultures. We restrict our use of *sex* to biological phenotypes and use *sexualities* for the range of behaviors called "homosexuality," "heterosexuality," "bisexuality," "trisexuality," and the like. The studies extend beyond psychological and sociological normative studies of years past to encompass the vast complexity of human desire, eroticism, and self-definitions of personhood.

Cross-cultural comparative studies have shown that genders and sexualities are not always fixed into only two marked categories. Institutionalized gender diversity is found throughout the world but not in all cultures. In Native North America, there were and still are cultures in which more than two gender categories are marked. There is more than a hundred years of writing on this subject (albeit sporadic until the mid-twentieth century). Contemporary studies of Native American gender diversity and sexuality are situated squarely within larger academic and public interests.

Two-spirit is the term that all but one of the contributors to this book have agreed to use—for the time being—when writing about those who have previously been termed "berdache" [*sic*] by anthropologists, historians, sexologists, sociologists, psychologists, and other writers on the subject of sexuality and gender. The term *two-spirit* (or *two-spirited*) was coined in 1990 by Native American individuals during the third Native American/First Nations gay and lesbian conference in Winnipeg (LaFortune [Anguksuar] 1993). Originating as a term for contemporary Native American gays and lesbians as well as people who have been referred to as "berdache" by anthropologists and other scholars, it has come to refer to a number of Native American roles and identities past and present, including

* contemporary Native Americans/First Nations individuals who are gay or lesbian;
* contemporary Native American/First Nations gender categories;
* the traditions wherein multiple gender categories and sexualities are institutionalized in Native American/First Nations tribal cultures;
* traditions of gender diversity in other, non-Native American cultures;[1]
* transvestites, transsexuals, and transgendered people; and
* drag queens and butches (cf. Tietz 1996:205).

The decision by Native Americans (indigenous people of the United States) and those of the First Nations (indigenous people of Canada) who attended the Winnipeg and subsequent conference to use the label *two-spirit* was deliberate, with a clear intention to distance themselves from non-Native gays and lesbians. It seems to us of interesting coincidence that this marked distancing happened at a time when the governments of United States and Canada were just beginning to respond to the AIDS epidemic in the gay community. Many urban Native American men attempted to return home to their reservations to spend their last years with their families before dying from complications of HIV infection. Each of us has heard personal stories from men who were not welcome "home" because they had that "white gay man's disease" and that gayness was not part of traditional culture. Using the word "two-spirit" emphasizes the spiritual aspect of one's life and downplays the homosexual persona (see Little Thunder, Red Earth, Tafoya, and Robertson in this volume). Homophobia may not be completely thwarted by using the term, but it may be held off in some instances.

"Berdache" is now considered to be an inappropriate and insulting term by a number of Native Americans as well as by anthropologists. To indicate that fact, it will be put in quotation marks whenever used in this book (for example, when the authors quote or refer to older sources where the term is used). The English phrase *two-spirit,* which originated primarily in urban Native American/First Nations contexts where English serves as a lingua franca to bridge cultural and linguistic differences, is not meant to be translated into Native American languages and terms. To do so may change the common meaning it has acquired since the early 1990s by self-identified two-spirit Native Americans. In some cultural contexts, translating it to a Native language could even be dangerous. For example, if "two-spirit" were translated into one of the Athapaskan languages (such as Navajo or Apache) the word could be understood to mean that such a person possesses both a living and a dead spirit—not a desirable situation (see Thomas in this volume). If "two-spirit" were translated into Shoshone, the literal translation would be "ghost" (Hall 1994). As a generic term for Native American gays, lesbians, transgendered individuals, and other persons who are not heterosexual or who are ambivalent in terms of gender, it is used in urban and rural environments, but not by all Native Americans who are, for example, self-identified as "gay," "lesbian," "bisexual," "transgender," or "third gender" (that is, people who are neither women nor men within systems of multiple genders). Some reject the term just as others reject "berdache."

"Berdache" has been employed to refer to special gender roles in Native American cultures that anthropologists have interpreted as ceremonial transvestism, institutionalized homosexuality, and gender variance/multiple genders. "Gender variance" is defined by Jacobs and Cromwell (1992:63–64) as "cultural expressions of multiple genders (i.e., more than two) and the opportunity for individuals to change gender roles and identities over the course of their lifetimes." We use *gender variance* and *gender diversity* interchangeably.

Detailed historiographies of the use of "berdache" are contained in Callender and Kochems (1983), Jacobs (1968), Roscoe (1987), and Williams (1986). The earliest use of the term Jacobs could find when doing research for "Berdache: A Brief Review of the Literature" (1968) was in the *Jesuit Relations* (from the 1700s), where such individuals were condemned. "The word originally came from the Persian *bardaj* [*barah*], and via the Arabs [*bardaj*] spread to the Italian language as *bardasso* [*berdasia*], and to the Spanish as *bardaxa* or *bardaje* [*bardaja*] by the beginning of the sixteenth century. About the same time the word appeared in French as *bardache*. . . [and] refers to the passive homosexual partner" (Williams 1986:9; alternative spellings from Jacobs 1968 and elsewhere appear in brackets). The term has also been translated as "kept boy" or "male prostitute" (Angelino and Shedd 1955:121–22). The *Oxford English Dictionary* gives a cross-reference for "berdache" to "catamite," which is translated as "a boy kept for unnatural purposes." With this etymology, it should come as no surprise that many Native American gay, lesbian, transgender, and other two-spirit people consider the term "berdache" derogatory and insulting.

The French term *bardache* became transliterated to *berdache* by later writers who entered it into the anthropological literature. There are also instances of the word being spelled as *broadashe, bundosh/bowdash, berdach, berdash, bredache, bredaches, bardash, berdêches, bird-ash, birdashes,* and *bradaje,* among others (this comes largely from Will Roscoe's 1993 compilation of frontier terms for two-spirits; see also Williams 1986 and contemporary dictionaries). Regardless of its spelling, the word has been used in anthropological writings not to imply that the individuals so labeled were "kept boys" or "male prostitutes" but to refer to what the writers perceived to be transvestism, homosexuality, hermaphrodism, and transgenderism as institutions viewed positively in Native American cultures (especially Blackwood 1984; Callender and

Kochems 1983, 1986; Jacobs 1968; Williams 1986). This sometimes ide-
alizing view has led to a relatively recent romanticization of purported positively sanctioned pan-Indian gender or sexual categories that do
not fit the reality of experiences faced by many contemporary gay, lesbian, third-gender, transgender, and otherwise two-spirit Native Americans who have had to leave their reservations or other communities
because of the effects of homophobia. Some of the earlier writings have
led them, as well as non-Native anthropologists and other scholars and
non-Native lesbians, gays, bisexuals, transsexuals, transgenders, and
others, to seek the primordial bliss of the supposed acceptance or even
revered status of "berdaches" in Native American cultures (see Cromwell, Jacobs, and Kochems and Jacobs in this volume; for an equally
inclusive interpretation that is completely opposite see Trexler 1995).

The fact is that in only some instances are third-gender people recognized as such with a specific linguistic marker and honored, accepted, and raised "to be the way they are" (see Farrer in this volume). The
same holds true of other two-spirit people, such as gays and lesbians,
who sometimes are supported by their families and communities (see
Anguksuar, Red Earth, Robertson, and Thomas in this volume). Homophobia in Native American communities is being addressed by
scholars and activists within the gay Native American and two-spirit
movements. At annual local and international gay/lesbian/two-spirit
gatherings they report on varying degrees of success in overcoming
homophobia in diverse locations (on the gatherings, see Lang in this
volume).

Nearly all academic publications investigating Native American sexuality or gender diversity have tended to emphasize male homosexualities (e.g., Williams 1986) or male gender blending (e.g., Roscoe 1991).
Hardly anything has been written in readily accessible social science literature about manly women, female homosexualities, or female-bodied
third or fourth genders, even though they have been documented in
tribes that range from the Southwest through the Plains and the Great
Lakes to the Subarctic (the exception is Williams 1986, ch. 11, concerning female gender variance). By the mid-1990s some of these females
were self-named "lesbians"; some were "berdaches" as defined by Blackwood (1984), Callender and Kochems (1983), and Lang (1990) in relation
to women; some used "dyke" (Allen 1986); others used the word *amazon*
(Williams 1986); and some identified themselves as two-spirit.

Until the later 1980s "berdache" was used sporadically by Native
Americans themselves. We know of several gay Native American orga-

nizations and one support group for non-Native transsexuals and trans-vestites (Bolin 1988:xi, 2, passim) who called themselves the "Berdache Society." Throughout North America, however, there are urban Native Americans who have come to refer to themselves as "two-spirit people," a term that is the result of research by them into traditions of gender diversity and homosexuality in their respective tribes. "Two-spirit" is used to include mainly Native American gays and lesbians as well as those individuals who identify with traditional tribal gender categories, as opposed to Western gay and lesbian identities (Burns [with Woods] 1993; Pahe 1993; Tafoya 1992).

Whereas Native Americans in some instances found writings by non-Native anthropologists a source of positive identity, others have ac-cused them of presenting an over-romanticized, misrepresented picture of the life circumstances of people who are not heterosexual or who are third gender in Native American cultures (Allen 1986; Gutiérrez 1989). As has already been suggested, "berdache" has largely become conflat-ed with the Western concept of homosexuality in the writings of a number of non-Natives. In fact, some have gone so far as to claim "ber-daches" as antecedents to contemporary gays in Western culture (e.g., Grahn 1984; Roscoe 1988a). This has occurred in spite of Callender and Kochems's article (1983), in which the differences between homosexu-ality as defined in Western culture and same-sex relationships within the context of gender diversity in Native American cultures were com-pellingly pointed out. Furthermore, it appears that social scientists in general are still confused about Native American gender diversity and sexualities, as evidenced by an article written by Robert Fulton and Steven W. Anderson, who are sociologists, in late 1992, and Ralph Bol-ton's discoveries (1995) of the use of "berdache" constructs in introduc-tory anthropology, sociology, and sexology books. The work leading to the publication of this book was inspired by our recognition of such problems.

Our Origin Story

The idea for this project grew from conversations we began in Seattle, Washington, in the spring of 1992. In March 1992, Sabine Lang had come to the United States from Hamburg, Germany, on a postdoctoral grant from the Deutsche Forschungsgemeinschaft to undertake a year-long study of "female berdaches" in contemporary Native American cultures. Soon after embarking on her project, she decided to include other kinds of two-spirit people (gays, lesbians, bisexuals, and transgenders) in her research. Lang had written her Ph.D. dissertation on the "North American berdache," alternative gender roles for women, and homosexuality in Native American cultures (Lang 1990, 1997). Walter L. Williams, whose seminal work *The Spirit and the Flesh: Sexual Diversity in American Indian Culture* had been published 1986, had agreed to be her academic sponsor and arranged for Lang to hold the position of affiliated scholar at the University of Southern California in Los Angeles, where he is a professor of anthropology.

Lang's travels led her to Seattle late in April 1992, and Wesley Thomas introduced her around the Seattle Native American lesbian/gay/two-spirit community. Over the course of some four weeks she met some women but mostly men in this community. From there she went to San Francisco to resume conversations with members of the Gay American Indians organization; then to Arizona for the Womyn's Sun Dance conducted by Beverly Little Thunder (Lang in this volume); then back to Los Angeles to write fieldnotes; and then to New Mexico to join Thomas and his family and try to locate Navajo *nádleeh* people.[2] From there, she and Thomas decided to attend the international two-spirit gathering in British Columbia in August 1992.

After Lang and Thomas attended the gathering, they joined Jacobs in Seattle, and we began exploring the differences between our understanding of the life experiences of two-spirit friends and the ways their lives had been characterized in anthropological and historical writings. Many of these writings center around individuals, statuses, and roles that were alive decades ago, a hundred years ago, and sometimes even three hundred years ago (e.g., Trexler 1995) when tribal cultures and traditions of gender diversity were different, and scholars' gazes were framed by the intellectual and clerical-philosophical thinking of their eras.

Hardly any writing has dealt with two-spirit people who live now. The most notable exception is Medicine's "Changing Native American Sex Roles in an Urban Context" (chapter 6 in this volume). That paper, written in 1979, often cited as a manuscript, and circulated widely among academic and community colleagues, has never been published and is included in this book because its insights and challenges are as relevant now as when they were written.

We became intrigued by the near absence of contemporary Native American voices in writings published in scholarly journals and by academic and trade presses. Although *Living the Spirit,* an edited collection, appeared in 1988 (Gay American Indians comps., ed. Roscoe), we seldom saw it cited. We agreed with two-spirit friends that for too long discussions of Native American gender diversity and sexuality had taken place without benefit of shared discourse with Native Americans, in spite of the fact that activism on the topic, as well as research and publications by Native people, had increased for a decade.

Thus, we decided to approach anthropologists and historians who were well known for their work in this area and see whether they would be willing to participate in an American Anthropological Association (AAA) meeting session at which Native Americans would also be invited to participate. Simultaneously, contact was made with Gay American Indians (GAI) in San Francisco to see if they would be willing to meet with us while we were there for the 1992 AAA meeting to discuss our idea and help plan such a session. In response, GAI sent out a dinner invitation to all Native American anthropologists and non-Native anthropologists and others who had written about Native Americans (especially about the "berdache") and who planned to attend the AAA meeting. Only those we three had contacted personally (and not all of them) accepted the invitation. The evening was devoted to dinner, discussion, and the showing of numerous private videotape presentations documenting aspects of gay, lesbian, and two-spirit Native Americans' lives. Before we were given the privilege of viewing the videotapes, but after we were fed, the non-Native anthropologists were interrogated about their motives, interests, experiences, and ambitions in investigating Native American gender diversity and sexuality. Major concerns of the Native Americans included what they perceived to be the continuous misuse of the derogatory term "berdache" for Native lesbians, gays, third-gender, and two-spirit people and the lack of thorough research on the traditional roles of "berdaches," contemporary gay, lesbian, and two-spirit people, and contemporary gender diversity and sexualities in Native American communities. At the end of the meeting, GAI members encouraged us to proceed with the planning of the session for the AAA annual meeting in 1993, and several agreed to participate.

Then Jacobs had the occasion to talk with Sydel Silverman, president of the Wenner-Gren Foundation for Anthropological Research in New York City, about the possibility of funding a conference where non-Native anthropologists would "face the Nations" and clearly articulate their theories and other ideas about Native American sexuality and gender diversity, past and present. We wanted a one-day, private, "closed" conference where we could sort out differences that might appear in our papers before we read them in public at the AAA session. Even before the last point was spoken, Silverman anticipated the need and suggested that we apply for funding. We did, and the foundation funded our conference on "Revisiting the 'North American Berdache' Empirically and Theoretically," held in Washington, D.C., on November 17, 1993, a day before the AAA session that used the same title. It was followed by a second conference held at the Field Museum of Natural History in Chicago in May 1994.

Our Goals

The primary goal of the 1993 Wenner-Gren Conference and AAA session was to convene both Native American and non-Native academic and community scholars of gender studies and sexuality for a shared discourse on matters concerning constructions of gender, gender diversity, and sexualities in Native American cultures. There also was a need to de-romanticize the concept of "berdache" without depriving contemporary two-spirit Native Americans of role models critical for their identities and the establishment of their roles and places within their communities.

We assume the universality of homosexual behavior. We also assume, for research purposes, that transvestism or cross-dressing occurs everywhere in some form or another and that transgender behavior occurs either for a lifetime (e.g., among the Chuckchee of Siberia [Bogoras 1904–8]) or for a certain period or function (e.g., manly-hearted women [Lewis 1941] and women who go to war [Medicine 1983]). These latter categories are not related to sexual object choice (see Kochems 1993 and Kochems and Jacobs in this volume, which both elaborate and update aspects of Callender and Kochems 1983) or to sexuality and sexual identity. They center on diversity in gender identities, roles, and statuses.

Four principal issues for further discussion emerged at the end of the first conference:

1. areas of conflict between native terminologies and concepts relating to gender and sexual identities and the way anthropologists, historians, and others have misread these as "berdache";
2. a redress of failed accountability to Native American consultants who have worked willingly and sometimes unwittingly with anthropologists;

3. the ethics of fieldwork in the study of homosexuality, gender diversity, and sexuality in general in Native American cultures; and

4. our collective challenge to the "berdache" canon and the establishment of priorities in research. The term was challenged by both Native and non-Native participants as being derogatory and inappropriate and as not reflecting gender roles, identities, and sexualities as lived by Native Americans.

It was emphasized during the conference that some urban non-heterosexual Native Americans have come to refer to themselves as "two-spirit (or two-spirited) people." In some cases people who are not heterosexual and who are searching for a meaningful label that ties them to traditions of their cultural past choose to use the historically appropriate term in order to validate their experience in life as the only way they can satisfy their desire to be socially recognized in their culture (cf. Herdt in this volume). Some of the culturally appropriate terms being used are *winkte* (Siouian speakers; see Robertson and Red Earth in this volume); *kwidó* (Tewa speakers; see Jacobs in this volume); and *nádleeh* (Navajo speakers; see Pahe 1993; Epple, House, and Thomas in this volume). In any case, Native Americans self-identify in terms of native categories rather than embrace terminologies and categories that anthropologists and others impose on their behaviors.

The empirical issues raised at the first conference were those to be addressed at the second, also funded by the Wenner-Gren Foundation. Most papers from 1993 were revised and distributed before we gathered in Chicago for three days of intensive discussion and work that was the basis for further revision.

Our work has centered on locating data that would confirm (or disprove) earlier writing and more recent writing by anthropologists, historians, and Native American scholars on Native American constructions of genders and sexualities. For example, Arnold Pilling's contribution investigates the Zuni census data and places the work of historian Will Roscoe (1991) in a new light. Wesley Thomas presents the first Navajo critique of non-Navajo writings on Navajo constructions of gender and sexuality, thereby challenging the earlier writings of Gifford (1940), Hill (1935, 1938), Matthews (1897), O'Bryan (1956), Reichard (1950), Witherspoon (1977), and others about *nádleeh* (spelled variously *nadle, natli,* and *nutli'*). Erna Pahe (1993), also Navajo, in turn challenged Thomas's and others' interpretations of Navajo gender categories, arguing that discussions that enumerate genders do not clarify the simplicity or the complexity of gender diversity within and across cultures. Michael Red Earth, Doyle Robertson, Anguksuar (all in this volume) and Randy Burns (with Woods, 1993) presented original narratives surrounded by theoretical arguments which, in part, support Williams's *The Spirit and the Flesh,* but they also disagree with some of his conclusions.

HIV/AIDS

The HIV/AIDS pandemic is one issue not addressed in the contributions to this volume because the emphasis in this first phase of our work has been to document the shift from European and Euro-American control of the discourse to Native American and First Nations self-naming, critical theory, and activisms. Yet the AIDS pandemic is of great concern to contemporary Native American gays, lesbians, and two-spirits, as it is to everyone else with any social conscience. The HIV virus is spreading rapidly on reservations, as it is everywhere. Tribal councils, the Indian Health Service, and communities-at-large face (often belatedly) the unwelcome necessity of coping with same-sex behavior rather than denying its existence (see Thomas in this volume for a commentary about Navajo male sexuality related to this issue). As everywhere else, it is by no means only gay or bisexual males or *winkte, nádleeh,* and *kwidó* who become infected; women, children, and heterosexual males also do so (Givan 1993). Still, there is a lot of fear and denial on the reservations concerning HIV/AIDS (Burns [with Woods] 1993) even though some tribal councils are beginning to invite Native American specialists on AIDS or activists from GAI and related organizations to educate them on the issue and various risk factors for infection, including those associated with the use of alcohol and controlled substances (drugs). Urban Native American health boards usually now have someone who specializes in HIV/AIDS education and support. Since approximately 1988 such health boards have published educational brochures specifically directed at Native American women and men.

National as well as regional and local conferences have dealt with Native American work on HIV/AIDS. In September 1994, for example, the National Institutes of Health and the Indian Health Service held a national conference, "HIV/AIDS in Native Communities: Maintaining Our Balance in the Circle of Life," in Albuquerque. Since 1990 the Navajo Nation AIDS Network has also had an annual conference to address all aspects of HIV infection, spread, and prevention and AIDS care, support, and treatment. And since 1988 the Tulalip Tribes have held numerous educational workshops and spiritual healings that emphasize HIV/AIDS. Native Americans who have worked with many different types of HIV/AIDS programs present papers at the conferences, and some hold workshops intended to explain why and how HIV transmission and AIDS-related diseases are not restricted to homosexuals or third-gender males.

Native people making presentations or holding workshops in Native communities (theirs or others) usually encounter conflicts with local people because of the lack of appropriate information concerning sexual behaviors of both heterosexual and homosexual males. It is rarely understood, for example, that in some cultural traditions third-gender male-bodied people do not have sex with one another—doing so would be considered homosexuality. They do have sex with straight or male-bodied men, which is considered to be heterosexual sex by people who conceptualize three (or more) gender categories (e.g., Thomas in this volume). But some Native American gay men do have sex with one another and understand that this is the accepted meaning of the word *homosexual* in the larger society and for many people in their own communities, especially those who use Western cultural concepts. This is a critical issue for understanding the difference between gay males and those whose cultural framework contains an active contemporary concept of third gender.

Native Americans who no longer have (or never had) multiple-gender categories within their traditional cultures have come to conflate gender identity and sexuality, assuming, for example, that persons who identify themselves as heterosexual men will not contract HIV or other sexually transmitted diseases even when occasionally engaging in same-sex behavior. We know of at least one AIDS educator who has told people in his community that *"nádleeh* only have sexual relationships with one another" and that "homosexual behavior does not exist outside of that context." Clearly, such a statement does not reflect the cultural construction of homosexuality as described in the preceding paragraph; nor does it acknowledge the male-to-male-to-female transmission pattern of HIV infection. Such false information contributes to the increasing spread of HIV infection. An understanding of the sexualities and gender constructions various Native peoples use is critical for intervention and prevention programs that concern the genital transmission of HIV and other sexually transmitted diseases.

Even though HIV/AIDS is not discussed by anyone in this volume, it is likely that the book will contribute to a better understanding of Native American sexualities, especially for those who are on the frontlines, helping people in the Native communities both on and off reservations cope with the impact of this pandemic. Thomas continues to work in the field, and Jacobs has done applied work in this regard.

Summary and Conclusions

Some contributors to this volume tend to emphasize terminology, classifications, and categories of gender (e.g., Cromwell, Epple, Lang, and Thomas); others focus on personhood, spirituality, and contextualization within their societies (e.g., Farrer, Hall, Anguksuar, Little Thunder, Robertson, and Tafoya). Goulet combines these approaches. Some address the issue of homophobia and its effect on the actualization of the full range of being a person in society (e.g., Jacobs, Robertson). We all know someone who desires to be able to be the revered person described by Blackwood (1984), Callender and Kochems (1983), Jacobs (1968), Lang (1990), and Williams (1986) when they write about the kind of social status once held by *winkte* (Lakota), *nádleeh* (Navajo), *kwidó* (Tewa), *tainna wa'ippe* (Shoshone), *dubuds* (Paiute), *lhamana* (Zuni), and the other marked individuals of the past who were not called words that mean "woman" or "man" in their respective societies. Some people come from traditions where there is so much power associated with and evoked by using a categorical term (e.g., *nádleeh*, medicine man, or clown) that to use the term signals other members of the culture that the person either is not what they are naming or that they are completely assimilated (Kehoe 1993; Tafoya 1994; Thomas in this volume). Others search for a meaningful label to tie them to their cultural traditions, and they may have no choice but to use some historically appropriate term in order to validate their experience in life as the only way to satisfy their desire to be socially recognized (cf. Herdt in this volume). Furthermore, it may be necessary to reject all association with historical terms and use another culture's system of markings for gender categories; for example, urban Navajos may find it more respectful of their tradition to define themselves as "gay males" or "lesbians" than as *nádleeh*. Still further, they may seek an intermediary way by rejecting both "lesbian" or "gay" and the traditional term by choosing the label "two-spirit."

Some of the issues that remain arise from conflicts inherent in conducting anthropology in Native American communities in the 1990s: the right of outsiders to name Native people and "tell everything they see" when working in Native American communities and the legal problems that emerge as intellectual property is appropriated. What happens when indigenous knowledge is taken without informed consent, full remuneration and attribution, and the acknowledgment of rights of ownership? Other issues arise from differences in perspectives associated with being academically oriented and community- (and individual-) oriented in research. No final resolutions to such disagreements are achieved in these pages.

There is much more work to be done in order to achieve understanding about the many textures, qualities, characteristics, and aspects of Native American gender identities and sexualities. As Clyde Hall (1994) cautions, "This is just the beginning, it is just the first step" of trying to open, establish, and maintain dialogue among "Native American two-spirit people and anthropologists." For some, there are life-threatening reasons why this work must proceed.

Jacobs and Farrer have known elder men on their respective reservations who appeared to live the "traditional berdache" roles as described by Allen (1986), Gay American Indians comps., ed. Roscoe (1988b), Martin and Voorhies (1975:84–107), and Williams (1986). But we also both know young men (boys) who have suffered grievously at the hands and words of people on their reservations, including relatives. In both instances, however, the boys' aunt or mother has protected them and tried to help them through the stages of ritual development. Homophobia stands firmly in the way for these boys. Did the elders we knew in the 1970s and 1980s go through the terrors of homophobia when they were boys? Were they "feminine" boys, "girlish" boys, or androgynous? How were they socialized to assume an accepted, sometimes revered, status in their communities?

Farrer and Jacobs have each spent almost a quarter of a century, and Thomas has spent a lifetime, in sustained relationships with a segment of the populations on the reservations where they have conducted fieldwork and continue to do so. That fieldwork could not have been done without the loving support of those Native Americans into whose families they have been incorporated. Thus, their perspective comes from living in a culturally defined (if not bounded) society where tradition informs current practice and is labeled proudly "Mescalero

Apache" (for Farrer), "San Juan Pueblo Tewa" (for Jacobs), and Diné, or Navajo (for Thomas). That there is homophobia in these tribal communities should come as no shock, yet it does because social scientists and others who have bought into the myth of the "primal bliss of the life of the ancient berdaches" were not present in that ancient past to see how manly women and womanly men were treated.

Recently, an Akimel O'odham (Pima) elder told Jacobs, "We have always had some of 'them' around, nobody really hurt them. Oh, they were always teased [a slight chuckle], especially as children, but they are just part of life so no one really thinks anything about it. They are just part of the community."

Notes

1. Jacobs and Cromwell have stopped using gender "variance" and now wish they had used "gender variability" in their 1992 paper. The word *variance* implies subjective departure from a norm; "variability," however, implies agency operating in context of a range of possibilities. Gender *diversity* has this same meaning and appears more often than "variance" in this volume.

2. In this volume, there are various spellings of *nádleeh;* all mean different things. *Nádleehí* refers to one person of the gender class *nádleeh. Nadleehe* refers to more than one *nádleehí. Nádleehé* appears in older spellings of *nádleehí.*

References Cited

Allen, Paula Gunn. 1986. *The Sacred Hoop: Recovering the Feminine in American Indian Traditions.* Boston: Beacon Press.

Angelino, Henry, and Charles L. Shedd. 1955. "A Note on Berdache." *American Anthropologist* 57(1): 121–26.

Blackwood, Evelyn. 1984. "Sexuality and Gender in Certain Native American Tribes: The Case of Cross-Gender Females." *Signs: Journal of Women in Culture and Society* 10(1): 1–42. Reprint. Wayne R. Dynes and Stephen Donaldson, eds. 1992. *Studies of Homosexuality.* Volume 2: *Ethnographic Studies of Homosexuality,* 23–38. New York: Garland.

Bogoras, Waldemar. 1904–8. "The Chuckchee." Reprint. F. Boaz, ed. 1975. *Memoirs of the American Museum of Natural History* 11(2), and in *Publications of the Jesup North Pacific Expedition* 7: 448–57. New York: G. E. Stechert.

Bolin, Anne. 1988. *In Search of Eve: Transsexual Rites of Passage.* New York: Bergin and Garvey.

Bolton, Ralph. 1995. Personal communication with Sue-Ellen Jacobs.

Burns, Randy (with Cayenne Woods). 1993. Untitled. Paper presented at "Revisiting the 'North American Berdache' Empirically and Theoretically." 92d annual meeting of the American Anthropological Association, Washington, D.C.

Callender, Charles, and Lee M. Kochems. 1983. "The North American Berdache." *Current Anthropology* 24(4): 443–70. Reprint. Wayne R. Dynes and Stephen Donaldson, eds. 1992. *Studies in Homosexuality.* Volume 2: *Ethnographic Studies of Homosexuality,* 273–88. New York: Garland.

———. 1986. "Men and Not-Men: Male Gender-Mixing Statuses and Homosexuality." In Anthropology and Homosexual Behavior, *Journal of Homosexual Behavior* 11 (3–4): 165–78. Republished. Evelyn Blackwood, ed. 1986. *The Many Faces of Homosexuality: Anthropological Approaches to Homosexual Behavior,* 165–78. New York: Harrington Park Press.

Fulton, Robert, and Steven W. Anderson. 1992. "The Amerindian 'Man-Woman': Gender, Liminality and Cultural Continuity." *Current Anthropology* 33(5): 603–10.

Gifford, Edward W. 1940. *Culture Element Distributions Twelve: Apache-Pueblo.* University of California Anthropological Records 4(1).

Givan, Janice Marie. 1993. "American Indian/Alaska Native Women with HIV Infection." Master's thesis, University of Washington-Seattle.

Grahn, Judy. 1984. *Another Mother Tongue: Gay Words, Gay Worlds.* New York: Beacon Press.

Gutiérrez, Ramón. 1989. "Must We Deracinate Indians to Find Gay Roots?" *Out/Look* 4: 61–67. Reprint. Wayne R. Dynes and Stephen Donaldson, eds. 1992. *Studies in Homosexuality.* Volume 2: *Ethnographic Studies of Homosexuality,* 175–81. New York: Garland.

Hall, Clyde. 1994. Personal communication with participants in the second Wenner-Gren Conference on "Revisiting the 'North American Berdache,'" Field Museum, Chicago.

Hill, Willard W. 1935. "The Status of the Hermaphrodite and Transvestite in Navaho Culture." *American Anthropologist* 37: 273–79.

———. 1938. "Note on the Pima Berdache." *American Anthropologist* 40(2): 338–40.

Jacobs, Sue-Ellen. 1968. "Berdache: A Brief Review of the Literature." *Colorado Anthropologist* 1(2): 25–40. Reprint. Wayne R. Dynes and Stephen Donaldson, eds. 1992. *Studies in Homosexuality.* Volume 2: *Ethnographic Studies of Homosexuality,* 273–88. New York: Garland.

Jacobs, Sue-Ellen, and Jason Cromwell. 1992. "Visions and Revisions of Reality: Reflections on Sex, Sexuality, Gender and Gender Variance." *Journal of Homosexuality* 23(4): 43–69.

Kehoe, Alice. 1993. Discussion. In the session "Revisiting the 'North American Berdache' Empirically and Theoretically." 92d annual meeting of the American Anthropological Association, Washington, D.C.

Kochems, Lee M. 1993. Discussion. In the session "Revisiting the 'North American Berdache' Empirically and Theoretically." 92d annual meeting of the American Anthropological Association, Washington, D.C.

LaFortune, Richard [Anguksuar]. 1993. Discussion. In the session "Revisiting the 'North American Berdache' Empirically and Theoretically." 92d annual meeting of the American Anthropological Association, Washington, D.C.

Lang, Sabine. 1990. *Männer als frauen—Frauen als männer: Geschlechtsrollenwechsel bei dei Indianern Nordamerikas.* Hamburg: Wayasbah.

———. 1997. *The Other Way: Gender Variance and Homosexuality among Contemporary Native Americans.* Austin: University of Texas Press.

Lewis, Oscar. 1941. "Manly-hearted Women among the Northern Piegan." *American Anthropologist* 43(n.s.): 173–87.

Martin, M. Kay, and Barbara Voorhies. 1975. *Female of the Species.* New York: Columbia University Press.

Matthews, Washington. 1897. *Navaho Legends.* Boston: Houghton Mifflin. Reprint. 1995. Salt Lake: University of Utah Press.

Medicine, Bea. 1983. "'Warrior Women'—Sex Role Alternatives for Plains Indian Women." In *The Hidden Half: Studies of Plains Indian Women,* 267–80. Edited by Patricia Albers and Beatrice Medicine. Lanham: University Press of America.

O'Bryan, Aileen. 1956. *The Diné: Origin Myths of the Navaho Indians.* Bureau of American Ethnology Bulletin 163. Washington, D.C.: Government Printing Office. Reprint. 1993. New York: Dover.

Pahe, Erna. 1993. Comments on papers read at "Revisiting the 'North American Berdache' Empirically and Theoretically." 92d annual meeting of the American Anthropological Association, Washington, D.C.

Reichard, Gladys A. 1950. *Navaho Religion: A Study of Symbolism.* New York: Bollingen Foundation. Reprint. 1990. Princeton: Princeton University Press.

Roscoe, Will. 1987. "Bibliography of Berdache and Alternative Gender Roles among North American Indians." *Journal of Homosexuality* 14(3–4): 81–171.

———. 1988a. "The Zuni Man-Woman." *Out/Look* 4: 56–67. Reprint. Wayne R. Dynes and Stephen Donaldson, eds. 1992. *Studies in Homosexuality.* Volume 2: *Ethnographic Studies of Homosexuality,* 358–69. New York: Garland.

———, ed. 1988b. *Living the Spirit: A Gay American Indian Anthology.* Compiled by Gay American Indians. New York: St. Martin's Press.

———. 1991. *The Zuni Man-Woman.* Albuquerque: University of New Mexico Press.

———. 1993. "Was We'wha a Homosexual?": Native American Survivance and the Two-Spirit Tradition." Paper read by Mildred Dickemann in the session, "Revisiting the 'North American Berdache' Empirically and

Theoretically" at the 92nd Annual Meeting of the American Anthropological Association, Washington, DC.

Tafoya, Terry. 1992. "Native Gay and Lesbian Issues: The Two-Spirited." In *Positively Gay: New Approaches to Gay and Lesbian Life,* ed. Betty Berzon. Berkeley: Celestial Arts Publishing.

———. 1994. Personal communication with Sue-Ellen Jacobs.

Tietz, Lüder. 1996. "Modern Rückbezüge auf Geschlechtsrollen Indianischer Kulturen." Master's thesis, University of Hamburg.

Trexler, Richard C. 1995. *Sex and Conquest: Gendered Violence, Political Order, and the European Conquest of the Americas.* Ithaca: Cornell University Press.

Williams, Walter L. 1986. *The Spirit and the Flesh: Sexual Diversity in American Indian Culture.* Boston: Beacon Press. Reprint 1991, with a new preface.

Witherspoon, Gary. 1977. *Language and Art in the Navajo Universe.* Ann Arbor: University of Michigan Press.

Part 1: Rebuilding Anthropological
Narratives Concerning
Two-Spirit People

Is the "North American Berdache" Merely a Phantom in the Imagination of Western Social Scientists?

Sue-Ellen Jacobs

Origins are in principle inaccessible to direct testimony; any voice from the time of origins is structurally the voice of the other who generates the self.
Haraway (1989:11)

In 1992, nearing the twenty-fifth anniversary of the publication of "Berdache: A Brief Review of the Literature" (Jacobs 1968), it became important to me to questions whether the "berdache" [*sic*] enterprise of the 1980s had been part of a movement for remasculinization of certain American and European men (white heterosexual males with classic education) through the exotification of "others" (particularly males of color and males living in exoticized cultures).[1] I also wondered if the recent non-Native interest in Native American sexuality and gender diversity was a phantasmagoric adventure of white homosexual males (with their emphasis on sexuality [Thayer 1980]) who were either appropriating cultural elements from Native cultures (in a "new age" epistemological fashion) or imputing to Native cultures characteristics that would resolve their heartfelt desires to be recognized fully as productive and important members of their own society.

I knew that for many non-Native individuals the "berdache" had become a liberating icon of possibilities in a society that has often denigrated, and in recent years had begun to trivialize, the hardship of their daily lives (e.g., male-to-female transsexuals, gay males, lesbians, and transgenders and bisexuals within diverse cultural traditions). At the same time, the use of "berdache" became anathema to Native American gay activists (including AIDS prevention community work-

berdache = liberating for some,
nowid for others ⇒ so use
"two-spirit"

ers) who wished to distance themselves from white, gay male culture and began to use the expression *two-spirit* or *two-spirited* people to identify their special qualities.

The irony is that as the "berdache" became an honored figure in the reconstructed romantic history of Native American cultures, lesbian, gay, two-spirit, and transgender people of various American Indian heritages were being beaten, disowned, and disavowed on their reservations. Some commit suicide, and others leave their reservations and seek new lives in a city. There, they join the ebb and flow of urban Indians who have established new "Native American" identities and often find more acceptance (although not necessarily personal comfort) in the multigendered, sexually diverse urban enclaves of the United States (and elsewhere) than they do in their natal communities. Some do go home to die in old age, or of AIDS, or to teach the home folks about gender and sexuality traditions—now condemned or lost—that they have read about in books not generally available in their communities. Others quietly reincorporate into their communities and work to reestablish the importance of their particular gender category. Only on a few reservations has resistance to white values spared homosexual, bisexual, and transgender people from ridicule, even though such resistance may have spared customary or traditional kinship structures, child-rearing practices, gender equity, and religions of great antiquity.

It is possible that anthropology's benign neglect of the wider, culturally defined domains of gender has privileged hierarchically situated, heterosexual male dominance models of sexuality and gender roles (male as well as female) and that these models, when applied to studies of Native Americans by non-Native homosexual males as well as lesbian anthropologists, are found "empirically and theoretically" comfortable. This intellectual hegemony has obscured the harsh realities experienced by diverse people in cultures written about. Just as such a stance has made violence against women invisible in anthropological writing, it has also made sexual violence against girls and boys—now being described in raw detail in some well-publicized non-anthropological stories—invisible, whatever the children's gender identities and potential sexualities.[2]

In 1968 I overlooked (for the most part) the evidence of punishment and maltreatment of "berdaches" as I prepared my paper. Published in an obscure, short-lived departmental journal conceived of by the faculty and students at the University of Colorado, that paper has been the most requested of all those I have written. It has also had a life of its own; it was copied frequently and circulated in the lesbian and gay underground for at least four years before I received news of its widespread distribution. After I had sent out photocopies for years, it was finally reprinted in a collection that included twenty-three other papers (Dynes and Donaldson, eds. 1992). That collection formed part of the foundation for cross-cultural anthropological studies of sexuality and gender diversity. It is from this perspective that I question the intent of research into Native American gender diversity and sexualities.

Politicizing and Romanticizing Native American History and Sexualities

By the time I had concluded the research requested by Omer C. Stewart at the University of Colorado that resulted in my paper, I was in awe of cultural systems that accommodated sexual and gender diversity. My experience growing up as a "different" female ("tomboy," "tough," and such) had been difficult. Even as an adult woman (who could not call herself a lesbian in 1968), my personal life was kept closeted; passing as straight was ritualized and routine. In my innocence and admiration, I concluded my paper:

> The incidence of berdache among North American Indian tribes [was] quite widespread. The only areas lacking reference to berdache in the United States were the north-eastern, north-central, and east-central states' tribes. It is possible that the overt manifestations of berdache have diminished because of the imposition of white values on the Indian's way of life. Surely the fact that agents tried to force berdaches to change their ways with threat of punishment if they did not, and the fact that the berdaches were so ridiculed by white people, has influenced this diminution. In some cases however, the berdache continued to exist amid ridicule and scorn, as [among] the Pima and Papago. . . .
>
> As with so many other institutions of Amerindian culture that served as means of social coordination by providing a place for even "deviant" members of the society, this position of berdache seems to have succumbed to the pressures of the white man. This pressure, in all cases, has forced the berdache into a position of a stigmatized member of society. (Jacobs 1968:31)

I had reacted to what anthropologists and other social scientists had written about Native American cultural institutions; no Indian voices were in the writing I found.

My observation was that European American colonialism and impe-

rialism has resulted in the loss of status for members of society reported to have previously held specific, accepted positions in their tribes.
It was a sad conclusion to the project. I assumed that even though Professor Stewart knew some people he called "berdaches" they surely
experienced discrimination in their communities on reservations, or
else they had gone underground (i.e., become closeted) and no longer
fulfilled traditional community roles. I was only partially right about
that.

In 1970 I met Harry Hay at San Juan Pueblo when the vehicle I was
driving overheated about three miles from the Pueblo center. Harry and
his partner, John Burnside, invited me and my traveling companion to
visit with them and some of the Pueblo people. After an wonderful
evening of discussing emerging feminist theory and issues of lesbian
and gay liberation, my companion and I stayed overnight. The next day
we were on our way back to California, where I resumed teaching at
Sacramento State College. A few months later, Hay called to say that it
had been suggested at a local Pueblo women's meeting that I might be
willing to help untangle a mystery framed by the question, "When did
we women lose our rights in this Pueblo?" After giving the matter some
thought and clearing up other applied anthropology projects to which
I was committed, I agreed to spend a summer on this community-
defined ethnohistorical project (Jacobs 1991; Timmons 1990).

During the course of my research in the summer of 1972 I met an
individual whom I was told was "the last traditional *kwidó* (or *kweedó*)
in the Tewa world." My comprehension of the significance of this first
meeting, and of later conversations and other encounters, was shallow
at best and ethnocentric at worst. At the least it was naive. I did not yet
know enough Tewa to understand the word being used. Consequently, I misspelled the term when I used my fieldnotes to respond to Callendar and Kochems's 1983 article in *Current Anthropology* (Jacobs
1983:460). When Harry Hay read my commentary he was furious and
wrote, "By this misspelling you have hidden the Tewa berdache from
the children of San Juan and other Tewa pueblos, thus denying them
part of their traditional heritage!" (Hay 1986). We then debated the
correct way to spell *kwidó* or *kweedó,* a term for which no written record
exists.[3] I thus reasoned that these spellings are more or less accurate
because they suggest contraction of the words *kwiyó* (old woman, wife)
or *kwee* (woman, wife) and *sedó* (old man, husband), the resulting terms
similar to others that, when translated to English, become "woman-
man"; or, as in Roscoe's translation (1991), "[the Zuni] man-woman";

or, in Greek, "androgynous."[4] Given my conversations in the 1980s with Tewa-speaking women and men about third-gender individuals—and until I am corrected by someone who speaks Native Tewa—I stand by these spellings.

Until 1989, the concept of a "woman-man" was still something I could explore with community people. After the individual whom I had met in 1972 died during the 1980s, however, people (elders and other individuals) began denying that the concept was truly Tewa. I was told on several occasions that I had misunderstood. They had "never had any people like that here." I was also told that people "like that" had learned such ways from white people. I was told these things in spite of the facts that at least three lesbians (two in their early twenties and one in her forties) lived at the Pueblo, one highly regarded lesbian (elder) from the Pueblo lived elsewhere and came home often for ceremonies and other occasions, and two gay males (one of whom has had classic androgynous characteristics since he was an infant) also lived at the Pueblo.

What happened? Why did the death of the traditional *kwidó* cause the disappearance of his status? Why has the child who should have been his spiritual successor been tormented by the male members of his family, staunchly protected by women relatives, and physically assaulted by other males in the community? In the summer of 1992, an angry male at a party "carved open" this young man's stomach. He survived this most recent and the most deadly of all the assaults he has suffered since he became a teenager. It will come as no surprise that this beautiful child's self-esteem is at rock bottom, and he is a serious alcoholic whose life is at risk in many ways.

What familial and community circumstances make it possible for the two twenty-year-old lesbians to be rather open at their parents' homes about their partnership yet require that they be careful about how they interact in public? Why is the young male-bodied person I etically label *kwidó*, and Harry Hay calls *kweedo*, treated more harshly than the women I etically label "lesbians"? I cannot come to an understanding of what's going on when people I have known for more than twenty years do not want to talk about these issues with me. My original job was to try to help answer a question about women's status and rights losses. My interest in the gay youth is part of that study.

Some of these questions are raised rhetorically and do not have simple—if any—answers. My altruistic answer has always been, "If I can find answers to the larger questions, maybe the young people will stop hurting; maybe they will stop killing themselves, maybe they will be respected instead of denigrated and beaten up in their communities." My selfish answer is, "If it can be 'fixed' abroad, maybe we can fix it at home." For those not deeply involved in this work, such a statement could be interpreted to be orientalism in its most racist form: looking at others in order to find reflected images of myself (Camaroff and Camaroff 1992; Haraway 1989:10–13; Lewis 1996; Said 1978). Because this is still a Colonial society, however, change must come before Western, Colonial America and Native America can break the mirror images we sometimes hold of one another.

Although it has felt like it at times, I am not alone in the search for alternative truths about gender diversity, nor am I alone in seeking answers within cultural contexts that may help remove stigma associated with being homosexual, alternatively gendered, or both. But why focus on the "North American berdache," especially when some American Indian scholars, academics, political leaders, and others are not sympathetic with this research and in fact would prefer that the matter be dropped? What, for example, are the ethical implications of continuing to write and teach about an alternative gender category (and real persons) at San Juan Pueblo when in 1988 some tribal members asked me not to do so? In the 1993 and 1994 Wenner-Gren Conferences we debated some of these issues and agreed that it is important that our research proceed and be conducted with the best possible scholarship, in the most detailed analytical and theoretical fashion, and with direct and full collaboration among Native American and non-Native scholars and activists in gay/lesbian/"berdache"/two-spirits studies as well as those involved in HIV/AIDS programs. We also agreed that there are specific areas and issues needing much more deliberate attention.

Some Current Issues

By 1988 a number of non-Native anthropologists and others had published articles about Native American homosexuality that were based on library research and fieldwork in Native American communities. Few of these studies were done in collaboration with Native Americans. Most were by men and were unabashedly androcentric; some even went so far as naming and claiming the right to define issues of sexuality and gender diversity for female-bodied Native Americans. The exceptions to this rule even to the present are found only in Albers (1988), Allen (1981, 1986), Blackwood (1984a, 1984b), Lang (1990), Medicine (1979, 1983), and the American Indian women contributors to *Living the Spirit:* Paula Gunn Allen (Laguna), Beth Brant (Mohawk), Erna Pahe (Navajo), Debra O'Gara (Tlingit), Chrystos (Menominee), Anne Waters (Seminole/Choctaw/Chickasaw/Cherokee), Mary TallMountain (Koyukon-Athabascan), Nola Hadley (Appalachian Cherokee), Carole LaFavor (Ojibwa), and Janice Gould (Maidu).

Living the Spirit was the first collection of Native American writing on the subject of sexual diversity in American Indian cultures. By the time it appeared in 1988, sexuality, sex, and gender were understood by some anthropologists, sexologists, and other academics to be cultural constructions that could be investigated separately. Gender became a central theoretical domain for those still trying to understand how societies engender social and personal identities, roles, and responsibilities. It was also understood that, in some cultures, "homosexuality" and "gender alternatives" are not synonymous, as evidenced by the fact that many Native epistemologies or worldviews (language and cognitive domains) mark them as separate. In such epistemological systems, sex is something people have and do; it is biophysiological. Gender is how people are classified along a continuum from female to male (or vice-versa), using endogenous criteria that may include only a few, or all, of the following characteristics: phenotype (body appearance, including primary and secondary sex characteristics); genotype (chromosomal makeup); hair distribution and style; clothing and other body adornments; kinesthetics, or "body language" (walking, the use of hands, head movements); vocalization in everyday speech and in formal public settings (pitch, or the use of "gendered" phrases or speech forms, as in Koasati Muskogean where women and men have different speech styles [Haas 1944], or in song); the use of tools, instruments, and other aspects of material culture; occupation or work; and place of residence and age. In other words, genders and sexualities are multidimensional and vary within and among cultures, sometimes over time and space and sometimes over the life course. But how?

Those who work with this particular theoretical orientation are more interested in learning Native categories of reality than imposing those developed in Western social and other sciences. In trying to understand categories of persons I am more interested in sociocultural managements of gender (as a multidimensional analytical category) than in sexual behaviors attributed to men (the latter being the emphasis of most studies of male-bodied "berdaches"). At the same time, I am interested in those characteristics attributed to gender categories that range from "real women" to "classificatory women," from "real men" to "classificatory men," and that may include three, four, or even more categories of gendered persons. This, of course, will also require consideration of those persons' sexualities.

When I come back from the field to write for my colleagues and students, I have to use the concepts and code words of my disciplines if I am to influence how others think about and understand the ways non-Westerners and Westerners construct meaning. When I do this, I sometimes shift cognitive domains as I seek words to help explain ideas, understandings, and concepts encountered in fieldwork. After three decades of such work, I must confess that things that readily make sense while I am at San Juan Pueblo or other field sites sometimes lose meaning when I get back to my workspace in Seattle. Sometimes I become confused as I try to establish a cross-cultural cognitive link between what I think I have learned in the field and what I have lived in my life, both at the field site and away from it.

In Seattle, I use a number of techniques for trying to recreate logical environments, or cognitive spaces, within the places where I conduct fieldwork: I talk with colleagues and students, telephone friends in the field to talk about puzzles or dilemmas, and read about the topic. Still, I am forever questioning whether I "have gotten it right" as my work goes to press or is incorporated into my lectures. The only way I can feel secure about my writing is to ask people in the community to read it and let me know their opinions, advice, and concerns. This procedure helps me understand more. My reports and papers have occasionally been useful for tribal community (e.g., social service) staff workers and sometimes have been interesting to other tribal members who work in non-related fields. Once or twice, someone has become angry and told me off when I have written about something they felt "should be kept at home." So far, the majority of readers have told me to go ahead and publish, but they did so for topics other than sexuality, a subject that can hurt if done wrong.

Were "Berdaches" Homosexuals, Transgender, Neither, or Both?

Definitions of homosexuality have temporal and spatial limitations as well as epistemological parameters based in sacred and secular philosophies. For cultural systems that recognize only two sexes and genders, "homosexuality" refers to sexual relations between people of the same sex and/or gender. Again, according to the belief system, such relationships may be tolerated or condemned. The relationships may be temporary or long-term. If a cultural system recognizes more than two sex or gender categories (Jacobs and Cromwell 1992; Martin and Voorhies 1975; Plato), then the definition of homosexuality may broaden to encompass cross-sex, same-gender sexual relationships yet it may not include same-sex, cross-gender sex (Thomas and also Kochems and Jacobs in this volume). The sexuality of individuals originally classified as "berdache" (whatever the term's spelling) turns out to be not exclusively homosexual, nor exclusively transgendered, nor transvestite. Some males were (and still are) classificatory women, and some females were (and still are) classificatory men for life or for shorter, specified periods.

Kroeber observed that generally "a berdache was not judged by his erotic life but by his social status. 'Born a male, he became accepted as a woman socially'" (1940:210). Thayer writes that "the 'problem' of the berdache has developed, I believe, from an overemphasis on its sexual aspects. This is due, no doubt, to an obsession on the part of Western travellers, missionaries, and even ethnographers with primitive and sexual 'odd customs'" (1980:293). This is important information for people interested in cross-cultural studies of gender diversity; for Wesley Thomas and Carolyn Epple in their work with *nadleehé* and *nadleehí*, respectively (each uses a different emic spelling); for Arnold Pilling's work with the Zuñi census data; and for Jason Cromwell in his work with female-to-male transgender people. It is also important to remember that Devereux (1931) noted the difference between transvestism or, using the language of the transvestite/transsexual/transgender (TV/TS/TG) movement, "transgendered" persons and homosexuals at Mojave. Likewise, Devereux's description of Mojave gender diversity and sexuality informs the theoretical work of Sabine Lang, Terry Tafoya, Michael Red Earth, Claire Farrer, Wesley Thomas, Jean-Guy Goulet, and mine as well. Still more observations from earlier writing inform current efforts to comprehend gender and sexuality and changing values or opinions about gender diversity in Native American communities. Perhaps the early writing should be reexamined; but those are historical studies rather than studies of the time in which these authors live and sometimes deliberately participate in making changes.

More recently, Gutiérrez has asked, "How do we reconcile the ridicule and low status the berdaches had in Zuñi society with the high status and praise others [especially non-Indian gay males] lavish on them?" (1989:66). He was not referring to the idea of using ethnographic and ethnohistorical materials to write about the "Zuni man-woman"

(We'wha). Instead, Gutiérrez was referring to what he perceived to be Roscoe's (and others') romanticization and embellishment of We'wha's status, extrapolations from We'wha's unique cultural position to all potential Zuñi "berdaches" (real and imagined), and an imagined "gay role in American Indian histories" (61).

The ethnographic and ethnohistorical record that Roscoe so carefully investigated and presented makes it clear that We'wha was unique—but perhaps that was a function of the cultural markings for gender diversity. Gutiérrez's query is important to my understanding of what seem to be changes at San Juan Pueblo. He, Roscoe, and I share intellectual mentoring from Harry Hay on the subject of "berdache," but that we have each read our time with him differently is obvious from our published recollections and the way we have constructed our gay, gay/"berdache," and feminist/lesbian-feminist orientations to theoretical and empirical approaches to issues of gender and sexuality.

My reading of the historical material has led me to conclude that "the lesson of the [old-time] berdache is that gender may have little or nothing to do with sexuality" (Jacobs and Cromwell 1992:54) and, conversely, that sexuality may have little or nothing to do with gender.[5] In other words, the ideology of gender and sexuality promotes (or at least tolerates) extraordinary flexibility of expression in sex, sexuality, and gender behaviors in some cultural situations. These three terms are not always coterminous, interdependent, or otherwise connected, but not everyone agrees with me.

What about Women?

From the perspective of a feminist lesbian, I question why two Anglo female anthropologists (Brettell and Sargent 1993) have used Walter Williams's chapter from *The Spirit and the Flesh* (which designates American Indian lesbians, manly-hearted women, and warrior women as "amazons") in an introductory textbook for cross-cultural studies of women. Why did they not use Native American Indian women's own terms for themselves (cf. Allen 1981; Allen 1986; Allen 1992; Blackwood 1984a; Blackwood 1984b; Brant 1993)? If Native American women call themselves "lesbian," "dyke," or a multitude of native terms, why should anyone privilege Williams's use of the term *amazon*? Is it because the white male voice (whether gay or straight) is assumed to have authority in all scholarly and other matters? Where are Native American women's voices in anthropological writing on this subject? Many are hidden, as many women's voices—irrespective of race, ethnicity, class, sexuality, and age—are made invisible by absence of reference in articles cited or used for theory-building. They are also left out of the published discourse (cf. Lutz 1990). Beth Brant, a Native American lesbian writer, has observed:

> If you ask why you have not read or heard of [Native Lesbian Writers], ask it of yourself. The answer lies in the twin realms of racism and homophobia. Some of us cannot get published. And this has nothing to do with the excellence of our work. It has to do with who will be courageous enough to see us in all of our facets of being. And of course, this has to do with power and who has it and who exercises it over us. . . .
>
> And what of the Native lesbian writers who have internalized homophobia to the extent of feeling they have to hide in order to be published and therefore offer up diminished pieces of themselves. They suffer. We suffer.
>
> And what of Native lesbians who put their mark on paper for the first time or one-hundredth time, believing their work will never be published because they are Indian and gay? I long for these sisters. Their words can feed a Nation. Just as our labor, our constancy, our faith has kept our Nations strong.
>
> For what we do, we do for generations to come. We write not only for ourselves but also for our communities, for our People, for the young ones who are looking for the gay and lesbian path, for our Elders who were shamed or mythologized, for [all of life, including our relatives] who gave us our Indian blood and the belief system that courses through that blood. (1993:946)

As I reflect upon the ways American Indian women have been characterized in the old "berdache" and other literature, I am intrigued by the frequency with which male writers masculinize females as the result of some observed or purported behavior. It appears, for example, that because of their daring and alleged unfeminine qualities (by privileged Western male standards) some observers assumed that Plains warrior women were the Native North American counterpart to the mythical Amazons of Scythia (as described in Greek and, subsequently, Western mythologies). Strong women—independent, brave, courageous warriors entering battle astride horses—they were certainly not the genteel ladies of the worlds from whence came the learned white men of religious orders, world travels, anthropology, and other fields. What the early male observers failed to notice was that courageous, strong, daring, warrior women existed worldwide (cf. Weigle 1982) without emic attributions of masculinity. Such traits and behaviors are part of the range of female characteristics within and across many cultures. Women who carry out brave deeds may, in some cultures, be granted masculine status by the rules of their society, but that does not necessarily mean an improvement in status. Some writers, however, consider masculinization of such females to be the only way to explain their behaviors and statuses. Indeed, "Kay Stone [a folklorist] observed in studies of European traditions in the New World that male narrators cast female heroes in masculine roles more often than women did" (as told to Mills 1985:189). I extend this observation as a hypothesis that has bearing on what, to me, is the surprisingly frequent and adamant use of the word *amazon* by European American males writing about strong women, Native and other.[6]

Such writing reflects a continued preoccupation with an image of femaleness that is bounded by the absence of attributes considered exclusively masculine. To use only one example, what Williams calls "amazon" behavior for a constructed class, "American Indian women" (both North and South American), is really a lumping of diverse and complex traits, experiences, beliefs, and sociocultural roles in cultures that (in some cases) are extremely different. Unless one is talking about the tribe of Scythian women imagined in Greek mythology and not about real, living women of Native America (and elsewhere), there is no single group that could be classed as "amazon" and have bounded, shared traits; nor could a single group be classed as "Indian woman" and have bounded, shared traits; nor, for that matter, are there single, worldwide, bounded classes of "lesbians," "dykes," "gay men," "berdaches," "warrior women," "men," or "women." To rearticulate the point about Plains warrior women, more recent writing, such as that by Beatrice Medicine, a Lakota anthropologist (1983 and in this book), and Patricia C. Albers, a non-Native (especially her teaching module on "female gender variance in American Indian societies" [1989:149–54]) are explicit about the flexibility of Native women's roles and statuses within and across Native cultures. The image of warrior woman shifts when told by women who have lived in cultures where such women are the norm.

Reconstructing Gender Images

"Tewa Warrior Woman" (Figure 1-1), painted by Camille Lacapa (Hopi-Tewa/Lac Court Orielle Ojibwe), appeared on the cover of the first issue

Figure I-I. "Tewa Warrior Woman." (Camille Lacapa 1991; courtesy of the artist)

of the magazine *Indigenous Woman* and delighted Native American and non-Native friends of mine (gay, lesbian, straight, bi, men, women, and other). Tewa Warrior Woman has her hair up on the left side and down on the right. An unmarried Hopi "maiden" wears her hair in this fashion; young girls, boys, and some men wear their hair long, flowing, uncut, and unbraided. The image in Lacapa's painting conveys a clear message of dual character. But which characters? By her title, Lacapa indicates that this is a Tewa warrior *woman,* an image "inspired by a story about a women who defends her people and their village" (*Indigenous Woman* 1991:i). She is as much a heroine as the Navajo warrior woman who once struck out on her own to reclaim her son who had been kidnapped and upon her successful return was proclaimed "(her name with the suffix)-baa'"—a term of honor rather than that used for an occupational category or a tribal sodality—a warrior woman of the Navajo nation (personal communication, Wesley Thomas, 1994; cf. Carrie House, this volume, 226). Lacapa's painting is striking in its simultaneous conveyance of womanly strength and power and the naive, innocent determination of youth.

Another painting has similar features but is marked deliberately to reflect a woman-man person (Figure 1-2). This work is by Joe Lawrence Lembo (Cherokee), "an artist living in San Francisco. During his travels in the Southwest, he became inspired by the Hopi Indians, producing works that have been shown in a variety of local exhibitions" (Gay American Indians comps., ed. Roscoe 1988:225). The painting, entitled simply but profoundly "Berdache," leaves no question about the gendered intent of the artist. The sun (the male sign in Pueblo cultures) is on the person's left; the moon (the female sign in Pueblo cultures) is on the person's right; the left hand holds bow and arrow (a symbol of male hunting/warrior occupation as well as deity in some Pueblo cultures), the right holds ears of corn (a female deity symbol in many Native American cultures); the *manta* or "woman's dress" covers the breast and legs on the right, and the hair is pulled up into a fashion that could mean unmarried female (as in Lacapa's painting) or the bun style worn by married women; the left breast, thigh, and upper calf are exposed above and below the "breechcloth"; on the left, the hair is either braided or cut, and a decorative band encircles the left upper arm. It is clear that this "berdache" is female on the right side and male on the left, an interesting opposition to, or perhaps a mirror image of, the habitually used "metaphors of men-right/women-left in the overall scheme of cultural life" (Miller 1982:286).

Figure 1-2. "Berdache." (after Joe Lawrence Lembo 1987)

What do these images and those images included in Arnold Pilling's work (1993 and in this volume) tell us about gender blending, gender mixing, gender ambiguity, and gender diversity in Native North American communities of the present as well as in the past? Do they reflect the broader notion of two-spirit people as defined by many of the Native contributors to this volume: individuals who combine feminine and masculine traits and are culturally both female and male yet not so biologically? Harry Walters has remarked that "the world is made of two: woman and man. But there have always been the third one who is both, the *nádleehi"* (1995; see also Callendar and Kochems 1983; Jacobs and Cromwell 1992; and Schnarch 1992 for additional comments on third-gender categories). Thomas (1993 and in this volume) and Epple (1993 and in this volume) provide a slightly different picture of Navajo gender diversity. They strongly disagree with one another on major issues; there is not always agreement within a linguistic and cultural community about the way diversity is constructed, never mind trying to achieve parity across linguistic and cultural domains.

Images conveyed through words may assume as much importance and power as these paintings, yet in each case there is no certainty of meaning beyond that the artist intends—except for that constructed by viewers' imaginations. How much of reconstruction of positively sanctioned gender diversity and sexualities is based on the idiosyncrasy of historic moments, as in the lives of We'wha of Zuni, "Woman Chief" of the Crow tribe, "Old Doctor" of northern California, "Qúquonok palke" (also known as "Qángon" and "Madame Boisverd") of the Kutenai, and the "Tewa Warrior Woman"? Their stories are based on tales of the past.

What do the stories of today tell us about tolerance (or intolerance) for gender and sexual diversity in Native North American communities, as well as in communities throughout the world? Ask the people who are openly living their homosexual, gay, lesbian, queer, bisexual, or transgendered lives in their own or other communities. Many will agree with Stoller about "observations long since noted on the deterioration in American Indians of techniques for ritualizing cross-gender behavior. No longer is a place provided for the role—more, the identity—of a male-woman, the dimensions of which are fixed by custom, rules, tradeoffs, or responsibilities. The tribes have forgotten. Instead, this role appears as a ghost" (1985:177).

Much has been said about purported and romanticized history. Paraphrasing the epigram from Haraway (1989:11), many contemporary retrospective studies have become voices of the present, generating images of the authors, who are usually white male descendants of colonizers who rarely tolerated—and generally abhorred—gender diversity and homosexuality (see also Trexler [1995] for a extensive review of the colonial writing about male "berdaches" that supports this point and Greenberg [1985] for evidence of intratribal ridicule of male "berdaches").

Conclusion

Many aspects of gender diversity are puzzling. For answers, I depend largely on published writing by Native Americans, non-Indians, anthropologists, psychologists, sexologists, and others. I remain entranced by the diversity of gender constructions and human sexualities embedded within them (where this occurs). I am also entranced by the myriad ways in which people account for their identities and lives and the many ways in which humanity finds affection, love, companionship, and reproductive success.

Is the "North American Berdache" merely a phantom in the imagination of Western anthropologists? Yes—and no. I use the words *imagination* (Camaroff and Camaroff 1992) and *phantom* in the postmodern sense (preferring this metaphor to Stoller's "ghost"), noticing that not only anthropologists but also a lot of other people (academics as well as nonacademics) use the idea of the "North American berdache" to represent a cultural category of significance to American Indians. Yet that category's counterparts in Western culture (lesbian, gay, homosexual, transsexual, gender-blender, and transvestite) are despised by European Americans and others who have integrated European values into their cosmologies.

Like the phantom of the opera, references to "berdache" figures have appeared and disappeared at irregular intervals on the stage of anthropological writings and are seldom linked to major analytical categories. As such they occupy positions of theoretical and empirical marginality and are rarely given importance in anthropological grand theories about sex roles, sexuality, or gender diversity. They have become icons of "difference" and of the "other" in the creative, curiosity-driven Western imagination found in introductory textbooks, elaborated encyclicals (Roscoe 1994; Williams 1986), and other writing. And I, for one, give up the use of the word "berdache" with great reluctance (my contradictory remarks in the introduction notwithstanding), for it has been an important symbol of potential liberation from gender identity construction, homophobia, and sexuality containment for some lesbian/gay/two-spirit First Nations/Native American Indian activists as well as for myself and other non-Natives.[7]

In the 1990s, however, the "North American berdache" has been redefined, described, renamed, and brought forward in clear empirical realities by diverse Native Americans throughout North America as

"two-spirit people of the First Nations." Accurately situating anthropological and other studies of Native American sexualities has urgent
meaning in American Indian and other Native American communities
faced with rapidly increasing HIV-positive and AIDS cases. Romantic
references to the past do not ameliorate the realities that need documentation at this critical moment. Paraphrasing Clyde Hall (1993 and
in this volume), contemporary studies of Native American sexualities
and gender diversity are not at an end; the work has barely begun.

Notes

A previous version of this chapter was read as the "Introduction" to the
Wenner-Gren Foundation Conference on "Revisiting the 'North American
Berdache' Empirically and Theoretically" at the 92d annual meeting of the
American Anthropological Association, Washington, D.C., November 17,
1993, as well as to the AAA session of the same name held in Washington
on November 18, 1993. Both events were organized and cochaired by Wesley K. Thomas, Sabine Lang, and me.

   1. Susan Jeffords has explored the role of film media in creating a new
definition of masculinity through the decades of the Reagan presidency
and immediately thereafter: "The hard body that emblematized a renewed
national and international strength has been repudiated, not for a return
to the soft body of the Carter years, but for the creation of a body in which
strength is defined internally rather than externally, as a matter of moral
rather than muscle fiber. This body is then positioned as a domestic rather than as an international hero, defending the rights of women and people of color across the country. . . . these heroes prove themselves through
their isolation from other men, deriving their power . . . alliances with the
larger institutional systems of justice to which they turn for the solution
of social problems" (1994:136–37). In addition to providing a renewed white
masculine image that makes the white male an institutional hero, the films
also redefine the "otherness" of men of color.

   See Tiffany and Adams (1994) for a thunderous criticism of Napoleon
Chagnon's films and writings about the Yanomani (Native Americans of
the Amazon region of Brazil) and subsequent use of his materials in introductory and other anthropology courses. The extent to which some have
gone for exoticizing "others" is shown in a 1995 *National Geographic* photograph of five white males from New York painted in bright red, yellow,
and green, adorned with headbands, armbands, and waistbands of the
same colored "feathers," and wearing straw-colored "grass skirts" that hang

over barely visible shorts or swim trunks. The men stand in knee-to-thigh-high water, their hands tied behind them. They are laced to trees in the Amazon River. Part of the caption reads: "American salesmen endure a mock tribal initiation. . . . rewards [for] star [real estate] agents" who get to "play Indian" in the ethnotourism and ecotourism worlds of Brazil (Van Dyk 1995:20–21). For a treatment of ethnic tourism in Mexico, see Van Den Berghe (1994).

2. Recent films and teaching videos, for example, describe incidences of sexual abuse of boys in boarding schools in St. Johns, Newfoundland, and Alkali Lake in Saskatchewan, Canada. Other media document the overall picture of cultural abuse that happened in select boarding schools in the United States (Lomawaima 1993; Lomawaima 1994; Mishesuah 1991).

3. Rio Grande Tewa became a written language in the 1960s as a result of the work of Randy Speirs and Anna Speirs of the Summer Institute of Linguistics; the examples presented here are in the practical orthography used in the *San Juan Pueblo Tewa Dictionary* (Martinez 1983). Esther Martinez, a Native Tewa-speaker and tribal linguist, has told me that there are two words for third and fourth gender people. These are the words used when she was growing up: *kweep'ąą* (glossed as "man like a woman") and *senp'ąą* (glossed as "woman like a man").

4. Greek mythology, as recounted by Plato (428–348 B.C.) in the *Symposium,* enumerates three original types of humans. The introduction of the word *androgynous* begins first, along with the listing of the three types: "The sexes were not two as they are now, but originally three in number; there was man, woman and the union of the two, having a name corresponding to this double nature, which had once a real existence, but now is lost, and the word 'Androgynous' is only preserved as a term of reproach" (190).

Plato describes the origins of the "original state of man": "Now the sexes were three, and such as I have described them, because the sun, moon, and earth are three; and the man was originally the child of the sun, the woman of the earth, and *the man-woman of the moon,* which is made up of sun and earth, and they were all round and moved round and round like their parents. Terrible was their might and strength, and the thoughts of their heart were great, and they made an attack upon the gods" (191, emphasis added). Zeus decided to stop the challenge to the pantheon by cutting each person in half, giving them legs on which to stand, and shaping them into forms we see or know today. The division left each half longing to be rejoined with the other. Thus, people are always looking for their missing half: "Men who are a section of that double nature which was once called Androgynous are lovers of women; adulterers are generally of this breed, and also adulterous women who lust after men; the women who are a section of the woman do not care for men, but have female attachments; the female companions are of this sort. But they who are a section of the male follow the male, and while they are young, being slices of the original man, [192] they hang about men and embrace them, and they are themselves the best of boys and youth, because they have the most manly nature [193]" (Plato 1952:157–58).

5. I am grateful to Sharon Slebodnick, a student in one of my courses at the University of Washington, for asking if the converse were possibly true, thereby putting the obvious squarely in my face.

6. See especially Williams (ch. 11:1986) for the most salient reductionism concerning this topic. Of the "Kutenai Female Berdaches," Schaeffer has noted: "One of the most prominent *of the native amazons* was the 'Woman Chief' of the Crow Tribe" (1965:225, emphasis added). In his discussion of Kootenay "berdaches" Miller observes, *"The females acted like Amazons* in that they became important war and diplomatic figures. In the most famous instance, a Kootenay woman assumed a full range of male roles in marriage, military, political, and religious areas" (1982:281, emphasis added).

7. The transsexual community in which Anne Bolin conducted her research in the 1980s, for example, called one of their support organizations the "Berdache Society" (Bolin 1988:102–3), and in Seattle, Washington, there was a short-lived, mixed Native, non-Native "berdache club" made up of lesbians and gay men.

References Cited

Albers, Patricia C. 1989. "From Illusion to Illumination: Anthropological Studies of American Indian Women." In *Gender and Anthropology: Critical Reviews for Research and Teaching,* ed. Sandra Morgen, 132–70. Arlington: American Anthropological Association.

Allen, Paula Gunn. 1981. "Beloved Women: Lesbians in American Indian Cultures." *Conditions: Seven,* 67–87. Revised version in *Women-Identified Women,* ed. Trudy Darty and Sandee Porter, 1984, 83–96. Palo Alto: Mayfield.

———. 1986. *"Hwame, Koshkalaka,* and the Rest: Lesbians in American Indian Cultures." In *The Sacred Hoop: Recovering the Feminine in American Indian Traditions,* 245–62. Boston: Beacon Press.

———. 1992. "Lesbians in American Indian Cultures." In Wayne R. Dynes and Stephen Donaldson, eds. 1992. *Studies in Homosexuality.* Volume 2: *Ethnographic Studies of Homosexuality,* 1–21. New York: Garland.

Blackwood, Evelyn. 1984a. "Cross-Cultural Dimensions of Lesbian Relations." Master's thesis. San Francisco State University.

———. 1984b. "Sexuality and Gender in Certain Native American Tribes: The Case of Cross-Gender Females." *Signs: Journal of Women in Culture and Society* 10(1): 127–42.

Bolin, Anne. 1988. *In Search of Eve: Transsexual Rites of Passage.* New York: Bergin and Garvey.

Brant, Beth. 1993. "Giveaway: Native Lesbian Writers." *Signs: Journal of Women in Culture and Society* 18(4): 944–47.

Brettell, Caroline B., and Carolyn F. Sargent. 1993. *Gender in Cross-Cultural Perspective.* Englewood Cliffs: Prentice-Hall.

Callendar, Charles, and Lee M. Kochems. 1983. "The North American 'Berdache.'" *Current Anthropology* 24(4): 443–70.

———. 1985. "Men and Not-Men: Male Gender-Mixing Statuses and Homosexuality." *Journal of Homosexuality* 11(3–4): 179–90.

Camaroff, John, and Jean Camaroff. 1992. *Ethnography and the Historical Imagination.* Boulder: Westview Press.

Devereux, George. 1937. "Homosexuality among the Mohave Indians." *Human Biology* 9: 498–527. Reprint. Wayne R. Dynes and Stephen Donaldson, eds. 1992. *Studies in Homosexuality.* Volume 2: *Ethnographic Studies of Homosexuality.* New York: Garland.

Dynes, Wayne R., and Stephen Donaldson, eds. 1992. *Studies in Homosexuality.* Volume 2: *Ethnographic Studies of Homosexuality.* New York: Garland.

Epple, Carolyn. 1993. "Navajo Worldview and *Nádleehí:* Implications for Western Categories." Paper presented at "Revisiting the 'North American Berdache' Empirically and Theoretically." 92d annual meeting of the American Anthropological Association, Washington, D.C. Revised for this volume.

Greenberg, David F. 1985. "Why was the Berdache Ridiculed?" *Journal of Homosexuality* 11(3–4): 179–90.

Gutiérrez, Ramón A. 1989. "Must We Deracinate Indians to Find Gay Roots?" *Outlook* 4 (Winter): 61–67. Reprint. Wayne R. Dynes and Stephen Donaldson, eds. 1992. *Studies in Homosexuality.* Volume 2: *Ethnographic Studies of Homosexuality.* New York: Garland.

Haas, Mary R. 1944. "Men's and Women's Speech in Koasati." *Language* 20: 147–49.

Hall, Clyde. 1993. "You Anthropologists Make Sure You Get Your Words Right." Paper presented at "Revisiting the 'North American Berdache' Empirically and Theoretically." 92d annual meeting of the American Anthropological Association, Washington, D.C. Revised for this volume.

Haraway, Donna. 1989. *Primate Visions: Gender, Race, and Nature in the World of Modern Science.* New York: Routledge.

Hay, Harry. 1986. Personal correspondence with author.

Jacobs, Sue-Ellen. 1968. "Berdache: A Brief Review of the Literature." *Colorado Anthropologist* 1(2): 25–40. Reprint. Wayne R. Dynes and Stephen Donaldson, eds. 1992. *Studies in Homosexuality.* Volume 2: *Ethnographic Studies of Homosexuality.* New York: Garland.

———. 1983. Commentary on "The North American 'Berdache,'" by Charles Callendar and Lee M. Kochems. *Current Anthropology* 24(4): 443–70.

———. 1991. "The Predicament of Sincerity: From Distance to Connection in Long Term Research." *International Journal of Moral and Social Studies* 6(3): 237–45.

Jacobs, Sue-Ellen, and Jason Cromwell. 1992. "Visions and Revisions of Reality: Reflections on Sex, Sexuality, Gender and Gender Variance." *Journal of Homosexuality* 23(4): 43–69.

Jeffords, Susan. 1994. *Hard Bodies: Hollywood Masculinity in the Reagan Era.* New Brunswick: Rutgers University Press.

Kroeber, A. L. 1940. "Psychosis or Social Sanction?" *Culture and Personality* 8: 204–15.

Lacapa, Camille. 1991. "Tewa Woman Warrior." *Indigenous Woman* 1(1): cover.

Lang, Sabine. 1990. *Männer als Frauen—Frauen als Männer: Geschlechtsrollenwechsel bei den Indianern Nordamerikas.* Hamburg: Wayasabah.

Lembo, Joe Lawrence. 1988. "Berdache." In *Living the Spirit: A Gay American Indian Anthology,* ed. Will Roscoe, 14. Compiled by Gay American Indians. New York: St. Martin's Press.

Lewis, Reina. 1996. *Gendering Orientalism: Race, Femininity, and Representation.* New York: Routledge.

Lomawaima, K. Tsianina. 1993. "Domesticity in the Federal Indian Schools: The Power of Authority over Mind and Body." *American Ethnologist* 20(2): 227–40.

———. 1994. *They Called It Prairie Light: The Story of Chilocco Indian School.* Lincoln: University of Nebraska Press.

Lutz, Catherine. 1990. "The Erasure of Women's Writing in Sociocultural Anthropology." *American Ethnologist* 17(4): 611–27.

Martin, M. Kay, and Barbara Voorhies. 1975. *Female of the Species.* New York: Columbia University Press.

Martinez, Esther. 1983. *San Juan Pueblo Tewa Dictionary.* San Juan Pueblo: San Juan Pueblo Day School.

Medicine, Bea. 1979. "Changing Native American Sex Roles in an Urban Context." Unpublished ms.

———. 1983. "'Warrior Women': Sex Role Alternatives for Plains Indian Women." In *The Hidden Half: Studies of Plains Indian Women,* ed. Patricia C. Albers and Beatrice Medicine, 267–80. Lanham: University Press of America.

Miller, Jay. 1982. "People, Berdaches, and Left-Handed Bears: Human Variation in Native America." *Journal of Anthropological Research* 38: 274–87.

Mills, Margaret. 1985. "Sex Role Reversals, Sex Changes, and Transvestite Disguise in the Oral Tradition of a Conservative Muslim Community in Afghanistan." In *Women's Folklore, Women's Culture,* ed. Rosa A. Jordan and Susan J. Kalčik, 187–213. Philadelphia: University of Pennsylvania Press.

Mishesuah, Devon A. 1991. "Too Dark to Be Angels: The Class System among the Cherokees at the Female Seminary." *American Indian Culture and Research Journal* 15(1): 29–52.

Pilling, Arnold. 1993. "Cross-Dressing and Shamanism among Selected Western North American Tribes." Paper presented at "Revisiting the 'North American Berdache' Empirically and Theoretically." 92d annual meeting of the American Anthropological Association, Washington, D.C. Revised for this volume.

Plato. 1952. "Symposium." In *Great Books of the Western World.* Volume 7: *Plato,* 149–73. Chicago: Encyclopedia Britannica.

Roscoe, Will, ed. 1988. *Living the Spirit: A Gay American Indian Anthology.* Compiled by Gay American Indians. New York: St. Martin's Press.

———. 1991. *The Zuni Man-Woman.* Albuquerque: University of New Mexico Press.

———. 1994. "How to Become a Berdache: Toward a Unified Analysis of Gender Diversity." In *Third Gender, Third Sex,* ed. Gilbert Herdt, 329–71. New York: Zone Books.

Said, Edward W. 1978. *Orientalism.* New York: Random House.

Schaeffer, Claude E. 1965. "The Kutenai Female Berdache: Courier, Guide, Prophetess, and Warrior." *Ethnohistory* 12: 193–236.

Schnarch, Brian. 1992. "Neither Man nor Woman: Berdache—A Case for Non-Dichotomous Gender Construction." *Anthropologica* 34: 105–21.

Stoller, Robert. 1985. "Two Feminized Male American Indians." In *Presentations of Gender,* 171–80. New Haven: Yale University Press.

Thayer, James Steel. 1980. "The Berdache of the Northern Plains: A Socioreligious Perspective." *Journal of Anthropological Research* 36(3): 287–93.

Thomas, Wesley. 1993. "Navajo Cultural Constructions of Gender and Sexuality." Paper presented at "Revisiting the 'North American Berdache' Empirically and Theoretically." 92d annual meeting of the American Anthropological Association, Washington, D.C. Revised for this volume.

Tiffany, Sharon W., and Kathleen J. Adams. 1994. "Anthropology's 'Fierce' Yanomami: Narratives of Sexual Politics in the Amazon." *NWSA Journal* 6(2): 169–95.

Timmons, Stuart. 1990. *The Trouble with Harry Hay: Founder of the Modern Gay Movement.* Boston: Alyson.

Trexler, Richard C. 1995. *Sex and Conquest: Gendered Violence, Political Order, and the European Conquest of the Americas.* Ithaca: Cornell University Press.

Van Den Berghe, Pierre. 1994. *The Quest for the Other: Ethnic Tourism in San Cristobal, Mexico.* Seattle: University of Washington Press.

Van Dyk, Jere. 1995. "Amazon: South America's River Road." *National Geographic* 187(2): 3–39.

Walters, Harry. 1995. Personal communication with colleagues in seminar on "Gender in American Indian Cultures," Newberry Library, Chicago.

Weigle, Marta. 1982. *Spiders and Spinsters: Women and Mythology.* Albuquerque: University of New Mexico Press.

Williams, Walter. 1986. *The Spirit and the Flesh: Sexual Diversity in American Indian Culture.* New York: Beacon Press. Reprint 1991, with a new preface by the author.

★ ★ **2**

The Northern Athapaskan "Berdache" Reconsidered:

On Reading More Than There Is in the Ethnographic Record

Jean-Guy A. Goulet

Recent claims have been made that the Native North American status of "berdache" [*sic*] existed among Northern Athapaskans in the Canadian Subarctic. Those who advance this idea read into the ethnographic record more than is there, however, and generally fail to take sufficient account of how Northern Athapaskans construct their worlds and gendered lives. This misreading can be found in the use Broch (1983), Callender and Kochems (1983a), Roscoe (1987), and Williams (1986, 1996) have made of Honigmann's 1954 report of a Kaska girl raised as a boy.[1] An analysis of accounts of cross-sex reincarnation reveals how the Dene Tha of Chateh in northwestern Alberta, Canada, constitute some individuals as male in female form and others as female in male form.[2] This view of Dene Tha individuals is found in accounts of cross-sex reincarnation in which Dene Tha individuals present themselves as having died and deciding to come back to a kinswoman, to "be made again" in a sex other than the one of their previous life. Dene Tha, like many Northern Athapaskans, construct gender identities that transcend the male/female, man/woman dichotomies so familiar to Euro-Americans. This does not mean that Northern Athapaskan "berdaches," unrecognized in the past, should be added to a growing list of Native North American populations for which this status is already reported.

The Recent "Discovery" of the Northern Athapaskan "Berdache"

When Callender and Kochems submitted "The North American Berdache" to *Current Anthropology* (1983a), it contained no references to

Northern Athapaskan "berdaches." Their view supported the earlier report of Jacobs (1968): There was no mention in the literature of "berdache" among Northern Athapaskans. In the published version of their paper, however, Callender and Kochems argued that, contrary to their earlier views, "berdaches were probably widespread among Northern Athapaskans" (464). Their change of mind is due to Broch (1983), who in his comment on their article called attention to five cases of what he considered instances of "berdaches" among Northern Athapaskans, past and contemporary: the Kaska girl raised as a boy to become a hunter, three Dene women who played "manly" roles in the context of the fur trade in the eighteenth century, and a contemporary Hare firefighter who "acted" like a woman at a fire camp.

Although they accepted Broch's point of view, Callender and Kochems commented on the absence of male "berdaches" in Arctic and Subarctic societies of the past in general and in Northern Athapaskan societies of the past in particular. They suggested that in northern subsistence economies "the contributions of males was too valuable to promote their transformation" into females (1983a:445). By implication, the value of the male contribution among hunters and gatherers would similarly explain the transformation of some girls into hunters. In particular, there is an account of a "Kaska couple who wanted a daughter to become a hunter" and consequently "dressed her as a boy and gave her masculine work" (Honigmann 1954:129–30).

This rather recent identification of "berdaches" among Northern Athapaskans, particularly the reference to the Kaska girl, has found its way into Williams (1986; 1996) and Roscoe (1987). The "discovery" is based on an unwarranted reading of Honigmann and, in the case of Broch, a dubious interpretation of observations made during fieldwork among the Hare. It is my purpose to challenge the current anthropological interpretation of Honigmann's report. Elsewhere, I have discussed all of the alleged cases of Northern Athapaskan "berdaches" that Broch submitted to Callender and Kochems (Goulet 1996).

The Case of the Kaska Girl

Honigmann's ethnographic report of a Kaska girl raised as a hunter is worth repeating at length. On the basis of this account, Callender and Kochems concluded that a "real berdache category" exists among the Kaska (1983a:444). Following Honigmann's report, Williams likewise concluded that one finds among the Kaska strong evidence that the assignment of a child to "be" a gender can proceed "independently of a person's morphological sex and can determine both gender status and erotic behavior" (1986:285). The source of their information on the girl is a paragraph found in Honigmann. Significantly, the context in which Honigmann presents his information is a discussion of homosexuality. The paragraph follows an extensive discussion of heterosexual activity among youths and adolescents, and then among married heterosexual couples. It ends with comments on wife exchange and polygyny. The paragraph deals first with male homosexuality, then with female homosexuality, and, finally, with the presumed homosexuality of the girl raised as a hunter. The paragraph begins in the following manner:

> *In one reported case* of homosexuality a man, disinclined to heterosexual relations, sought young men as sexual partners, with whom he secured orgasm by apposing the glans of penes. In the morning the homosexual rewarded his lovers with gifts, treating them "just as good as women." Although dressing as a man, the homosexual removed his clothing during sexual relations. Once he tried to secure anal intromission with a sleeping man who had been eating fat and who defecated against his would-be seducer. (1954:129–30, emphasis added)

The information is scant. It concerns one man disinclined to heterosexual relations and who rewarded young lovers the morning after having had sex with them. The inclusion of an account of attempted anal intromission with a sleeping man who defecates against his would-be lover may reflect the informant's view that the man could not find mature men who would willingly engage in homosexual activity.

The paragraph then moves on to the topic of female homosexuality, which is dealt with in a sentence and a half: *"Female homosexuals simulated copulation by 'getting on top of each other.' Such women were often transvestites,* but *no male transvestites could be recalled"* (130, emphasis added).

The paucity of information on female homosexuality and the nature of its presentation probably reflects the fact that both Honigmann and his informants were males. He offers no references to any reported cases of women's homoerotic behaviors, which are simply described as a simulation of heterosexual activity. He assures readers that although male homosexuals were not transvestites, female homosexuals often were. It is then that Honigmann introduces the case of the daughter "raised as a boy, dressed in masculine attire," performing "male tasks," and later in life presumably entering "homosexual relationships."

Sometimes if a couple had too many female children and desired a son to hunt for them in later years, they selected a daughter to be "like a man." When she was about five years old the parent tied the dried ovaries of a bear to her inner belt. She wore this amulet for the rest of her life in order to avoid conception. The girl was raised as a boy. She dressed in masculine attire and performed male allocated tasks, often developing great strength and usually becoming an outstanding hunter. She screamed and broke the bow and arrows of any boy who made sexual advances to her. "She knows that if he gets her then her luck with game will be broken." Apparently such a girl entered homosexual relationships. (Honigmann 1954:130)

It is noteworthy that Honigmann completes this presentation with a comment that "apparently such a girl entered homosexual relationships." He appears to believe that if some female homosexuals were transvestites then it not only followed that some female transvestites were homosexuals but that it was also probably the case that the girl raised as a boy and made a transvestite was also homosexual. Nowhere does Honigmann say that he had met Kaska parents who were raising a girl as a hunter nor that he had encountered women who had been raised as a male to become a hunter later in life. He simply reports, without specifying the source of his information (perhaps one or more male informants), that "sometimes" this occurred.

The first question that comes to mind concerns why Honigmann could not be more specific about the girl's sexual orientation. The answer, in brief, is that he was writing his ethnographic reconstruction of Kaska culture three years after he had left the field, and he had no further access to his Kaska informants, all of them English-speaking males. Honigmann spent two periods of fieldwork among the Kaska, at Lower Post on the Liard River of the Yukon. The first, to which he refers as "13 happy weeks" from mid-June to early September 1944, were in preparation for a five-month period the following year, including part of the winter of 1945. At Lower Post, Honigmann experienced little of "the reticence, diffidence, and disinterest" so often reported by anthropologists for Northern Athapaskans. To the contrary, "Willing male informants were easy to secure." He describes them as "most cooperative" as well as "possessing considerable facility of English" (1954:6). One must keep in mind that his Kaska informants, all males, were so disposed and qualified because of the years they had worked with the formidable Northwest Division of the U.S. Army, building the Alaska Highway through the Kaska homeland. Also noteworthy is the fact that Honigmann's main informant and host was a Kaska Indian identified as Old Man, "an Upper Liard Indian of mixed Indian ancestry who was early orphaned and spent the greater part of his youth in the serve of white men," a man who "married three times, his first two wives being sisters and half-Cree women from Fort Nelson" (1949:29).

When he initiated his fieldwork among the Kaska, Honigmann's intention was "to acquire gradually an intimate knowledge of their contemporary culture and personality by approaching them with questions about their aboriginal way of life" (1954:5). Contemporary culture and personality on the one hand, and aboriginal way of life on the other, thus became the topic of two books. The first, *Kaska Culture and Ethos* (1949), was written in the vein of the then-important American school of culture and personality. The second book, *The Kaska Indians: An Ethnographic Reconstruction* (1954), was written in the tradition of salvage ethnography in the ethnographic present. The data he did not include in his first publication, such as the information concerning Kaska girls raised as boys and hunters, found its way into the second. Although he completed that book in 1951, he had begun to write it in 1948 when he found himself isolated among the James Bay Cree of Attawapiskat, Ontario, during the course of "a relatively lonely winter" (1954:6). Hence, in 1948 Honigmann was writing on the basis of fieldnotes that he had collected four years earlier.

In his delayed reconstruction of Kaska pre-contact culture Honigmann introduces information about the girl raised as a boy in the context of a discussion of homosexuality. This may or may not be the context of the information offered to him. I suspect it was not; had it been, he would most probably have been clear about the sexual orientation of the girl in adult life. Honigmann interviewed informants on a number of predetermined topics, including heterosexuality, homosexuality, transvestism, and sexual sadism. The mention that "no male transvestites could be recalled" is telling, as is "behavior corresponding to sexual sadism, masochism, and exhibitionism could not be recalled" (1954:130). Recollections or admissions on the part of adult male informants were prompted by Honigmann's interviewing techniques, alluded to when he writes that the informant "agreed that both male and female homosexuality sometimes occurred" (1954:130).

During his first visit to the Kaska Indians, Honigmann interviewed informants at Lower Post in the Yukon, at the confluence of the Dease and Liard rivers, where the Dease River Kaska were spending the summer with other Upper Liard Kaska Indians. In his 1954 publication Honigmann carefully distinguishes the information he obtained from Upper Liard Kaska Indian and the Dease River Kaska. What is found among one group is not necessarily present among the other. For instance, he summarizes the information he received on sexual activity among the Dease River Kaska in the following way: "In coitus the women lay on her back. Cunnilingus was denied but a rare woman performed fellatio as a preliminary to intercourse. Berdaches were unknown but the informant agreed that both male and female homosexuality sometimes occurred. Homosexual men engaged in sodomy, oral contacts being carefully avoided. Two women achieved orgasm through clitoral friction" (1954:130). This is the standard pattern of presentation: heterosexual activity first, male homosexuality second, and female homosexuality last. Had the Dease River Kaska homosexual men and women been transvestites, Honigmann would have identified them as "berdaches."

When he presents his information for the Upper Liard Kaska, Honigmann refers to female transvestites in the context of a discussion of homosexuality. That discussion logically leads to the presentation of the girl raised as man, a context not necessarily that in which his Kaska informants mentioned her. Honigmann writes that *"apparently* such a girl entered into homosexual relationships" (130, emphasis added). He is not definite, nor can he be. He does not say whether he has inferred this while writing up his ethnographic notes or whether an informant suggested it to be the case.

A number of features of Honigmann's presentation call for clarification: the girl being dressed as a boy; the intent to avoid conception by the means of an amulet; the performance of male allocated tasks and the acquisition of outstanding hunting skills; and her resistance to the sexual advances of boys, a fact attributed to her alleged homosexuality. I will explore each characteristic to show that the Kaska girl raised as a boy was not that much different from other Kaska girls not so raised and that no evidence supports whether she did or did not enter homosexual relationships.

The Girl Was Dressed as a Boy

What does Honigmann mean when he says that the five-year-old girl was "dressed in masculine attire" because she was chosen to become a hunter?" From his own account of pre-contact Kaska culture we learn that among the Upper Liard Kaska a woman "manufactured clothing for her husband, children and herself" (1954:63). What is striking about this manufactured clothing is its similarity for both sexes, in childhood and in adulthood. During the summer, "infants who spent a great deal of time in the moss bag needed no garment other than the container," and they were protected "in baby bags doubled and interlined with eiderdown" during the winter (1954:64). When young children began to walk, they "wore shirts of caribou skin reaching to below the stomach" (1954:64).

Honigmann makes no mention of sex-specific garments for infants and children. On the basis of his information on traditional Kaska dress, the significance of his statement that the girl was dressed in "masculine attire" is lost. She did not differ much in dress from her female peers who were not raised in that manner. All children, boys and girls, were dressed basically the same, as were adults: "In summer each sex wore a tanned-skin breech cloth supported from an inner belt, a tailored coat or dress with sleeves reaching to just below the elbow and girdled by a belt of tanned-skin or woven porcupine quills, trousers of the same material suspended at the hips from the inner belt, and moccasins" (Honigmann 1954:63). In winter the adjustments made to this basic dress consisted in the main of additional covers: "The breech cloth became a length of plaited rabbit skin, while over the coat both sexes slipped a parka made of caribou skin or a sheep skin tanned with the hair on" (1954:63). Men and women both wore leggings, "those of the man reaching to the knee and those of the woman ending somewhere lower." Although there were "hats of woven spruce roots lined with feathers" and headgear made "from the head of the caribou" that appear to have been restricted to men, "both sexes wore hats of beaver or rabbit skin with flaps extending below the ears to tie under the chin (1954:64). Variation in dress for adult men and women thus appear to vary minimally in form and material. Among the Kaska, clothing was not a significant marker of gender. To state that the Kaska girl was dressed as a boy is meaningless. There was no gender-specific Kaska clothing.

The Girl's Avoidance of Conception

The attire of the girl raised as a boy, however, differs from that of other girls in one important respect. Kaska parents who intended a daughter to become a hunter also intended her not to conceive later in life. To this end, they prepared a belt to which the dried ovaries of a bear were attached, a belt their daughter would wear "for the rest of her life in order to avoid conception." Elsewhere Honigmann writes of other means by which Cree and Kaska women sought to avoid conception.

For instance, he reports that a girl who "following a miscarriage decides she did not again want to conceive . . . sought to induce sterility by piercing the afterbirth of the stillborn fetus with porcupine quills," thus following a custom "restricted to the Nelson Indians" (1949:231).

Because two of Old Man's wives were Cree from Fort Nelson. Old Man was probably the source of this account, as well as of the following information concerning the Upper Liard Indian custom of avoiding conception. Honigmann's reference to this second custom is worth quoting in full, for once again it appears that a sole male informant was the source of his ethnographic data: "When Mary Wiley sought to prevent conception, she followed an Upper Liard custom. Taking a three foot long piece of a bear's small intestine, she tied it around her abdomen next to the skin. This belt was worn for ten days. Although married for three years, Old Man reported, Mary has not yet produced a child" (1949:232). The intent of the Fort Nelson Indian and Upper Liard Indian customs was to avoid conception, not to prevent menstruation or interfere with sexual intercourse with males. It seems reasonable to presume that this was also the function of the dried ovaries attached to the waist of the Upper Liard girl raised as a boy.

In fact, Honigmann does not write that the purpose of the amulet was to prevent menstruation, and presumably the girl menstruated as do all other girls. Honigmann does not say that all girls raised to be hunters shun heterosexual relationships. Presumably—and assuming that the Kaska view was that the dried ovaries were worn to avoid conception—the parents and the girls must have assumed that somehow sexual intercourse could or would occur, whether a matter of mutual consent, forced by a male, or forced by the girl upon a male. According to Honigmann, such a girl often developed "great strength" (1954: 130), and a "strong woman also could throw down a man, undress him, and by sitting astride his thighs force intromission" (128). If so, Honigmann's presumption that she engaged in homosexual relationships could make the girl bisexual, that is, not adverse to sexual activity with either male or female.

Assuming, for the moment, that the girl raised as a boy to be a hunter menstruated and engaged in heterosexual activity, did she avoid conception throughout her life and always shun motherhood? We are not told, and perhaps Honigmann was also never told. Perhaps he did not ask or his male informants did not know. Assuming that some of these girls raised as boys to become hunters did become wives and mothers, would they continue to be the regular hunting and trapping partners of other males? Probably not any more than other wives and mothers. Even if girls raised as boys to become hunters did not become wives and mothers, the notion of menstrual blood as detrimental to successful hunting would constitute an important impediment to an uninterrupted partnership with male hunters. Menstrual sequestration—"camping 'way back' and then never in the company of the opposite sex" (1954:123)—was a regular feature of a woman's life from menarche to menopause. When Kaska moved camp, "the menstruant followed a distance behind the group in the company of her mother. Young men dared not followed in her footsteps if they valued their dream power" (123). Similarly, a married male avoided the camp where his menstruating wife was, "fearing that close contact with menstrual blood would cause his legs to become sore and thus render him incapable of hunting or performing other work." Similar prohibitions are mentioned for many other Native North American populations (Allen 1992:46–47, 252–54; Ryan 1995:46–47; Williams 1996:207–8). Surprisingly, Honigmann and, following him, Broch, Callender and Kochems, and Williams, do not consider the implication of such prohibitions on the Kaska girl who "performed male allocated tasks" and became a hunter.

The Girl Performing Male Tasks

How then did the activities of the girl raised to be a hunter differ from those of other girls? To answer this question we must first note that among the Kaska, "each family constituted an independent economic unit, capable of preparing required artifacts and carrying out all the routines necessary for survival" (Honigmann 1954:40). Households were expected to survive on their own, as were adults, male or female. More than a strict sexual division of labor, autonomy and competent management in the bush all year around were emphasized for both males and females. A young married couple generally trapped together, but once children were born the man looked to a "related or unrelated youth" for trapline companionship and assistance (1954:124). Women and their daughters as they grew nevertheless pursued trapping and hunting: "The general practice is for every adolescent [male and female] in a family to set traps in a territory agreed upon as his part of the trap line. . . . only unmarried girls and, sometimes a man's wife confine their trapping to within a day's journey from the winter settlement" (1954:68, 70). This is in contrast to the couple's eight-to-fifteen-mile treks before their first child. Moreover, "if adolescent girls or married women set traps given to them by a husband or father, the fur caught becomes their own" (1954:68). The furs were generally sold by the men at the trading post, but the proceeds went to their wives and daughters. Where, one may ask, is the difference between the girl raised as a boy to become a hunter and her sisters not so raised? The difference is that she accompanies her father on longer journeys away from home and probably engages in big-game hunting—when not menstruating. It is a significant difference but not beyond the reach of other women.

In childhood and early adolescence the life of the girl raised as a boy to become a hunter differed little from that of other boys and girls. Thus Honigmann can write that "for the girl puberty is accompanied by a few major changes in her economic role. She has been using a small rifle for a year or two and has already been given the task of running her mother's rabbit line" (1954:189). She and her brother hunted the same small game: "A girl who can shoot rabbits, chicken, and porcupine is flattered and may be called 'my little boy.' A boy who begins to hunt is praised less lavishly for small game (although his bag is always welcome), but his first moose or caribou marks an occasion of considerable excitement" (190). Presumably, the girl raised as a boy to become a hunter was similarly met as she progressed from small-game to big-game hunting, but Honigmann also reports that many other Kaska women also hunted and shot big game. Significantly, Honigmann writes that "men are reluctant to hunt or trap for long periods without the company of their wives," whereas women "show a greater readiness to live independently and, as widows, do not show the eagerness to remarry which is revealed by men" (1949:197). Indeed, "a widow, perhaps with the aid of a daughter or sister, often becomes economically self-supporting, hunting moose and trapping as well as tending to female allocated duties."

Here is the key difference in the socialization of Kaska male and females: "The women's greater capacity for independence is probably related to the fact that men rarely do women's work, while as children women are in a position to learn many of the duties of the opposite sex and are better prepared to be self-sufficient" (1949:197). Hence, when we read that a girl was raised as a boy to become a hunter we need not infer that when she began to perform tasks allocated to males she was atypical in doing so. Nor should we infer that in doing so she ceased performing the activities that men rarely do and that women always do. In the end, the mature girl raised as a boy to become a hunter, the newly married woman with her husband on eight-to-fifteen-kilometer treks in the bush to trap and hunt, and the independent widow pursuing the hunting mode of life in the company of other females differed little in terms of abilities and life-style.

The Girl's Resistance to the Sexual Advances of Boys

When Honigmann mentions that the girl would resist the sexual advances of boys, the context suggests that her resistance is an expression of her homosexuality (1954:128). But he also observes that "as is so common in North America, a [Kaska] girl walking along away from camp always proved a fair target for sexual advances provided she did not come under an incest rule." Among the Kaska, however, "most girls hung back shyly from physical intimacy." A girl "had first to be caught and 'forced' into submission." Seen in this light the girl-hunter who resists the sexual advances of boys is responding typically. Honigmann offers no evidence to support the view that this resistance was due to the girl's homosexual orientation. His suggestion that such a woman "apparently . . . entered homosexual relationships" probably comes from his assumption that because some female homosexuals were transvestites the girl raised and dressed as a boy was probably homosexual. He does not substantiate this inference.

To the girl who "struggled in the arms of her lover," continues Honigmann, "the boy promised I'm not going to leave you alone. I'm going to fight you," words "calculated to make her surrender, perhaps by stressing how little resistance would avail" (1954:128). So certain is Honigmann (and perhaps his male informant) of the willingness of the girl to give in to her assertive lover that he writes, "The struggle in which a girl's ambivalence toward sex relations was overcome did not constitute rape in the eyes of the youths." He then admits that "sometimes it happened that a girl truly resisted a boy's advances" and quotes an informant telling him, "When a girl does not want a man she hits the man." Even in such circumstances a male would persist in his advances. "To subdue such a girl, the rapist punched her leg about halfway above the knee thereby relaxing the thigh sufficiently to force them apart" (128).

The girl raised as a boy may differ from other Kaska girls insofar as "she knows that if he [the boy] gets her than her luck with game will be broken." According to Honigmann, Kaska closely associate hunting and sexuality, "sexual intercourse being equivalent to the successful killing of game" (1954:294). If that is the case, the girl might resist being taken as "game" by other boys in order to maintain her status as a taker of prey. If this is the symbolic association underlying her behavior, it might not necessarily preclude her taking the active role in pursuing sexual intercourse with boys, for she would then act in keeping with a hunter's ethos. But we do not know that. Honigmann is silent on the subject, as on many others, because he failed to follow up on his Kaska informants' construction of their world and their accounts of their behavior.

In the end, Honigmann's reconstruction of sexuality and gender variance in traditional Kaska culture becomes a collage of answers to a list of predetermined topics. It is a presentation of patterns of sexual behaviour from the perspective of English-speaking Kaska males and a configuration of often ill-defined recollections of past practices written up in the ethnographic present. Moreover, because "all field work was conducted in English and no interpreters were employed" (1949:19), there was no opportunity to compare and contrast accounts of the "same" event in Kaska and in English, an exercise that has been extremely revealing in work with the bilingual Dene Tha (Goulet 1988:8; Goulet 1994b:164–70).

A Recent Paraphrase of Honigmann

In the light our understanding of Honigmann's ethnographic report, we can now critically read Walter Williams's paraphrase (1986:235; 1996:202–13) of Honigmann and note what Williams had added:

> Among the Kaska Indians of the Subarctic having a son was extremely important because the female depended heavily on big-game hunting for food. If a couple had too many female children and desired a son to hunt for them in their old age, they would simply select a daughter to "be like a man." When the *youngest daughter* was about five years old, and it was obvious that the mother was not going to produce a son, *the parents performed a transformation ceremony.* They tied the dried ovaries of a bear to a belt which she always wore. That was believed *to prevent menstruation,* to protect her from pregnancy, and *to give her luck on the hunt. According to Kaska informants,* she was dressed like a male and trained to do male tasks, "often developing great strength and usually becoming an outstanding hunter." . . . if a boy made sexual advances to such a female, she reacted violently. Kaska people explained her reaction thus: "she knows that if he gets her then her luck with game will be broken." *She would have relationships only with women, achieving sexual pleasure through clitoral friction, "by getting on top of each other."* (1996:235, emphasis added)

Williams has not only added to Honigmann's Kaska data in a number of significant ways, but he has also reconfigured part of Honigmann's information to create a more definite picture of the Kaska girl as an "amazon" in the making.

In the first place there is no basis for the statement that it was the "youngest daughter," five, who was chosen to become a hunter. More likely, the five-year-old would have been chosen when following births had failed to produce a hoped-for son. The expression *transformation ceremony* is entirely Williams's. Honigmann refers to such practice simply as Indian customs used to "avoid conception." Williams appears to use the term *transformation* to signify the presumed change in the girl's gender and erotic orientation. Williams writes that the dried ovaries of a bear were also intended to prevent menstruation and give her luck on the hunt, whereas Honigmann simply mentions that the amulet was intended to prevent conception. Surprisingly, Williams does not consider the possibility that the girl might menstruate in due time, nor does he explore the implications of this development for her status as a hunter.

Second, there is nothing in Honigmann's account to confirm, as Williams writes, that informants (plural) told him that the girl would be dressed like a male and trained to do male tasks. The attribution of the information to many informants is a literary device to increase its validity. As we know from many other instances, however, Honigmann often writes of Kaska practices on the basis of information obtained from a single male informant. This may also be the case concerning the status of girls raised as boys.

Finally, Williams's statement that such a girl "would have relationships only with women" is a far cry from Honigmann's comment that "apparently such a girl entered homosexual relationships." Williams goes further; he writes that in these relationships the girl and her female partner "achieved sexual pleasure through clitoral friction." This is almost word for word what Honigmann reports for two women among the Dease River Kaska: "two women achieved orgasm through clitoral friction." This, once again, is based on the report of a single male informant who denied there were any transvestites among his people, either male or female. Williams writes that the girl and her partner achieved clitoral friction "by getting on top of each other," the words that Honigmann uses to refer to the Upper Liard female homosexuals "simulating copulation," a topic he covers briefly before turning to the discussion of girls raised as boys. A pattern of behavior reported for two Dease female homosexuals and another reported for an un-determined number of Upper Liard Kaska female homosexuals are at-tributed to the girl, now clearly identified as a homosexual.

In his paraphrase of Honigmann, Williams amalgamates different pieces of information pertaining to two groups of Kaska. As a result, the girl's sexual behavior and orientation become definite in a way they are not in the original ethnographic data. Gone is Honigmann's account, with its inherent ambiguities in content and structure. The original account appears to have been in need of revisions; of itself, it would not, as Williams claims, strongly demonstrate *"the extreme malleability* of people with respect to gender roles" nor strongly support the notion that "such assignment operates independently of a person's morpho-logical sex and can *determine both gender status and erotic behavior"* (1986:235; 1996:203, emphasis added). I do not intend to dismiss such views here, but to simply point out that they are not supported by Honigmann's record concerning the Kaska.

In brief, we know that Kaska couples might raise a daughter to become a hunter when they "had too many female children and desired a son."[3] The exceptional socialization of a girl into the role of hunter is an adap-tive strategy in the context of particular life circumstances. Honigmann recognizes that when he mentions that, as is the case among the Kaska, "in Montenegro and in other Balkan countries it was not uncommon for a girl to swear virginity and occupy the role of a son in a family without boys" (1954:130n20; cf. Cromwell in this volume). In other words, "so-cietal structure can call forth what appears to be cross-dressing or occu-pational crossing when a household needs but lacks a person of a certain social category (e.g., an 'eldest sister' in Zuni households, or 'inheriting son' in Albanian households)" (Kehoe 1993:3).

Callender and Kochems (1983a:443) recognize the Kaska girl as a "berdache" because she "combined social attributes of male and fe-male." To reach this conclusion is to miss the point that all Kaska fe-males combine these attributes to a varying degree, as do many men to a lesser degree, if only for brief periods of their lives when living in the bush without their wives. Thus Honigmann's data do not support Callender and Kochems's claim that "a real 'berdache' category" exists among the Kaska (1983a:444).

To reiterate, to write that a Kaska girl dressed and worked as she would have done had she been a male child is to say little. Both sexes differed little in dress and occupation. A strict sexual division of labor was not observed, especially by Kaska females. Among the Kaska, male and female were not the dichotomized categories found in Western culture. The ideal person in Kaska culture, whether male or female, is the autonomous and independent individual. In a society in which women routinely "learn many of the duties of the opposite sex" and whose dress styles are not marked in opposition to men's, gender differences tend to be blurred. There is a lesson to be drawn from this critical examination of the unwarranted use of Honigmann's data by contemporary anthropologists. The interest in Northern Athapaskan gender variance is legitimate, but attention should be on the diverse social and cultural contexts within which Northern Athapaskans construct their world and gendered lives. This is the intention of the following examination of Dene Tha ethnographic data.

Being Both Male and Female among Contemporary Dene Tha

To discuss gender in cases of cross-sex reincarnation among contemporary Dene Tha may suggest to some that the Dene Tha are exotic folk, far removed from the modern world. On the contrary, the Dene Tha contemporary life-style is modern, and, over the past two hundred years they have lived through all the changes described for the Slave by Asch (1981; 1984:14–27). The semi-nomadic bands of the past who traveled across the land with horse wagons, canoes, and dog sleighs have now settled permanently on a reservation to live in government-built houses serviced with electricity. A household is most often constituted of three generations living under one roof. Sources of income are many: income generated by trapping, wages earned in and outside of the reservation through part-time work, and family allowance, old-age pension benefits, and social welfare provided by different levels of government. Cars, trucks, motorboats, and snowmobiles are the means of transportation to traplines or nearby towns. Dene Tha families buy much of their food in the local store, but big-game meat, fowl, fish, and small-game meat procured by men, and fish and berries harvested by women, are also prominent parts of the diet. A local public school teaches children in English, although they speak their native language on the school's playground. At home, children converse with each other and other family members in their own language while listening to the omnipresent television.

The Dene Tha, who have been the subject of intense missionary activity over the last century, continue to shape their lives according to a distinctive Northern Athapaskan religious tradition (Goulet 1982; Goulet 1994a). In this tradition, a distinction is drawn between "this land" or "our land" (*ndahdigeh*) and the "other land" (*ech'uhdigeh*), also referred to as *yake* (heaven) and *Ndahxota digeh* (God's land). Human beings live in both of these lands, and communication through dreams and visions between those who live in "our land" and the deceased in the "other land" is possible and normal. Communication between the deceased and their relatives in "this land" often occurs when the soul of the deceased, rather than journeying to the "other land," seeks on its own to enter the womb of a woman to be born again in "this land" in a sex of his or her choice (Goulet 1982:9–10; Goulet 1988:8–11; Goulet 1994b:156–62). Sightings of souls of deceased individuals seeking to be born again are often reported.[4] For instance, speaking of her recently deceased brother, a woman told me, "He has been to our house and wants to be a baby again. He came at night and around the school too he was seen." When returning to Chateh after a six-month absence, I was told that "right now there are lots of people going around who want to be reincarnated." In Chateh, a reincarnation is thus commonly foreseen and foretold by a parent-to-be or a relative of a child yet to be born.

When speaking of these events, Dene Tha speakers seldom use the expression *reincarnation*. They may use English phrases such as "he or she was done to us again" or "he or she was done again," expressions that are almost literal translations of the Dene phrase denoting such a person: *Dene andats'indla* (a person who was made again by others). The process of reincarnation and the process of human reproduction are intimately linked. Dene Tha often pointed out to me that a sexually active couple often remained without a child for a few years and that conception then occurred after either the wife or husband "saw" a deceased relative coming back to them to be born again. Sexual intercourse thus appears as a necessary, but not sufficient, condition for human reproduction.

As one Dene Tha woman put it, "There is always somebody who knows who it is going to be, they see the spirit going into you." From Dene Tha accounts of reincarnation, I understand that the spirit going into a woman belongs to an individual with a clear sexual identity—it is a known male or female who has come back to a kinswoman to be born again. When the child is born, its sex may or may not coincide with the individual's previous sex. When the child is born in a sex opposite to its previous sex, the previous sex determines what kinship terms of address are used. A man might address his brother's son as "my daughter" and address him/her as such because he "knows," as does everyone else, that the child is his daughter reincarnated. In turn, these kinship terms trigger a wide range of accounts of the child's previous life that progressively enter that child's sense of identity. These accounts of a previous life enter all kinds of conversations—those in houses, at the local store, and at the band administration building. For instance, in the local store I heard Dene Tha men jokingly remind a mature Dene Tha woman of the time she had been a male among them and could join them in all-male drinking bouts in the bush. She was not expected to join them in her present gender because that would not be consistent with her present life as a wife, mother, and grandmother. She, like others identified as cases of cross-sex reincarnation, was normally not expected to dress and behave as a member of the sex characteristic of her previous incarnation. Household members may, however, ask such individuals to momentarily manifest more clearly their underlying sexual identity through changes in hair-style, manner, and the use of cosmetics, as illustrated in the following case.

Being Male and Female

In May 1980, Paul, twenty-seven, told me, "You know, I am really the sister of Mary." Mary, in her forties, is his cousin (his father's sister's daughter) and neighbor. Paul was sharing the knowledge that he shared with the other Dene in the community: He was not the man he appeared to be, he was really Mary's sister. I asked Paul to explain further. He first recorded a statement in Dene and then made the following translation of his Dene recording:

> I am Denise, Mary's sister. I came back, that is what I was. One day, all of a sudden, Denise and her sister [Rose] came to my mother. Rose said: "My big sister, I bring her [Denise] with me, that is what I am doing." After Rose went, I (Denise) stayed. My mother says: "Denise grabbed me and I fell unconscious." It will be a baby girl they thought. But I was. Now, they knew I had come back, and they loved me very much. If I put my hair behind, from a distance I am as a woman, and they tell me I am a girl. I colour my eyes and my mouth, and sometimes they ask me to put my hair behind, like this, and they tell me: "yes, you look like a woman!"

In this account Paul begins by identifying himself as Denise, Mary's sister, and then refers to himself/herself in the third person: "All of a sudden, Denise and her sister [Rose] came to my mother." Denise thus appeared to Paul's mother before she was born as Paul, a boy. Paul explains that Denise, a baby girl, had died shortly after birth and that soon after her death her ghost had appeared frequently to Paul's mother in her house in Chateh. The apparition Paul mentions occurred in the Camsell hospital in Edmonton, where Paul's mother was hospitalized. Paul's home is more than eight hundred kilometers from Edmonton. It was Rose (also a ghost) who took her younger sister, Denise, to Paul's mother. When Denise grabbed Paul's mother she fell unconscious. Back home, Paul's mother discovered she was pregnant. She and her relatives expected Denise to be born again. Everyone expected a girl, but a boy was born. Everyone nevertheless knew who she was, he was Denise.

"They knew I came back as Denise." Paul added, "They always told me who I was." Because this is so, he was not treated as other boys and men in the community. Girls did not and would not date him. In his late twenties he was still single. When young men congregated in the bush for all-male beer parties, Paul was not invited. Paul did not join the young unmarried men and women in the abandoned house they used for parties and sex. The walls of this house are covered with drawings of male and female figures having sexual intercourse, along with drawings of hearts and genitals. Among the drawings I noticed two hearts, one surrounding a cherry and the other surrounding a penis. The two hearts, one next to the other, were surrounded by the following inscription: "Paul never broke his cherry. I don't know how to break Paul's cherry, but someday I break his cherry for her."

Although he did not take part in the parties held in this house, sex was certainly on Paul's mind, as shown in the following account of a dream he had shortly before his first experience of sex with a young woman. The dream involves John, his very close friend, who has fathered children with a number of young Dene Tha women. In the opening scene of the dream, Paul sees John holding a woman lying in thick, dry grass: "They were on a big prairie; I am there too, and there is a woman I want. I tell John, 'There are no women for me, not one of them likes me.' But John says, 'Go for it, that woman is your woman, go play with her over there.' And I woke up. Those women. I knew who they were, but when I woke up I did not remember." Immediately following the account of his dream, Paul asked me, "Is it bad to do witchcraft on somebody?" I asked, "Why would you want to do witchcraft on someone?" He answered, "I want some people to do something I want them to do." He showed me a pocket-size magazine advertising witchcraft spells and love potions for sale. "Like I would make love with them, I would make them turn into lovers, it's for myself, " he said. Paul then added that he had recently had a private encounter with a young woman who had kissed him. He attributed her attitude and behavior to someone's "power" making her interested in him.

The drawing of the two hearts publicly stated the problem as Paul's peers saw it. His body was obviously that of a male, yet he carried within his personal identity that of a female. His "cherry," the marker of his female identity, had to be broken; his penis, the sign of his male identity, had to be affirmed. Paul's dream and his secret encounter with a young woman who kissed him in the privacy of a small house reflected his inclination to change his past. A radical transformation was called for if Paul were to evolve in adulthood in the expected relationship with an opposite-sex partner. This was initiated by his peers. In the mid-1980s news circulated around the community that Paul's cherry had finally been broken. Young men and women had finally succeeded in having Paul join them at a drinking party where they had him have sex with a young woman from the group. For a week or so after the event, Paul was constantly teased in public, in the store, at church, and on the road, with people asking him in Dene Dháa if he had enjoyed himself. Paul would invariably laugh with them, acknowledging that the experience had, indeed, taken place and that it had given him much pleasure. Following his sexual initiation, Paul emerged in the community with a complete personal identity that he did not have before, that of an active heterosexual male who had enjoyed himself with an opposite-sex partner.

Paul's account of his life reveals that there is more to a person's identity than meets the eye. Seeing Paul as a female in a male body is possible in the context of a belief system in which it is taken for granted that a person can be reborn. Northern Athapaskan knowledge allows for cross-sex reincarnation, and it therefore follows that looking upon a male as a female reincarnated, or a female as a male reincarnated, illustrates a truth about human life. As among the Tlinkit, "Sex is apparently not an unchangeable attribute of a person" (de Laguna 1954:187).[5] Within the Dene Tha framework of knowledge, Paul's close kin identify him as a she, address her accordingly when using kinship terms, and at times ask her to part her hair behind, color her eyes and lips, to "look like a woman." Contemporary Dene Tha also generally expect that regardless of one's antecedent sexual identity, as an adult one eventually engages an opposite-sex partner in the procreative business of life.

It appears that Paul's peers arranged to start Paul on the road of hetero-sexual activity.

Conclusion

The ethnographic record contains references to Northern Athapaskan women who dressed and/or behaved "just like a man" and to Northern Athapaskan men who at times behaved "just like a woman." People who are not Northern Athapaskan generally read more than there is in the ethnographic record because they lack an in-depth grasp of the manner in which Northern Athapaskans themselves understand such phenomena. Euro-Canadian (and other Western-based) dichotomized categories of male and female gender roles are not those of the Northern Athapaskans. The Kaska girl raised as a boy shared dress with other boys and girls, as well as occupation. This was so because Kaska emphasized individual autonomy more than a strict sexual division of labor. Euro-Canadian (and other Western-based) dichotomized categories of male and female gender roles are not those of the Kaska. It is easy to read more than is warranted into the ethnographic record, and one can paraphrase it in ways that add details to reflect particular propositions about gender and sexual malleability rather than the original source.

The pursuit of identifying hitherto unknown "berdaches" and "amazons" among Northern Athapaskans is a dubious one. It is more fruitful to examine local conceptions of personhood and gender, as I have done for the Dene Tha, and show how individuals come to self-identify as woman, as man, or as both (as is the case for some Dene Tha) in cooperation with others as they jointly create and maintain these identities. Social identities, like any other social reality, are created and sustained in and through linguistic and social practices. Among the Dene Tha, personal identities are more complex than those of Euro-Canadians; one's life history often includes an episode in the "other land," from which one has chosen to come back to "this world" to be made again. A Dene Tha is an individual whose soul is believed to travel from "this land" to the "other land" in the dream state or in death. In the Dene Tha experience of the world—and of themselves—sexual identity is not unchangeable. For many, the journeys from "this land" to the "other land" and back allow individuals to accumulate many lives, as male or female or as both.

Notes

A revised and condensed version of the discussion of the Kaska girl raised like a man, and an expanded presentation of Dene Tha culture and cross-sex reincarnation, appear in Goulet (1996). The article also contains a theoretical discussion of the construction of gender identities by anthropologists and Northern Athapaskans and a discussion of other alleged cases of "berdache"/two-spirit among Northern Athapaskans.

The extensive research time among the Dene Tha (six months a year for five consecutive years, beginning in January 1980, with regular visits since) was made possible by the Canadian Research Centre for Anthropology, Saint Paul University (Ottawa). I am indebted to Sue-Ellen Jacobs, Sabine Lang, and Graham Watson for their comments on earlier drafts of this essay presented at the Wenner-Gren Conferences "Revisiting the 'North American Berdache' Empirically and Theoretically." Their insightful questions and requests for additional information, as well as their criticism, were very helpful. In the end, however, I am responsible for the views expressed in this essay. Above all, my gratitude goes to the people of Chateh who shared their stories and welcomed me into their lives and homes.

1. Gender identities, whether of Euro-Americans or of Native North Americans, like any other social reality, are created and sustained in and through social practices. It is possible to show that every reality, including those of the hard sciences and mathematics, is constructed, thus undermining the implicit claim of many epistemological positions that reality exists prior to, and independent of, the discourse that constitutes it (Watson and Goulet 1992). The fashionable distinction between sex (the biological givens) and gender (the sociocultural roles ascribed to individuals on the basis of their sex) wrongly assumes that culture interprets or assigns social significance to natural (biologically given) distinctiveness. The historical and anthropological record, however, shows much variability in European and non-European taxonomies of sexual organs. Broch-Due, Rudie, and Bleie write: "The body can hardly be seen to occupy a pure prediscursive space in society, directly interpretable through the senses. Rather, sexed bodies are lived in culture, mediated and molded by its values and its discourse" (1993:32). This is illustrated in a statement by a traditional Dine scholar to Carolyn Epple: "Even the [sexual] organs are male and female, inseparable and distinct. At the tip of the penis is a little vagina, while on the vulva is a little penis. That is how it is said in Navajo" (1993:19). What is mostly missing in Callender and Kochems's discussion of the "berdache" is the conceptualizations in other cultures of sexuality and gender. In its absence, it makes little sense to recognize more and more "berdaches," past and present, in more and more societies.

2. In the anthropological literature, people of this community are referred to either as Slavey (Asch 1981:348) or as "the Dene Tha branch of the Beaver Indians" (Smith 1987:444). Chateh is the name of the reservation also known as Assumption (Asch 1981:338). The Department of Indian and Northern Affairs Canada (1987:91) lists the reservation as Hay Lake, with a population of 809 in December 1986. Linguistically, *Dene Dha* is a more appropriate spelling, but the people of Chateh have retained the old spelling, *Dene Tha,* and I follow suit. Quotations of informants are verbatim, and all individual names are fictive to protect anonymity.

3. Similar practices are reported for the Dogrib. Ryan notes that "as with hunting, men chose partners with whom to go out on the trap lines. Occasionally, a man and his wife might be 'partners' by themselves out on the land. Some women also had partnerships with their fathers and reported that they worked 'just like a man.' This was usually the case when a man had older daughters but no sons old enough to go out with him" (1995:31). A few years ago I had a Cree student who was similarly raised by her father. Although she recognized that the experience of having lived as a hunting and trapping companion certainly marked her off from her sisters, she did not see herself as occupying a special gender status in Cree society and culture.

4. Views concerning reincarnation differ considerably from one Northern Athapaskan community to another. In Chateh, not everyone comes back to be born again, only those who cannot find the path to heaven or those who had not wanted to die in the first place. In principle this could result in successive reincarnations by the same individual. In practice, Dene Tha appear to focus on the most recent identity of the one reincarnating. As the daughter of a Dene Tha dreamer explained, "Like half-way to heaven there is a door and they look at heaven on the other side and they look back on this earth. Sometimes they do not want to leave this earth, they come be reborn." Among the Dunne-za of northeast British Columbia, however, "All people are said to be the reincarnation of souls who have been on earth before" (Mills 1988:25). This is also in contrast to the Chipewyan, who "believe that new souls are always entering the world" (Sharp 1976:31), which explains why the majority of Chipewyans do not recall having had a previous life on earth. The Dunne-za account differently for the fact that some individuals do not remember a previous reincarnation. They say that after reaching heaven "the disincarnate person's soul is washed," making "their memories of their past life, of specific people and places, and of their likes and dislikes" largely unrecoverable when reborn (Mills 1988:25). But some souls "never get past that place where you have to grab hold of the cross" to continue on the path to heaven (Mills 1988:25). These souls are reborn quickly and are known as "special children." These souls bring with them some of the knowledge, preferences, and aversions, and the personality they had manifested in previous lives (Mills 1988:25).

5. I thank Sabine Lang (1994) for having brought to my attend Frederica de Laguna's "Tlingit Ideas about the Individual," in which she discusses gender variance in the context of reincarnation beliefs: "Sex is apparently not an unchangeable attribute of a person. Thus, not only may sex be changed at reincarnation, but at menopause (according to the interior Tlingit) the women 'changes back to a man again'" (de Laguna 1954:187). The reference to Tlingit women who after menopause revert to being a man calls to mind Honigmann's description of Kaska women, who at a similar stage pursue a manly life, living independently and hunting big game with other women as companions.

References Cited

Allen, Paula Gunn. 1992. *The Sacred Hoop: Recovering the Feminine in American Indian Traditions.* Boston: Beacon Press.

Asch, Michael. 1981. "Slavery." In *Handbook of North American Indians,* ed. J. Helm, 6:338–49. Washington: Smithsonian Institution.

———. 1984. *Home and Native Land: Aboriginal Rights and the Canadian Constitution.* Toronto: Methuen Publications.

Broch, Harald Beyer. 1983. Comments on "The North American 'Berdache,'" by Charles Callender and Lee M. Kochems. *Current Anthropology* 24(4): 467.

Broch-Due, Vigdis, Ingrid Rudie, and Tone Bleie. 1993. "Carved Flesh-Cast Selves: An Introduction." In *Carved Flesh-Cast Selves: Gendered Symbols and Social Practices: Cross-Cultural Perspectives on Women,* ed. Vigdis Broch-Due, Ingrid Rudie, and Tone Bleie. Volume 8. Oxford: Berg.

Callender, Charles, and Lee M. Kochems. 1983a. "The North American 'Berdache.'" *Current Anthropology* 24(4): 443–70.

———. 1983b. Reply. *Current Anthropology* 24(4): 464–67.

De Laguna, Frederica. 1954. "Tlingit Ideas about the Individual." *Southwestern Journal of Anthropology* 10(2): 172–91.

Department of Indian and Northern Affairs, Canada. 1987. *Schedule of Indian Bands, Reserves and Settlements Including—Membership and Population, Location and Area in Hectares.* Ottawa: Department of Indian and Northern Affairs, Canada.

Epple, Carolyn. 1993. "Another 'Berdache' Headache; or, *Nádleehí* in Navajo Worldview: Implications for Western Constructs." Paper presented at "Revisiting the 'North American Berdache' Empirically and Theoretically." 92d annual meeting of the American Anthropological Association, Washington, D.C.

Goulet, Jean-Guy A. 1982. "Religious Dualism among Athapaskan Catholics." *Canadian Journal of Anthropology/Revue Canadienne d'Anthropologie* 3(1): 1–18.

———. 1988. "Representation of Self and Reincarnation among the Dene Tha." *Culture* 8(2): 3–18.

———. 1994a. "Ways of Knowing: Towards a Narrative Ethnography of Dene Tha Experiences." *Journal of Anthropological Research* 50(3): 113–39.

———. 1994b. "Reincarnation as a Fact of Life among Contemporary Dene Tha." In *Amerindian Rebirth,* ed. Antonia Mills and Richard Slobodin, 156–76. Toronto: University of Toronto Press.

———. 1996. "The 'Berdache'/Two-Spirit: A Comparison of Anthropological and Native Constructions of Gendered Identities among the Northern Athapaskans." *Journal of the Royal Anthropological Institute* 2(n.s.): 1–20.

Honigmann, John H. 1949. *Culture and Ethos of Kaska Society.* New Haven: Yale University Press.

———. 1954. *The Kaska Indians: An Ethnographic Reconstruction.* New Haven" Yale University Publications in Anthropology 51.

Jacobs, Sue-Ellen. 1968. "Berdache: A Brief Review of the Literature." *Colorado Anthropologist* 1(2): 25–40. Reprint. Wayne R. Dynes and Stephen Donaldson, eds. 1992. *Studies in Homosexuality.* Volume 2: *Ethnographic Studies of Homosexuality.* New York: Garland.

Kehoe, Alice. 1993. Comments on papers presented at "Revisiting the 'North American Berdache' Empirically and Theoretically." 92d annual meeting of the American Anthropological Association, Washington, D.C.

Mills, Antonia, 1988. "A Preliminary Investigation of Cases of Reincarnation among the Beaver and Gitksan Indians." *Anthropoligica* 30: 23–59.

Roscoe, Will. 1987. "Bibliography of Berdache and Alternative Gender Roles among North American Indians." *Journal of Homosexuality* 14(3–4): 81–171.

Ryan, Joan. 1995. *Doing Things the Right Way: Dene Traditional Justice in Lac LaMartre N.W.T.* Calgary: University of Calgary Press.

Sharp, Henry Stephen. 1976. "Man: Wolf: Woman: Dog." *Arctic Anthropology* 13(1): 25–34.

Smith, J. G. E. 1987. "The Western Woods Cree: Anthropological Myth and Historical Reality." *American Ethnologist* 14(3): 434–48.

Watson, Graham, and Jean-Guy A. Goulet. 1992. "Gold In; Gold Out: The Objectification of Dene Tha Accounts of Dreams and Visions." *Journal of Anthropological Research* 48(3): 215–30.

Williams, Walter L. 1986. *The Spirit and the Flesh: Sexual Diversity in American Indian Culture.* Boston: Beacon Press. Reprint 1992, with a new preface.

———. 1996. "'Amazons' of America: Female Gender Variance." In *Gender in Cross-Cultural Perspective,* ed. Caroline B. Brettell and Carolyn F. Sargent, 202–13. 2d edition. Englewood Cliffs: Prentice-Hall.

★ ★ 3

Cross-Dressing and Shamanism among Selected Western North American Tribes

Arnold R. Pilling

This chapter reevaluates some of the concepts relating to what the older anthropological literature designates as "berdache" [*sic*]. My comments are derived, in part, from my research into U.S. census coverage of Zuni cross-dressers (transvestites) who lived on that reservation between 1880 and 1900 (Cushing 1880; Greason 1898). In 1916 Elsie Clews Parsons wrote an article on Zuni transvestites, one of the earliest extensive discussions of cross-dressing in any North American Indian community. She referred to her paper as a contribution to the study of "Indian berdache."

Today, following the usage of contemporary urban Native American communities, the inappropriately applied older term *berdache* has been dropped, and the new Native American/Indian term of *two-spirit* has been adopted. "Two-spirit" refers to persons who are a blend of the feminine and the masculine, the woman and the man. Clearly, the cross-dressers of the past fall into this category.

Readers may find this discussion singularly dry, clinical, and "scientific" in its phrasing, devoid of the warmth now associated with two-spirit people. That is the nature of most census data, however. For instance, it would appear that American legal usage concerning federal censuses bars questions on religion or spirituality, areas central to the thinking of today's two-spirit persons. Yet by looking at census sources we can glimpse what life was like for earlier two-spirit persons, into what type of kinship household they fitted, and how they seem to have continued to be accepted in their homes of origin.

I do not want to romanticize the lives of two-spirit persons late in the last century, however. The Zuni cross-dresser Kasinelu was initially opposed by his mother's father, Nayuchi, a kind of head of his household, when he wanted to start dressing as a woman. Nayuchi's opposition was possibly an early occurrence of what might today be termed homophobia. But in Zuni it is the mother's mother and the mother of a person who have the primary say concerning their behavior, and Kasinelu, supported by her/his mother and mother's mother, remained in his household and cross-dressed (Parsons 1916:523; Roscoe 1991:195; Stevenson 1904:38).

Early on, it should be noted that every four years, including 1896 and 1916, the Zuni performed a ceremony in which there was a Kachina that Roscoe has identified as a "berdache" (1991:24, 78, 147–69). She/ he held a yucca bloom in each hand and wore in her/his hair a white eagle feather, one of the symbols of an elite (ceremony-controlling) family in much of western North America. In 1896 a female whom Elsie Clews Parsons identified as "Nancy" represented this Kachina.[1] I strongly suspect that the name was Parsons's pseudonym for Nina, the first cousin of the person Parsons (1939) designated as the last Zuni transvestite, Kasinelu.[2] Also in Kasinelu's kin group was a female named Ener-citu, who in 1920, at about sixty-five, had her gender identification changed from female to male.[3] In the decennial U.S. census for Zuni, taken on February 4, 1920, "Enaseta" is designated as "F[emale]" and a "herder . . . of sheep" (van der Beek 1920:sheet 10a, line 43), an occupation otherwise at Zuni restricted to males. She was living with her brother Halian, Nina's father, and her cousin Kasinelu (van der Beek 1920:sheet 10a, lines 42–45). In the Bureau of Indian Affairs census of June 30, 1920, "Enasetah" is said to be a "M[ale]," living alone (Bauman 1920:present #187). That is, there is some evidence that the ceremonial role of "Berdache Kachina" passed down one family line and that lineage or kin group contained several special-gendered persons.

In her 1916 account, Parsons mentioned an aged Zuni heterosexual male who could remember nine male Zuni cross-dressers. This man, named "Tsaliselu" (Parsons 1917:306), was reported by the 1910 census-taker (Davis 1910:sheet 8a, line 4) to have been about sixty, suggesting a birth year of 1850 and a memory covering events back to 1860. Parsons did not list all nine of these Zuni "men-women" (la'mana). She did mention Kasinelu (1880–fl. 1946), Kwiwishidi (1872–fl. 1900), Tsalatit-se (1873–1918), U'k/Yuka (1884–1937), and We'wha (1849–96), the subject of Will Roscoe's The Zuni Man-Woman (1991).[4]

Mary Dissette, who taught school for several years at Zuni starting in 1888 and continuing until at least February 18, 1898 (Roscoe 1991:23, 118, 246n80), gave the name "Manna" for an early Zuni man-woman. This designation is probably no more than a variant of *la'mana*. What Dissette writes of this person suggests that her "Manna" was actually We'wha.

The 1898 Bureau of Indian Affairs census taken by Elmira R. Greason (1898:#1551) also notes transvestite "Tsi a muna" as an "in woman clothes M[ale]." This designation, however, is one of the names known for Parsons's Tsalatitse (1873–1918) (1939:338). That is, two *la'mana* who might be thought of as additional, named two-spirit persons are in fact only instances of known men-women who had two different names and designations.

In contrast, reference to early U.S. censuses identifies two more *la'mana*. The decennial U.S. census taken by Frank Hamilton Cushing of the Bureau of Ethnology in October 1880 specifies not only We'wha, whom Cushing (1880:26, line 42) identifies as a "Hem F [Hermaphrodite Female]," but also Na-wi-ko (ca. 1848–fl. 1880; 7, line 11) and Kisi-a-us-ti (ca. 1843–fl. 1880). Cushing designated both Na-wi-ko and Kisi-a-us-ti as "hermaphrodites" (5, line 29). That is, both the aged Zuni male of 1916 and the census data indicate that there were at least seven men-women living in Zuni sometime between 1880 and 1900.

Parsons (1916) suggested that two men-women were briefly married to men. Greason reported 1898 census data that specified that Kwiwishidi lived in a two-person household within the Zuni farming settlement of Nutria, a unit that consisted of Kwiwishdi, thirty-five, and her/his twenty-six-year-old nephew. Parsons (1916), who never observed this household as a functioning unit, referred to it as a marriage. Matilda Coxe Stevenson, who lived at Zuni when the relationship existed, referred to it in a more circumspect, and probably more accurate, fashion; she wrote of this "couple . . . living together" and stated that the *"ko'thlama* [the same as *la'mana*] . . . allied himself to a man" (1904:406). The household in Nutria, however, seems most accurately described as nothing other than a family's farm-settlement suburban household.

What was probably the other "marriage" referred to by Parsons concerned a co-residence of "Manna" in the early 1890s. Parsons was not witness to this household, nor was her chief source of data, her hostess Mrs. Lewis, and details of Manna's living arrangement are unclear. There is no census entry covering the occurrence; that is, there is no firm evidence that any Zuni cross-dresser was ever married to a man.

A study of the composition of each Zuni man-woman's household shows a shared structural feature. Among the predominantly uxorilocal, matrilineal Zuni, women seem to have controlled household operations. With few exceptions, daughters remained in their birthright household at marriage, each bringing her husband into her matrilineal household. Aged Zuni, both female and male, were dependent upon the young females of their household for help. Therefore, it is not surprising that all cross-dressers except U'k, who was retarded (Parsons 1916), lacked an elder sister. It seems that the emergence of a cross-dresser in a Zuni household was nearly always a response to the lack of a sister or female matrilateral cousin in the household. The cross-dressing occurrences seem, in part, to have been a reaction to a gap in the multigenerational Zuni household structure.

I would note that my recent research in Zuni documents shows that We'wha and all *la'mana* of 1898 lived most, or all, of the time in one or another of the farming communities, with We'wha apparently in Nutria (Broder 1990:173, illus. 179; Wittick 1890/1894; see also Figure 3-1), as were Kwiwishdi and Kasinelu; U'k at Oja Caliente; and Tsi a muna/Tsalatitse at Pescado (Greason 1898).

Review of the occurrence of cross-dressing at Zuni suggests an increase of such persons in the 1890s. Perhaps that increase correlated with the termination of the Ute (and Mexican) slave trade in children on January 31, 1852, as a product of its aggressive suppression by Mormon leaders (Sonne 1962:136). Perhaps the increase in cross-dressing was a form of resistance to the increase of white ways at Zuni village. Or maybe We'wha's travel to Washington and meeting with Grover Cleveland served as a model of success for some young Zuni males.

There remains the question of the extent to which Zuni cross-dressing patterns may be related to shamanism. Conner lists the activities of shamans: "communicating with deities and spirits, divining the future, diagnosing and healing illnesses, working magic (especially bringing rain), and guiding the souls of the deceased to the next life . . . ancestor reverence, sacrifice, reaching altered states of consciousness via drumming, dancing, and other techniques" (1993:48). A hint of this type of activity among the Zuni is noted in passages by Matilda Coxe Stevenson (1904:195) describing the Rain Dance and the burial of prayer plumes.

The occurrence I have encountered in the Zuni literature that links a cross-dresser with shamanistic behavior is to be found in relation to

Figure 3-1. We'wha in front of her/his home in the Zuni farming suburb of Nutria. Note We'wha's loosely hanging hair. (Ben Wittick, 1890 [Wright 1894:2d leaf after 444])

We'wha's burial of prayer feathers while in Washington (Roscoe 1991:69–70, 90, citing Mason 1886), a behavior pattern that does not seem distinctively shamanistic but rather a general adult male practice among the Pueblos. That is, among the Zuni, cross-dressing does not seem to have had any special tie to shamanism.

The 1898 Bureau of Indian Affairs census records nearly a .22 percent occurrence of cross-dressers among Zuni about June 28, 1898 (Greason 1898). The rate seems, in part, to have been a reflection of specific structural and historical developments at Zuni, where the concept of cross-dressing was already present as part of Kachina rituals but not part of a curing or shamanistic role.

Another occurrence of cross-dressing was described in the fieldnotes of Joel V. Berreman (1934, 1935), who reported on the Wapato group of Tualatin in northern Lincoln County, Oregon, where Jack Nance—Shimkin (or Simpkin), a shaman—had lived at Grand Ronde Reservation. Berreman's notes described Jack Nance as habitually dressing as a woman, riding sidesaddle, and having been rumored to have had a husband; he was coarse-featured and large-handed. His curing dance was somewhat idiosyncratic when compared with that of the three other male and three female shamans at Grand Ronde. Unlike the other six shamans, Jack Nance did not enter the house that was the site of a curing until near the end of his doctoring dance. Unlike Zuni cross-dressers, he was not reported to be part of a more general Grand Ronde pattern but seems to have worked out his own cross-dressing definition.

It is possible that Jack Nance's surname, "Nance," is a reference to his passive homosexuality. Consider, for example, President James Buchanan's personal relationship with Franklin Pierce's vice president William Rufus King (1786–1853): "Former President Andrew Jackson dubbed the lifelong bachelor [William Rufus King] 'little Miss Nancy' after King took fellow politician James Buchanan as a roommate—an arrangement that lasted over twenty years" (Aylson 1990:129). I have also heard "Nance" and "Nancy" used interchangeably among gay men in the Detroit area to refer to one another.

Two cross-dressing shamans were reported from the nineteenth-century Tolowa of northwestern California. Roscoe indicates that such shamans were labeled *minhushre* in their native Tolowa language (Gay American Indians, comps., ed. Roscoe 1988:51, apparently inaccurately citing Gould 1978:131). The earlier of these two was a person designated as "Old Doctor" (Costelloe 1870:26, line 32). Stephen Dow Beckham (1971:86; see also Figure 3-2) reproduces a photograph of Old Doctor taken "before 1874"; in 1971 an original of that photograph survived in the collections of the Smithsonian Institution's Office of Anthropology. In this studio shot, a wooden post acts as a prop in front of Old Doctor, whose left arm is raised from the elbow upward at the left of his body. Old Doctor is wearing a woman's hat shaped like a sugar loaf, as was known for the southern Oregon Coast. Fur-wrapped—probably otter-skin-wrapped—pendant locks hang at each side of his face. He also is wearing a dentalia necklace as owned by the wealthy of both genders of Tolowa, Yurok, and Hupa.

A second, very similar, image of Old Doctor was reproduced in the 1877 version of Stephen Powers's work, *The Tribes of California* (the 1872 version of the work is not illustrated). The biography of Powers notes that "during the summers of 1871 and 1872, [Powers] traveled some thousands of miles on foot and on horseback among the California Indians" (Park 1975:13). The earliest of the articles deriving from these trips concerned northern California Indians and were published in the

Figure 3-2. Old Doctor. (Beckham 1971:86, from a negative in Office of Anthropology, Smithsonian Institution)

Overland Monthly in late 1872 (Heizer, ed. 1976:6), suggesting that the second image of Old Doctor probably derived from 1871. This image was etched, almost certainly from a photograph, by an artist signing himself H. H. Nichols, and it was labeled "Figure 23. The old Charcoal Artist" (Heizer, ed. 1976; Powers 1877:opposite 246; see also Figure 3-3). This image of Old Doctor is almost identical to the photograph reproduced by Beckham. It differs in its lack of a post in front of the old man and the position of the left arm and hand, the latter being held by the right hand in the second image. The same basketry cap is at the same cant as that in the first image; indeed, the second image may have been drawn from the first image.

The third image of Old Doctor (Figure 3-4), like the other image (or other images were) taken by an unknown photographer, is a halftone reproduced in the U.S. Census report for 1890, *Indians Taxed and Not Taxed* (Wright 1894:opposite 206). Its top is arched, and the lower edge is square. Such a photographic outline is most commonly found on stereographs (McCulloch 1981; Taft 1938/1964), although it is occasionally found on daguerreotypes (Newhall 1976:#61, #93), *cartes de visite* (Darrah 1981:#198, #362), and cabinet mounts (Taft 1938/1964:343, lower left). It seems likely that this third image of Old Doctor derives from a stereograph.

In the shot Old Doctor wears the same loaf-shaped cap and has fur-wrapped locks on each side of his face. He appears to be wearing dentalia, one through the wing on each nostril, much as was later worn by Doctor Medicine (Gould 1966:140–41; Gould 1978:132; Gay American Indians, comps., ed. Roscoe 1988:52, citing Smithsonian Institution, National Anthropological Archives, neg. 81–2130; W. Williams 1986:pl. 13). Old Doctor appears to have a square abalone ornament hanging from his nose septum (or the item could be a white clay European pipe).

Old Doctor is bare-chested, as are his arms. At his neck is a loose cloth choker that seems to be unpatterned and monochrome. Pendant from his neck are two necklaces, one a standard northwestern California dentalia necklace and another that hangs to his waist and is many-stranded. Each strand is made up of white and dark, probably blue, beads. The bottom of the necklace at his waist is dark, then come a series of white beads on each strand about eight inches long, and then a band of dark beads disappears under Old Doctor's wrapped locks about three inches above the previous white band of the necklace.

At Old Doctor's waist is a buckskin band perhaps ten inches wide. Its upper six inches or so are plain, then comes an apparent three-inch

Figure 3-3. Old Doctor. (Heizer 1976: Figure 23, from original labeled "Figure 23. The old Charcoal Artist" [Powers 1877])

Figure 3-4. Old Doctor. (Wright 1894: opposite 206, from original labeled "Klamath Indian Shaman [Medicine Man], Crescent City")

band of what appears to be river otter fur that seems to have been sewed onto the buckskin waistband. Another four inches below, the fringe at the bottom of the waistband begins: grass that varies from four to eight inches in length. At the end of many fringe strands are pendant thimbles; the ends of other woven grass fringes appear to have been wrapped. The waistband is worn over a knee-length ceremonial skirt made of grey squirrel skins, white bellies out. The pendant tails of some cat species hang from the joining site of each squirrel skin to about his ankles (Figure 3–4). This skirt is worn over heavy jeans. His feet seem to be in doeskin-wrapped moccasins.

A note on this ceremonial skirt is appropriate. Lee Davis, the modern scholar of the Hoopa, has told me that such cat skirts were considered to have a great deal of spiritual power. A similar skirt is pictured in the same *1890 Indians Taxed and Not Taxed* (Cantwell 1890/1894:opposite 204; see also Figure 3-5) and is made of grey squirrel pelts with cat tails hanging between them. That skirt is worn by a middle-aged Hoopa White Deerskin "hook man" dancer demonstrating how obsidian "show" blades are carried when being paraded in the White Deerskin Dance. As far as is known, the cat from which the skirt was made has been extinct in northwestern California for many decades, possibly nearly a century.

Old Doctor lived in a Yurok/Tolowa village south of Crescent City, just north of Endert's Beach, at Cushion Creek. A photograph labels him as "KLAMATH [Yurok] INDIAN SHAMAN (MEDICINE MAN), CRESCENT CITY" (Wright 1894:opposite 206). Lowana Brantner, the Yurok oral historian who died in May 1984, suggested that the Cushion Creek Village was a historic phenomenon, being the daughter village of an older settlement at Endert's Beach, a Yurok village north of the southernmost Tolowa village at Wilson's Creek.

Old Doctor's household was included in the 1870 decennial U.S. census, which normally lacks any kinship designation for the relationship between the head of a household and its members. The entry for Old Doctor's household was an exception, however. Old Doctor was reported to have been sixty-five; his wife, who was "keeping house," was stated to be sixty. Old Doctor's co-resident sister was thirty and worked as a laborer; his son, twenty-five, was also a laborer. Other members of the household were a female named Sally, estimated to be forty-five and listed as a "Basketmaker"; another female, designated "Mary" and estimated to be thirty-five, another "Basketmaker"; a second female called "Mary," a laborer and estimated to be eighteen; a three-year-old

Figure 3-5. Hupa "hook man," as in Deerskin Dance, photographed in 1890 by Herbert C. Cantwell, 40 Eddy Street, San Francisco. (Wright 1894; opposite 204, from originial labeled "Hoopa Valley Agency, California. Leader of White Deerskin Dance, with Crown of Horns and Medicine Stone")

named Jim; and a six-year-old labeled "Dick." How these persons were related to Old Doctor, beyond being members of his household, is not known.

According to the statement of one of my Yurok friends, Old Doctor disappeared during a trip in which he took a boy into the wilds. Neither body was ever found. Such an episode would have been consistent with the lad's death during spiritual training; after such a death, the sponsor was obliged to commit suicide.

Data on the other Tolowa cross-dressing doctor comes mainly from the memory of Joseph Francis Endert (1878–1968), son of a long-time Del Norte County, California, sheriff, Joseph B. Endert (Del Norte County 1968); his was a Catholic family. In his youth, Joe the younger lived with his father and mother next to the Catholic parish house next to the church. In that context, he was able to observe much about the other Tolowa cross-dressing shaman. This nineteen-century Tolowa shaman was known, in English, as Doctor Medicine, or Pebble Beach Doctor, or Wolf Doctor (Pilling 1992–94:185). His name in Tolowa was Tsoi'tsoi. Doctor Medicine was also known to the whites as Cha Cha Naw-wemo (Endert ca. 1965:173) and Cha Cha Mowena, Old Man of Chonchoy, "Chonchoy" being the Yurok name for the village on the bluff overlooking Pebble Beach at its south end, just north of Crescent City's pioneer cemetery. The Tolowa name for this village was *melexdn* (Gould 1966:140) or *meʔsɬteɬdən* (Heizer 1978:131, Figure 6), meaning "village down on the flat" (Endert ca. 1960). Doctor Medicine attended the Catholic church for awhile, wearing his Yurok woman's half-orange-shaped basketry cap (Warburton and Endert 1966:166–67); he did not drink alcoholic beverages (Endert ca. 1965:173).

Cha Cha Mowena had a Yurok-style family house in which he doctored; it was called, in Yurok, *sæʔ-soi* (house of the South) (Pilling 1992–94:101, citing Loren Bommelyn, Tolowa oral historian). Next to Doctor Medicine's doctoring house at Pebble Beach was his small, one-story, chimneyless European-style shack/barn. Nearby but further west were two larger structures, both shacks. The one the farthest east was a residential building with a chimney; the one the farthest west was a two-story, chimneyless barn with a second-story hayloft entry door. A photograph (Del Norte County Historical Museum negative 147) shows this building complex (Pilling 1991–92:173; see also Figure 3-6).

Only one photograph of Doctor Medicine survives, taken about 1910 (Figure 3-7). Walter Williams (1986: pl. 13; see also Gould 1966:140–41; Gould 1978:132; Gay American Indians, comps., ed. Roscoe 1988:52, cit-

Figure 3-6. Tolowa Doctor Medicine's old and new barn, residential shack, and the Yurok-style family house where he did his curing, located at south end of Pebble Beach near Crescent City, California. (Main museum, Del Norte County Historical Society, Crescent City)

ing Smithsonian Institution, National Anthropological Archives, neg. 81–2130) provides the best reproduction of the shot and labels Doctor Medicine as a "Tolowa berdache shaman." He is shown wearing a Yurok woman's cap (*l'cah*, apparently in Yurok) (Endert ca. 1965:173). His other attire was typical of a wealthy Tolowa/Yurok male in ritual costume: two necklaces from which pierced silver coins were suspended and a heavy dentalia necklace and a bandolier hung from his right shoulder downward, Sam Browne fashion, from which top-perforated silver thimbles and perforated coins were pendant. From his waist, alleged marten and mink pets hung, and he wore a deerhide wrap skirt that covered jeans. His staff reached well above his waist. A dentalia shell was suspended from each side of his nose septum, and there were vertical dentalia through each wing of his nose. Endert describes an undiscernible part of Doctor Medicine's garb: "Moccasins, upper tanned hide from neck of elk; soles are rawhide from neck of elk" (ca. 1965:174).

Figure 3-7. Doctor Medicine. (Main museum, Del Norte County Historical Society, Crescent City, California)

Doctor Medicine had a sister named Yu-an-na in Tolowa; her English name was Alice Charlie, and she was married to Wharf Charlie. Their children were Clara; Maggie, who was first the wife of Joe Seymour and then the wife of a man named Billie; and Fred Wharf Charlie/Charles, the father of Margaret Mathews (Pilling 1992–94:101).

Doctor Medicine is reported by one present-day medicine person with northwestern California training as having had "wolf power," power or a guarding spirit he gained while seeking it on Sawtooth Ridge or Sawtooth Peak southeast of Crescent City. My source was told this fragment of data by a youthful present-day Tolowa historian (Pilling 1992–94:184). Medicine Grizzlybear Lake (publishing under the name Robert G. Lake) mentions "sources of power . . . includ[ing] Wolf . . . that live in a mountain" (Lake 1991:3). Elsewhere, he describes a curing that he and his wife conducted in which they use the power of wolves (120–21).

Doctor Medicine was tormented by white hoodlums who called him "Boy Die," a reference to his profound depression following the death of his son at about the age of nineteen. The elder Doctor was training the youth to be a curer (Endert ca. 1965:173). He was also reported to have supervised high-mountain doctor training, possibly on Sawtooth Ridge, for Fanny Flounder, the famous Yurok curer from Gold Bluffs and Requa. On other occasions, her training was supervised by her female doctor relatives at a sea cave that had an entrance below ocean surface beneath Split Rock a few miles south of Requa.

The two Tolowa shamans seem to have followed almost identical patterns. Their cross-dressing consisted primarily of wearing women's caps from an adjacent tribe; otherwise, each dressed mainly in male ritual costume while curing. Both also at times wore dentalia shell horizontally through the wing of each nostril. The Tolowa cross-dressing pattern seems to have been part of what Conner (1993:221) has called "mixed-dressing" in contrast to "cross-dressing." Both Old Doctor and Doctor Medicine had a female wife and a son. In behavior, the men seem not to have followed women's patterns; their transvestitism, or mixed-dressing, was, at most, minimal.

My final example of a cross-dressing medicine man is Sam Brown, a half-white Hoopa who was the son of Dan McCloud and Hupa Judy Hostler, born on December 15, 1879 (California 1959 and 1987). The first record of him dates from 1886, when he was about eight. He lived in "Hostler Ranche" in a household headed by his mother, Judy, reported age of sixty. Also in the household were Judy's daughter, Annie (Bridle Annie), twenty-two; Judy's son Oscar, twelve; and her two grand-daughters, presumably daughters of Annie. These granddaughters were Louisa, three, and a baby, one. Also in the household was Old Annie, Judy's aunt, about seventy-five (Michel 1886:11, #212–18).

The 1887 census of Hostler Ranche shows the same household com-position, but Judy is given as fifty and Old Annie is listed as seventy. The baby is still listed as one, and Sam Brown is nine (Michel 1887:11, #218–24). The 1888 census of the rancheria shows the same household composition as 1886 and 1887. Judy, however, is listed as fifty-seven, whereas Old Annie is noted as seventy-one; Sam is ten, and the baby girl, two, is now named Blanche (Michel 1888:2). The 1889 census and later censuses (Root and Dougherty 1890:#224–49) give no data on rancheria affiliation. The household composition is unaltered except for the fact that Old Annie is no longer a member, probably having died (Dougherty 1889:#231–36).

By 1890 the household has lost Annie, sister of Oscar and Sam, but still retains her daughters Louisa and "Blanch." Judy's name has changed; that designation is crossed out, and the name "Judith Brown" is written above it. Her age is given as fifty-five. Oscar Brown, Sam Brown, Louisa Brown, and Blanch Brown make up the rest of the household. Sam first was listed as Sam Cloe, but the word *Cloe* was struck out and *Brown* substituted. Added to the household is a niece, Hebe Brown, twenty-five (Root and Dougherty 1890:#244–49). The 1891 Bureau of Indian Affairs census shows Annie Brown, twenty-eight, to have re-turned to her mother's household. Sam Brown is twelve, and Hebe Brown, his cousin, is eighteen (Beers 1891:#37–#43).

The bureau's 1892 census reports upon "Julia" Brown's ten-person household (Beers 1892:#207–16). Julia is listed as a fifty-seven-year-old widow. Annie Brown, now twenty-nine, is present, as are her two daughters. Oscar Brown, eighteen, is now married to Maggie Kane Brown, sixteen; they have a three-month-old daughter. Another daugh-ter of Julia Brown, Effie, nineteen, has returned to the household with her husband, Steve Redwood, also nineteen. Sam Brown is listed as thir-teen. The 1893 census of Hoopa Valley Agency states the membership of Julia Brown's nine-person household (Harlow and Doherty 1893: #208–16). The only change results from the death of Effie; her widow-er husband, Steve Redwood, is still part of the household. Oscar and Maggie Brown's daughter is listed as Stella, and Sam Brown is fourteen. The 1894 census of Hoopa Valley indicates that Julia Brown's eight-person household has lost Steve Redwood; "Samuel" Brown is specified as fifteen (Harlow 1894:#242–49). Apparently, no Hoopa census survives from the period between 1895 and 1900.

According to the 1900 decennial U.S. census, Sam Brown lived with his brother Oscar Brown, born in 1873; the latter's wife, Maggie Kane Brown, who married him in 1892; and their son Fred, four, and daughter Julia, two. Also in the household was Judy Brown, a sixty-five-year-old widow, mother of Oscar and Sam. No Hoopa Valley census is known for the period between 1900 and 1910. In October of 1902 Sam Brown was recorded, apparently in Hoopa, by the ethnographer Pliny Earle Goddard (Keeling 1991:224, citing Hearst Museum's 24-1852-24-1855).

Some years later, Sam, dressed as a female, lived as a self-employed seamstress in Blue Lake, a predominantly white mill town near Hoopa, until her/his logging boots gave him away as a male during a community dance. On May 11, 1910, Sam Brown was living in a two-person household with his single, allegedly full-blood niece Blanche, then listed as twenty-three and an English-speaker; the census lists their relationship as that of brother and sister. Sam worked as a laborer at odd jobs (Underwood 1910:sheet 8a, lines 4 and 5). By July 1 of that year he was back living in the household of Oscar and Maggie Brown (Martsolf 1910:1, unnumbered lines 15–20). That household then consisted of Oscar, thirty-seven; his wife, Maggie, thirty-five; their daughter, Stella, eighteen; and sons Fred, fifteen, and Herman, ten. Sam was thirty-one.

Sam Brown is shown as living alone in 1911 through 1916 (Holden 1913:unnumbered 1; Holden 1914:#12; Martsolf 1911:2; Martsolf 1912: unnumbered 1, last entry; Martsolf 1915:#13; Martsolf 1916:#12). Entries for 1911 through 1913 suggest that Sam Brown may have lived adjacent to Oscar and Maggie Brown, for his is the next household after theirs, but he is listed as "Bro." (Holden 1913:unnumbered 1; Martsolf 1911:2; Martsolf 1912:unnumbered 1, last entry) rather than as "single" as in later years (Martsolf 1915:unnumbered 1, #12; Martsolf 1915:unnumbered 1, #13; Martsolf 1916:unnumbered 1, #12).

In 1917 Sam Brown moved back into the household of Oscar and Maggie Brown (Martsolf 1917:#9–#12). This living arrangement continued from 1917 into 1928 (Keeley 1926:114, #36–#38; Keeley 1928:#37–#39; Martsolf 1917:#9–#12; Martsolf 1918:#9–#12; Martsolf 1919:#8–#11; Martsolf 1920:#6–#8; Martsolf 1921:#6–#8; Martsolf 1922:#6–#8; Martsolf 1923:#6–#8; Randell 1924:#6–#8; Randell 1925:#34–#36; Underwood 1920:sheet 2b, lines 27–29).

In 1927 Edward Sapir recorded Sam Brown and wrote of him "as a man caught between two worlds" (Keeling 1992:19, citing Golla in press; see also Keeling 1992:21). Victor Golla (1984:141) noted that "Sam Brown (Hupa) stated that many of the texts were based upon dream experiences and that the text typically mentioned clouds, fog, birds, or other themes related to the sky" (Keeling 1992:115). Apparently, Sapir recorded only two songs from Sam Brown: one (D-23) was a formula and song for good luck with words referring to "Dawn Maiden, who lives in the east where the sun rises" (262); the other (G-18) was a formula and war song concerning Black Hawk, who lives with his sisters on Redwood Ridge. Both recordings apparently have been lost (273–74).

From 1929 through 1937 Sam Brown is listed as living alone and being single (Boggess 1930:#051; Boggess 1931:#43; Boggess 1932:#43; Boggess 1933:#42; Boggess 1937:#93; Keeley 1929:#39). The year 1937 is the last Bureau of Indian Affairs census that lists Sam Brown. The decennial U.S. censuses for 1930, 1940, and 1950 are not yet available to the public. From the 1930s into the 1950s Sam Brown was the main Hoopa formulist/medicine man. In the mid-1940s he was interviewed by ethnographers William Wallace and Edith Taylor.

Sam Brown died on February 18, 1958. His death certificate listed his last occupation as cook at Brizard's Restaurant in Hoopa. Also on the certificate is the entry "never married," provided by his "nephew" James Jackson, a judge (California 1959). Several who knew Sam Brown have mentioned that he was gay; the records give no indication that he ever lived as other than a member of his natal household or alone.

Sam Brown's cross-dressing seems to have been an idiosyncratic pattern of a half-white male; it was much later in life that he became a "medicine man," as the community formulists for the White Deerskin and Jump Dances are called in northwestern California—men who were also specialists in mental health and spiritual curing.

In summary, the four instances of cross-dressing—Zuni, Wapato, Tolowa, and Hoopa—consisted of Wapato and Hoopa occurrences that seem to have been individualistic, as were the two dissimilar usages followed by Zuni females, whereas nearly all of the male Zuni and both Tolowa instances were part of more generally practiced local traditions.

Notes

1. As is discussed later, "Nancy," or its variant "Nance," was a name used in the nineteenth century to designate what urban Indians now refer to as a two-spirit person. Whether Parsons intentionally, or unintentionally, chose the pseudonym with that usage in mind cannot be determined.

2. Data on Nina are present in the following censuses: Bauman (1917: present #1602; 1918:present #1620; 1919:present #1146; 1920:present #1172; 1921:present #1250; 1922:present #110; 1923:present #107; 1924:present #107; 1926:present #111); Davis (1910:sheet 16b, line 22); Graham (1900: sheet 12a, line 7; 1904:#339; 1905:#351); Greason (1898:#195); Oliver (1907: #941); Trotter (1927:present #1540; 1928:present #889; 1929:present #92890; 1930:present #00904; 1931:present #900; 1932:present #923); van der Beek (1920:sheet 6b, line 68); and M. C. Williams (1887:#1347; 1888:#1350; 1889:#1347).

Additional information on Kasinelu is present in the following censuses: Bauman (1917:present #541; 1918:present #546; 1919:present #338; 1920: present #345); Davis (1910:sheet 11b, line 31); Graham (1900:sheet 12a, line 5; 1904:#337; 1905:#349); Greason (1898:#1050, #1785); Oliver (1907:#940); Segura (1891:#1350); Trotter (1928:present #891; 1929:present #93941; 1930:present #00906; 1931:present #902; 1932:present #925); van der Beek (1920:sheet 10a, line 44); and Williams (1887:#1350; 1888:#1354).

3. Information on Ener-citu is reported in the following censuses: Bauman (1917:present #540; 1918:present #545; 1919:present #186; 1920: present #187; 1921:present #214; 1922:present #232; 1923:present #224; 1924:present #227; 1926:present #240); Davis (1910:sheet 11b, line 30); Graham (1900:sheet 12a, line 4; 1904:#336; 1905:#348); Greason (1898:#1051); Oliver (1907:#939); Segura (1890:#1352; 1891:#1352); van der Beek (1920: sheet 10a, line 43); and Williams (1887:#1352; 1888:#1856; 1889:#1352).

4. For census data on Kwiwishdi, see Greason (1898:#1688), and possibly Graham (1900:sheet 21b, line 26). For a census entry for Tsalatitse, see Greason (1898:#1551). Further data on U'k/Yuka are in the following censuses: Graham (1900:sheet 16b, line 27); Greason (1898:#1255); and possibly van der Beek (1920:sheet 12a, line 46). Further data on We'wha are to found in the following censuses: Robertson (1892:#48); Segura (1890:#338); and Williams (1887:#338; 1888:#339; 1889:#338).

References Cited

Alyson. 1990. *The Alyson Almanac: A Treasury of Information for the Gay and Lesbian Community.* Boston: Alyson Publications.

Bauman, R. J. 1917. *Census of Zuni Indians of Zuni Indian Agency, N.M., on June 30th, 1917.* National Archives Microfilm Publications, microcopy 595, "Indian Census Rolls 1885–1940," roll 689: "Zuni, 1904, 1905, 1907, 1915 (letter), 1916–20." Washington: National Archives, National Archives and Records Service, General Services Adminstration, 1965.

———. 1918. *Census of Zuni Indians of Zuni Indian Agency, N.M., on June 30th, 1918.* National Archives Microfilm Publications, microcopy 595, "Indian Census Rolls 1885–1940," roll 689: "Zuni, 1904, 1905, 1907, 1915 (letter), 1916–20." Washington: National Archives, National Archives and Records Service, General Services Adminstration, 1965.

———. 1919. *Census of Zuni Indians of Zuni Indian Agency, N.M., on June 30th, 1919.* National Archives Microfilm Publications, microcopy 595, "Indian Census Rolls 1885–1940," roll 689: "Zuni, 1904, 1905, 1907, 1915 (letter), 1916–20." Washington: National Archives, National Archives and Records Service, General Services Adminstration, 1965.

———. 1920. *Census of Zuni Indians of Zuni Indian Agency, N.M., on June 30th, 1920.* National Archives Microfilm Publications, microcopy 595, "Indian Census Rolls 1885–1940," roll 689: "Zuni, 1904, 1905, 1907, 1915 (letter), 1916–20." Washington: National Archives, National Archives and Records Service, General Services Adminstration, 1965.

———. 1921. *Census of Zuni Indians of Zuni Indian Agency, N.M., on June 30th, 1921.* National Archives Microfilm Publications, microcopy 595, "Indian Census Rolls 1885–1940," roll 690: "Zuni, 1921–24, 1926–29." Washington: National Archives, National Archives and Records Service, General Services Adminstration, 1965.

———. 1922. *Census of Zuni Indians of Zuni Indian Agency, N.M., on June 30th, 1922.* National Archives Microfilm Publications, microcopy 595, "Indian Census Rolls 1885–1940," roll 690: "Zuni, 1921–24, 1926–29." Washington: National Archives, National Archives and Records Service, General Services Adminstration, 1965.

———. 1923. *Census of Zuni Indians of Zuni Indian Agency, N.M., on June 30th, 1923.* National Archives Microfilm Publications, microcopy 595, "Indian Census Rolls 1885–1940," roll 689: "Zuni, 1921–24, 1926–29." Washington: National Archives, National Archives and Records Service, General Services Adminstration, 1965.

———. 1924. *Census of Zuni Indians of Zuni Indian Agency, N.M., on June 30th, 1924.* National Archives Microfilm Publications, microcopy 595, "Indian Census Rolls 1885–1940," roll 690: "Zuni, 1921–24, 1926–29." Washington: National Archives, National Archives and Records Service, General Services Adminstration, 1965.

———. 1926. *Census of Zuni Indians of Zuni Indian Agency, N.M., on June 30th, 1926.* National Archives Microfilm Publications, microcopy 595, "Indian Census Rolls 1885–1940," roll 690: "Zuni, 1921–24, 1926–29." Washington: National Archives, National Archives and Records Service, General Services Adminstration, 1965.

Beckham, Stephen Dow. 1971. *Requiem for a People: The Rogue River Indians and the Frontiersmen.* Norman: University of Oklahoma Press.

Beers, Isaac A. 1891. *Census of the Hoopa Indians of Hoopa Valley Agency, California, June 30th, 1891.* National Archives Microfilm Publications, microcopy 595, "Indian Census Rolls, 1885–1940," roll 182: "Hoopa Valley (Hupa or Hoopa and Klamath Indians), 1885–97, 1899–1907." Washington: National Archives, National Archives and Records Service, General Services Administration, 1965.

———. 1892. *Census of the Hoopa Indians of Hoopa Valley Agency, California, June 30th, 1892.* National Archives Microfilm Publications, microcopy 595, "Indian Census Rolls, 1885–1940," roll 182: "Hoopa Valley (Hupa or Hoopa and Klamath Indians), 1885–97, 1899–1907." Washington: National Archives, National Archives and Records Service, General Services Administration, 1965.

Berreman, Joel V. 1934. "Field Notes, Grand Ronde—Summer 1934 (Oregon)." Manuscript kindly made available by Gerald D. Berreman.

———. 1935. "Cultural Adjustment of Indian Tribes." Manuscript kindly made available by Gerald D. Berreman.

Boggess, O. M. 1930. *Census of the Hoopa Valley Reservation of the Hoopa Valley Jurisdiction, April 1, 1930.* National Archives Microfilm Publications, microcopy 595, "Indian Census Rolls, 1885–1940," roll 185: "Hoopa Valley (Hupa or Hoopa, Klamath, and Other Indians), 1930–32." Washington: National Archives, National Archives and Records Service, General Services Administration, 1965.

———. 1931. *Census of the Hoopa Reservation of the Hoopa Valley Jurisdiction, April 1, 1931.* National Archives Microfilm Publications, microcopy 595, "Indian Census Rolls, 1885–1940," roll 185: "Hoopa Valley (Hupa or Hoopa, Klamath, and Other Indians), 1930–32." Washington: National Archives, National Archives and Records Service, General Services Administration, 1965.

———. 1932. *Census of the Hoopa Reservation of the Hoopa Valley Jurisdiction, April 1, 1932.* National Archives Microfilm Publications, microcopy 595, "Indian Census Rolls, 1885–1940," roll 185: "Hoopa Valley (Hupa or Hoopa, Klamath, and Other Indians), 1930–32." Washington: National Archives, National Archives and Records Service, General Services Administration, 1965.

———. 1933. *Census of the Hoopa Reservation of the Hoopa Valley Jurisdiction, April 11, 1933.* National Archives Microfilm Publications, microcopy 595, "Indian Census Rolls, 1885–1940," roll 186: "Hoopa Valley (Hupa or Hoopa, Klamath, and Other Indians), 1933–35." Washington: National Archives, National Archives and Records Service, General Services Administration, 1965.

———. 1937. *Census of the Hoopa Reservation of the Hoopa Valley Jurisdiction, January 1, 1937.* National Archives Microfilm Publications, microcopy 595, "Indian Census Rolls, 1885–1940," roll 187: "Hoopa Valley (Hupa or Hoopa, Klamath, and Other Indians), 1936–39." Washington: National Archives, National Archives and Records Service, General Services Administration, 1965.

Broder, Patricia Janis. 1990. *Shadows on Glass: The Indian World of Ben Wittick.* Savage, Md.: Rowman and Littlefield.

California. 1959. Certificate of Death; Affidavit to Correct a Record. Sacramento: State of California Department of Health Services, Certificate of Vital Records [ca. 1987], Samuel Brown. Cited in Index to the Death Record, microfiche, as register 117, file 59–15506. Sacremento: California Department of Health.

Cantwell, Herbert C. 1890. "Hoopa Valley Agency, California/Leader of White Deerskin Dance with Crown Horns and Medicine Stone." In Wright, Carrol D. 1894. *Report on Indians Taxed and Not Taxed in the United States (Except Alaska) at the Eleventh Census: 1890.* U.S. House of Representatives, 52d Cong., 1st sess., Miscellaneous Document 340, pt. 15. Washington: Government Printing Office.

Conner, Randolph P. 1993. *Blossom of Bone: Reclaiming the Connections between Homoeroticism and the Sacred.* San Francisco: HarperSanFrancisco.

Corran, W. H. L., comp. 1889. *Langley's San Francisco Directory for the Year Commencing May, 1889.* San Francisco: Francis, Valentine and Compant, Printers.

Costelloe, Peter. 1870. "Crescent Township." In *Population Schedules of the Ninth Census of the United States, 1870: California.* Volume 2: *Colusa, Contra Costa, and Del Norte Colonies,* 265–483. U.S. National Archives Microfilm Publications, microcopy 593, roll 71. Washington: National Archives, National Archives and Records Service, General Services Administration, 1965.

Cushing, Frank Hamilton. 1880. "Schedule 1. Inhabitants in Zuni (Shi wi na), County of Valencia, State of New Mexico." F. H. Cushing, enumerator. In *Tenth Census of the United States, 1880: New Mexico.* Volume 3: *Santa Fe, Socorro, Taos, [and] Valencia [Counties].* Washington: U.S. Bureau of Census, Microfilm Laboratory.

Darrah, William Culp. 1981. Cartes de Visite *in Nineteenth Century Photography.* Gettysburg: W. C. Darrah.

Davis, Edward Jackson. 1910. "Zuni." In *Population Schedules of the Thirteenth Census of the United States, 1910: New Mexico.* Microfilm 1472, reel 915: "McKinley [County], Supervisor's District 181, Enumeration District 124." Washington.

Del Norte County. 1968. Certificate of Death . . . Joseph Francis Endert. Crescent City, Calif.

Dougherty, William E. 1889. *Census of the Hoopa Indians of Hoopa Valley Agency, California . . . June 15th, 1889.* National Archives Microfilm Publications, microcopy 595, "Indian Census Rolls, 1885–1940," roll 182: "Hoopa Valley (Hupa or Hoopa and Klamath Indians), 1885–97, 1899–1907." Washington: National Archives, National Archives and Records Service, General Services Administration, 1965.

Endert, Joseph Francis. [ca. 1960.] "Chonchoy Mewimor." Text of un-
signed label adjacent to large, oval-framed photograph of Doctor Medicine hung on the east wall of the Indian Room of the main Del Norte
County Historical Museum; probably dictated by Joseph Francis Endert.
Copy of text in Pilling, Arnold Remington. 1991–92. "Yurok Notebook
62: October 20, 1991–August 14, 1992," 177.

———. [ca. 1965]. "Cha-cha Naw-wemo." Label adjacent to a photographic postcard of the only known image of Doctor Medicine and signed
"Sco-ith-may-gaw." In Indian Room of the main Del Norte County Historical Museum. Display spindle 2, center, "Indian 26." Copy of label in
Pilling, Arnold Remington. 1991–92. "Yurok Notebook 62: October 20,
1991–August 14, 1992," 173–74.

Golla, Victor K., ed. 1984. *The Sapir-Kroeber Correspondence.* Survey of California and Other Indian Languages. Special Report 6. Berkeley: University of California.

———. In press. *The Collected Works of Edward Sapir.* Volume 14: *Northwestern California.* Berlin: Mouton de Gruyter.

Gould, Richard A. 1966. *Archaeology of the Point St. George Site and Tolowa
Prehistory.* Volume 4. University of California Publications in Anthropology. Berkeley: University of California Press.

———. 1978. "Tolowa." In *Handbook of North American Indians,* ed. Robert
Fleming Heizer and William C. Sturdevant. Volume 8: *California,* 128–
36. Washington: Smithsonian Institution.

Graham, Douglas D. 1900. "Zuni Pueblo, Zuni Reservation Pueblo and Ji-
carrila Agency." In *Twelfth Census of Population 1900, New Mexico.* Volume 9: *Valencia County.* Washington: Bureau of the Census, Micro-film
Laboratory.

———. 1904. *Census of Zuni Training School . . . Indians of Zuni, N.M. Agency.* National Archives Microfilm Publications, microcopy 595, "Indian
Census Rolls, 1885–1940," roll 689: "Zuni, 1904, 1905, 1907, 1915 (letter),
1916–20." Washington: National Archives, National Archives and
Records Service, General Services Administration, 1965.

———. 1905. *Census of the Zuni Pueblo . . . Indians of Zuni Agency, N.M.* National Archives Microfilm Publications, microcopy 595, "Indian Census
Rolls, 1885–1940," roll 689: "Zuni, 1904, 1905, 1907, 1914 (letter), 1916–
20." Washington: National Archives, National Archives and Records
Service, General Services Administration, 1965.

Greason, Elmira R. 1898. *Census of the Zuni Indians of Pueblo and Jicarilla
Agency.* National Archives Microfilm Publications, microcopy 595, "Indian Census Rolls, 1885–1940," roll 400: "Pueblo (Pueblo Indians 1898,
1899, Jicarilla-Apache Indians 1893–95, 1897–99)." Washington: National
Archives, National Archives and Records Service, General Services Administration, 1965.

Harlow, F. W. 1894. *Census of the Hoopa Valley Indians of Hoopa Valley Agency, California, June, 1894.* National Archives Microfilm Publications, microcopy 595, "Indian Census Rolls, 1885–1940," roll 182: "Hoopa Valley (Hupa or Hoopa and Klamath Indians), 1885–97, 1899–1907." Washington: National Archives, National Archives and Records Service, General Services Administration, 1965.

Harlow, F. A., and William Doherty. 1893. *Census of the Hoopa Valley Indians of Hoopa Valley Agency, California.* National Archives Microfilm Publications, microcopy 595, "Indian Census Rolls, 1885–1940," roll 182: "Hoopa Valley (Hupa or Hoopa and Klamath Indians), 1885–97, 1899–1907." Washington: National Archives, National Archives and Records Service, General Services Administration, 1965.

Heizer, Robert Fleming, ed. 1976. *Tribes of California,* by Stephen Powers. Berkeley: University of California Press. Reprint. *Contributions to North American Ethnology.* Volume 3. 1877. Washington: Government Printing Office, for the Department of the Interior, U.S. Geographical and Geological Survey of the Rocky Mountain Region.

———, ed. 1978. *Handbook of North American Indians.* Volume 8: *California.* Washington: Smithsonian Institution Press.

Holden, E. J. 1913. *Census of the Hupa Indians of Hoopa Valey Agency, on June 30th, 1913.* National Archives Microfilm Publications, microcopy 595, "Indian Census Rolls, 1885–1940," roll 13: "California Special, 1912–13." Washington: National Archives, National Archives and Records Service, General Services Adminstration, 1965.

———. 1914. *Census of the Hupa Indians of Hoopa Valey Agency, June 30th, 1914.* National Archives Microfilm Publications, microcopy 595, "Indian Census Rolls, 1885–1940," roll 14: "California Special, 1914–15." Washington: National Archives, National Archives and Records Service, General Services Adminstration, 1965.

Keeley, John D. 1926. *Census of the Hoopa Valley Indians of Hoopa Valley Agency, California, June 30th, 1926.* National Archives Microfilm Publications, microcopy 595, "Indian Census Rolls, 1885–1940," roll 184: "Hoopa Valley (Hupa or Hoopa, Klamath, and Other Indians)/1923–29." Washington: National Archives, National Archives and Records Service, General Services Administration, 1965.

———. 1928. *Census of the Hoopa Valley Indians of Hoopa Valley Agency, California on June 30th, 1928.* National Archives Microfilm Publications, microcopy 595, "Indian Census Rolls, 1885–1940," roll 184: "Hoopa Valley (Hupa or Hoopa, Klamath, and Other Indians)/1923–29." Washington: National Archives, National Archives and Records Service, General Services Administration, 1965.

———. 1929. *Census of the Hupa Tribe of the Hoopa Valley Reservation of the Hoopa Valley Jurisdiction, June 30, 1929.* National Archives Microfilm

Publications, microcopy 595, "Indian Census Rolls, 1885–1940," roll 184: "Hoopa Valley (Hupa or Hoopa, Klamath, and Other Indians)/1923–29." Washington: National Archives, National Archives and Records Service, General Services Administration, 1965.

Keeling, Richard. 1991. *A Guide of Early Field Recordings (1900–1949) at the Lowie Museum of Anthropology*. Volume 8. University of Calfornia Publication: Catalogs and Bibliographies. Berkeley: University of California Press.

———. 1992. *Cry for Luck: Sacred Song and Speech among the Yurok, Hupa, and Karok Indians of Northwestern California*. Berkeley: University of California Press.

Lake, Medicine Grizzlybear Staff. 1991. *Native Healer: Initiation into an Ancient Art*. Wheaton, Ill.: Theosophical Publishing House. Reprint. 1993. New York: Harper Collins.

Martsolf, Jesse B. 1910. *Census of the Hupa Indians of the Hoopa Valley Agency, California, July 1, 1910*. National Archives Microfilm Publications, microcopy 595, "Indian Census Rolls, 1885–1940," roll 12: "California Special, 1907–11." Washington: National Archives, National Archives and Records Service, General Services Administration, 1965.

———. 1911. *Census of the Hupa Indians of the Hoopa Valley Agency, California, June 30, 1911*. National Archives Microfilm Publications, microcopy 595, "Indian Census Rolls, 1885–1940," roll 12: "California Special, 1907–11." Washington: National Archives, National Archives and Records Service, General Services Administration, 1965.

———. 1912. *Census of the Hupa Indians of the Hoopa Valley Agency, California, June 30, 1912*. National Archives Microfilm Publications, microcopy 595, "Indian Census Rolls, 1885–1940," roll 13: "California Special, 1912–13." Washington: National Archives, National Archives and Records Service, General Services Administration, 1965.

———. 1915. *Census of the Hupa Indians of the Hoopa Valley Agency, California, June 30, 1915*. National Archives Microfilm Publications, microcopy 595, "Indian Census Rolls, 1885–1940," roll 183: "Hoopa Valley (Hupa or Hoopa, Klamath, and Other Indians)/1915–22." Washington: National Archives, National Archives and Records Service, General Services Administration, 1965.

———. 1916. *Census of the Hupa Indians of the Hoopa Valley Agency, California, June 30, 1916*. National Archives Microfilm Publications, microcopy 595, "Indian Census Rolls, 1885–1940," roll 183: "Hoopa Valley (Hupa or Hoopa, Klamath, and Other Indians)/1915–22." Washington: National Archives, National Archives and Records Service, General Services Administration, 1965.

———. 1917. *Census of the Hupa Valley Indians of the Hoopa Valley Agency, California, June 30, 1917*. National Archives Microfilm Publications, microcopy 595, "Indian Census Rolls, 1885–1940," roll 183: "Hoopa Valley

(Hupa or Hoopa, Klamath, and Other Indians)/1915–22." Washington: National Archives, National Archives and Records Service, General Services Administration, 1965.

———. 1918. *Census of the Hupa Indians of the Hoopa Valley Agency, California, June 30, 1918.* National Archives Microfilm Publications, microcopy 595, "Indian Census Rolls, 1885–1940," roll 183: "Hoopa Valley (Hupa or Hoopa, Klamath, and Other Indians)/1915–22." Washington: National Archives, National Archives and Records Service, General Services Administration, 1965.

———. 1919. *Census of the Hupa Indians of the Hoopa Valley Agency, California, June 30, 1919.* National Archives Microfilm Publications, microcopy 595, "Indian Census Rolls, 1885–1940," roll 183: "Hoopa Valley (Hupa or Hoopa, Klamath, and Other Indians)/1915–22." Washington: National Archives, National Archives and Records Service, General Services Administration, 1965.

———. 1920. *Census of the Hupa Indians of the Hoopa Valley Agency, California, June 30, 1920.* National Archives Microfilm Publications, microcopy 595, "Indian Census Rolls, 1885–1940," roll 183: "Hoopa Valley (Hupa or Hoopa, Klamath, and Other Indians)/1915–22." Washington: National Archives, National Archives and Records Service, General Services Administration, 1965.

———. 1921. *Census of the Hupa Indians of the Hoopa Valley Agency, California, June 30, 1921.* National Archives Microfilm Publications, microcopy 595, "Indian Census Rolls, 1885–1940," roll 183: "Hoopa Valley (Hupa or Hoopa, Klamath, and Other Indians)/1915–22." Washington: National Archives, National Archives and Records Service, General Services Administration, 1965.

———. 1922. *Census of the Hoopa Indians of the Hoopa Valley Agency, California, June 30, 1922.* National Archives Microfilm Publications, microcopy 595, "Indian Census Rolls, 1885–1940," roll 183: "Hoopa Valley (Hupa or Hoopa, Klamath, and Other Indians)/1915–22." Washington: National Archives, National Archives and Records Service, General Services Administration, 1965.

———. 1923. *Census of the Hoopa Indians of the Hoopa Valley Agency, California, June 30, 1923.* National Archives Microfilm Publications, microcopy 595, "Indian Census Rolls, 1885–1940," roll 183: "Hoopa Valley (Hupa or Hoopa, Klamath, and Other Indians)/1923–29." Washington: National Archives, National Archives and Records Service, General Services Administration, 1965.

Mason, Otis T. 1886. "The Planting and Exhuming of a Prayer." *Science* 8 (179): 24–25.

McCulloch, Lou W. 1981. *Card Photographs: A Guide to Their History and Value.* Illus. Thomas R. McCulloch. Exton, Pa.: Schiffer Publishing.

Michel, William M. 1886. *Census of the Hoopa Valley Indians, June 1886.*

National Archives Microfilm Publications, microcopy 595, "Indian Census Rolls, 1885–1940," roll 182: "Hoopa Valley (Hupa or Hoopa and Klamath Indians), 1885–97, 1899–1907." Washington: National Archives, National Archives and Records Service, General Services Administration, 1965.

———. 1887. *Census of the Hoopa Valley Tribe of Indians, June 30th 1887.* National Archives Microfilm Publications, microcopy 595, "Indian Census Rolls, 1885–1940," roll 182: "Hoopa Valley (Hupa or Hoopa and Klamath Indians), 1885–97, 1899–1907." Washington: National Archives, National Archives and Records Service, General Services Administration, 1965.

———. 1888. *Census Role of the Hoopa Indians.* "Census / of / Hoopa Tribe of Indians. Hoopa Valley. Cala / July 1st 1888 . . . by Wm. M. Michel / Census Marshall." National Archives Microfilm Publications, microcopy 595, "Indian Census Rolls, 1885–1940," roll 182: "Hoopa Valley (Hupa or Hoopa and Klamath Indians), 1885–97, 1899–1907." Washington: National Archives, National Archives and Records Service, General Services Administration, 1965.

Newhall, Beaumont. 1976. *The Daguerrotype in America,* 3d ed. New York: Dover Publications.

Oliver, William J. 1907. *Census of the Zuni Indians of the Zuni Agency, New Mexico.* National Archives Microfilm Publications, microcopy 595, "Indian Census Rolls, 1885–1940," roll 689: "Zuni, 1904, 1905, 1907, 1915 (letter), 1916–20." Washington: National Archives, National Archives and Records Service, General Services Administration, 1965.

Park, Susan. 1975. "Stephen Powers, California's First Ethnologist." In *Stephen Powers: California's First Ethnologist and Letters of Stephen Powers to John Wesley Powell Concerning Tribes of California,* ed. Robert Fleming Heizer, 1–44. Contributions of the University of California Archaelogical Research Facility, 28.

Parsons, Elsie Worthington Clews. 1916. "The Zuni La'mana." *American Anthropologist* 18(4): 521–28.

———. 1917. "Notes on Zuni." *Memoirs of the American Anthropological Association* 4(3–4):151–327.

———. 1939. "The Last Zuni Transvestite." *American Anthropologist* 41(2):338–40.

Pilling, Arnold Remington. 1991–92. "Yurok Notebook 62: October 20, 1991–August 14, 1992." Arnold R. Pilling Papers, Wayne State University Library, Detroit.

———. 1992–94. "Yurok Notebook 63: August 15, 1992, into May 1994." Arnold R. Pilling Papers, Wayne State University Library, Detroit.

Powers, Stephen. 1872. "The Northern California Indians." *Overland Monthly* 8: 325–33, 425–35, 531–39.

———. 1877. *Tribes of California.* Contributions to North American Ethnology. Volume 3. Washington: Government Printing Office, for the Department of the Interior, U.S. Geographical and Geological Survey of the Rocky Mountain Region.

Randell, C. W. 1924. *Census of the Hoopa Valley Indians of Hoopa Valley Agency, California, June 30th, 1924*. National Archives Microfilm Publications, microcopy 595, "Indian Census Rolls, 1885–1940," roll 184: "Hoopa Valley (Hupa or Hoopa and Klamath Indians), 1923–29." Washington: National Archives, National Archives and Records Service, General Services Administration, 1965.

———. 1925. *Census of the Hoopa Valley Indians of Hoopa Valley Agency, California, June 30th, 1925*. National Archives Microfilm Publications, microcopy 595, "Indian Census Rolls, 1885–1940," roll 184: "Hoopa Valley (Hupa or Hoopa and Klamath Indians), 1923–29." Washington: National Archives, National Archives and Records Service, General Services Administration, 1965.

Robertson, John H. 1892. *Census of the Pueblo of Zuni—Indians of Pueblo and Jicarilla, New Mexico*. National Archives Microfilm Publications, microcopy 595, "Indian Census Rolls, 1885–1940," roll 399: "Pueblo (Pueblo Indians 1891, 1892, Jicarila-Apache Indians, 1892)." Washington: National Archives, National Archives and Records Service, General Services Administration, 1967.

Root, E. S. S., and William E. Dougherty. 1890. *Census of the Hoopa Valley Reservation Indians of Hoopa Valley Agency, California, June 30th, 1890*. National Archives Microfilm Publications, microcopy 595, "Indian Census Rolls, 1885–1940," roll 182: "Hoopa Valley (Hupa or Hoopa and Klamath Indians), 1885–97, 1899–1907." Washington: National Archives, National Archives and Records Service, General Services Administration, 1965.

Roscoe, Will, ed. 1988. *Living the Spirit: A Gay American Indian Anthology*. Compiled by Gay American Indians. New York: St. Martin's Press.

———. 1991. *The Zuni Man-Woman*. Albuquerque: University of New Mexico Press.

Segura, Jose. 1890. *Zuni, Pueblo Agency, Santa Fe, NM*. National Archives Microfilm Publications, microcopy 595, "Indian Census Rolls, 1885–1940," roll 398: "Pueblo 1889, 1890." Washington: National Archives, National Archives and Records Service, General Services Administration, 1965.

———. 1891. *Census of the Zuni Pueblo, Indians of Pueblo Agency, New Mexico*. National Archives Microfilm Publications, microcopy 595, "Indian Census Rolls, 1885–1940," roll 399: "Pueblo (Pueblo Indians 1891, 1892; Jicarila-Apache Indians, 1892)." Washington: National Archives, National Archives and Records Service, General Services Administration, 1967.

Sonne, Conway Ballantyne. 1962. *World of Wakara*. San Antonio: Naylor.

Stevenson, Matilda Coxe Evans. 1904. "The Zuni Indians: Their Mythology, Esoteric Fraternities, and Ceremonies." In *Twenty-third Annual Report of the Bureau of American Ethnology, 1901–1902*, 1–608. Washington: Government Printing Office.

Taft, Robert. 1938/1964. *Photography and the American Scene: A Short History, 1839–1889.* New York: Macmillan. Reprint. New York: Dover Publications.

Trotter, G. A. 1927. *Census of the Zuni Indians of Zuni Indian Agency, N.M., on June 30th, 1927.* National Archives Microfilm Publications, microcopy 595, "Indian Census Rolls 1885–1940," roll 690: "Zuni, 1921–24, 1926–29." Washington: National Archives, National Archives and Records Service, General Services Administration, 1965.

———. 1928. *Census of the Zuni Indians of Zuni Indian Agency, N.M., on June 30th, 1928.* National Archives Microfilm Publications, microcopy 595, "Indian Census Rolls 1885–1940," roll 690: "Zuni, 1921–24, 1926–29." Washington: National Archives, National Archives and Records Service, General Services Administration, 1965.

———. 1929. *Census of the Zuni Tribe of Zuni Reservation as of June 30th, 1929.* National Archives Microfilm Publications, microcopy 595, "Indian Census Rolls 1885–1940," roll 690: "Zuni, 1921–24, 1926–29." Washington: National Archives, National Archives and Records Service, General Services Administration, 1965.

———. 1930. *Census of the Zuni Tribe of Zuni Reservation as of April 1, 1930.* National Archives Microfilm Publications, microcopy 596, "Indian Census Rolls 1885–1940," roll 691: "Zuni, 1930–32." Washington: National Archives, National Archives and Records Service, General Services Administration, 1965.

———. 1931. *Census of the Zuni Reservation of the Zuni Jurisdiction as of April 1, 1931.* National Archives Microfilm Publications, microcopy 596, "Indian Census Rolls 1885–1940," roll 691: "Zuni, 1930–32." Washington: National Archives, National Archives and Records Service, General Services Administration, 1965.

———. 1932. *Census of the Zuni Reservation of the Zuni Jurisdiction as of April 1, 1932.* National Archives Microfilm Publications, microcopy 596, "Indian Census Rolls 1885–1940," roll 691: "Zuni, 1930–32." Washington: National Archives, National Archives and Records Service, General Services Administration, 1965.

Underwood, Norman O. 1910. "Hoopa." In U.S. Department of Commerce, *Thirteenth Census of the United States: 1910—Indian Population,* Reel T624:77: "California, Humboldt [County], Klamath Township, Supervisor's District no. 1, Enumeration District 14." Washington.

———. 1920. "Hoopa Valley." In U.S. Department of Commerce, *Fourteenth Census of the United States, 1920,* "California, Humboldt County, Klamath Township, Hoopa Valley Indian Reservation, Supervisor's District No. 1, Enumeration District 57." Washington.

van de Beek, Meindert. 1920. "Zuni Indian Reservation." In U.S. Department of Commerce, *Fourteenth Census of the United States, 1920,* microcopy T625, reel 1074: "State of New Mexico, County of McKinley, Township 10N, Range 19W, Supervisor's District no. 2, Enumeration District no. 82." Washington: National Archives, National Archives and Records Service, General Services Administration.

Warburton, Austen D., and Joseph F. Endert. 1966. *Indian Lore of the North California Coast.* Santa Clara: Pacific Pueblo Press.

Wilber, George B. 1891. *Langley's San Francisco Directory for the Year Commencing May, 1891.* San Francisco: United States City Directories, 1882–1901.

Williams, M. C. 1887. *Pueblo of Zuni 1887.* National Archives Microfilm Publications, microcopy 595, "Indian Census Rolls, 1885–1940," roll 397: "Pueblo, 1887, 1888." Washington: National Archives, National Archives and Records Service, General Services Administration, 1965.

———. 1888. *Zuni.* National Archives Microfilm Publications, microcopy 595, "Indian Census Rolls, 1885–1940," roll 397: "Pueblo, 1887, 1888." Washington: National Archives, National Archives and Records Service, General Services Administration, 1965.

———. 1889. *Zuni Pueblo, Pueblo Agency, New Mexico.* National Archives Microfilm Publications, microcopy 595, "Indian Census Rolls, 1885–1940," roll 398: "Pueblo, 1889, 1890." Washington: National Archives, National Archives and Records Service, General Services Administration, 1965.

Williams, Walter. 1986. *The Spirit and the Flesh: Sexual Diversity In American Indian Culture.* Boston: Beacon Press. Reprint with new preface, 1991.

Wittick, Ben. 1890/1894. "House of "We-Wa: Pueblo of Zuni, 1890." In *Report on Indians Taxed and Not Taxed in the United States (Except Alaska) at the Eleventh Census: 1890,* ed. Carrol D. Wright, unnumbered p. 2 after p. 444. U.S. House of Representatives, 52d Cong., 1st sess. Miscellaneous Document 340, Part 15. Washington: Government Printing Office.

Wright, Carrol D., ed. 1894. *Report on Indians Taxed and Not Taxed in the United States (Except Alaska) at the Eleventh Census: 1890.* U.S. House of Representatives, 52d Cong., 1st sess. Miscellaneous Document 340, Part 15. Washington: Government Printing Office.

★ ★ 4

Various Kinds of Two-Spirit People:

Gender Variance and Homosexuality in Native American Communities

Sabine Lang

Ever since Europeans came into contact with North American Indian cultures, there have been reports on Native American males who partially or completely take up the culturally defined roles of women in their respective communities, doing women's work and feminine arts or crafts such as beadwork, pottery, and basketry; sometimes wearing women's clothes; and often entering into sexual relationships or marriages with men. Beginning with the early decades of this century, sources also increasingly started to mention females in Native American cultures living, to varying degrees, the lives of men. In the sources, such individuals have usually come to be referred to as "berdaches" [*sic*], less commonly (and mostly in older writings) as transvestites or hermaphrodites. In the following, the term *two-spirit* will replace "berdache" and be used to refer to alternatively gendered people of either sex whenever it may be necessary to talk about gender variance cross-culturally. Whenever talking about gender variance in a particular tribe, the term or terms existing in that tribe will be used, such as *nádleehé* (Navajo), *winkte* (Lakota), *warharmi* (Kamia), and *hwame* (Mohave).

Because male two-spirits often entered into sexual relationships with men, anthropologists and other writers on the subject for a long time interpreted two-spirit roles as institutionalized male homosexuality, as a way to integrate homosexual and therefore "deviant" males into North American Indian cultures (Benedict 1934; Ford and Beach 1968; Katz 1985; Kiev 1964; Minturn, Grosse, and Haider 1969; Stewart 1960; Werner 1979). Females taking up the ways of men were usually not in-

cluded in discussions of the two-spirit, with some exceptions (Blackwood 1984; Callender and Kochems 1983; Lang 1990; Medicine 1983;
Roscoe 1988b; Whitehead 1981; Williams 1986a). The same holds true,
by the way, for lesbians (see Little Thunder in this volume). The sad
truth is that hardly anything has ever been written about Native American lesbians, with the exception of a few contributions by Native
American lesbians themselves in women of color anthologies (e.g.,
Brant 1984; Silvera, ed. 1991). Volumes of prose and poetry have been
published by authors such as Chrystos (Menominee), Beth Brant (Mohawk), and Paula Gunn Allen (Laguna/Sioux). The voices of contemporary Native American lesbian and two-spirit women are not as volumi-
nous as they could be.

A close look at the sources reveals that there is much more to two-
spirit roles than sexual behavior, as has been pointed out by a number
of authors since the late 1970s (Callender and Kochems 1983; Jacobs
and Cromwell 1992; Kessler and McKenna 1977; Lang 1990; Martin and
Voorhies 1975; Medicine 1979 and in this volume; Whitehead 1981;
Williams 1986a; Williams 1986b). Becoming a "berdache" apparently is
not a matter of sexual orientation but of occupational preferences and
special personality traits. An even closer look at the sources also reveals
that the culturally defined roles for individuals who one way or another
are reversing or blending gender roles in Native American cultures are
as diverse as those cultures themselves (Lang 1990). In more recent
anthropological writings, the "berdache"/two-spirit roles are seen as
manifestations of constructions of gender in Native American cultures
that differ from Western ways of defining and constructing gender (cf.
Callender and Kochems 1986; Jacobs and Cromwell 1992).

Because individuals hitherto called "berdache" in anthropological
writings often lived in culturally sanctioned and approved relationships
with partners of the same sex, urban Native American gays and lesbians have, in many cases, come to refer to "berdaches" as their immediate predecessors in American Indian cultures as well as role models
and sources of specific identities that differ from Western gay and lesbian identities. In the following, I will first discuss "berdache" roles as
traditionally defined in American Indian cultures and then explore the
concept of two-spirit in the creation of contemporary Native American
gay and lesbian identities. This chapter is based on written sources as
well as data gathered in the course of a twelve-month fieldwork project
conducted in 1992 and 1993, followed by another ten-week stay in the
United States in the summer of 1993.[1]

Two-Spirit Sexualities

Before discussing two-spirit roles and identities past and present, I would like to start by recapitulating some "two-spirit basics." The role of womanly, two-spirit males in Native American cultures (i.e., American Indian and Inuit/Eskimo) has long been viewed as institutionalized (male) homosexuality. The fact that quite a number of reports mention "berdache" males living with women and/or who had sexual relationships with women has been overlooked or played down by most writers. The same interpretation was, more implicitly, applied to two-spirit females even though such females were hardly ever included in discussions of the "North American 'berdache.'" Yet a survey of the literature shows that there are about twenty tribes in North America where two-spirit males reportedly live with or have sexual relations with women; there are at least as many references to "berdache" males who are said to have had no sexual relationships with men or, in some instances, no sexual relationships at all. The same holds true for two-spirit females who might have relationships both with women or men (Lang 1990:222ff, chapters 5.9., 6.1.4).

Regarding the relationships entered into by two-spirit females and males, Native consultants in some cases undoubtedly told heterosexual white researchers what they perceived the latter wanted to hear. When asked by Omer C. Stewart, a white anthropologist, about the existence of "berdaches" in his or her tribe, a Paiute consultant once answered in the negative, "because our Indians were good and taught their children right" (Stewart 1941:440). It must also be kept in mind that (to my knowledge) most anthropologists who collected data on the lives and sexual relationships of "berdaches" never talked to a two-spirit person but interviewed members of a given tribe who were knowledgeable as far as their tribe's culture was concerned and were willing to cooperate. In any case, the existing accounts of "berdache" males having sexual relationships with women cannot simply be ignored under the assumption that they are the result of interview situations involving Native American consultants and potentially homophobic heterosexual white researchers, as is suggested by Williams (1986a:105). Native American consultants, including two-spirit people, do tell heterosexual researchers of their same-sex relationships or desires; Claire Farrer's contribution to this volume is an example.

According to my data and research, it seems highly likely that a number of both male and female two-spirits did enter relationships with partners of the opposite sex for a number of reasons. First, the traditional two-spirit roles such as the *nádleehé,* the *winkte,* the *lhamana* (Zuni), and the *hwame* are apparently not defined in terms of sexual preference; they are defined in terms of gender according to the way a given Native American culture constructs gender and gender roles, as well as appropriate sexual behavior relating to these roles. Cultural constructions of gender and gender roles varied, and still vary, widely in Native American cultures given the diversity among these cultures. Regardless of specific differences in the construction of gender and gender roles, a majority of Native American cultures define gender in a way that allows for the cultural construction of more than two genders, which has come to be termed *gender variance* in recent anthropological writings. Gender variance is defined by Jacobs and Cromwell (1992:63) as "cultural constructions of multiple genders (i.e., more than two) and the opportunity for individuals to change gender roles and identities over the course of their lifetimes."

Thus, in many Native American cultures there existed—and in a number of instances still exists—three or four genders: women, men, two-spirit/womanly males, and, less frequently, two-spirit/manly females. In each Native American culture that acknowledges multiple genders there also exists specific words to refer to people who are of a gender other than woman or man. Terms referring to two-spirit people in Native American languages usually indicate that they are seen as combining the masculine and the feminine (cf. Lang 1990:299–302, 312–13; Roscoe 1988a; see also Callender and Kochems 1983). The Shoshoni term *tainna wa'ippe,* for example, translates as "man-woman" (Hall 1992); "tainna" in Shoshoni means "man," and "wa'ippe" means "woman" (Miller 1972:136, 146). Exceptions to this include the Navajo word *nádleehé,* which refers to someone in a constant process of change (see Wesley Thomas in this volume), or the Siouan word *winkte* (see Doyle Robertson in this volume).

These terms do not refer to sexual behavior even though certain kinds of sexual behavior may be considered culturally appropriate for an individual belonging to any gender category. Data from a number of Native American cultures indicate that hermaphrodites are classified as belonging to the same genders as two-spirit males and females (Lang 1990:162ff). Two-spirit statuses and roles reflect worldviews found widely in Native American cultures, which appreciate and recognize ambivalence and change both in individuals and in the world at large, as becomes apparent from origin stories, stories relating to the Trickster

Cycle, and many other stories from different tribes. There are also what might be called supernatural two-spirit role models in the religious oral traditions of, among others, the Navajo, Zuni, Bella Coola, and several Yuman tribes (Lang 1994). The fact that two-spirit females and males are seen as a mixture of the masculine and the feminine, and not something completely different from both, does not imply that they are not seen as separate genders different from both man and woman. On the contrary, two-spirit males and females are seen as genders of their own regardless of whether their status and roles may be largely a combination of the culturally defined women's and men's and, in some cases, special roles appropriate to them because of their dual nature.

It seems that in order to understand the nature of the sexual relationships entered into by males and females in Native American cultures, one question must be asked over and over: What implications do systems of multiple genders have on cultural constructions of homosexuality and heterosexuality? In Western culture, a homosexual relationship is defined as being between two men or two women—two individuals who are of the same sex and the same gender. In Native American cultures, a relationship entered into by a male two-spirit, for example, may involve two individuals of the same biological sex but not of the same gender. The two-spirit partner is classified as belonging to what Callender and Kochems (1983, 1986) as well as I term an alternative, or mixed, gender—neither a man nor a woman but a *nádleehé* or a *winkte* (cf. Callender and Kochems 1983; Jacobs and Cromwell 1992; Lang 1990; Williams 1986a, 1986b; for a critique of the term *alternative/mixed gender,* see Weston 1993 and Blackwood in this volume).

In other words, a same-sex relationship in many Native American cultures, at least traditionally, is not necessarily at the same time a same-gender relationship. ("Traditionally" in this chapter refers to Native American cultures before the massive impact of Western culture and ideas, as well as to contemporary Indian communities and families that still remember and respect those "old ways.") Thus, a relationship between a male two-spirit and a man, or between a female two-spirit and a woman, may be seen as homosexual on the physical level but not on the level of gender: "If you are a man and you have a sexual relationship with a 'berdache,' you're not having sex with another man. You're having sex with a 'berdache.' And if you're a woman who has sex with a 'berdache,' you're not having sex with a man, you're having sex with a 'berdache,' you're not having sex with a woman, you're having sex with a 'berdache.' So the partners of the 'berdache' technically are never homosexual because they're not having sex with their same gender" (Terry Tafoya in Levy, Beauchemin, and Vogel 1991). Tafoya's remark also holds true for two-spirit males and females, of course, who, regardless of whether they are involved with a woman or a man, are having sex or a relationship with a person who may be of the same sex but not of the same gender.

Which sexual relationships are culturally acceptable depends on the way each Native American culture defines appropriate sexual behavior on the one hand and genders on the other. This can be illustrated by briefly looking at two examples.

Navajo male *nádleehé* (two-spirit males) generally confine their sexual relations to heterosexual men (that is, men who otherwise exclusively enter into relationships with women), and female *nádleehé* may generally confine theirs to heterosexual women.[2] (The statement concerning female *nádleehé* is only hypothetical, however, because no female-bodied *nádleehé* have yet been interviewed). All other kinds of sexual relationships might be considered inappropriate (Thomas 1992; Thomas 1993). In this context it becomes apparent that a concept of homosexuality indeed may have existed in a number of North American Indian cultures; behavior considered homosexual, however, is defined in those cases in a way that differs from the Western construction of homosexuality. In Navajo culture, any relationship between two men, between two women, between a male *nádleehé* and a woman, between a female *nádleehé* and a man, between two male *nádleehé*, or between two female *nádleehé* is considered homosexual because two individuals of the same gender or of closely related genders (female-bodied two-spirit and man, male-bodied two-spirit and woman) are involved. Those kinds of relationships are culturally viewed with disapproval, whereas relationships between *nádleehé* and partners of the same sex (but not of the same gender) are condoned and sanctioned, at least among traditional Navajo families (see Thomas 1993 and in this volume).

In the definition of the *nádleehé* role and gender, there is a strong emphasis on occupational aspects as opposed to the visionary experiences that are so central in many Plains Indian cultures. A male two-spirit, for example, is allowed by his family to grow into the *nádleehé* role and gender because as a young child he shows interest in work activities that are defined as feminine within the division of labor between the sexes. His being of an alternative gender is legitimized by his occupational activities. His nonmasculine gender in turn becomes central in determining which sexual relationships are appropriate for him in a society that does not condone same-gender relationships.

Among the Shoshoni, on the other hand, *tainna wa'ippe* (two-spirit males and females) are acting on a powerful vision. The vision causes them to adopt the ways and clothing of the other sex, but their *tainna wa'ippe* status largely does not limit their choices as far as sexual partners are concerned. Male and female *tainna wa'ippe* can have relationships with both men or women. The only sexual relationship that is considered inappropriate is between two *tainna wa'ippe*. Such a relationship seems to be viewed as incestuous because at least male *tainna wa'ippe* regard each other as "sisters" (Hall 1992). Yet here, as among the Navajo, any relationship entered into by a *tainna wa'ippe* is heterogender regardless of his or her partner's sex. A gay person, as opposed to a *tainna wa'ippe,* is defined as lacking the spiritual element, acting on personal preference instead of manifesting spiritual power. Homosexuality, in this case, is defined on the basis of the presence or absence of a manifestation of spiritual power. A gay relationship is a relationship between two persons of the same sex and the same gender that does not involve a *tainna wa'ippe.*

While the occupational aspect is crucial in defining and identifying a Navajo *nádleehé,* the spiritual aspect is central in defining the gender status of a *tainna wa'ippe.* The expression of occupational interests associated with the role of the other sex is a manifestation of that spiritual aspect (for a similar distinction between gays and *winkte* among the Lakota, see Williams 1986b). "Some of those people, or two-spirited people, were married people. They dressed in feminine clothes, they dressed in women's things, but they were married. Some of them even had children. One person told me, 'Well, those old time "berdaches," they were nothing but drag queens, weren't they?' And I said, 'No they weren't!' Because they didn't dress in women's clothes just of personal preference. It was because of the manifestation of Spirit. They *had* to do it" (Hall 1992).

Because most anthropological researchers classified relationships between two-spirit males and men and two-spirit females and women as homosexual, when doing fieldwork in North American cultures they failed to look for relationships involving two persons of the same sex and the same gender. Thus, hardly anything is known about the way homosexual relationships in the Western sense were seen in Native American cultures at a time when the two-spirit roles were still largely intact and about concepts of homosexuality that may have existed in

American Indian cultures before the massive impact of Western influences. It seems, however, that there was generally no way to acknowledge a sexual relationship between two men formally, or between two women, the way various kinds of heterogender relationships (woman and man, male two-spirit and man, or female two-spirit and woman) were acknowledged formally. Some authors contend that there probably were homosexual relationships in Native American cultures but they involved women or men who otherwise led married lives (cf. Allen 1981). Scant references in anthropological literature also hint at the possible existence in a number of tribes of homosexual relationships viewed as something different than a relationship between a two-spirit and a person of the same sex (Lang 1990:375–83).

Two-Spirit People: Gay and Lesbian Native Americans Looking for Identities

Before the massive impact of Western culture and its belief systems on North American Indian cultures, gender variance existed in most tribes from Alaska to what is now the border between the United States and Mexico (Callender and Kochems 1983; Lang 1990; Roscoe 1987; Roscoe 1988a). Whereas since the mid-1980s a number of publications have discussed the old-time two-spirit roles of the pre-reservation and early reservation tribal cultures, starting with Callender and Kochems's article published in *Current Anthropology* (1983) and including books such as Williams's *The Spirit and the Flesh* (1986a) and Roscoe's *The Zuni Man-Woman* (1991), much less attention has been paid to the lives and concerns of contemporary gay, lesbian, and two-spirited Native Americans on and off the reservations. This also holds true for my dissertation, an ethnohistorical work based on the written sources (Lang 1990). The sometimes enormous problems faced by gay and lesbian Indians in both settings are pointed out in the chapter in this volume by Bea Medicine, the first version of which was written in 1979. There, she strongly suggested that the subject could be a good research topic. When doing fieldwork research in 1992 and 1993 on Native American gender variance as well as on homosexual roles, I found the situation of lesbian and gay Native Americans to be in many respects still very similar to that which Medicine had described and analyzed in 1977 and 1979.

Although two-spirit individuals and their same-sex relationships seem to have been freely accepted in those Native American cultures that provided multiple genders, the attitude toward sexuality in general and same-sex relationships in particular has changed dramatically on many reservations due to long-term exposure to Western religion, boarding schools, and, more recently, the media, most notably television. As Medicine has pointed out, the "wholesale denigration of native belief systems in which individuals with this sexual inclination [two-spirit] could manifest actualization has affected the attitudes of Indian persons in the present day. [The] learning of new cultural and sexual mores in the Christianization process also has relevance for attitudes regarding 'perversion'" (1979:7).

In many cases the traditions of gender variance have been forgotten or repressed. Most of my data indicate that very few individuals who live in the role of the opposite sex and who other members of their community classify as belonging to an alternative gender still live on reservations. Among the Navajo, for example, according to Wesley Thomas (1992), "The traditional *nádleehé* is a person who is the true *nádleehé*, but I think only very few exist. A true *nádleehé* or traditional *nádleehé* is somebody who is 100 percent a woman, [who] was born a man but is a woman in Navajo society—not in their sexual preferences or sexual persuasions, but as an occupational [status]."

When I asked a Navajo woman who identifies as a lesbian and who, although she lives in a city close to the reservation, grew up on the reservation and still has strong ties to and extensive knowledge about her culture, about female *nádleehé*, she replied that she had never met one. Erna Pahe (Navajo), when asked the same question during a taped conversation in 1992, told me about a woman who used to compete with the men in rodeos, work as a female cowboy, and hang out with the men in the 1950s or early 1960s. Apart from those Lakota *winkte* encountered by Williams in the early 1980s, the last "true" *winkte* who fully functioned in a traditional two-spirit gender role are said to have lived in the 1930s (Hall 1992). This is confirmed by a Lakota woman elder who during a brief conversation in 1991 said that the last *winkte* she remembered had lived on Pine Ridge reservation when she was a child. The last "old-time" Shoshoni *tainna wa'ippe* were alive in the 1920s, and even then some people viewed them with suspicion due to the influence of boarding schools and missionaries (Hall 1992). Among the Native cultures of Winnipeg in Canada, gender variance reportedly disappeared by the twentieth century, probably being "repressed by the Natives in the face of contempt evinced by Whites" and "losing its social significance through the challenge to traditional sex roles in the destruction of the Native social order" (Steffenson 1987:29).

Because of the influence of white ideas and Christianity, gender variance and homosexuality have come to be seen as identical by many Native Americans themselves, and both phenomena are consequently met with strong disapproval. Although there still are some males and females on reservations who manifest traits of an alternative gender and who are accepted and sheltered by their families and local communities, and even though families may accept a homosexual daughter or son, in many cases Native American gays and lesbians as well as persons of an alternative, two-spirit gender face rejection and discrimination, not only in white surroundings but also on their reservations (Calvin 1993; Robles 1992).

Traditional gender roles for two-spirit individuals have disappeared on many reservations, and young people who grow up to be "different" in terms of occupational preferences and/or sexual orientation often find themselves at a loss for role models. This holds true even more for urban Native Americans. It seems that both on and off the reservations, the only way a two-spirit male or female can identify is as a gay person. There are exceptions, of course. In some cases relatives, usually grandmothers, are still familiar with the traditions of gender variance in their tribe and will recognize a child who manifests personality traits of a two-spirit and see to it that the child is allowed to grow up to fulfill a two-spirit gender role. The touching autobiographical chapters by Michael Red Earth and Doyle Robertson elsewhere in this volume show that even when old-time traditions of gender variance may be gone from a community or family there still may be an appreciation and recognition of a child who is different. It is as if a memory from a more or less distant cultural past has been carried through acculturation, helping that child grow up and find an identity that blends the old and the new or elements from a mixed heritage.

Rejection by their parents and family, however, is a far more recurrent theme in the life histories of Native American women and men who identify as being gay/lesbian/two-spirit, even though the gay or lesbian person and his or her family rarely reconcile as the years pass. Thus, a considerable number of gays and lesbians leave their reservations to join Native American gay and lesbian communities in the cities even though they may return to the reservations periodically to see relatives, which often also means going back into the closet while they are there (Burns 1992). A "gravitation of those individuals of native ancestry with homosexual proclivities to urban centers, especially San Francisco, for actualization and appreciation of their sexual orientations" has been observed (Medicine 1979:9), with mostly male gays from varying tribal backgrounds having "sought an urban lifestyle in contrast to sexual repression on the reservation" (Medicine 1979:10). That gravitation is also prompted by better educational and job possibilities in cities than on reservations.

The foundation of the organization Gay American Indians (GAI) in 1975 has been instrumental in the search of Native American gays and lesbians for acceptance and an identity: "In San Francisco sixteen years ago, we had to fight like hell to be recognized. We had to fight to be at the table along with our 'straight' leadership, and if we came to the table they would get up and walk out of the room. And that was kind of an insult, but that's how they dealt with us in that urban leadership and communities around Indian country. Today we sit right at that table with them as equal" (Burns 1992). Even though GAI was founded as an organization that would bring together gay and lesbian Native Americans so they could socialize, its activities soon were no longer limited to gay and lesbian issues and included issues that concerned the Indian community at large: civil rights, land rights, water rights, and fishing rights (Burns 1992). Among its other activities, GAI, together with straight members of the San Francisco Indian community, is involved in efforts to found a new Indian center there, and membership has increased substantially. In 1984 the GAI history project was formed, resulting in the publication of *Living the Spirit,* an anthology containing essays on the two-spirit traditions as well as contemporary Native American gay and lesbian prose and poetry (Gay American Indians comps., ed. Roscoe 1988b).

In the face of discrimination, urban gays and lesbians finally turned to their Native cultures, searching for an identity, role models, and predecessors. In their search, contemporary Native American gays and lesbians rediscovered two-spirits, whose gender statuses were freely accepted and who, moreover, often were respected members of their communities. For some, the two-spirit roles of the *winkte, heemaneh, tainna wa'ippe,* and *warharmi* came to be interpreted as gay roles in traditional American Indian cultures: "Our tribes occupied every region of this continent. Gay American Indians were a part of all these communities. We lived openly in our tribes. Our families and communities recognized us and encouraged us to develop our skills. In turn, we made special contributions to our communities. As activists, providers, and healers, our traditional gay ancestors had important responsibilities. Gay and Lesbian Indians of today represent the continuity of this tradition. We are living in the spirit of our gay Indian ancestors" (Burns 1988:1–2).

Consequently, in many cases the word *gay* has disappeared from the names of Native American gay and lesbian organizations, groups, and events. It has been replaced by the term *two-spirit/two-spirited,* a reference to the men-women and women-men in traditional Native American cultures who combined both masculine and feminine activities and personality traits and who, unlike modern gay and lesbian Native Americans, were respected by the other members of their communities (for the provenance of the term, see Anguksuar in this volume).

It would be a mistake, however, to see the use of the term *two-spirit* as just a political move to gain acceptance within the Native American communities. Urban Native American gays and lesbians, as well as homosexual women and men on reservations, have long found themselves without any sources of identities that were specifically Indian/Native American, as opposed to the white lesbian and gay identities prevalent in the cities. A number of conversations gave me the impression that Native Americans often experience prejudice and discrimination within urban white gay and lesbian subcultures. They also sometimes feel alienated by the more radical white-dominated gay groups, feeling that there is not enough sensitivity to and respect for the cultural background and personal experiences of Native Americans in the language that such groups use and the actions they take (Burns 1992).

Native American gays and lesbians, when talking about priorities in their self-identification, will usually say that they see themselves first as Indians/Native Americans/First Nations (or as members of their particular Native American culture/tribe); their sexual orientation is part of their identity but not as important as their ethnic background. The concept of two-spirit seems to have emerged from an increasingly positive attitude toward being Native American and gay and the rediscovery of the acceptance—and sometimes even privileges—once enjoyed by two-spirit people, with an emphasis on same-sex relationships of the latter. Two-spirit is a specifically Native American homosexual identity, differing both from white gay and lesbian identities that emphasize sexual orientation and traditional two-spirit roles that emphasize gender and occupation. Rather than combining masculine and feminine characteristics and genders in tangible ways (such as occupations), as many alternatively gendered people used to, contemporary two-spirit people seem to regard a combination of the masculine and the feminine as a more abstract quality that is inherent in homosexual individuals.

While some Native Americans who identify as two-spirit in this sense have considerable knowledge about the traditional roles of two-spirit people in the specific tribes of their ancestry, others, mostly of urban and of mixed descent, have to rely on information contained in written sources. Some activists in the Native American gay and lesbian movement are of mixed heritage and do not know their tribe of origin. Therefore, it is difficult for them to refer to role models in a specific tribe. Native American gay and lesbian communities all over the United States and Canada are made up of people from various tribes as well as those of mixed descent. Perhaps for that reason, the two-spirit identity seems to be basically pan-Indian; participants at two-spirit gatherings, for example, are united by common symbols and actions, mainly of Plains provenance, regardless of the participants' specific tribal background. These symbols and actions include the use of sage or other plants ritually used by Native Americans for smudging, sweat lodges, talking circles, pow-wows, and giveaways. Certain values are also emphasized, such as respect for elders, support of the needy, care for the sick, and respect for and keeping of Native American traditions in general. At meetings and events by Native American two-spirit groups and organizations, there is also an emphasis on sobriety, and alcohol and drugs are often banned.

Two-spirit gatherings have been held since 1987, with the purpose of bringing Native American gays/lesbians/two-spirit people together to share their specific experiences and concerns, which in many respects differ from the experiences and concerns of gays and lesbians from other ethnic groups in the United States and Canada. In addition to these gatherings, there is also a recognition of the special needs of Native American women. A space has been created for them within a ceremony based on one of the Lakota Sun Dance traditions. Each July since 1987 there has been a Womyn's Sun Dance meant to strengthen Native American lesbians, as well as other lesbians of color, spiritually. The two founders of the Womyn's Sun Dance split up in 1991, and now (1994) two dances are held, at two different locations. The southern ceremony is led by a Lakota woman who originally founded the Womyn's Sun Dance because of a vision. The northern Sun Dance is led by her former partner, who is part Lakota. In the Southern Womyn's Sun Dance, only women of color are permitted to pledge to be dancers.

Not all Native American lesbians and gays identify as two-spirit. A considerable number still choose an identity closer to Western homosexual identities and try to merge into gay and lesbian urban subcultures, where gays and lesbians can socialize and look for potential partners at bars and other gathering places. Lesbians and gays who live on reservations sometimes frequent gay-friendly bars in the towns and cities closest to their reservations. Two-spirit identities and roles have primarily been emerging among Native Americans in urban environments and at nationwide gatherings of gay and lesbian Native Americans/First Nations from the United States and Canada.[3]

There is more to Native American two-spirit identities than sexual orientation. While both traditional two-spirit people (such as *winkte, nádleehé, tainna wa'ippe, lhamana, hwame,* and *kwerhame*) and contemporary two-spirit people are viewed by urban Native American gays and lesbians as manifesting gay roles in their sexual preferences, gay/lesbian/two-spirit people see themselves as carrying two-spirit traditions far beyond sexuality. A two-spirit person is seen as someone actively living, preserving, and honoring Native American cultures. Gays and lesbians are also seen as especially gifted people who can make important contributions within the Indian communities. A number of formal and informal conversations with two-spirit people reflect their opinion that "some of us continue to fill traditional roles in our tribal communities; others are artists, healers, mediators, and community organizers in urban areas; many of us are active in efforts to restore and preserve our cultural traditions" (Burns 1988:2).

Radical white lesbian and gay groups seem to have a tendency to reject Western culture, which discriminates against them. Instead of rejecting contemporary Native American culture, which often also does not accept gays and lesbians, two-spirit people tend to work toward acceptance in Native communities, in part by referring to the traditional acceptance of womanly males and manly females and also by stressing the special contributions, as Burns has observed, that lesbians and gays can make to Indian communities at large.

In expressing and promoting their specific experiences, goals, and identities, two-spirit people in the Unites States and Canada have become more verbal. The history of gender variance and homosexuality in Native American cultures is no longer written and interpreted solely by white anthropologists or historians. In addition to works of prose and poetry published since the early 1980s by various gay and lesbian authors (e.g., Brant 1984; Chrystos 1991; contributions in Moraga and

Anzaldúa, eds. 1983; Silvera, ed. 1991), a number of book projects have been planned by Native American gays and lesbians, including an updated version of *Living the Spirit* (Gay American Indians, comps., ed. Roscoe 1988b). Another example is an anthology, *The Basket and the Bow,* announced in 1993 (Wahsquonaikezhik and Deschamps 1993:1). GAI members are also talking about publishing a book for and by Native Americans who live with serious diseases such as HIV/AIDS, cancer, or Lupus (Burns 1992). Beverly Little Thunder, in a discussion of the invisibility of Native American gender variance and lesbianism, has mentioned that she wants to "try and compile stories from my sisters and my own story. [I] feel the need to help my sisters take their place in unwritten history, and it needs to be told by Native wimmin" (Little Thunder 1993).

Conclusions

Three kinds of roles and identities of Native Americans who predominantly or exclusively enter same-sex (but not necessarily same-gender) relationships have been discussed in this chapter. Two-spirit roles (formerly referred to as "berdache" roles in anthropological writings) were available in most Native American cultures to individuals who took up the culturally defined role of the other sex partially or completely and who manifested, in varying degrees, personality traits culturally attributed to the other sex. Becoming a two-spirit male or female, such as a *winkte, lhamana, nádleehé, hwame,* or *warharmi,* was, and is, a matter of occupational preferences and personality traits, not of sexual orientation. Two-spirit people are seen as being neither men nor women, but as belonging to genders of their own within cultural systems of multiple genders. Therefore, relationships between two-spirit individuals and persons who are of the same sex may be seen as homosexual on the physical level from a Western perspective but not on the level of gender in Native American cultures. The acceptance of gender-variant individuals in Native American cultures can be seen as part of a worldview that realizes and appreciates transformation, change, and ambiguity in the world at large as well as in individuals.

The roles and identities of two-spirit people in Native American cultures traditionally are defined in terms of gender. The roles and identities of gay individuals in the Western sense of the word, on the other hand, are mostly defined in terms of sexual orientation even though some lesbians and gays will manifest gender blending (cf. Devor 1989) to varying degrees, and even though there are other aspects—such as spirituality—to a number of Western lesbian and gay identities. Lacking any other role models, Native American women and men on and off the reservation, feeling attracted to members of the same sex, often will identify as gay, that is, as individuals who enter homosexual relationships.

The contemporary Native American gay/lesbian/two-spirit identities differ from both traditional two-spirit (*winkte, nádleehé, tainna wa'ippe,* or *hwame*) and white gay identities in being defined primarily neither in terms of gender, nor sexual preference. At the core of contemporary two-spirit identities is ethnicity, an awareness of being Native American as opposed to being white or being a member of any other ethnic group in the United States and Canada, even though solidarity with other so-called ethnic minorities is expressed by two-spirit organizations. Whereas white gay and lesbian activists often feel alienated from white society and its homophobia, two-spirit activists will usually not reject Native American cultures, even though such cultures may manifest homophobia just as intensely as does white society. By tracing their ancestry to the traditional two-spirit roles and pointing out the significance of those roles in Native American cultures, two-spirit people try to reconcile themselves with their respective communities and create a role for themselves within those communities instead of withdrawing from them. Instead of seeing themselves as sexual renegades fighting back at a society that does not accept them, two-spirit people tend to emphasize their Indian/Native American identity and the special potential and skills they as lesbians and gays can contribute for the benefit of the community at large.

Notes

I would like to thank all who so generously shared their time, insights, and suggestions: Walter L. Williams, who encouraged me to realize my fieldwork project; Sue-Ellen Jacobs and Wesley Thomas, my unofficial advisory team; Wesley Thomas and Clyde Hall, who invited me to their reservations; Mildred Dickemann, Evelyn Blackwood, Will Roscoe, Joan Weibel-Orlando, Alice Kehoe, and Peter Bolz, who supplied help and advice at various stages of my project; Beverly Little Thunder and the women who participated in the Womyn's Sun Dances in 1992, 1993, and 1994; and Bonnie Fabian (Canadian Métis), my friend and unofficial advisor. I would also like to thank my mother, Ruth Lang, who always has loved and accepted a daughter who did not choose to walk a "straight" way in life.

1. Research was made possible by two grants by the Deutsche For-schungsgemeinschaft: a postdoctoral grant (La 752/1-1) paying for my twelve-month project (March 1992–March 1993) and a travel grant (La 752/3-1) that enabled me to spend ten more weeks (June 14–September 1, 1993) in the United States to do further research.

2. According to more recent and still ongoing research by Wesley Thomas, *nadleeh* (personal name) *baa'* may be a more appropriate term for females taking up the ways of men in Navajo culture. See Thomas's contribution in this volume for an analysis of the word *baa'*.

3. Lüder Tietz (University of Hamburg) has been working with a two-spirit organization in Canada. Many of his findings and interpretations parallel the results of my work, although in some aspects his approach and conclusions differ from mine. Our approaches as researchers in many ways complement each other (Tietz 1994; Tietz 1996). Tietz has completed his master's thesis on Canadian two-spirits' identities and situations.

References Cited

Allen, Paula Gunn. 1981. "Beloved Women: Lesbians in American Indian Culture." *Conditions* 7: 67–87. Revised version in *Women-Identified Women*, ed. Trudy Darty and Sandee Porter, 1984, 83–96. Palo Alto: Mayfield.

Benedict, Ruth. 1934. "Anthropology and the Abnormal." *Journal of General Psychology* 10: 59–82.

Blackwood, Evelyn. 1984. "Sexuality and Gender in Certain Native American Tribes: The Case of Cross-Gender Females." *Signs: Journal of Women in Culture and Society* 10(1): 1–42.

Brant, Beth, ed. 1984. *A Gathering of Spirit*. Ithaca: Firebrand Books.

Burns, Randy. 1988. "Preface." In *Living the Spirit: A Gay American Indian Anthology*, ed. Will Roscoe, 1–5. Compiled by Gay American Indians. New York: St. Martin's Press.

Burns, Randy. 1992. Taped conversation with Sabine Lang, April 10, 1992.

Callender, Charles, and Lee M. Kochems. 1983. "The North American 'Berdache.'" *Current Anthropology* 24(4): 443–70.

———. 1986. "Men and Not-Men: Male Gender-Mixing Statuses and Homosexuality." In *The Many Faces of Homosexuality: Anthropological Approaches to Homosexual Behavior*, ed. Evelyn Blackwood, 156–78. New York: Harrington Park Press.

Calvin, Susan. 1993. "AIDS and the Navajo: An Interview with an HIV-Positive Navajo." *The Sacred Fire* (Spring-Summer): 10–12.

Chrystos. 1991. *Dream On*. Vancouver: Press Gang Publishers.

Devor, Holly. 1989. *Gender Blending*. Bloomington: Indiana University Press.

Ford, Clellan S., and Frank Beach. 1968. *Formen der Sexualität*. Hamburg: Rowohlt.

Hall, Clyde. 1992. Taped conversation with Sabine Lang and Randy Burns, April 22.

Jacobs, Sue-Ellen, and Jason Cromwell. 1992. "Visions and Revisions of Reality: Reflections on Sex, Sexuality, Gender and Gender Variance." *Journal of Homosexuality* 23(4): 43–69.

Katz, Jonathan. 1985. *Gay American History: Lesbians and Gay Men in the USA.* New York: Harper and Row.

Kessler, Suzanne, and Wendy McKenna. 1977. *Gender: An Ethnomethodological Approach.* New York: Wiley.

Kiev, Ari. 1964. "The Study of Folk Psychiatry." In *Magic, Faith, and Healing: Studies in Primitive Psychiatry,* ed. Ari Kiev, 3–35. New York: Free Press of Glencoe.

Lang, Sabine. 1990. *Männer als Frauen—Frauen als Männer: Geschlechtsrollenwechsel bei den Indianern Nordamerikas.* Hamburg: Wayasbah.

———. 1994. "Hermaphrodite Twins, Androgynous Gods: Reflections of Gender Variance in Native American Religions." Paper presented at the 93d annual meeting of the American Anthropological Association, Atlanta.

Levy, Lori, Michel Beauchemin, and Gretchen Vogel. 1991. "Two-Spirited People: The Berdache Tradition in Native American Culture." Video. University of California, Berkeley.

Little Thunder, Beverly. 1993. Personal correspondence with author.

Martin, M. Kay, and Barbara Voorhies. 1975. *Female of the Species.* New York: Columbia University Press.

Medicine, Beatrice. 1979. "Changing Native American Sex Roles in an Urban Context." Unpublished ms.

———. 1983. "'Warrior Women': Sex Role Alternatives for Plains Indian Women." In *The Hidden Half: Studies of Plains Indian Women,* ed. Patricia Albers and Beatrice Medicine, 267–80. Lanham: University Press of America.

Miller, Wick. 1972. "Newe Natekwinappeh: Shoshoni Stories and Dictionary." *University of Utah Anthropological Papers* 94.

Minturn, Leigh, Martin Grosse, and Santoah Haider. 1969. "Cultural Patterning of Sexual Beliefs and Behavior." *Ethnology* 8: 303–18.

Moraga, Cheríe, and Gloria Anzaldúa, eds. 1983. *This Bridge Called My Back: Writings by Radical Women of Color.* New York: Kitchen Table-Women of Color Press.

Pahe, Erna. 1992. Taped conversation with Sabine Lang, April 12.

Robles, Jennifer Juarez. 1992. "Tribes and Tribulations." *The Advocate,* Nov. 17, 40–43.

Roscoe, Will. 1987. "Bibliography of Berdache and Alternative Gender Roles." *Journal of Homosexuality* 14(3–4): 81–171.

———. 1988a. "North American Tribes with Berdache and Alternative Gender Roles." In *Living the Spirit: A Gay American Indian Anthology,* ed. Will Roscoe, 217–22. Compiled by Gay American Indians. New York: St. Martin's Press.

——, ed. 1988b. *Living the Spirit: A Gay American Indian Anthology.* Compiled by Gay American Indians. New York: St. Martin's Press.

——. 1991. *The Zuni Man-Woman.* Albuquerque: University of New Mexico Press.

Silvera, Makeda, ed. 1991. *Piece of My Heart: A Lesbian of Color Anthology.* Toronto: Sister Vision Press.

Steffenson, Kenneth. 1987. *Manitoba Native Peoples and Homosexuality: Historical and Contemporary Aspects.* Winnipeg, Manitoba: Council of Homosexuality and Religion.

Stewart, Omer C. 1941. "Culture Element Distributions 14: Northern Paiute." *Anthropological Records* 4(4): 362–440.

——. 1960. "Homosexuality among the American Indians and Other Native Peoples of the World." *Mattachine Review* 6(1): 9–15, 6(2): 13–19.

Thomas, Wesley. 1992. Taped conversation with Sabine Lang, April 25.

——. 1993. "A Traditional Navajo's Perspectives on the Cultural Construction of Gender in the Navajo World." Paper presented at "Revisiting the 'North American Berdache' Empirically and Theoretically." 92d annual meeting of the American Anthropological Association, Washington, D.C.

Tietz, Lüder. 1994. "Two-Spirited People in Canada: Between Triple Discrimination and Empowerment." Paper presented at the 93d annual meeting of the American Anthropological Association, Atlanta.

——. 1996. "Moderne Rückbezüge auf Geschlechtsrollen Indianischer Kulturen." Master's thesis, University of Hamburg.

Wahsquonaikezhik, Sheila, and Gilbert Deschamps. 1993. "The Basket and the Bow Anthology." *The Sacred Fire* (Spring/Summer): 1.

Werner, Dennis. 1979. "A Cross-Cultural Perspective on Theory and Research on Male Homosexuality." *Journal of Homosexuality* 4(4): 345–62.

Weston, Kath. 1993. "Lesbian/Gay Studies in the House of Anthropology." *Annual Review of Anthropology* 22: 339–67.

Whitehead, Harriet. 1981. "The Bow and the Burden-Strap: A New Look at Institutionalized Homosexuality in Native America." In *Sexual Meanings: The Cultural Construction of Gender and Sexuality,* ed. Sherry Ortner and Harriet Whitehead, 88–115. London: Cambridge University Press.

Williams, Walter L. 1986a. *The Spirit and the Flesh: Sexual Diversity in American Indian Culture.* Boston: Beacon Press. Reprint 1991, with a new preface.

——. 1986b. "Persistence and Change in the Berdache Tradition among Contemporary Lakota Indians." In *The Many Faces of Homosexuality: Anthropological Approaches to Homosexual Behavior,* ed. Evelyn Blackwood, 191–200. New York: Harrington Park Press.

★ ★ 5

Traditions of Gender Diversity and Sexualities:

A Female-to-Male Transgendered Perspective

Jason Cromwell

> I am dismayed that whenever I read about TSs [transsexuals] in mainstream publications there seems to be a fascination with genitalia and a lack of interest in the social construction of gender.
>
> Green (1994:52)

Nearly all gender-variant individuals in searching for their identities turn to the past. Some may even look to other cultures. Unlike many male-to-female transgendered people (i.e., male transvestites or cross-dressers and male-to-female transsexuals), very few female-to-male (FTM) transgendered people identify with the concept of Native American "berdache" [*sic*]. Nor do they identify with its linguistic cousins: female "berdache," amazons, cross-gender females, manlike women, "manly women," female "man-woman," or dykes.[1] Although the ethnographic and historical descriptions of these categories may strike an initial chord, it dissipates quickly. This chapter discusses the androcentrism, heterosexism, and phallocentrism of these categories that render female gender diversity invisible. Such terminology is inappropriate, and as such "berdache" has no symbolic meaning or significant relevance for contemporary U.S. female-to-male transgendered individuals. Insights gleaned from transgender studies, however, may shed light on the puzzles and complexity of studies of Native American gender diversity and sexualities.

There are striking similarities between studies of homosexuality and transgenderism. First, like the concepts of sex and gender, they become conflated: Where there is transgendered behavior, there is a presumption of homosexuality. Beginning with some of the earliest literature on Native American gender diversity, individuals who displayed trans-gendered behaviors have been called "sexual inverts" (Hill 1938:338) or "homosexuals" (Devereux 1937:500; see also Gilbert Herdt in this volume). For example, Devereux states, "The Mohave recognize only two definite types of homosexuals. Male transvestites, taking the role of the woman in sexual intercourse, are known as *alyha*. Female homosexuals, assuming the role of the male are known as *hwame*" (1937:500). Angelino and Shedd note that "in the literature the term ["berdache"] has been used in an exceedingly ambiguous way, being used as a synonym for homosexualism, hermaphroditism, transvestism, and effeminism" (1955:121). Callender and Kochems, attempting to clarify the ambiguity surrounding the status of gender diversity and sexualities, have observed that "its frequent equation with homosexuality, even by explicitly gay writers, distorts the sexual aspects of berdachehood" (1983:444). More recently, this remains the case even when clear evidence for homosexuality is lacking. For example, Roscoe concludes that We'wha, a Zuni "berdache," was "a traditional gay role" (1988:64; see also Roscoe 1991). Fulton and Anderson have inferred that the attribution of homosexuality is a result of "a tendency to conflate gender and sexuality" (1992:608).

Second, it is assumed, for both homosexuality and transgenderism, that what was and is true for males was and is true for females. Concerning lesbianism, Mary McIntosh notes: "The assumption always is that we can use the same theories and concepts for female homosexuality, and that, for simplicity, we can talk about men and assume that it applies to women" (1981:45). This is the case also for male-to-female and female-to-male transgendered persons. Devor, for example, states, "By definition, a transsexual is a person whose physical sex is unambiguous, and whose gender identity is unambiguous, but whose sex and gender do not concur" (1989:20).

Note the clear lack of sex or gender markers. Frequently, when such markers are noted, they quickly disappear once discussion is underway. Concerning gender identity and transsexualism, for example, Nanda states, "Gender identity refers to the inner psychological conviction of an individual that *he* or *she* is either a *man* or a *woman*. The concept of gender identity allows transsexuals to maintain that, in spite of a *male* body, they are and always have been *women*" (1990:137, emphasis added). Again note the use of sex or gender markers from those that include both male and female to those that gloss over the female-to-male case.

Just as researchers once assumed that lesbianism is "the mirror-image of male homosexuality" (Blackwood 1985:6), many researchers now assume that female transgenderism is the mirror image of male transgenderism. To paraphrase Evelyn Blackwood (1985), it is time to break the mirror.

Cross-Cultural and Historical Studies of Female-to-Male Transgenderism

René Grémaux reports having found "some 120 cases" in the ethnographic literature (1994:243) for females living as men in the Balkans (the present-day Albania, Serbia, and Croatia). The reports begin in the 1800s and continue into the summers of 1985 through 1988, when Grémaux conducted interviews with two "masculine sworn virgins" as well as others concerning individuals "now deceased" (243). There are two distinctive "social" male types: those who have been reared as such from infancy, and those who "reconstruct" themselves later in their lives. Regardless of when they begin living as males, they "abstain from matrimony and motherhood" and are therefore referred to in native terms as "virgins." Some native terminology, however, stresses their manhood, such as the "South Slavic 'muskobanja' which is translated as 'manlike woman'" (Grémaux 1994:244).

Four "case histories" are provided, three of whom Grémaux refers to using male gender markers. Mikas was legally "registered under" a male name (1994:250) and since childhood had lived as a man (247). He referred to himself in male terms, and in 1934 at his death he was "buried like a man" (251, 253). Tonë, following the death of two brothers at nine years of age, reportedly "decided" to become a man; he did not adopt a "masculine name" (253, 254), however. In 1971, like Mikas, Tonë was buried in men's clothing (256). At the time of Grémaux's research, Stana was "fifty years old" (256) and had been "encouraged by the parents to adopt the male role" at a very young age (257). Like Tonë, Stana did not adopt a male name (261); in an interview with a reporter, however, Stana declared, "Most of all I detest being a female . . . nature is mistaken" (262). Durgjane was the only individual who referred to herself in female terms (263) and who lived during Grémaux's research. Durgjane claimed that no one encouraged her, but rather, "I wanted it that way. I started to dress and behave like a boy. As far as I remember I have always felt myself more like a male than a female" (265). Stana's and Durgjane's comments are like those of Euro-American female-to-male transgendered persons.

Grémaux argues that the Balkan practice is unique in relation to other cultural areas where female men have lived. It resulted in a "more permanent and institutionalized social crossing . . . [and] . . . concerned crossing gender identities rather than merely cross-dressing, since the individuals assumed the male social role with the tacit approval of the family and the larger community" (242). Despite Grémaux's claim, many Native American tribes as well as the Siberian Chukchis have had institutionalized social roles for females as men. Furthermore, females have lived as men throughout history and continue to do so. Cross-culturally, Evelyn Blackwood reports forty-four cultures that have instances of cross-gender behavior in females, with thirty-four of these found among Native American tribes and the remainder in South America, Africa, Polynesia, and Melanesia (1984a:112–15). The earliest case was reported in 1901 (1984a:114). The Portugese explorer Pedro de Magalhaes de Gandavo, however, reported seeing females dressed and living as men in 1576 among the Tupinamba Indians of Brazil (Williams 1986:233).

Rudolf Dekker and Lotte van de Pol have documented "119 'women living as men' in the Netherlands between 1550 and 1839" (1989:xi). Most (105) were female soldiers or sailors, another twenty-two joined the "land army," and the remainder were civilians (9, 10). The possibility of discovery in the military was extremely high (9), which leads to the observation that "many archives have been lost and many others have not been researched. Moreover, we do not know how many cross-dressers left no trail behind them in written source-material. We can make a guess that this especially concerns those women who transformed themselves so successfully that they were never unmasked. For these reasons, we presume that our 119 cases are only the tip of the iceberg" (1989:3).

When discovered, these females provided various motivations for living as men: a desire to remain with their husbands, to search for them, or to avoid detection while traveling in dangerous areas; encouragement by other people; poverty; patriotism; adventure; and a belief that it was their "nature" (1989:25–27). "The decision to start dressing as a man was never for one reason alone" (Dekker and van de Pol 1989:27). In at least one case, however, it is possible that the individual was a transsexual "before the introduction of the word by modern science" (69). Not unlike contemporary female-to-male transgendered people or Grémaux's examples of the nineteenth and twentieth centuries (Stana and Durgjane), Maria van Antwerpen ("Jan van Ant" or

"Machiel van Antwerpen") stated in 1769, when asked to what sex "she" belonged, "By nature and character, a man, but in appearance, a woman. . . . It often made me wrathful that Mother Nature treated me with so little compassion against my inclinations and the passions of my heart" (68).

Julie Wheelwright (1990) has documented twenty cases extensively, and referred to thirty-five others, of females who lived as males in Europe (primarily England), Russia, and the United States. As the title of her book—*Amazons and Military Maids*—indicates, the majority were soldiers or sailors. Curiously, Wheelwright does not mention Charlotte Charke, whose "narrative" was first published in 1755 in London. It is possible that Wheelwright has discounted Charke's narrative as less than truthful; as the anonymous editor of the second edition proclaimed, "Ungrammatical, insanely inconsequent, braggart and fantastic, the *Narrative* is not literature. . . . If the swagger has a quaver in it, it is against her will: barefaced beggar that she is, it is your purse she asks, never your pity" (1827:10). Charke lived as a man for much of her life, although she acted on stage in both female and male roles (Bullough 1976:490).

Indeed, many of the tales of female men seem fantastic. Those who served in the military often suffered wounds so severe that they led to death, and many individuals were captured and imprisoned. Both wounds and capture lead to discovery. For many, cross-dressing ended after their military service ceased or they were discovered, although some continued to dress as men throughout their lives. Such was the case with Angélique Brulon, who was born in 1771, served in the military for seven years, received three wounds, was awarded Legion of Honor, and wore her uniform frequently in civilian life until her death (Gilbert 1932:87–91). For others, dressing as men was a life-style choice. For example, Queen Christina of Sweden, who abdicated her throne in 1654, declared her independence and "to demonstrate [it] she abandoned the female, and adopted a male, attire . . . [and] took the name of Count Dohna" (Gilbert 1932:95). She was "always strangely attired, partly as a man, partly as a woman, sometimes completely as a man, but never entirely as a woman" (1932:101). This was to be true until her death in 1689.

Although many females, including Deborah Sampson ("Robert Shurtliff"), fought in the American Revolutionary War (Medlicott 1966:xv), records for that period are scarce and less well documented than later cases. By the 1850s, however, there was an extensive history

of females living as men. One of the most famous cases is that of Ca-
lamity Jane, who was born in 1847 and died in 1901. In 1877 Jane is reported to have abandoned "the society of women forever, and joined
the male sex" (Horan 1952:176). "She was completely devoid of a female
figure. Her body was slim and hard. . . . [but] it is difficult to obtain a
reliable physical description of Jane. Her pictures show her to be more
of a man than a woman" (Horan 1952:172, 173). Although James Horan
seems extremely doubtful about many of Jane's exploits, he states,
"There is no doubt that Jane was tragically miscast by nature in sex.
There is little doubt she should have been a man. [Men] accepted her
as one of their own kind" (172).

A less famous case but one brought to our attention by a fictional-
ized account of his life in film is that of Little Jo Monoghan, who was
born around 1857 and died in 1903. Monoghan arrived in a small Idaho town in 1868, where he staked a mining claim, herded sheep, broke
horses, and became a homesteader, working a sawmill and horse ranch
on his property. When he died thirty-five years later, it was discovered
that Monoghan had a female body (Horan 1952:305–10).

Louis G. Sullivan, a female-to-male transsexual who died in 1991,
collected numerous clippings from San Francisco and Milwaukee newspapers. The earliest, from the *San Francisco Daily Morning Call,* is dated
January 1, 1870, and concerns a female who committed suicide dressed
in men's clothes. Details of this person's life are scant. Other clippings
in Sullivan's collection, however, detail how several individuals lived
following their discovery, among them Frank Dubois, Milton B. Matson, Frank Blunt (or Blount), Ralph Kerwineo, and Jack Garland.[2] According to the newspaper accounts, these individuals assumed men's
ways in order to increase their chances of employment and draw better wages, to experience adventure or travel unfettered, and to marry
women. But seldom were the individuals allowed to speak for themselves; therefore, with the exception of a few rare cases, it is difficult to
be certain of what motivated them to assume the statuses, roles, and
life-styles of men. Some individuals' motivations may have been as the
news accounts report, but others may have believed that they were men
with female bodies.

Contemporary Female-to-Male Transgendered People

In my work with female-to-male transgendered people, I have observed
several areas in which they differ from male-to-female transgendered

people. As I have discussed elsewhere (Cromwell 1995), the transgendered community can be only loosely described as a community in that there is no single locale where individuals live, work, or socialize. Because of this, gathering data is also a loose endeavor. Even though transgendered people do not live together in socially isolated enclaves, many do gather for support groups, social events, and to attend national conferences. These social contexts, as well as personal contacts, were the means through which the data for this chapter were gathered in Seattle, San Francisco, Philadelphia, and Atlanta. Informal interviews were conducted individually as well as within small groups that ranged from three to ten individuals; thirty people were interviewed. The interviews occurred in private and in public locations such as restaurants, hotel rooms and lobbys, private homes, and, on one occasion, in a law office. Interviews lasted an average of an hour, although some (telephone interviews) were as brief as fifteen minutes, whereas others (large-group interviews) went on for two hours.

Interviewees ranged from individuals who practiced occasional transvestism to postsurgical transsexuals, as well as variations between these two. All interviewees identify as men. Ethnic and racial diversity was also varied and included eighteen Caucasians, three Caucasian/Native Americans, three Latinos, three African American/Native Americans, one Asian American, one Caucasian/Hawaiian, and one Native American/Latino. Incomes ranged from $9,000 to $80,000 a year. There were substance abuse counselors, computer programmers, and waiters, as well as a lawyer, paralegal assistant, prison guard, systems analyst, construction worker, cable installer, postal clerk, postal carrier, technical writer, small business manager, lab technician, salesperson, teacher, and social sciences graduate student. Just over half (seventeen) of the interviewees were married or in long-term relationships, either with women or men. Thus sexual orientation also varied such that individuals identified as heterosexual, gay, bisexual, or queer. Ages ranged from twenty-three to forty-eight.

The initial research for this chapter began with the question of why FTMs (a "native," insider, or emic term for female-to-male transgendered people) rarely mention "berdache" or "passing women" when discussing the historical evidence for FTMs. The question arose from my observation that male-to-female transgendered people often turn to "berdache" as a symbol of affirmation and a historical image that lends credence to their modern-day identities. For example, it is not uncommon to hear a male transvestite or a male-to-female transsexual express the sentiment, "There was a time when people like us were revered." Yet I have rarely heard a similar sentiment expressed by FTMs. In fact, there is no mention of Native American traditions in *Information for the Female to Male Cross Dresser and Transsexual* (Sullivan 1990b), the primary published source for FTMs (although in addition to others all of the historical cases mentioned earlier appear in it). Initially, I thought this might be a result of the fact that females are rarely mentioned in cross-cultural literature as manifesting transgendered behavior. This turns out not to be the case; rather, it is an instance of FTMs not relating to the few cases mentioned. As a Cherokee/Caucasian FTM told me, "FTMs don't have a history." When I asked, "What about female 'berdache' and 'passing women'?" He replied:

> As I understand the term, "female berdache" is a complete misnomer. "Berdaches" were males who were labeled "berdache" by outsiders. From what I've read, *berdache* means "kept-boy" or "male prostitute." How, then, can there even be such a thing as a "female berdache"? What would that be? A female "kept-boy?" A female "male prostitute?" I can't identify with such a term. First, because I'm not female, except biologically. Second, I'm not a "kept-boy" or a "male prostitute."
> "Passing women" also seems like a strange term. We're talking about females, right? Why did they have to pass as women, they already were women, weren't they? Whatever their reasons were, they were females passing as men. Why aren't they called "passing men?" I guess that somewhat I can identify with passing women, but I'd identify even more strongly with them if they were called passing men. I'm a man who was born female, in this sense, I pass as a man not as a woman. (Cromwell 1996:139–40)

These are legitimate questions, and some are worth reiterating. How can there be such thing as a female "berdache"? What would that be? Why aren't they called "passing men?" More to the point, Why are the female (as in biophysiological) counterparts to "berdache" given androcentric terms such as "man-woman" rather than "woman-man" or "female-man?" The answer may be as simple as a Latino FTM's statement: "Female 'berdache' is an oxymoron and it seems like a means in which to make FTMs or an FTM counterpart invisible. For most people, the bottom-line is that a man has to have a penis" (Cromwell 1996:140).

Indeed, most of the literature concerning Native Americans is phallocentric, androcentric, and heterosexually oriented; as such, it frequently overlooks or only mentions the existence of females who have histories and life-styles similar to male gender variance.[3] As Callender and Kochems note, "Evidence for a cross-cultural examination of the 'berdache' status is scanty, fragmentary, and often poor in quality" (1983:443). This is even more so the case for female gender diversity. Harriet Whitehead, for example, states, "The vast majority of reported cases are ones of anatomic males assuming aspects of the status of women. For these the term 'berdache' . . . has come down to us in the ethnographic literature. Female deviations into aspects of the male role were far from infrequent, but in most areas . . . these excursions were not culturally organized into a named, stable category comparable to that of 'berdache'" (1981:86).

It is not uncommon in the literature for an entry to consist of nothing more than a statement that says, in essence, "Oh, by the way, females have been known to do this also." Blackwood notes critically: "Most anthropological work on the cross-gender role has focused on the male 'berdache' with little recognition given to the female cross-gender role. Part of the problem has been the much smaller data base available for a study of the female role. Yet anthropologists have overlooked even the available data. This oversight has led to the current misconception that the cross-gender role was not feasible for women" (1984b:29).

In spite of the oversights or lack of data as well as the still current misconception that females did not or could not manifest transgendered behavior, there is no reason to doubt that females did indeed transcend and/or transgress gender boundaries and continue to do so. As the Latino FTM stated:

It is possible FTMs or what might be our counterparts were overlooked. Given the rugged lifestyle and the [physical] similarities between men and women in Native cultures a FTM person who worked the fields or was a hunter-warrior [in nomadic tribes] would not have stood out. In cultures where males did not have heavy beards and might have only a few whiskers, females who took on male tasks would not stand out. To an outsider such a person would have "passed" as a man without question. I imagine this would be like what happened with Billy Tipton [a jazz musician who died in 1989]. No one knew until he died that he had a female body. Those who lived within the tribe would have known but would an outsider? I doubt it! (Cromwell 1996:141–42)

One case does appear in the literature that supports this position. As Claude Schaeffer concluded concerning a Kutenai female who dressed in male clothing, "She seems to have had little or no difficulty adapting herself to the new garments, since she evaded detection in such garb at Fort Astoria for an entire month" (1965:197). It is likely the individual would have continued to pass as a man had a former acquaintance not returned to the fort and revealed her identity. Male observers seemed to be acutely aware of the male in woman's dress, but it is very likely they would not have noticed the female who appeared as a small boy or as a young man participating with the other boys or men in tribal societies.[4] Given the Euro-American consciousness wherein what females do is unimportant, why would female gender diversity be noticed? To androcentric observers, it would be completely inconceivable that a female person could successfully live as a man, so females who manifest gender diversity usually escape attention.

Ironically, when such persons have been noted, the individuals are described as "physically large, tall, and robust . . . and matched this size and strength with assertive personalities" (Miller 1982:281). Schaeffer notes that the Kutanai female "was said to have been quite large and heavy boned" (1965:195). Schaeffer also notes that although she was not a transvestite, "Crow Woman Chief [was] taller and stronger than most women" (1965:226). Gifford states that "such females [do] not menstruate or develop large breasts. Like men in muscular build, but external sex organs of women" (1933, in Katz 1976:325). Likewise, Honigmann reports that such females "often develop[ed] great strength" (1964, in Katz 1976:327). Not surprisingly, nearly all of the published cases of female gender diversity report female-men to be "outstanding hunters" (Williams 1986:235) and providers, doing "all the work a husband is supposed to do" (Devereux ca. 1850–95, in Katz 1976:305). Yet, Judith Brown concludes that the reasons so few female hunters exist is because, first, game animals react adversely to menstrual blood, and second, hunting is incompatible with child care (1983:457; cf. Whitehead 1981:86).

When I asked my consultants about menstruation and reproduction, most thought the issue of menstruation was irrelevant. As one FTM stated, "Females don't bleed all the time. So what, they didn't hunt for one week out of the month" (Cromwell 1996:143). Concerning reproduction, another FTM concluded, "Granted there was the need to reproduce, especially so, for females. But children weren't the property of individuals, they belonged to the community. So after giving birth, a female would not be restricted to 'mothering' activities and could take on so-called 'male tasks.' You know, many Native cultures did not have strict social roles" (ibid.).

The assumption that female-to-male transgendered people are incapable of hunting, being warriors, or prevented from being men within their societies because of mothering activities is, ironically, a biologically deterministic (cf. Blackwood 1985:7) and heterocentric argument. This position is not surprising given the sources of these writings. As Paula Gunn Allen has observed, "The discussions are neatly ordered according to middle-class white views about where [females] fit into social schemes. It is clear, I think, that the ground we are exploring here is obscure: [females] in general have not been taken seriously by ethnographers or folklorists, and explorations that have been done have largely been distorted by the preconceptions engendered by a patriarchal world-view, in which lesbians are said not to exist" (1986:252).

Allen's remarks apply to transgendered females as well as lesbians. Although much of the literature contends that transgendered females did not exist, other accounts are nothing more than hearsay. Callender and Kochems note that "most accounts are retrospective, based on memory or tradition and describing phenomenon no longer subject to observation" (1983:443). For example, much of Pedro de Magalhaes de Gandavo's description of the so-called amazon warrior is hearsay and not firsthand information:

> There are some Indian women who determine to remain chaste: these have no commerce with men in any manner, nor would they consent to it even if refusal meant death. They give up all the duties of women and imitate men, and follow men's pursuits as if they were not women. They wear the hair cut in the same way as the men, and go to war with bows and arrows and pursue game, always in company with men; each has a woman to serve her, to whom she says she is married, and they treat each other and speak with each other as man and wife. (Williams 1986:233)

As such, it is amazing that Williams would call Native American female gender-variant people "amazons": "Because I have some disagreements with the concept of gender crossing, and also because 'cross-gender female' is linguistically awkward, I prefer the word *amazon*" (1986:234, emphasis in the original).

During the research for this chapter, a Cherokee/African American FTM called me to say that he had just finished reading Williams's *The Spirit and the Flesh*. Although he found it interesting, he was disturbed by the term *amazon* to describe the female counterpart to male "berdache." He disagreed vehemently with Williams's contention that amazon is "parallel to berdache" (Williams 1986:234):

There is no parallel. Amazons were females who identified as women. Cutting off a breast in no way negates an identity as female. Nor does it imply a male identity. He's way off base. I also think that to name Native American FTMs amazons which were probably mythical somehow implies that we are too. It negates the validity of our existence. What does he mean when he says that "amazon" isn't "subservient to male definitions"? He's a man. He decided these folks were amazons. In my mind this makes amazon subservient to his definitions. (Cromwell 1996: 145)

Clearly, contemporary FTMs do not identify with powerful females or "amazons." Nor do they identify with the terms *cross-gendered females* (Blackwood 1984b) or *manlike women* (Williams 1986:239). As a Blackfoot/African American FTM put it, "When I was younger and had to wear girl's or women's clothing I felt cross-gendered. That kind of clothing made me feel odd. People reacted to me as though I was a girl, but I knew I wasn't. I only felt normal when I wore boy's or men's clothes. I may be physically female, but I'm not cross-gendered when I wear men's clothes. Nor am I manlike. I am a man" (ibid.).

While terminology is central to contemporary FTMs' lack of identification with Native American gender-variant females, it is not the only factor. Most FTMs do not identify with the female counterparts of "berdache" because too often these roles were temporary, involved gender mixing or gender blending, or did not involve complete change-overs. The Latino FTM stated this clearly, "Although I haven't had any surgery and probably won't, I don't mix or blend my gender. What I am is a man with a female body. A lot of people really get hung up on that. But I can't see having surgery for something that is so inadequate" (Cromwell 1996:146).

Another factor is the conflation of homosexuality with transgenderism. Almost all references and discussions regarding female gender diversity are equated with lesbianism (cf. Blackwood 1985:9). The argument goes something like this: If the individual adopted the behaviors, manners, and dress of the other sex and also had relationships with people of their biological sex, then they must have been homosexual. Not only does this argument conflate sex and gender, but it also shows homocentric bias and transgender-phobia.[5] What is missing is the individual's personal sense of identity. When viewed from a contemporary transgendered person's perspective, identity is key to understanding. Although most FTMs' partners are female, FTMs do not identify as lesbians. They identify as men. Nor do their partners identify as lesbians. They identify themselves as either "straight" or bisexual women and identify their FTM partners as men. By linking transvestic behaviors with homosexuality, transgendered persons are made invisible.

It appears to be beyond most writers' imagination to envision females as men. As Blackwood has pointed out, some have even gone so far as to state that "it is impossible" for females to assume male roles "because such behavior poses a threat to the gender system and the very definitions of maleness and femaleness" (1985:14). This attitude is rooted in androcentrism and phallocentrism. It is androcentric in its relentless assumptions that females cannot possibly "pass" as men, thus they become "passing women" or other related terms. It is phallocentric because the attitude that prevails is that without male genitalia a person cannot be a man. What is a man without a penis? Merely a "passing woman," an "amazon," a "cross-gendered female," or a "manlike woman." Yet contemporary FTMs make the impossible a daily reality, and many do so for years without surgical or hormonal intervention. As a Caucasian FTM stated, "When I started out living as a man I was only eighteen. I tried but couldn't find a physician to prescribe hormones for four years. I didn't have any problem 'passing' except people assumed I was younger than I actually was. I even got carded for cigarettes until I was twenty-five, but no one doubted I was male. Heck, people thought I was male long before I started living as a man" (Cromwell 1996:147).

Repeatedly throughout the course of my research, FTMs concluded that terms such as "female berdache," "amazon," "cross-gendered females," and "manlike women" were inappropriate and hold no significance for their identities. Furthermore, such terminology denies the existence of female gender diversity by assuming that all females who manifest transgendered behaviors are lesbians. As one FTM stated, "I have no doubt that some females who had relationships with other females were lesbians. But some were also simply men" (Cromwell 1996:147).

Some theorists have concluded that transgendered people could not exist before medical technology's ability to transform individuals surgically. For example, Janice Raymond states, "Without its [surgery's] sovereign intervention, transsexualism would not be a reality. Historically, individuals may have wished to change sex, but until medical science developed the specialties, which in turn created the demand for surgery, sex conversion did not exist" (1979:xv). Although Raymond's position is that of a radical separatist feminist, she is not alone in her contention. Vern Bullough notes, "The subject of transsexualism poses special problems for a historian since it raises the question of whether it is possible to look to history for a phenomenon that was not described until a few decades ago" (1975:561).

Although it is true that terminology surrounding transsexualism did not come into being until the early 1950s, it is erroneous to assume that transgendered individuals did not exist before the terminology or the medical technology (Cromwell 1987).[6] Denying the existence of transgendered persons is akin to denying the existence of homosexuality before the late 1890s, when the term came into being (cf. Halperin 1990). From an anthropological perspective, medical intervention was not necessary for an individual to transcend gender boundaries. All that was required was social recognition. At least one society, the Siberian Chukchi, recognized transgendered females as "true" men (Bogoras 1904–8:455; Cromwell 1987:27; Jacobs and Cromwell 1992:51). Throughout history, and cross-culturally, transgendered people have existed and continue to exist.

Some have questioned whether transgendered persons are a third (or fourth) gender and whether "berdache" should be equated with transgenderism. For example, Williams states, "What is most noticeable in all the outpouring of new research is that gender studies scholars basically agree with the thesis of *The Spirit and the Flesh:* that 'berdachelike' traditions in other cultures should not be defined as 'transvestites' or 'transsexuals' but as an alternative or intermediate gender. That is, scholars now agree that 'berdaches' are accepted by their societies as being distinct from both women and men" (1986:xiv).

On one level I agree with Williams and others: We must be cautious in our assumptions concerning the status of "berdache" as well as the status of transgendered females. As Fulton and Anderson note, "Imposing Western labels (such as 'male' and 'homosexual') on the aboriginal 'man-woman' imbues the role with Westernized meanings for which, we suggest, there was no context in aboriginal society" (1992:608). This applies also to "female berdache." But on another level, one must ask what transvestites, transsexuals, and transgenders are if they are not alternative or intermediate genders. Transvestites fall into the alternative category of genders in that they alternate between male and female. By at least one definition, transsexuals are an intermediate gender in that the label obtains only while in transition from male to female (and vice-versa). Transgenders are an intermediate gender category by virtue of their morphology coupled with their gender presentation, which is usually in opposition to their biology. In varying degrees all individuals within these categories transcend or transgress their societies' boundaries of sex and gender. All three categories are distinct from both female/women and male/men. That is, they are marked as other. The view, in Western society, that there are two, and only two, genders is obfuscated by transvestite, transsexual, and transgender. To maintain the myth of only two genders, however, transvestites and transsexuals are considered "abnormal," "deviant," and "nonconforming gender" and as such are considered pathological. Transgenders are thus rendered invisible by the medico-psychological establishment's refusal to acknowledge individuals who maintain an intermediate status. The exception is Richard Docter, a psychologist, who defines transgender in his own terms, without regard to its origins or its definition by transgendered persons themselves (1988:21–22).[7]

Williams's statement, and others like it, are examples of cultural blindness. It is like looking at two apples and calling one an orange. "Berdache" or transgendered behavior in other cultures is normalized, yet in U.S. culture it is "deviant." Because of cultural biases, we refuse to call another culture's accepted third, fourth, or more genders by our stigmatized terms of transvestite or transsexual.

It could be argued that transvestite and transsexual are different than "berdache" and other multiple genders because the latter are constructed genders. But what are transvestites, transsexuals, and transgenders if not constructed genders? To define "berdachelike traditions" as transvestite or transsexual is to admit the existence of more than two genders. Furthermore, we must admit that we are willing to accept as normal those in exotic cultures but not those in our own cultures. Finally, by refusing to recognize transgendered behaviors for exactly what they are—transcending and transgressing sex or gender boundaries—in every culture and in every time, we continue to stigmatize contemporary transgendered people.

Sabine Lang wisely discusses the "female berdache" tradition as encompassing at least four categories: "berdaches," "independent women," "alternative feminine gender roles," and "lesbians" (1991:9–17). Even so, these categories may not be enough; at least they are not enough for contemporary female-to-male transgendered persons.

Although the various categories may not be enough, the actions of individuals persist beyond the obsfucation of androcentrism, phallocentrism, heterosexism, and homocentrism. As a Latino FTM stated, "I've been rethinking what I said before. I still can't identify with the terms but I can identify with the people and what they did. I can identify with how they lived their lives. I take pride in what they did and how they lived their lives as men in their societies without hormones or surgery. In this sense, they are a part of my history" (Cromwell 1996:151).

Summary and Conclusion

History is important to understanding Native American, Balkan, early European, and U.S. FTMs within gender studies. As Kochems has suggested, it is necessary to "unpack the system of gender related categories, statuses, roles and features and [to] examin[e] how they stand in relation to one another" (1993:13 and in this volume). Clearly, within certain Native American cultures and in the Balkans, Europe, and the United States, females took on the statuses, roles, and features of men—as is the case with contemporary FTMs. In all of these systems of gender, individuals are seen as men even though they have female bodies; for FTMs this varies by degrees and is based on the extent of surgery (cf. Dickemann 1993:16). As such, studies of contemporary FTMs and their historical as well as cultural predecessors have much to offer in understanding Native American gender systems.

Like Native Americans and individuals in the Balkans, contemporary FTMs have their own terminology that allows them to live within their specific gendered systems. I have repeatedly used the term *transgendered* throughout this chapter. Notwithstanding the recent emergence of the term in the humanities and social sciences literature (e.g., Rubin 1992; Weston 1993), "transgender" and its derivatives arose out of the transvestite and transsexual community (Lynn 1984; Lynn 1988), where the term is used in two ways. First, it designates individuals who do not fit into the categories of transvestite and transsexual. That is, transgendered persons are individuals who live as social men or as social women but do not desire or have sex reassignment surgery (Cromwell 1992:6). As such, transgender is viewed as a "viable option *between* crossdresser [transvestite] and transsexual" (Holly 1991:31, emphasis in the original). Second, it is used as an encompassing term for transvestites and transsexuals as well as those who do not fit neatly into either category, that is, the first definition (Cromwell 1995:6). Thus, members of the "transgendered community" are individuals (of any biological sex) who identify themselves as preoperative or postoperative transsexuals, crossdressers/transvestites, and transgenderists. Anne Bolin argues that the transgender community is in the process of creating not just a third gender, but the possibility of numerous genders and multiple social identities. As such, they challenge the dominant American gender paradigm with its emphasis on reproduction and the biological social body as the *sine qua non* of gender identity and role. As a political movement the transgender community views gender and sex systems as relativistic structures imposed by society and by the privileged controllers of individual bodies, the medical professions. The transgenderist is disquieting to the established gender system and unsettles the boundaries of bipolarity and opposition in the gender schema by suggesting a continuum of masculinity and femininity, renouncing gender as aligned with genitals, body, social status and/or role. Transgenderism reiterates what the cross-cultural record reveals, the independence of gender traits embodied in a Western biocentric model of sex. (1994:447–48)

Clearly, gender diversity among Native American females and contemporary transgendered FTMs has created numerous genders and identities.[8] Although some may find both disquieting, it is time to move beyond the androcentrism, phallocentrism, heterosexism, and homocentrism that have rendered, and continue to render, female gender diversity invisible.

Several small, incremental steps are being made toward ending the various "isms." The first step concerns academic writing about transgendered people and how its tone has changed. An example is found in two articles by Grémaux concerning transgendered females in the Balkans. The first article appeared in 1989 and, although Grémaux proposed to explicate "to what extent do they actually identify themselves with the male gender" (144), identities were obscured by his choice of gender markers. In fact, the article provides an excellent example of the androcentrism, heterosexism, phallocentrism, and biological determinism found in earlier writings on gender diversity. Grémaux insists upon the femaleness of individuals' bodies as being their "true sex"; thus, no matter what he was told by or about these transgendered females, he insists that they are women. In another article, however, Grémaux (1994) drops female markers and uses male markers for three of four cases where individuals clearly expressed a male gender identity. It is impossible to say what engendered this change in gender markers, but it would not surprise me if it resulted from the activism of the transgender community.

The second step concerns the activism of the transgender community. A recent issue of *TV/TS Tapestry Journal* lists 283 transgendered organizations worldwide, including in the United States, Canada, Japan, Australia, New Zealand, Turkey, Pakistan, Nigeria, South Africa, and throughout Europe. Many but not all of these organizations are active in making changes for the betterment of transgendered persons. As Bolin notes:

> The transgendered community is viewed here as a reflection of the expanding concerns of the individuals involved who wanted a voice in treatment, in defining themselves and in offering activities, conferences, support groups and other events to further their interests and needs as a growing community. The social construction of identities has become the property of a community with a political agenda. (1994:465)

> Ideally, the interests of no single group are privileged and the political focus can be kept on common concerns rather than differences. This realignment illustrates the shifting of identities as part of a strategy for empowerment and extends the national level to the local level. (1994: 471)

Strategies for empowerment include not only the expansion of gender identity possibilities but also challenges to "media stereotypes" (Bolin 1994:471), to destigmatizing medico-psychological categorizations (cf. Bolin 1988; Bolin 1994; Cromwell 1992), and to legal issues such as those concerning employment and housing discrimination (Frye 1994).

The third, and most important, step concerns the actions of FTMs themselves. A half-dozen or more FTM scholars are completing doctoral dissertations that focus on FTM issues, and each is publishing and publicly presenting research findings. Furthermore, many FTMs outside of academia also are publishing and speaking publicly on behalf of the transgender community. Most of the public presentations (regardless of the medium) focus on dispelling myths and generalizations about FTMs as well as explaining what FTMs are. The necessity for demythologizing and degeneralizing is because many, if not most, FTMs do not pursue complete sex changes, and by doing so they create "intermediate bodies, somewhere between male and female" (Rubin 1992:476). FTMs refuse complete sex changes because, as James Green has stated, "We are aware of the limitations of surgery and aware of our masculinity in a deeper, more spiritual way" (1994:52). Thus, regardless of how we construct our bodies or lives, from a female-to-male transgendered perspective what needs to be kept in mind is that "some females are not women. We are not pretending to be men. We are men" (Cromwell 1993:6).

Notes

This is a revised version of my paper "Not Female Berdache, Not Amazons, Not Cross-Gender Females, Not Manlike Women: Locating Female-to-Male Transgendered People within Discourses on the Berdache Tradition," presented at the Wenner-Gren Foundation Conference on "Revisiting the 'North American Berdache,' Empirically and Theoretically" at the 92d annual meeting of the American Anthropological Association, Washington, D.C., Nov. 17, 1993, as well as to the AAA session of the same name held in Washington on Nov. 18. My appreciation to Sue-Ellen Jacobs for encouraging me to write the paper and to "hang in there" for the second Wenner-Gren Conference held May 26–29, 1994. Thanks also go to all the other conference participants whose encouragement was gratefully appreciated, especially Terry Tafoya, who convinced me that a transgendered perspective was needed. I am grateful to all FTMs who have entrusted me with their voices, especially James Green, Sky Renfro, Michael Hernandez, J.H., B.L., P.B., C.J., Miles, and T.A. The interpretations, and final rendering, of their voices remain my responsibility.

1. Although many contemporary transgendered people view their identity as having a spiritual dimension, it is difficult to say whether they will or should identify with the concept of "two-spirit." It is reasonable to assume that those who identify with the concept of "berdache" will likely identify with two-spirit. It is also quite possible that those who have not identified with "berdache" may find two-spirit a more descriptive conception of their identity. I know of no research, however, that would confirm either of these suppositions.

2. Articles concerning each of these cases appeared in the following newspapers: *Milwaukee Sentinel,* March 8, Oct. 30–Nov. 28, 1883 (Frank Dubois); *San Francisco Call,* Jan. 27–Feb. 15, 1895; *San Francisco Chronicle,* Jan. 28–29, 1895; *San Francisco Examiner,* Feb. 7, 10, 1895 (Luisa Matson, alias Milton B. Matson); *Milwaukee Daily News,* July 13–17, 1893; *Milwaukee Sentinel,* July 14–17, 1893 (Frank Blunt, née Annie Morris); *Milwaukee Journal,* May 3, June 14, 1914; *Milwaukee Sentinel,* May 4–15, 1914 (Cora Anderson, alias Ralph Kerwineo); the [Stockton] *Evening Mail,* Aug. 2, 1897–Oct. 22, 1900; the *Bakersfield Californian,* May 12, 1898; the *Sacramento Evening Bee,* Sept. 16–21, 1936; *Berkeley Daily Gazette,* Sept. 21, 1936; *Los Angeles Times,* Sept. 21–29, 1936. Newspapers in Hawaii, Oakland, and San Jose also carried stories of Jack Garland. For more about Jack Garland see Sullivan, *From Female to Male* (1990a).

3. Phallocentrism, androcentrism, and heterosexism all take males as the center. Specifically, phallocentrism centers manliness in the penis or male genitalia, and phallocentric positions argue that those who lack penises are "less than" men.

4. My appreciation to Anne Bolin for this formulation.

5. Homocentric biases take homosexuality as a central position such that even when individuals manifest only cross-gender behavior it is automatically assumed that they also have an homosexual orientation. Homocentrism is, as Dallas Denny has cogently stated, looking "through gay-colored spectacles [and] interpret[ing] berdache from a gay perspective" (1993:11). Transgender-phobia is manifested by skepticism about the existence of, or a dislike or hatred of—and occasionally hostility toward—transgendered persons (Denny 1993).

6. David O. Cauldwell coined the term *transsexual* in 1949 (Cauldwell 1949:275–80). It did not come into general use, however, until the 1950s following Christine Jorgensen's return to the United States after her sex change surgery in 1953. Cauldwell did not use the term in regard to Jorgensen in his commentary on her in *Sexology,* wherein he states unequivocally that only hermaphrodites ("true" and "pseudo") can change their sexes (1953:494–503).

7. Transgenderists define "transgender" as living either as a woman (with a biophysiology of male) or as a man (with a biophysiology of female) without genital surgery; living this way may, or may not, involve taking hormones to approximate the phenotype of a woman or a man ("full-time living"). Docter restricts the usage of the term to those who go "back and forth from one gender role to the other. Without such oscillations, the full-time cross-gender living would qualify in our definition as transsexual behavior. We prefer the term, *preoperative transsexual,* simply to indicate that reassignment procedures are anticipated" (1990:22, emphasis in the original).

I agree with Docter that some people who define themselves as transgendered may go back and forth between gender roles. He fails to recognize, however, that some who define themselves as transgenderists have no intention of—nor do they ever anticipate—having genital surgeries. Furthermore, he does not recognize that many individuals are quite content to be, and have purposely chosen, an intermediate category. Transgenderists are all too aware of the term *preoperative transsexual* but have rejected it as a defining category because it does not describe what they are doing in their lives. Those who define themselves as transsexual and have not yet had genital surgery (but anticipate doing so) often use the term to denote their presurgery status. Because many transgenderists live full-time in their roles, they do not view themselves as transsexuals or as preoperative transsexuals or transvestites. Furthermore, many within the transgender community have adopted the terms *transgender, transgenderist,* and *cross-dresser* specifically to distance themselves from the medico-psychiatricization, and the subsequent stigmatization, attached to the terms *transsexual, preoperative transsexual,* and *transvestite.*

8. Further analysis of the early European and U.S. cases are necessary before determining whether individuals created different genders and identities.

References Cited

Allen, Paula Gunn. 1986. *The Sacred Hoop: Recovering the Feminine in American Indian Traditions.* Boston: Beacon Press.

Angelino, Henry, and Charles L. Shedd. 1955. "A Note on Berdache." *American Anthropologist* n.s. (57): 121–26.

Blackwood, Evelyn. 1984a. "Cross-Cultural Dimensions of Lesbian Relations." Master's thesis, Stanford University.

———. 1984b. "Sexuality and Gender in Certain Native American Tribes: The Case of Cross-Gender Females." *Signs: Journal of Women in Culture and Society* 10(1): 27–42.

———. 1985. "Breaking the Mirror: The Construction of Lesbianism and the Anthropological Discourse on Homosexuality." *Journal of Homosexuality* 11(3–4): 1–17.

Bogoras, Waldemar. 1904–8. "The Chuckchee." Reprint. F. Boas, ed. 1975. *Memoirs of the American Museum of Natural History* 11 (2), and in *Publications of the Jesup North Pacific Expedition* 7: 448–57. New York: G. E. Stechert.

Bolin, Anne. 1988. *In Search of Eve: Transsexual Rites of Passage.* South Hadley: Bergin and Garvey.

———. 1994. "Transcending and Transgendering: Male-to-Female Transsexuals, Dichotomy, and Diversity." In *Third Sex, Third Gender: Beyond Sexual Dimorphism in Culture and History,* ed. Gilbert Herdt, 447–85. New York: Zone Books.

Brown, Judith. 1983. Comments on "The North American 'Berdache,'" by Charles Callender and Lee M. Kochems. *Current Anthropology* 24(4): 457–58.

Bullough, Vern L. 1975. "Transsexualism in History." *Archives of Sexual Behavior* 4(5): 561–71.

———. 1976. *Sexual Variance in Society and History.* Chicago: University of Chicago Press.

Callender, Charles, and Lee M. Kochems. 1983. "The North American 'Berdache.'" *Current Anthropology* 24(4): 443–56.

Cauldwell, David O. 1949. "Psychopathia Transexualis." *Sexology Magazine* (Dec.): 275–80.

———. 1953. "Man Becomes Woman." *Sexology Magazine* (March): 494–503.

Charke, Charlotte. 1827. *A Narrative of the Life of Mrs. Charlotte Charke, Written by Herself.* London: N.p.

Cromwell, Jason. 1987. "Transsexualism and Concepts of Gender." Unpublished ms. Seattle: Ingersoll Gender Center.

———. 1992. "Fearful Others: The Construction of Female Gender Variance." Unpublished ms., University of Washington.

———. 1993. "Default Assumptions; or, The Billy Tipton Phenomenon." Paper presented at Southern Comfort Conference, Atlanta. Reprint. *Cross-Talk: The Transgender News and Information Monthly* (67): 15–16, 23.

———. 1995. "Talking about without Talking about: The Use of Protective Language among Transvestites and Transsexuals." In *Beyond the Lavender Lexicon: Authenticity, Imagination, and Appropriation in Lesbian and Gay Languages,* ed. William L. Leap, 267–95. Amsterdam: Gordon and Breach.

———. 1996. "Making the Visible Invisible: Constructions of Bodies, Genders, and Sexualities by and about Female-to-Male Transgendered People." Ph.D. diss. University of Washington, Seattle.

Dekker, Rudolf M., and Lotte C. van de Pol. 1989. *The Tradition of Female Transvestism in Early Modern Europe.* London: Macmillan Press.

Denny, Dallas. 1993. "You're Strange, and We're Wonderful: The Relationship between the Gay/Lesbian and Transgender Communities." Unpublished ms. Atlanta: AEGIS.

Devereux, George. 1937. "Institutionalized Homosexuality of the Mohave Indians." *Human Biology* 9(4): 498–527.

———. 1976 [ca. 1850–95]. "The Case of Sahaykwisa." In *Gay American History: Lesbians and Gay Men in the U.S.A.,* ed. Jonathan Katz, 304–5. New York: Thomas Y. Crowell.

Devor, Holly. 1989. *Gender Blending: Confronting the Limits of Duality.* Bloomington: Indiana University Press.

Dickemann, Mildred. 1993. Comments on papers read at "Revisiting the 'North American Berdache' Empirically and Theoretically." 92d annual meeting of the American Anthropological Association, Washington, D.C.

Docter, Richard. 1988. *Transvestites and Transsexuals: Toward a Theory of Cross-Gender Behavior.* New York: Plenum Press.

Frye, Phyllis Randolph. 1994. "Legal Briefs: IFGE in Portland, Oregon." *TV/TS Tapestry Journal* 68: 9–10, 17–20.

Fulton, Robert, and Steven W. Anderson. 1992. "The Amerindian 'Man-Woman': Gender, Liminality, and Cultural Continuity." *Current Anthropology* 33(5): 603–10.

Gilbert, O. P. 1932. *Women in Men's Guise.* London: Bodley Head.

Gifford, Edward W. 1976 [1933]. "Female Transvestites." In *Gay American History: Lesbians and Gay Men in the U.S.A.,* ed. Jonathan Katz, 325. New York: Thomas Y. Crowell.

Green, James. 1994. "All Transsexuals Are Not Alike." *TV/TS Tapestry Journal* 68: 51–52.

Grémaux, René. 1989. "Mannish Women of the Balkan Mountains: Preliminary Notes on the 'Sworn Virgins' in Male Disguise, with Special Reference to their Sexuality and Gender-Identity." In *From Sappho to De Sade: Moments in the History of Sexuality,* ed. Jan Bremmer, 143–72. London: Routledge.

———. 1994. "Woman Becomes Man in the Balkans." In *Third Sex, Third Gender: Beyond Sexual Dimorphism in Culture and History,* ed. Gilbert Herdt, 241–81. New York: Zone Books.

Halperin, David M. 1990. *One Hundred Years of Homosexuality and Other Essays on Greek Love.* New York: Routledge.

Hill, W. W. 1938. "Note on the Pima Berdache." *American Anthropologist* n.s.(40): 338–40.

Holly. 1991. "The Transgender Alternative." *TV/TS Tapestry Journal* 59: 31–33.

Honigmann, J. J. 1976 [1964]. "Both Male and Female Homosexuality." In *Gay American History: Lesbians and Gay Men in the U.S.A.,* ed. Jonathan Katz, 327. New York: Thomas Y. Crowell.

Horan, James D. 1952. *Desperate Women.* New York: G. P. Putnam.

Jacobs, Sue-Ellen, and Jason Cromwell. 1992. "Visions and Revisions of Reality: Reflections on Sex, Sexuality, Gender, and Gender Variance." *Journal of Homosexuality* 23(4): 43–69.

Kochems, Lee M. 1993. Discussant. "Revisiting the 'North American Berdache' Empirically and Theoretically." 92d annual meeting of the American Anthropological Association, Washington, D.C.

Lang, Sabine. 1991. "Female Gender Variance among North American Indians: A Cross-Cultural Perspective." Unpublished ms. University of Hamburg.

Lynn, Merissa Sherrill. 1984. "Definitions Follow-Up." *TV/TS Tapestry Journal* 44: 60–61.

———. 1988. "Definitions of Terms Commonly Used in the Transvestite-Transsexual Community." *TV/TS Tapestry Journal* 51: 19–31.

McIntosh, Mary. 1981. "The Homosexual Role, with Postscript: The Homosexual Role Revisited." In *The Making of the Modern Homosexual,* ed. Kenneth Plummer, 30–49. Totowa: Barnes and Noble.

Medlicott, Alexander. 1966. "Introduction." In *The Female Marine; or, Adventures of Miss Lucy Brewer.* New York: Da Capo.

Miller, Jay. 1982. "People, Berdaches, and Left-Handed Bears: Human Variation in Native America." *Journal of Anthropological Research* 38: 274–87.

Nanda, Serena. 1990. *Neither Man nor Woman: The Hijras of India.* Belmont: Wadsworth.

Raymond, Janice G. 1979. *The Transsexual Empire: The Making of the She-Male.* Boston: Beacon Press.

Roscoe, Will. 1988. "The Zuni Man-Woman." *Out/Look* 1: 56–67.

———. 1991. *The Zuni Man-Woman.* Albuquerque: University of New Mexico Press.

Rubin, Gayle. 1992. "Of Catamites and Kings: Reflections on Butch, Gender, and Boundaries." In *The Persistence of Desire: A Femme-Butch Reader,* ed. Joan Nestle, 466–82. Boston: Alyson.

Schaeffer, Claude E. 1965. "The Kutenai Female Berdache: Courier, Guide, Prophetess, and Warrior." *Ethnohistory* 12: 193–236.

Sullivan, Lou. 1990a. *From Female to Male: The Life of Jack Bee Garland.* Boston: Alyson.

———. 1990b. *Information for the Female to Male Cross Dresser and Transsexual.* Seattle: Ingersoll Press.

Weston, Kath. 1993. "Lesbian/Gay Studies in the House of Anthropology." *Annual Review of Anthropology* 22: 339–67.

Wheelwright, Julie. 1990. *Amazons and Military Maids.* London: Pandora.

Whitehead, Harriet. 1981. "The Bow and the Burden Strap: A New Look at Institutionalized Homosexuality in Native North America." In *Sexual Meanings: The Cultural Construction of Gender and Sexuality,* ed. Sherry B. Ortner and Harriet Whitehead, 8–115. New York: Cambridge University Press.

Williams, Walter L. 1986. *The Spirit and the Flesh: Sexual Diversity in American Indian Culture.* Boston: Beacon Press. Reprint 1991, with a new preface.

Part 2: Questions of Terminology

★ ★ **6**

Changing Native American Roles in an Urban Context *and* Changing Native American Sex Roles in an Urban Context

Beatrice Medicine (Standing Rock Lakota)

Mitakuyepi oyasin chante waste ya nape chiyusa pe. I am greeting you in my Lakota language. When I am home, living on the reservation, this is the way I would normally speak to a gathering. I will translate this greeting because it very neatly, in my mind, encapsulates what has happened here. *"Mitaku yepi oyasin"* means "all my kinspersons," *"chante waste ya"* means "with a good heart," and *"nape chiyusa pe"* is "I shake hands with you." This is very symbolic because it speaks to the whole issue of kinship: *"Mitaku yepi oyasin"* includes not only other humans but also, as Black Elk states (and his words have been repeated often), the rest of the creatures—in the air, in the waters, and all around us. *"Chante waste ya"* means that we approach our respective work with good hearts. I am proud of my many tribespersons because they have done a wonderful job in opening their hearts on an issue of great sensitivity. *Oyasin* means that all variations of persons are seen as kin in the Lakota worldview. The greeting symbolizes the circle—the kinship circle. Metaphorically, all persons shake hands, and this, I think, is beautiful. The greeting indicates an inclusivity and acceptance of all persons.

Now perhaps I should begin with some designation: "Not a 'berdache' [*sic*], not a plastic medicine person, but an anthropologist and a Lakota woman." As an anthropologist, I have had to put up with a lot of nonsense from within the discipline and outside of it, and even from some Native communities other than my own. The chapters that follow that are written by Native people (and some of the others) contain the basis for some of the disenchantments that have made Native people doubt the value and veracity of anthropology. But in spite of these matters I am still an anthropologist, and I still maintain ties with Native communities throughout North America.

I became involved in gender studies after speaking with a handsome young Kiowa man many years ago. Later, another native woman from his "culture area" approached me and said, "Isn't it terrible that this good-looking man is gay? And that is what happened when the Europeans came to us." "No, you certainly don't know anything about your culture, if you can say this," I replied. This then motivated my work.

The fact is, in many communities in Native North America a growing homophobia is evident. That concerns me. I feel that we have to deal with this frightening situation in some way. I responded to the woman's remark by writing a paper in 1979, "Changing Native American Sex Roles in an Urban Context," which I never published but is provided as part of this chapter. I published on "Warrior Women of the Plains" (1983) and began to examine the contours of gender terms in my own Lakota language. By examining Native terms for gender classifications, the nuances of naming and behavior will become clearer.

Persons of Lakota or Dakota heritage, as well as others, might quote *"koshkalaka* [means] dyke" from Paula Gunn Allen's writings (1986:258). I did not correct her at the outset because at that time it was a sensitive issue. I knew that a lot of Native women who were just beginning to assert themselves as lesbians might say, "Oh, you're just lesbian-bashing." Being an anthropologist, being bashed by so many other Native people, I did not want to put anyone in that situation. *Koshkalaka* means simply "young man," "youth," or "post-pubescent male." We Lakota have another term, *wikoshkalaka,* which means "young woman," "a post-menarche female," or a "young woman who is *isnati* [lives alone or apart]," often referred to as living in a "menstrual hut" in the anthropological literature. Moreover, in talking with many of my elders (both male and female) and considering the analysis of words, I asked, "Is there a word for women who are like the *winkte?*" There was none. In 1993, when I discussed this, I heard the term *winkte winyan,* for some of the elder females had seen one. Here, again, the term *winkte* was used but with the term for woman, *winyan,* added.

Winkte, the Lakota/Dakota term for "gay or homosexual male," has assumed Pan-Indian or intertribal connotations and been translated as "wants [wishes] to be a woman." In a deeper, structural linguistic sense, it means to "kill women." This latter interpretation caused some ire among gender researchers when I first mentioned the translation (Medicine 1987). At the first Wenner-Gren Foundation conference and the subsequent American Anthropological Association session on "Revisiting the 'North American Berdache,'" we heard the term *koshkalaka winyan;* the word *winyan* had been added to Allen's use of *koshkalaka.* If we stick with Allen's meaning and usage, adding *winyan* might be considered redundant or, more often, emphatic: "dyke-woman" or, in other contexts, "lesbian-woman." Although Paula Gunn Allen has written me that the information given her was wrong, and the interpretation of *koshkalaka* was incorrect, the term is used unabashedly in women's studies courses as a result of the continued romanticization of Native American gender and sexuality.

Several other terms in the Lakota language are used to indicate gender characteristics. One, *bloka,* may be translated as the penultimate characterization of masculinity. It was a metaphor for the buffalo bull: ferocious, fearless, and fecund. The term was used to connote the best qualities of a provider and care-taker. *Winyan tanka* posed the desired characteristics of womanhood: virginity in maidenhood, industry and generosity in marriage, and priestliness in old age in order to receive the honored Bite the Knife ceremony without approbation. By contrast, *bloka* indicated men who exuded power on the vision quest, on the warpath, in horse raids, on buffalo hunts to provide for the *tiospaye* (extended family), and in protecting and cherishing women and children. These characteristics are mythic to the many contemporary men for whom the term means only sexual prowess. The term *bloka egla wa ke* has been translated as "thinks she can act like a man" in striving and excelling in such masculine achievements as riding horses and owning and providing for cattle and ultimately family and *tiospaye.* The term has been used to refer to women who indicate tendencies that may be construed as lesbian characteristics, or it might be considered to fit that constellation of behavior (Medicine:1993).

We must be very careful in using, or contriving, English translations for Native terms. We also must be aware of the ways language is changed and the meaning of Native terms altered and then used to meet the needs of disenfranchised groups and individuals as a possible response of self-interest. While I was in Canada, I investigated the Algonkin (Algonquian) term for "two-spirited." The use of "two-spirit" as a Pan-Indian term is not intended to be translated from English to Native languages, however. To do so changes the common meaning it has acquired by self-identified two-spirit Native Americans. Translating the word *two-spirits* into some languages could lead to misunderstandings that could have adverse effects on the person using the term. One should be cautious and careful to contextualize gender terms and how they are used in Native communities. *Spirit* is an extremely variable term, and in some Native languages connotes sacredness.

What follows was written in 1979 and, like Jacobs's essay (1968), it has had a life of its own, being copied and distributed among Native American women and men who, at that time and even now, call themselves "lesbian" and "gay." I have agreed to its publication here because what I said then still applies to many situations and because it provides historical roots to contemporary efforts.

I am pleased to have been part of the sessions that led to this book, and am pleased to be part of this book. The issues we are dealing with are very delicate in Native communities and in anthropology. What happened with the interaction of aboriginal people of all nations and anthropologists of all stripes during the course of the Wenner-Gren conferences was precedent-setting. We have set a model. I think that there should be more of this interaction in the anthropological profession. You should take very seriously what you read in these pages so that we may proceed with purpose and clarity, and an unknowing public can be informed.

[1993]

Changing Native American Sex Roles in an Urban Context*

Many Native American societies—especially the Plains tribes—have provided an outlet for male sexual deviancy in the institutionalized "berdache" (called *winkte* in Siouan and *hemaneh* among the Algonkian-speaking Cheyenne), which has been equated with homosexual in most introductory anthropology text books. Seemingly, there was no analogous role for Indian women. Reexamination and explication of sex roles in contemporary Indian societies indicate a shift in the feminine role to accommodate an emerging (or latent) lesbian orientation. Urban organizations such as GAI (Gay American Indians) will be analyzed as to their function in meeting actualized roles of Native Americans. Here I examine male and female roles in an urban, intertribal context and suggest further research needs.

*Editors' note: What follows is Medicine's now classic 1979 essay. As noted in the Introduction and in her remarks, the essay has been circulated in the Gay American Indian underground since it was first given, in much the same way that Jacobs's 1968 "berdache" paper was circulated in gay underground channels.

Contrary to popular belief, movements of Native Americans to urban centers have had a long history (Medicine 1973; Officer 1971). The Relocation Program sponsored by the Bureau of Indian Affairs in the 1950s greatly increased the trend toward urbanism as a way of life for Indians in contemporary society. This division of B.I.A., renamed the Employment Assistance Program, is still fostering the migration of reservation Indians to cities. The current population figures for urbanized Indians reads variously between 50 and 60 percent of an approximately one million Native inhabitants. This urban variation in census enumeration is typical of statistical data regarding Indians in all areas.

The literature on Native American urbanization has characteristically dwelt upon such problems as alcoholism, poverty, unemployment variables, family break-down, and the return rate to reservations, which form an integral part of the total picture in the life-styles of present-day Indians of all tribes.

Little has been done to deal with the coping strategies of individual Indians. This paper seeks to concretize some of the ideas advanced by Southall (1973) and utilizes data relating to changing sex roles of Indians in an urban context. Southall's neat, "vitamin-like"—(KEPLV)—representation of variables is an extremely challenging method for examining role relationships when applied to the urban experiences of certain self-ascribed Native Americans. Studies (Hirabayashi and Kemnitzer, eds. 1976; Price 1968) have stressed an unequal emphasis on the value of kinship and ethnic (K); economic and occupational (E); political (P); ritual and religious (L); and recreational, leisure-time, and voluntary (V) upon some of the discrete categories for analysis proposed by Southall in urban research. This is to suggest that a partitive analysis of role enactments by Native Americans in cities typifies much urbanization research. In general, therefore, the examination of role relationships has been uneven for the urban experiences of Native Americans.

Within the urban Indian experience, I shall attempt to examine the voluntary coming-out-of-the-closet process for individuals of Indian ancestry. The term is used to indicate the one that homosexuals use to vindicate a change in sex role orientation and actualization. This English equivalent is also preferable to such Native terms as the Siouan *winkte* (womanlike, or wishes-to-be-a-woman) which, like the Siouan term *washicu* (white person), assumes greater prevalence in intertribal vernacular in urban settings.

Many Native American societies—especially the Plains tribes—had traditionally provided an outlet for sexual "deviancy" in the institutionalized role of "berdache" (Jacobs 1968). Unfortunately, this social role—*winkte* among the Siouan Lakota-speakers (Hassrick 1964:133–35) and *hemaneh* among the Algonkian-speaking Cheyenne (Hoebel 1960: 77)—has often been equated with male homosexuals in most introductory anthropology texts and classes. Among the Lakota (Teton Sioux), there is evidence that other facets of action were bounded within the *winkte* gloss—ritualist, artist, specialist in women's craft production, herbalist, seer, namer of children, rejector of the rigorous warrior role, "mama's boy" (Hassrick 1964:134), and the designation commonly stated in anthropology books. Therefore, the multiplex categorizations in the following statement are extremely appropriate in the elucidation of such a role in an urban setting: "It is the conceptual idea of the particular, defined structural position which I call role and every instance in which it is played, whether by different persons, or by the same person to a number of others, I call role-relationship" (Southall 1973:75).

Additionally, Southall's reference to Banton's contention that "high moral density is associated with small population groups where everyone knows everyone else so that deviance in role performance by one person affects all the rest" (1973:80) has relevance to new role enactment on the part of some tribal individuals. The tightly constricted ethnic enclaves of reservations certainly present restrictiveness to role change. There are some instances of ritual role change in some tribes that are temporary and specialized. A certain surreptitiousness and secrecy has been evident in many reservation communities as far as these sexual "deviants" are concerned. Southall indicates, however, that he does not consider sex or age as roles for (his) present purposes, because neither is a universal generator of role relationships. "There is no question of the importance of sex and age in qualifying performance and attitude, but they do not in themselves give rise to basic role-relationships" he states (1973:76–77). It may be suggested that new role relationships in an urban context be examined. The fact that Native American homosexuals are coalescing and amplifying bonding mechanisms that fit into the (V) category may have implications for the urbanizing process and sex roles.

As indicated previously, the ethnological record concentrates primarily upon the examination of the male homosexual role. Apparently, if we rely upon the male-biased reporting of early anthropological accounts dealing with sex roles among Native Americans, there was no corollary expression for Indian females. Gender-based studies in socialization and role differentiation are greatly lacking in anthropological research upon contemporary Native American groups. Schaeffer (1965) presents most of the ethnohistorical data on a Kutenai "berdache" living in the nineteenth-century.* In most of the literature dealing with this perceived "deviancy" in Native societies, there are few data on female sexual expression. Seemingly, there is sparse information that can give us dimensions of feminine enactment of an analogous sex role. There are, however, narratives in the myth structure of some tribes which center upon lesbian behavior (i.e., Lowie [1909:51] for the Assiniboine and Jones [1907:151] for the Fox). There are other references to "female transvestitism" scattered throughout the ethnological literature on American Indians (Hill 1935). Hassrick (1964:135) writes: "Lesbianism seems to have played a much less obvious part in the life of the Sioux. Certain dream instructions given to young women in particular, the Double Woman's Appearance—hint at a kind of sanction for female perversion. . . . And yet there exists no record of old maids among the Sioux. Furthermore, there seem to be no examples of female inversion, and the role of women within the society appears to obviate the development of any meaningful causes."

Recent reexamination and explication of sex roles in contemporary Native American societies indicate an increase in overt actualization of homosexual roles. There is, in some instances, a shift in the feminine role to accommodate an emerging (or latent) lesbian orientation. The latency is seemingly more general in reservation communities than in urban areas. Acknowledgements of "gayness" have been indicated to me by Indian males and females, with males more predominant numerically. (I do not think that I am divulging secrets or breaches of trust but feel that such a statement is in order. I do not wish to give the impression of participant-observer.)

The dormant, or suppressed, sexual orientation in women is now (1977–79) being verbalized in reservation communities and may be due to the impact of Mental Health Programs among some Lakota and on other reservations. It may also be a function of the heightened awareness of the plight of women in general. Such new manifestations of sexual inequality as shelters for battered women and the formation of the White Buffalo Calf Women's Society are factors for consideration in a changing society. Enactment of the new sex role is still not salient

*Editors' note: The tribal name is also spelled as Kootenai, Kotanae, and Kootenay. See Nisbet (1994:134–38) for a brief account of Qánqon, a Kootenai female "berdache."

upon most reservations, however. There is evidence that the governmental agencies, as the Mental Health Programs of the Indian Health Service, are beginning to deal with the emotional trauma of Native people and there is the possibility that more cases involving lesbian tendencies may be forthcoming as the data is collected.

Again, the congealed interaction of small groups and the onus placed upon such individuals (males, historically, and now females) as the result of generations of an imposed ethical and moral system have apparently taken their toll on the participants in Native societies. Emphatically, the ritual roles of such tendencies, especially for the male actor, have been a part of the total religious repression, as with the Sun Dance among the Sioux. The wholesale denigration of Native belief systems in which individuals with this sexual inclination could manifest actualization has affected the attitudes of Indian persons in the present day. The learning of new cultural and sexual mores in the Christianization process also has relevance for attitudes regarding so-called perversion.

Psychologists in the Indian Health Service have mentioned lesbians among other Indian groups (Apache and Navajo, for example). These scattered inferences of Native lesbianism are reflected in the treatment modalities in the reservation health system. That is, the implication of "deviancy" is indicated, and mental health facilities are then utilized by the "deviant." This raises some interesting implications for the study of powerless people and administered human relations, and it also has significance for urban anonymity.

It is possible that overtness on the part of Native women homosexuals is more reflective of a change in the social climate in the larger, heterosexual white society. It is also significant that expression of lesbian sexual preference is more conspicuous in urban areas.

The lot of the Indian male homosexual in contemporary American Indian life has not been easy, just as it has been difficult for his white counterpart. Many Native American women in leadership positions have maintained that male homosexuality is a result of contact with Europeans and, mostly, have held such sexual "perverts" with disdain. In general, ridicule by fellow tribespersons has been the rule.

Moreover, male-male preference has been recognized and tolerated to various degrees in reservation communities. In some areas, particularly the Lakota-speaking areas, the aspect of *wakan* (power) has prevailed in some traditional communities. However, the orientation of most males to these persons has been one of intolerance. In addition, the male dominance and "macho-like" expressions of males in Indian militant and reform movements have placed these individuals—especially the males—in a triple bind. That is, there is not a sanctioned outlet in a changed and changing social milieu. The constraints of superimposed religious systems of the larger society have prevailed upon the ethical code of the reservation communities, and the marginal character of these individuals has fostered urban migration. To quote Randy: "I was like a lot of Indian people who came to the city. During the forties and fifties, the Bureau of Indian Affairs relocated many Indians to the cities. A lot of them were gay Indians who had 'lost' the respect of their tribes. They came to the cities and turned suicidal, alcoholic, and stereotypically cross-dressed" (Katz 1976:500–501).

This is not to say that the majority of migrants to urban areas fit this sexual designation. Nor is it possible at this time to say with certainty whether the urban atmosphere did allow the seeking of new sex roles. It is possible, however, to state with certainty that the urban milieu did offer greater avenues of accessibility to the homosexually oriented. This availability is highly valued by the participants. It is not possible to trace the transformation of individuals into this sexual role. The type of childhood experience (reservation, urban, or foster home), educational experience (parochial or federal boarding school or living at home), and early sexual experimentation (male and female prostitution) are all factors that are presently under investigation.

Of importance in the urbanization process is the formation of the San Francisco voluntary organization: GAI was formed in July 1975 to meet the needs of this displaced group, foster group interaction and solidarity, and provide a support system to meet the specialized needs of an ethnic group.

Equally interesting in the formation of this special interest group is that two persons—a Paiute male and a Lakota (Sioux) female—were instrumental in organizing the association. The male organizer is explicit in stating that he first became conscious of the institutionalized role of homosexuals in pre-contact societies by reading the gay press. Basic to organizing is a search for Indian pride and a mediation between tradition and change. They were also concerned with dispelling the "image of Indian as macho militant" (Katz 1976:502), which has been so prevalent in the Indian protest movements. Sexism is rampant in such movements as the American Indian Movement (AIM), where the militant men often say they are fostering Indian unity by having girl friends in each tribe and by fathering as many children as possible. The intolerance toward homosexuals has been equally enormous. Starting with a nucleus of ten members, GAI now numbers about thirty members representing some twenty tribes in an organization that is predominantly male. The association certainly shows variety in role relationships that transcend tribe and race, for the interaction extends to occupiers of other roles in an urban context.

Observations of the members of the group at Bay Area pow-wows and political meetings indicated that they were often ridiculed and taunted when they appeared at such functions. Certainly, the group has been involved in protests in the Bay Area, has attempted to educate Indians and others about their status and needs, and has presented radio shows in the greater metropolitan area.

At the present time (1979), the GAI group needs reassessment. Of significance in the arena of role relationships is the fact that individuals of Native ancestry who have homosexual proclivities appear to be gravitating to urban centers, especially San Francisco, for actualization and appreciation of their sexual orientations. Individuals mostly male from South Dakota (Sioux), Michigan (Ojibway), Washington state (Flathead), and Idaho (Nez Perce) have sought an urban life-style in contrast to the sexual repression they often find on the reservations. Significantly, face-to-face relationships in small communities are forfeited to urban masses and role-relationship differentiation.

Again, the "macho-like" attitudes of most Native Americans in the home communities are articulated toward these urban migrants, when some males state, "Yes, you can 'come out of the closet' when you are in San Francisco, but you have to 'go back in' when you come home."

The entire ramifications of homosexuality among Native Americans males and females in contemporary life on reservations and in urban settings have not been researched thoroughly. This paper has attempted to call attention to its dimensions as the problem is perceived by role participants and chart the social parameters.

[1979]

References Cited

Allen, Paula Gunn. 1986. *The Sacred Hoop: Recovering the Feminine in American Indian Traditions.* Boston: Beacon Press.

Hassrick, Royal B. 1964. *The Sioux.* Norman: University of Oklahoma Press.

Hill, W. W. 1935. "The Status of the Hermaphrodite and Transvestite in Navaho Culture." *American Anthropologist* 37: 273–79.

Hirabayashi, James, and Luis Kemnitzer, eds. 1976. *Urban Indian Research Project.* Unpublished ms. San Francisco State University.

Hoebel, E. Adamson. 1960. *The Cheyennes: Indians of the Great Plains.* New York: Holt, Rinehart and Winston.

Jacobs, Sue-Ellen. 1968. "Berdache: A Brief Review of the Literature." *Colorado Anthropologist* 1(2): 25–40. Reprint. Wayne R. Dynes and Stephen Donaldson, eds. 1992. *Studies in Homosexuality.* Volume 2: *Ethnographic Studies of Homosexuality.* New York: Garland.

Jones, William. 1907. *Fox Tests.* Publications of the American Ethnological Society. Volume 1. Leiden: E. J. Brill.

Katz, Jonathan. 1976. *Gay American History.* New York: Thomas Y. Crowell.

Lowie, Robert H. 1909. "The Assiniboine." *Anthropological Papers of the Museum of Natural History* 4: 42. New York: American Museum of Natural History.

Medicine, Beatrice. 1973. "The Native Americans." In *Outsiders, USA,* ed. Don Spiegel and Patricia Keith-Spiegel, 392–407. San Francisco: Rinehart Press.

———. 1983. "'Warrior Women': Sex Role Alternatives for Plains Indian Women." In *The Hidden Half: Studies of Plains Indian Women,* ed. Patricia Albers and Beatrice Medicine, 267–80. Lanham: University Press of America.

———. 1987. "New Perspectives on the Siouan Term: *Winkte.*" Paper presented at the New Gender Scholarship Conference, University of Southern California.

———. 1993. Fieldnotes in possession of the author.

Nisbet, Jack. 1994. *Sources of the River: Tracking David Thompson Across Western North America.* Seattle: Sasquatch Books.

Officer, James E. 1971. "The American Indian and Federal Policy." In *The American Indian in Urban Society,* ed. Jack O. Waddell and O. Michael Watson, 9–65. Boston: Little, Brown.

Price, John A. 1968. "The Migration and Adaptation of American Indians to Los Angeles." *Human Organization* 27: 168–75.

Schaeffer, Claude E. 1965. "The Kutenai Female Berdache: Courier, Guide, Prophetess and Warrior." *Ethnohistory* 12(3): 195–216.

Southall, Aidan. 1973. "The Density of Role Relationships as a Universal Index of Urbanization." In *Urban Anthropology,* ed. Aidan Southall, 71–106. New York: Oxford University Press.

★ ★ 7

Navajo Cultural Constructions
of Gender and Sexuality

Wesley Thomas (Navajo)

Multiple genders were part of the norm in the Navajo culture before the 1890s. From the 1890s until the 1930s dramatic changes took place in the lives of Navajos because of exposure to, and constant pressures from, Western culture—not the least of which was the imposition of Christianity. Religious leaders, medicine people, and others at variance from Christian norms started to be discrete about exposing their identities to the outside world. They moved underground due to the pressure from Western secular and religious beliefs (Spicer 1962). Due to the influence of Western culture and Christianity, which attempt to eradicate gender diversity, the pressure still exists (Thomas 1992).

Of the multiple genders still present in Navajo culture, composed in various degrees of traditional and contemporary people, the first two genders correlate with those acknowledged in Western culture. Westerners define heterosexual man/masculinity as the first gender and heterosexual woman/femininity as the second gender. "Male" and "female" are sexual terms. In Navajo society these two genders, man and woman, are reversed in priorities. In addition, the Navajo term *nadle* has been used as an example of a "supernumerary sex" (Martin and Voorhies 1975:84–107), classic "berdache" [*sic*] examples (Hill 1935), and as an alternative gender (Thomas 1992). To my knowledge, before my efforts no Navajo had ever undertaken an empirical study of the *nádleeh*. In this chapter I will provide a brief introduction to my research, which includes interviews with Navajo people of various degrees of traditionalism and other identifications; a review of the literature in English; and my experiences as a Navajo, including my interactions with *nádleeh*-identified Navajo.

Navajo Gender Concepts

Navajo sex-based gender categories are reflected in the language used to designate people at various stages of their life-cycles (Table 7-1).[1] Using the criteria of sex, terms are assigned to females and males according to age. There are also words used for females and males when sex is either irrelevant or unknown. The traditional social gender system, although based initially on biological sex, divides people into categories based on several criteria: sex-linked occupation, behaviors, and roles (Table 7-2; see also Kochems and Jacobs in this volume). "Sex-linked occupation" refers to expected work specializations associated with being female or male (e.g., women are generally weavers, men are generally hunters). "Sex-linked behaviors" include body language, speech style and voice pitch, clothing and other adornment, and those aspects of ceremonial activities that are sex-linked (e.g., women wear shawls in dancing and men do not; men use gourd rattles during dances and women do not). Women's sex-linked activities include those associated with childrearing, cooking

Table 7-1. Navajo Gender Terminology for Selected Age Groups

Age	Female	Neutral	Male
0–12 months		*'awéé'* (baby/infant)	
1–2 years	*'at' ééd yázhí* (little girl)	*'ałchíní* (children)	*'askii yázhí* (little boy)
3–13 years	*'at' ééd* (girl)	*chąąmą 'ii* (youngster)	*'askii* (boy)
3–13 years	*'at' ééké* (girls)	*dinééh* (youth)	*ashiiké* (boys)
13–30 years	*ch'kę́ę́h* (young woman)	*tsiłkę́ę́h* (youth)	*dinééh* (young man)
13–30 years	*ch'ikéí* (young women)	*diné* (people)	*tsiłkę́ę́h* (young men)
30–70 years	*'asdzáni* (woman)	*diné* (people)	*hastiin* (man)
30–70 years	*sáanii* (women)	*diné* (people)	*hastóí* (men)
70+ years	*'asdzą́ą́' sání* (old woman)	*diné* (people)	*hastiin sání* (old man)

Table 7-2. Navajo Gender System

Gender status	woman 'asdzáán	female nádleeh	hermaphrodite nádleeh	male nádleeh	man hastiin
Gender features					
sexual object choice	men and nádleeh	women	?	men	women and nádleeh
demeanor	feminine	masculine	androgynous	feminine	masculine
dress	female	male	androgynous	female	male
occupation	weaver	hunter	varies	weaver	hunter
Gender/sex category	female body		mixed genitalia	male body	

and serving meals, making pottery and baskets, and doing or overseeing other work associated with everyday aspects of the domestic sphere. For men, getting wood, preparing cooking fires, building homes, hunting, planting and harvesting various vegetables, and doing or overseeing work associated with the ceremonial aspects of everyday life are appropriate. A *nádleeh* mixes various aspects of the behaviors, activities, and occupations of both females and males. The older Navajo people recognize five traditional gender categories.

The Female Gender

The primary gender in the Navajo culture is *'asdzáán* (woman). *'Asdzáán* is a generic gender term for "woman." *'Áád* is the perfective root term referring to the female sex and is considered a secondary characteristic of a person. The term *'áád* is not a gender-identifier; it is commonly used as a referent for female sex identification of species other than humans. If it is used for humans, it carries a derogatory and an insulting connotation. When used to refer to sex of female humans, the term becomes *ba'áád*. The *ba'* prefix indicates "for it." *Ba'áád* is a sexual marker. It also means sexual partner and can be used to refer jokingly to one's wife/girlfriend/female friend, a man's wife/girlfriend/female friend, and it could also mean a woman's wife/girlfriend/female friend. The female gender is primary in the Navajo origin stories, and it has been established as the most important gender. It is not only appropriate but also necessary for the feminine gender to be primary according to the Navajo cultural construction of woman/female/feminine gender and sex. Women are the heads of households and the primary decision-makers among traditional Navajo people. All life emerges from the Earth and Earth Woman, and the principal female deity is *'Ásdzáá Nádleehí* (Changing Woman) (Reichard 1950:21; Witherspoon 1977:91).[2]

The Male Gender

The next gender is *hastiin* (man), a term used as a gender marker only. It is not a sexual marker. Man is defined by a range of terms from birth through old age (Table 7-1). *Ką'* is the sexual marker for male. Like the use of *'áád* for human females, the use of the term *ką'* for human males is considered derogatory and insulting. The utilization of sexual markers of *'áád* and *ką'* is normally limited to nonhumans. These terms are commonly used to define the sex of animals, insects, natural forces, plants, rain, rivers, mountains, inanimate objects, abstract ideas, thoughts, and ceremonies.

Nádleeh/Hermaphrodite

The third gender category is the *nádleeh*/hermaphrodite.[3] *Nádleeh* is a Navajo gender term, whereas *hermaphrodite* is a Western-defined biological term. Hermaphrodites have been briefly mentioned in Navajo origin stories, which describe no physical attributes of hermaphrodites but only characteristics, such as doing women's work (Haile 1981; Hill 1935; Matthews 1897; Reichard 1950).[4] Again, only the gender characteristics are presented. Western culture's definition of hermaphrodism has been applied to Navajo *nádleeh,* as illustrated in Hill's article in which he defines hermaphrodites as the "real *nadle*" and transvestites as "pretend to be *nadle*" (1935:273). From the Navajo view, until the turn of the century males who demonstrated characteristics of the opposite gender were known to fulfill their roles as *nádleeh.* Changes began to occur in the late 1800s, and the role of *nádleeh* had begun to disappear by the 1930s (Hill 1935:274).

The meaning of the word *nádleeh* has changed, too, although it is still powerful within traditional Navajo discourse.[5] The word is not used in day-to-day conversations. Historically, speech is the manifestation of thought, which is inherently powerful (Witherspoon 1977:16). Navajo traditionalists continually teach that "sacred begins at the tip of your tongue. Be careful when speaking. You create the world around you with your words" (Jim, ed. 1994:4). The majority of traditional Navajo families almost never speak the word *nádleeh* because of an appreciation for the power inherent in speech and careful usage of the word in appropriate context and by appropriate individuals. This is applicable within Navajo space, as defined within the four sacred mountains. When *nádleeh* is used outside this defined space, it is considered a label and similar to other Navajo or English words. Furthermore, *nádleeh* is intertwined with control, ambiguity, knowledge, and continuity of Navajo life and culture within Navajo space. Constructed Navajo behaviors to and with speech and thought are deemphasized in the academic world and in publication (Goulet 1994 and in this volume). Moreover, *nádleeh* is the gender marker for male-bodied individuals, although it has been misapplied to those who are female- bodied. *Nádleeh____baa'* is the proper term for them; a given family name is inserted between the words (Young and Morgan 1951:431–33). Another name for female-bodied *nádleeh* was *dilbaa'* (warrior girl) (Young and Morgan 1992:45, 976).

Further research is needed to clarify and justify adding another gender category, particularly applied to female-bodied *nádleeh* (*nádleeh____baa', dilbaa'*). The women's name, *baa',* does not belong in this category but is applied to the female gender. With the addition of *nádleeh* (prefix) and *baa'* (suffix) or *dilbaa',* the traditional Navajo gender categories increase to six.

Navajo persons today who identify with the general *nádleeh* gender category would be classified as female-bodied *nádleeh* or male-bodied *nádleeh.* Through the advancement of medical technologies, I doubt that there are any hermaphrodites; infants born with both genitalia are surgically assigned (often without the parents being informed) as either a male or, most often, a female in order to fit into America's medical classification of two sexual and gender categories (Fausto-Sterling 1993; Money and Ehrhardt 1972; Weeks 1985). Most Navajos now conflate concepts of gender and sexuality because of diversity and their unawareness of the multiple categories within the Navajo culture (Thomas 1994).

Kochems (in this volume and with Callender 1983) uses "gender mixing" to refer to *nádleeh* of either sex. Lang and I prefer *womanly male* and *manly female* to make a clear distinction between male-bodied and female-bodied *nádleeh.*[6] Others do not like the use of these terms because they are too close to the *Diagnostic and Statistical Manual III-R* (American Psychiatric Association 1989) typologies used under "gender dysphoria." In Navajo tradition, there is no concept of gender dysphoria; rather, as has been shown, there is a concept of gender diversity (meaning it is recognized that there are more than two genders).

The Masculine-Female Gender

The fourth gender category is one I hesitantly associate *nádleeh* concept and call masculine female. Masculine females are individuals who do not fit into the first two gender categories. Within the Navajo culture, masculine females are distinct from other female-bodied people because they are not involved in reproduction and their priorities are different from primary gender people (women). Even today, masculine females fill some occupational roles usually associated with the male gender, such as construction worker, firefighter, and auto mechanic, even though such occupations may also be taken up by women who are not of the masculine-female gender.

Historically, female-bodied *nádleeh*/masculine females had specific Navajo ceremonial roles that have disappeared through time. A few of the Navajo elderly medicine people I talked with alluded to these functions but refused to elaborate on them. Knowledge of ceremonial roles is not to be divulged to persons who are not Navajo medicine people. The masculine-female gender, however, necessitates a separate, additional gender category within Navajo society and culture because they are defined differently in Navajo discourse.

The Feminine-Male Gender

The last—for the time being—and fifth gender is the feminine male, who do not fit into the male gender category. Their gender identity is established by their definition and confirmed by Navajo origin stories as *nádleeh* (Haile 1981; Matthews 1994:217). Many traditional Navajo people believe that origin stories describe the foundation of their culture. Gender identification is derived from this foundation, and frequent mention of male-bodied *nádleeh*/feminine males is found in origin stories.

Feminine males identify with a concept of gender diversity. As one of the original people in the Navajo origin stories, feminine males performed and were responsible for work also performed by women. The tradition continues to an extent. Some of the work feminine-male people do includes cooking at religious gatherings, weaving, household chores, and tending children. It is socially acceptable for feminine males to do women's work in traditional Navajo society but not in other societies.

Adaptations

Navajo culture has frequently borrowed ideas from other cultures, including Euro-American culture which brought in the concepts of gay and lesbian identities. Today, many younger Navajos see themselves as gays or lesbians and have no interest in conforming to the traditional cultural definition of *nádleeh,* simply because of changes in time. As a result, Navajo gays and lesbians identify with the Euro-American notion of sexual identity rather than with the Navajo ideology of multiple genders. Because of Western schooling, extensive exposure to Western culture, and the lapsed transmission of Navajo tradition, the traditional role of both male-bodied *nádleeh*/feminine males and female-bodied *nádleeh*/masculine females is not widely known by young Navajos who would fit into these categories.

Types of Relationships

There are major differences between Western and traditional Navajo concepts relating to gender, sexuality, and sexual relationships. Neither a relationship between a female-bodied *nádleeh*/masculine female and a woman nor a relationship between a male-bodied *nádleeh*/feminine male and a man are considered a homosexual relationship by traditional Navajo people, although each is termed "homosexual" in Western culture. Relationships between two women, two men, two female-bodied *nádleeh*/masculine females, or two male-bodied *nádleeh*/feminine males are, however, considered to be homosexual and even incestual in traditional Navajo culture. Even though a small percentage of Navajo individuals are considered to be asexual or homosexual, the majority of their relationships are culturally classified as heterosexual. A relationship between a woman and a man is obviously heterosexual, for example; likewise, a relationship between a woman and a female-bodied *nádleeh*/ masculine female is given the same consideration and rights as a heterosexual relationship. Equally, a relationship between a man and a male-bodied *nádleeh*/feminine male is heterosexual (Table 7-3).

Table 7-3.   Sexual Relationships and Classifications I: Traditional and Transitional

Gender Categories	Feminine Female	Masculine Male	Masculine Female (*nádleehí*)	Feminine Male (*nádleehí*)
Feminine female	inconceivable	heterosexual	heterosexual	relationship rare
Masculine male	heterosexual	inconceivable	relationship rare	heterosexual
Masculine female (*nádleehí*)	heterosexual	relationship rare	inconceivable	relationship rare
Feminine male (*nádleehí*)	relationship rare	heterosexual	relationship rare	inconceivable

These relationships are seen primarily as gender issues and only secondarily as sexual issues. Again, this is because the Navajo cultural construction dictates how the gender relationship system functions. From my observation, it appears that only a small percentage of traditional Navajo people on the reservation who are female-bodied *nádleeh*/masculine females or male-bodied *nádleeh*/feminine males are seen by other traditional Navajos as being homosexuals. This is, again, because of Western influences. Likewise, female-bodied *nádleeh*/masculine females and male-bodied *nádleeh*/feminine males themselves do not identify with or associate themselves with homosexuality. They make a distinction between themselves and gay or lesbian Navajos. The majority of those who identify as gay or lesbian (i.e., homosexuals) have moved to urban settings. Instances of urban homosexual relationships involve women (two biological and cultural females) or men (two biological and cultural males) (Table 7-4).

Bisexuality and Transgenderism

I have found no separate linguistic category for bisexualism for either males or females, but I know that bisexuality as it is defined by Western traditions is practiced among Navajo contemporary males and females. When we consider that the English term *bisexuality* means that an individual is sexually active with both women and men, and when we consider further the permissible and inappropriate sexual relations based on Navajo gender categories other than sex, bisexuality does not occur. This particular area needs additional research for better clarification of how bisexuality functions within the context of Navajo culture. For purposes of HIV/AIDS education, however, the reality of male-to-male sex, both on and off the reservation, must be faced. Male-to-male sex is one of the leading causes of HIV infection among men and heterosexual women.

Table 7-4. Sexual Relationships and Classifications II: Contemporary, Acculturated, and Assimilated

Gender Categories	Feminine Female	Masculine Male	Masculine Female	Feminine Male
Feminine female	homosexual	heterosexual	homosexual	heterosexual
Masculine male	heterosexual	homosexual	heterosexual	homosexual
Masculine female	homosexual	heterosexual	homosexual	heterosexual
Feminine male	heterosexual	homosexual	heterosexual	homosexual

This reality must be understood at the personal level by health providers, AIDS educators, and lay people. Male extramarital sexual activity is a major source of HIV and other sexually transmitted disease (STD) infection of women (Givan 1993). More research is desperately needed in this area.

"Transgenderism" is defined by those who label themselves by this word as the processes involved in living one's life as the gender with which one's personal identity is congruent (see Cromwell in this volume). The term is intended to cover self-identified cross-dressers and other gender mixers, transvestites, and pre- and postoperative transsexuals. Navajos I would place in this category include those who refer to themselves as "drag queens" (see Epple in this volume), transsexuals who are in various stages of male-to-female sex reassignment, and women and men who cross-dress in their everyday lives or on special occasions, as well as those who live as the gender opposite their sex but are neither *nádleeh* or preoperative transsexuals.

Types of Female-Bodied *Nádleeh*/Masculine Females and Male-Bodied *Nádleeh*/Feminine Males

To facilitate better analysis, I have subdivided the female-bodied *nádleeh*/ masculine females and male-bodied *nádleeh*/feminine males (Table 7-5). In my research, I found it useful to create five categories to represent those who make up each of the female-bodied *nádleeh*/masculine-female and male-bodied *nádleeh*/feminine-male gender category: traditionalist, transitionalist, contemporary, acculturated, and assimilated.[7] These five categories are not derived from the Navajos' point of view; they were constructed as a heuristic device to further my analysis.

Table 7-5. Gender Diversity in Navajo Culture: Traditional-Assimilated Cultural Continuum

Gender Categories	Traditional	Transitional	Contemporary	Acculturated	Assimilated
Women	+	+	+	+	+
Masculine females	–	+	+	+	+
Nádleeh/ hermaphrodites	+	–	–	–	–
Feminine males	–	+	+	+	+
Men	+	+	+	+	+

Key: + = present; – = absent

The traditionalist is a person who lives on the reservation, usually at his/her mother's residence. The Navajo Nation is a matrilineal society, and Navajos are predominately matrilocal. If the mother is deceased, then the traditional *nádleeh* (for simplicity this term will be used) lives near a maternal aunt or older sister who would most likely be involved in some sort of traditional curative or religious ceremony. According to Hill (1935), a traditional *nádleeh* is considered wealthy, in a Navajo cultural sense not in a Western capitalist monetary sense, in comparison with siblings or relatives who are not *nádleeh*. In addition, that individual is considered to be an anchor within the extended family group. My observations confirm these points and add new ones. For example, the *nàdleeh* might be raising a child or children within the kin group. No traditional *nádleehí* I know identifies or associates with Western-identified gays or lesbians.[8] The traditional *nádleehí* is defined on the basis of the important occupational position or social role held within that person's particular families. The traditionalist is, first, defined on the basis of social role and/or occupational preference.

Historically, children who showed a keen interest in work tools and activities associated with the gender opposite their sex often were encouraged to develop skills in the occupational domains of their interest. Today, a male-bodied *nádleeh* may be encouraged by his female kin to become a weaver as opposed to a silversmith, and the female kin may also teach him/her cooking and sewing and other domestic skills and responsibilities. The traditionalist is frequently involved in religious activities and is a medicine woman, medicine man, herbalist, or diagnostician. As far as sexual identification is concerned, the traditional *nádleeh* is a heterosexual in Navajo terms. *Nádleeh* do not have sex with one another. Male-bodied *nádleeh* do have sexual relationships with men, but these relationship are not considered "homosexual relationships" by the *nádleeh* themselves, their partners, or the traditional Navajo society in general (see Epple in this volume for a contemporary *nádleeh*'s perspective on this issue).

The second category of Navajo person is the transitionalist, who generally lives on or off the reservation but still maintains strong family ties. The individual still retains many Navajo religious beliefs but is not as involved in Navajo culture as the traditionalist. Some transitionalist *nádleeh* identify with and associate with Western-identified gays and/or lesbians. Transitionalist *nádleehí* have typically been more exposed to Western culture than have traditionalists, and they usually have more Western education. Some transitionalists identify more with

Western-identified gays or lesbians than they do with *nádleeh.* Those who identify as *nádleehí* will usually base their identities primarily on occupational preference, as do traditionalists. For example, male-bodied *nádleeh* have obtained training that would prepare them for a cross-gender occupation such as secretary, nurse's aid, weaver, day-care provider, or other stereotypically female jobs. They retain family relationships that support their gender status and roles. A transitionalist is, however, less likely than a traditionalist to become deeply involved in religious activities. Like traditionalists, male transitionalist *nádleeh* have sexual relationships with men, and these relationships are generally classified by the transitionalist, his partner, and Navajo society as heterosexual unless the transitionalist is a self-identified gay male rather than a male-bodied *nádleeh* or feminine male.

Such classifications only hold true for traditional Navajo culture. Many Navajos have come to conflate gender diversity and homosexuality and make no distinction between male-bodied *nádleeh* and transvestitism and their respective relationships with men. In some Navajo communities or chapters on the reservation, knowledge about gender diversity has been repressed or officially forgotten due to Western secular colonial pressures (including forced education) and fundamentalist and evangelical conservative Christian influences.

The third category of Navajo personhood is the contemporary. This person has some or a little knowledge of traditional Navajo culture, religious beliefs, and social/occupational activities. The individual also has some or little contact with reservation life and usually returns to the reservation for very short visits. In addition, she or he has some knowledge of the Navajo language that is likely to be deteriorating gradually because most of the person's time is spent off the reservation. Many people in this group identify with urban gays and lesbians, which enables them to have a closer relationship with Euro-American gay and lesbian culture than with Navajo culture. There are others who self-identify not only as Navajo gays and lesbians but also as two-spirit—lesbian and gay Native American—a rapidly spreading Pan-Indian North American alternative concept intended to distance Native Americans from European-American-dominated lesbian and gay cultural norms.[9]

The fourth and fifth category of Navajos are the acculturated and assimilated. Both categories refer to Navajos who have lived away from the reservation (very few are on the reservation) for several generations as well as Navajo children born into interracial and intertribal families. A person in the acculturated category usually has little or no knowledge of the Navajo language. They are aware that their tribal heritage lies with the Navajo Nation, yet the assimilated are not aware of their tribal heritage and do not acknowledge it. Members of both categories have an identity similar to gay or lesbian. A few members of these two groups, especially the acculturated, may self-identify as two-spirit if their identity as Native American is strong and they do not want to merge into the white-dominated gay and lesbian urban cultures.

Sexual Relationships

Cultural taboos forbid sexual relationships among three of the five categories of Navajo gender. For example, the Western idea of a sexual relationship between a person who is a Navajo traditionalist *nádleeh* and a Navajo transitionalist *nádleeh* would be homosexuality and incestuous in Navajo culture because of the gender categories. People of the same sex and gender are not supposed to have sex with one another according to Navajo tradition, but *nádleeh* who are biologically males may have sex with women and with men who are not *nádleeh*. Gender classification, identity, and roles as prescribed by Navajo culture supersede sexual identification in these relationships (Table 7-6). Who may and who should not have sexual relationships is further illustrated in Tables 7-3 and 7-4. Of course, there will always be people who break the rules. And

Table 7-6. Permitted, Possible, and Inappropriate Sexual Relationships (Traditional-Transitional Navajo Culture)

Gender Categories	Feminine Female	Masculine Male	Masculine Female (*nádleehí*)	Feminine Male (*nádleehí*)
Sex: female Gender: woman	inappropriate	permitted	permitted	possible, inappropriate
Sex: male Gender: man	permitted	inappropriate	possible, inappropriate	permitted
Sex: female Gender: *nádleehí*	permitted	possible, inappropriate	inappropriate	possible, inappropriate
Sex: male Gender: *nádleehí*	possible, inappropriate	permitted	possible, inappropriate	inappropriate

Key: Permitted relationships are those between individuals who are of different sex and different gender or of same sex but of different gender. Inappropriate relationships are those between individuals who are of the same sex and same gender. Possible relationships are those conservative traditionalists would classify as inappropriate and transitional people would classify as permitted although rare.

so Navajo gay men and lesbians who are homosexuals and, consequently, often face discrimination, harassment, and other expressions of homophobia, both on and off the reservations (Deschamps, ed. 1993).

Politics of Location

Depending on the environment of someone's location, identity is negotiated and renegotiated according to a need to relate to the immediate locale. In the politics of location, a temporary adjustment is made to accommodate the needs of others or make a connection of relationships with others in a locale. For example, a Navajo person who grew up on the reservation will relate differently to non-Native people if placed in their environment. Another example would be a Navajo male who is a two-spirit-identified person; he will not see himself as a male-bodied *nádleeh* or as a feminine-male gender, or maybe—at a given, appropriate time—he might. This also can be referred to as "situational gender-identity." Likewise, a Navajo-identified person who grew up in an urban area will probably identify as a gay person or even as a two-spirit but not as a *nádleeh* or a male-bodied *nádleeh,* primarily because of the inability to relate to that concept of gender identity. Perhaps at one point the person could relate temporarily to the male-bodied *nádleeh.* This, too, is in need of further research for proper elucidation.

Conclusion

Most Navajos living in the United States today, whether on the reservation or off, are faced with the same kinds of issues concerning sexualities and gender identities that people of other nations, tribes, races, and ethnicities face. Some hold to traditional ways, and others anxiously embrace new ways that bring them into the one of the mainstreams of American society. These mainstreams include national and state politics, Western medicine, urban business practices, and the urban gay/lesbian/bisexual/transgender cultures. Navajos can be classified according to their degree of belief and participation in traditional Navajo culture. The classifications I have constructed range from "traditional" to "assimilated." In addition, because this chapter is about gender diversity within Navajo cultural constructions, people's location along this continuum is considered from the point of view of sexual category and gender identity. The names people use for themselves on the reservation may be different from those used in urban environments. Some will refer to themselves as lesbian or gay regardless of where they are; others will confine the use of those terms to urban situations. Such choices generally reflect individual awareness and practice of the politics of location. Yet shifting among several terms and therefore categories may reflect situational gender identity (as defined by Jacobs in this volume). As Jacobs notes, this is not unlike shifting ethnic identities found in various parts of the world as strategies for maximizing one's comfort among various kin and non-kin. Table 7-7 is intended to demonstrate how people's sex and gender categories are marked along the continuum from traditional to assimilated. Where a concept (marked by specific English terminology) is absent, a minus sign is shown in the appropriate cell; where a concept is found, a plus sign is shown.

To achieve a better understanding of the complexity of gender and sexuality in Navajo culture will take more time and research. Moreover, gender formulation and reformulation within the Navajo culture are ongoing processes that have been affected by the influence of Euro-American cultures. The Navajo world has always evolved by synthesizing traditional ideas and practices with new ones. The Navajo people are continuing to absorb new things and practices from the outside, as they have always done, without losing their identity and strength. This will continue if parents and the tribe teach the Navajo culture and tra-

Table 7-7. Gender Diversity in Navajo Culture from 1897 (Matthews) to 1997 (Thomas): Traditional-Assimilated Cultural Continuum

Gender Categories	Traditional	Transitional	Contemporary	Acculturated	Assimilated
Female-bodied					
Women	+	+	+	+	+
Lesbians	–	–	+	+	+
Masculine females	–	+	+	+	+
Both male and female *Nádleeh*/hermaphrodites	+	+?	–	–	–
Either male or female Two-spirits	–	–	+	+	+
Male-bodied					
Feminine males	–	+	+	+	+
Gay	–	–	+	+	+
Men	+	+	+	+	+

Key: + = present; – = absent

dition. Otherwise, the Navajo concept of gender and sexuality may be transposed by Western ideas and practices, something that is well on the way to happening. Preserving Navajo cultural concepts and beliefs will help keep respect for, and acceptance of, multiple genders within Navajo society. Knowing the Navajo people's acceptance might enable European-Americans to reformulate their understanding of cultural and gender diversity, a value espoused by many.

Notes

This chapter is a revised version of a presentation to the Wenner-Gren Foundation Conference on "Revisiting the 'North American Berdache' Empirically and Theoretically" at the 92d annual meeting of the American Anthropological Association, Washington, D.C., November 17, 1994, as well as to the AAA session of the same name held in Washington on November 18. The research upon which the chapter is based was specifically funded by the Royalty Research Fund and the Institute of Ethnic Studies in the United States Fund, both at the University of Washington-Seattle, during the summer of 1993. The chapter is but an introduction to my interest in Navajo culture, as a Navajo.

Additional funds were provided by the Danforth-Compton Fellowship, Ronald Olson Fellowship, Department of Anthropology, Graduate School Travel Fund, Minority Education Division, and Office of Minority Affairs (all at the University of Washington); the Wenner-Gren Foundation, New York City; the American Indian Graduate Center, Albuquerque; the Navajo Nation Scholarship, Window Rock, Arizona; and the Gilbert and Katheryn Wrenn Scholarship Fund, Tempe, Arizona.

Special thanks are due to my mentors: Sabine Lang, who provided comments on previous versions of the chapter, and Maureen Trudelle Schwarz, who provided consistent and determined support through my academic studies, providing inspiration and strong insights on my research. Thanks also to my Ph.D. committee members at the University of Washington: James D. Nason, who provided continuous encouragement; Gary Witherspoon, who cautioned me from the outset to insist on my right to conduct research from my cultural perspective; and Sue-Ellen Jacobs, who first suggested this project and stuck with me throughout its inception and the grant proposal process. Finally, K. Tsianina Lomawaima provided much-needed and valuable criticism.

1. Navajo infants are classified with animals as "callers" until they speak their first words (Witherspoon 1977:97). The gender marking commonly begins after the first word is spoken.

2. In the *Navajo Dictionary* (Young and Morgan 1987:843), this is how it is spelled. Other variations occur in this volume. *'Asdzáá Nádleehí* is a female of the primary gender who changes from White Shell Woman to Earth Woman to Sun Woman to Corn Woman (see Matthews 1994 and Witherspoon 1977 for additional information). If the words are reversed, as *Nádleehí 'Asdzaan,* it refers to "lesbian" (Young and Morgan 1987:935).

3. Before the invention of sex-assignment surgery and its habitual use throughout the United States for infants born with ambiguous genitalia, a "true" *nádleeh* was a hermaphrodite, a genitally androgynous person, recognized within a third category of sexed persons whose social behavior and social roles mixed expectations for both female-bodied and male-bodied persons. Other *nádleeh* ("those who pretend to be 'true'") were and still are recognized in traditional Navajo communities (Table 7-3 and the section on *nádleeh*/hermaphrodites).

4. In the *American Heritage Dictionary* (second college edition), "hermaphrodite" is defined as "one that has the sex organs and many of the secondary characteristics of both male and female."

5. *Báá* is defined as "warrior girl" in Young and Morgan (1951:431; 1967:20). *Báá* was and is still used as a girl's or woman's name. It has no relation with female-bodied *nádleeh* or masculine-female gender. Through my conversations with elderly Navajo women and Navajo linguistic analysis of the word *báá,* one can see that it refers to the masculine characteristic of a woman or girl. It pronounces the male aspect of a woman. It was an additional role for females (Hill 1936). The dichotomization of male/female within Navajo personhood, either a man or a woman, was researched by Maureen Trudelle Schwarz for her Ph.D. dissertation in anthropology at University of Washington in Seattle (1997).

6. The terms *womanly male* and *manly female* are the result of a number of discussions between Sabine Lang and I, during which we tried to develop descriptive terms that are more appropriate to referring to gender diversity than "berdache." Furthermore, it is not culturally appropriate to use the term *nádleeh* for present-day Navajo persons, even though they may identify as such. It has been reclassified as a label only.

7. The first three terms were introduced by Jennie Joe (Navajo), a medical anthropologist who lives in Tucson, Arizona.

8. The term *nádleeh* means constant state of change (as a verb), and *nádleehí* means one who is in a constant state of change (as a noun). Both are my translations.

9. *Two-spirit* is a self-label that grew from the Native American two-spirit movement (see Anguksuar and Jacobs in this volume) as a generic term that would embrace Native American gay, lesbian, and transgender people who either choose not to use their Native terms or whose Native terms been forgotten. The expression is not intended to be translated into Navajo or

other Native American languages. In Navajo, such a translation could be interpreted to mean a person with both a dead spirit and a living spirit within them—not a desirable situation.

References Cited

American Psychiatric Association. 1989. *Diagnostic and Statistical Manual of Mental Disorders.* 3d ed. Washington: American Psychiatric Association.

Callender, Charles, and Lee M. Kochems. 1983. "The North American 'Berdache.'" *Current Anthropology* 14(4): 443–70.

Deschamps, Gilbert, ed. 1993. "AIDS and the Navajo: An Interview with an HIV Positive Navajo." *The Sacred Fire* (Spring-Summer): 10–12.

Fausto-Sterling, Anne. 1993. "The Five Sexes: Why Male and Female Are Not Enough." *The Sciences* (March-April): 20–24.

Givan, Janice Marie. 1993. "American Indian/Alaska Native Women with HIV Infection." Master of nursing thesis, University of Washington.

Goulet, Jean-Guy. 1994. "The Northern Athapaskan 'Berdache' Reconsidered." Paper presented at "Revisiting the 'North American Berdache' Empirically and Theoretically." 92d annual meeting of the American Anthropological Association, Washington, D.C.

Haile, Berard. 1981. *Women versus Men: A Conflict of Navajo Emergence.* Lincoln: University of Nebraska Press.

Hill, Willard W. 1935. "The Status of the Hermaphrodite and Transvestite in Navaho Culture." *American Anthropologist.* 37(n.s.): 283–89.

———. 1936. *Navajo Warfare.* New Haven: Yale University Publication in Anthropology Series, volume 5.

Jim, Rex Lee, ed. 1994. *Dancing Voices.* White Plains: Peter Pauper Press.

Martin, M. Kay, and Barbara Voorhies. 1975. *Female of the Species.* New York: Columbia University Press.

Matthews, Washington. 1994 [1897]. *Navaho Legends.* Salt Lake City: University of Utah Press.

Money, John, and Anke A. Ehrhardt. 1972. *Man and Woman, Boy and Girl: The Differentiation and Dimorphism of Gender Identity from Conception to Maturity.* Baltimore: Johns Hopkins University Press.

Reichard, Gladys A. 1950. *Navajo Religion: A Study of Symbolism.* New York: Bollingen Foundation.

Schwarz, Maureen Trudelle. 1997. *Molded in the Image of Changing Woman: Navajo Views of the Human Body and Personhood.* Tucson: University of Arizona Press.

Spicer, Edward H. 1962. *Cycles of Conquest: The Impact of Spain, Mexico and the United States on the Indians of the Southwest, 1522–1960.* Tucson: University of Arizona Press.

Thomas, Wesley. 1992. "Alternative Gender of the Navajos." Paper presented at the International Gathering of Native Gays and Lesbians, Gold Bridge, B.C.

———. 1994. "Navajo Male Weavers' Perspective: Gender and Economics." Paper presented at "Navajo Weaving since the Sixties." Arizona State University and the Heard Museum, Phoenix.

Weeks, Jeffrey. 1985. *Sexuality and Its Discontents: Meanings, Myths and Modern Sexualities.* London: Routledge and Kegan Paul.

Witherspoon, Gary. 1977. *Language and Art in the Navajo Universe.* Ann Arbor: University of Michigan Press.

Young, Robert, and William Morgan. 1951. *A Vocabulary of Colloquial Navaho.* Phoenix: Phoenix Indian School Printing Department.

———. 1967. *The Navaho Language.* Salt Lake City: Deseret Book Company.

———. 1987. *The Navajo Language: A Grammar and Colloquial Dictionary.* 2d ed. Albuquerque: University of New Mexico Press.

———. 1992. *Analytical Lexicon of Navajo.* Albuquerque: University of New Mexico Press.

A Navajo Worldview and *Nádleehí:*

Implications for Western Categories

Carolyn Epple

Individuals among Native American people who may other-gender dress, perform occupations associated with both masculine and feminine genders, and possibly engage in same-sex sexual practices are often discussed in terms of Euro-American constructs, such as "berdache" or alternate genders—categories based on certain clusters of behaviors, cultural roles, and other traits (Callender and Kochems 1983; Jacobs 1968; Roscoe 1987; Williams 1986). For scholars who have explored the diversity of cultures and for individuals included in these categories it is a problematic endeavor. Too rigorous a definition excludes many people otherwise included, whereas too broad a definition can become meaningless. Furthermore, categories such as "berdache" or "alternate gender" are based on a-situational traits and nondynamic genders, concepts not necessarily upheld in the cultures described as having a "berdache" or "alternate gender." As a result, we (Euro-American and some Native American anthropologists) may be applying categorical notions that are not relevant to those we profess to describe, as Tafoya (1993:6) explains: "In cross-cultural research, one can have context or definition, but not both at the same time. The more one attempts to establish a context for a situation or process, the more one will blur a clean, simple definition. The more one strives to establish a clean, simple definition for a situation or process, the more one will lose a sense of context." A second difficulty occurs when we apply categories such as "berdache" or alternate gender to peoples' actual experiences, because the bases of these Euro-American constructs, a-situational traits and nondynamic genders, are not necessarily upheld in other cultures.

To elaborate on these points I will present recent ethnographic material on Navajo *nádleehí*—a group often referred to as "berdache" or alternate gender—in the context of a Navajo worldview.[1] This context is critical given that, unlike Euro-American categorical understandings, Navajo meanings and uses of the word *nádleehí* are not fixed. For example, Navajo definitions can vary from "a derogatory word used like 'fag,'" to "a homosexual," to "a hermaphrodite and only hermaphrodites," to "a very sacred word that can't just be talked about." Furthermore, the definitions will vary according to the age and sex of the speaker and audience, the individual's residence on the reservation, and degree of identification with Navajo traditional cultures.

The diversity of meanings also applies to the people themselves. Thus, although my *nádleehí* cultural teachers were similar—they were all males, approximately twenty-six to thirty-eight, maintained fairly close ties with traditional Navajo understandings, lived on or close to the Navajo reservation in "border towns," and used the terms *gay* or *queen* when referring to themselves or other *nádleehí*—they were by no means representative of all *nádleehí* (see Thomas in this volume). Hill (1935:273) further expands the definition, noting that *nádleehí* include both "real *nadle*" (hermaphrodites) or "those who pretend to be *nadle*" (anatomical males and females who engage in activities associated with both genders as well as those somewhat unique to *nádleehí*). Specific activities for both hermaphroditic and nonhermaphroditic *nádleehí* include hauling wood (usually done by men) and washing clothes (usually done by women), wearing other-gender dress, mediating conflicts between men and women, engaging in hetero- and same-sex sexual practices, and other social role aspects (Hill 1935; D.B.; H.A.; P.K.; B.H.; and others). Several of these features, such as spousal mediation, varying occupations, and varying sexual practices, were true for my *nádleehí* teachers as well.

The diversity of *nádleehí* is not surprising; Navajo understandings of the world, as I am learning them, speak of all things, including humans, as a dynamic process. I will explore understandings of process with a brief background on a Navajo worldview and therein present a culturally relevant framework with which to understand *nádleehí*. Based on this framework, I will also suggest an alternative understanding of *nádleehí* and challenge the relevance of the categories "berdache" and "alternate gender" to *nádleehí*.

A Navajo Worldview

A Navajo worldview is often discussed in terms of *sa'ąh naaghái bik'eh hózhǫ́* (SNBH), a cyclical processing by which and as which everything exists.[2] The following four points will be salient to what follows: (1) every person, thought, and action, and the universe itself, is a *sa'ąh naaghái bik'eh hózhǫ́* cycle; (2) everything is also in a larger overall *sa'ąh naaghái bik'eh hózhǫ́* cycle; (3) *sa'ąh naaghái bik'eh hózhǫ́* is a living system in which everything interconnects; and (4) *sa'ąh naaghái bik'eh hózhǫ́* cyclically processes everything into everything else.[3] These cycles are further described by D.B., a traditional Diné (Navajo) scholar, in terms of natural processes.[4]

> If you look at the times of day, it is the cyclical ordering, it is this natural process. At the east, where the sun first appears, there is the white air which is the color right at dawn. As you move in a sunwise direction toward the south, that is midday with the blue air. As you continue to the west, it is evening twilight, and on to the north it is dark air, the color of night. The sun continues its movement, on to the east, and the cycle starts all over. Everything can be talked about like this; everything is this natural process.

Everything in the universe, then, is a process, with the process being a cyclical movement. The dawn, midday, and so forth is each a unique cycle, and each also cycles into the others as part of the overall *sa'ąh naaghái bik'eh hózhǫ́* cycle. This understanding informs us of the individual's relationship to the universe, or of what I have learned of as "inseparable *and* distinct" (D.B.). For example, a dawn is *inseparable* from midday, given the larger diurnal cycle, so too is the individual inseparable from the air by which she or he survives or the ground on which she or he lives (D.B.).

Inseparability deals with the interconnectedness of the universe, as evidenced in, first, the existence of everything as the same thing, that is, the *sa'ąh naaghái bik'eh hózhǫ́* cycle, and, second, the cycling of everything into everything else, such as the cycling of ourselves into all interconnecting natural processes (D.B.). During the course of the cycles, individuals are also transformed into those processes, much as dawn transforms into midday. D.B. provides another example of this transformation: "Like corn in the valley, they breathe in air and release it back as oxygen. We then breathe that oxygen in and exhale carbon dioxide, returning it back to the corn. Over and over again, through all of these complex interconnections, that air cycle is going on."[5]

The interconnections can become more complex, as an extension of D.B.'s example indicates. Let us suppose that the carbon dioxide we exhale is used by a plant to produce fruit. The fruit is eaten by another person, who uses the energy to build a shelter. The shelter, in turn, protects the person's children, and so forth. But the cycling is more than simply the passing on of atoms. As I have learned it, we are the actual movement of SNBH's transformative cycle; thus, we are the very process by which dawn becomes midday and midday eventually becomes dawn (D.B.).

By focusing on the individual as a process through which all things cycle (a shift away from the immediately preceding focus on *sa'ąh naagháí bik'eh hózhǫ́* as a grand cyclical movement), we can begin to know of the individual as distinct. Briefly, distinctiveness arises out of one's unique connections to other processes (D.B.); thus, although everything is interconnected to the same processes, everything is also distinct in how those interconnections occur. Stated from a slightly different perspective, no two cycles (or things) interconnect with other processes in the exact same configuration. Each process is known by its specific set of interconnections or by how it relates to everything else.

A third aspect of this particular Navajo worldview is that everything exists as male and female, with each individual composed of male and female (D.B.).[6] The maleness and femaleness of all things, however, extends beyond the individual's physical makeup. Every process, including thought, speech, water, and air, is thus comprised. Indeed, we, as do all things, arise from and exist as *sa'ąh naagháí* (male) and *bik'eh hózhǫ́* (female), itself composed of both *sa'ąh naagháí* and *bik'eh hózhǫ́*.

Implications for *Nádleehí* and Western Constructs

D.B. states, "Your living is the repeated patterns of the natural systems," that is, one's existence is the workings of *sa'ąh naagháí bik'eh hózhǫ́*. Thus, to understand humans, specifically *nádleehí*, living concepts such as inseparability, distinctness, and the ubiquity of male and female are essential to the analysis. In so doing, we not only gain greater insight into the "patterns of the natural systems" but also learn of *nádleehí* within a culturally relevant framework.

Inseparability

Inseparability is about interconnections, which are like the anthropological concept of context. For example, the interconnections whereby dawn occurs are about the contextual arrangement of natural processes, such as sun and earth. When considering the individual as interconnected or inseparable, then, we are looking at a complex context in which the person exists and with which she or he is able to understand and respond to the world. D.B. and a *nádleehí* teacher, P.K., elaborate on *nádleehí* inseparability and contextuality:

> D.B.: Their identity is not only as *nádleehí*. For the older traditional people, in reality there is no separation of the mountains from the people.
>
> P.K.: In terms of types of queens, everyone is different here.[7] Time and events and classification and categories, that's how you Anglos try to put everything. You get so caught up, you don't see people as humans responding to situations.

P.K. continues with an example of *nádleehí* as "humans responding to situations": "When I went to college, I didn't want to be gay all my life. So I avoided gays, but still yearned so much. I met a woman, though, and we got drunk and ended up in bed. We were together for a while, but later on I felt really choked by her."

D.B.'s and P.K.'s comments indicate that any set of behaviors, such as sexual practices, must be seen in the context in which they occurred. Based on her interconnection with high school experiences, P.K., for example, decided to forego same-sex sexual practices. Once in college, she responded to that particular situation with a heterosexual relationship. When those interconnections became problematic, P.K. left and returned to same-sex sexual practices. Throughout her life, P.K. has existed as a process—cycling into other processes such as school settings and lovers and being the unique configuration of those and other processes cycling into her.

The situating of *nádleehí* behavior has clear implications for our classification of them and others who are possibly similar, particularly classifications that rely on such clusters of traits as attire, social role, occupation, and sexual partner preference to confer *nádleehí* or a possibly similar status (Katz 1976; Roscoe 1987; Williams 1986).[8] Frequently, we treat the traits as isolated features, void of cultural meaning and thus the same across cultures. As such, a male who just happens to do the tasks or wear the attire associated with the feminine gender can be erroneously labeled a "berdache." H.A. provides the following example:

> Male and female—it depends on the situation of which one it is that you are talking about. There are things that women do and men do, but that

depends on earlier and more recent teachings, and again on the situation.

[For example,] I had three sisters and one brother and I'm the oldest. Our mother died when I was nine, and my baby sister was ten months old. I had to take care of her, scrounge for cloth [for diapers], and had to learn to wash a baby.

I pretty much had to take care of the kids like I was their mother. I had to learn how to cook, to make dough, make frybread. I had to do all that a mother does to raise kids. All of those skills stayed with me.

When I got married, I taught my wife how to cook, make frybread, make potatoes. Time went on and my wife asked me to wash clothes, so I washed them. To me it was no big deal. I never thought of these things as woman's work. It was survival.

Were we to classify H.A.'s childhood, based on the first three paragraphs, we might conclude he is a "berdache." Clearly, he is a male who is (or was) heavily involved in other-gender social roles and occupations. When we consider the account in terms of its interconnections, however, it is not about "berdache," regardless of what "berdache" may be. H.A.'s activities were precipitated by the loss of parents, grandparents' lack of time, and basic survival needs; therein, his actions derive meaning.

Although the discussion on context has stemmed largely from Navajo understandings of worldview, it is nonetheless relevant for other cultures. If we are intent on accurately describing those we supposedly know, we must examine any trait or feature in its larger cultural situation to understand its significance. Without the background meaning, we risk unfounded conclusions, as is illustrated in the following classification of the Pueblo peoples' "berdaches."

Roscoe's (1987:86) highly informative bibliography includes the reference "Parsons 1939:765" as an example of "berdache" or alternate gender.[9] The citation appears to refer to Parsons's comments about wearing other-gender dress, specifically when a male in women's attire portrays the Acoma Pueblo Kachina, known as Komutina, in the Corn Clan Ceremony. A comparison of Komutina with another Acoma Kachina known as Storoka, however, suggests "berdache" or "alternate gender" may not be accurate labels for Komutina. Unlike Komutina, Storoka is, first, referred to as a *kokwima,* the Acoma term for a hermaphrodite (Gunn 1917:17) or a male who may take on the dress and task preferences usually attributed to women (White 1943:325); and, second, Storoka is described as wearing the attire of women *and* men (Parsons 1939:766; White 1943).

These findings raise two questions: First, if Komutina is a *kokwima,* why is he not referred to as such? Second, if Komutina is a *kokwima,* why is he dressed differently (i.e., women's attire only) than the known *kokwima,* Storoka, who wears both genders' clothing? One possibility is that Komutina is simply a Kachina who wears other-gender dress and not a "berdache." Certainly Parsons's (1920:98) work at the adjacent Laguna Pueblo suggests such; she notes that a male Kachina in female attire did not necessarily mean that the Kachina was a "man-woman." Unfortunately, by stripping the selected trait, attire, of its cultural meaning, the significance of Komutina's appearance remains unaddressed.

As P.K.'s, H.A.'s, and the Acoma examples indicate, traits are not isolated, a-contextual features but are responses or events embedded in the surrounding situations. The significance of the specific characteristic must be ascertained from within the cultural and individual interconnections. Studies of *nádleehí* (and possibly similar others) that extricate characteristics of dress, occupation, and sexual behavior from specific cultural and individual context risk misinterpretation and unfounded generalizations.

One other aspect on the importance of traits deserves consideration: Euro-American understandings of traits are not necessarily shared by the cultures from whom we learn and that we profess to describe. Reichard (1944:4) alluded to this when she stated, "We base classes on the unique, the distinctive; the Navajo bases [her/]his categories on the inclusive." Instead of determining exclusionary identities based on a-cultural features, many Navajos see the features as but a few aspects of the inclusive whole. As D.B. elaborates, the traits examined in "berdache" definitions are miniscule in the vastness of an individual's interconnectedness:

> Let's say you were to take a person who is nádleeh and have [her] looked at by a group of ten people. They concentrate on only [her] eye and those forces [processes] coming into [her], and [her] interconnections to those forces. That alone would fill up books and books.
>
> If you go through every part of [her] and do the same thing, you would fill up a library. Then you get to this one artificial part about [her] clothing. In a drawing of [her] as all of [her] interconnections, you'd have to magnify that artificial part a million times even to see it.

Thus, clothing or occupation or any of the other "berdache" traits are negligible in the overall makeup of an individual. To extend D.B.'s analogy, those who rely on trait-based definitions have mistaken one comma on one page in one book for the entire library. It is little wonder that many Native American colleagues at a recent "berdache" conference emphasized their individual differences, complexity, and richness of experience in response to Euro-American research.[10] As Robertson (1993, and in this volume) states, "I ask you, please do not limit the definition of me as 'berdache.' I am not and don't want to be a cross-dressing, man-woman, sexually anal passive, suited to sewing and beading while I carry in the wood for the fire I'm cooking supper on . . . I am Doyle."

Thus, inseparability questions one of the key features in "berdache" studies—the relative significance of specific features such as dress, occupation, and sexual practice. Instead of traits as discrete, self-contained features that are valid across cultures, we are reminded of an important anthropological tenet: All things are contextual or, in Navajo understandings, interconnected; therefore, the significance of dress and occupation depends on the situation. Inseparability also emphasizes that how we perceive and organize traits is not universal. Although we use traits to create exclusionary categories, many Navajo consider specific traits as "miniscule" in the overall connectedness of the individual to the universe (D.B.).

Distinctness

Who is *nádleehí* defies easy definition, a fact D.B. frequently acknowledged: "If you were to ask what is a *nádleehí,* no one could really say." This ambiguity is further apparent in *nádleehí* self-definitions and perceptions. As three *nádleehí,* B.H., P.K., and P.A., describe themselves:

> B.H.: Well, like in my case, I am different from a straight male, a heterosexual male, and from a homosexual male. [Later in the interview] I am a complete woman, just without the vagina. [And later yet] I'd rather have a woman [as a sexual partner] than a queen. I mean I do have some kind of maleness.
>
> P.A.: That's the funny thing about it, there's an in-between type of person. It's hard to understand. I don't want to be a drag queen, and I don't want to be a girl.
>
> P.K.: A queen is identified with a female. But I don't consider myself a girl. I'm a man and am attracted to men.

This illustrates several points. First, the definitions are in terms of those with whom the *nádleehí* interconnects, such as straights, heterosexuals, homosexuals, "drag queens," women, and men, and therein demonstrate that *nádleehí* are literally their specific configuration of inter-connecting processes.[11] Second, the variation between definitions is dependent on different kinds of interconnections. For example, the significance of a man or "drag queen" to a *nádleehí* self-description is relative to that *nádleehí* context. P.K.'s self-identification as a man may be a function, in part, of her interconnections with her bi-gender socialization. Elsewhere, B.H.'s seemingly disparate descriptions of "being a complete woman" while also having "some kind of maleness" are dependent on conversational context (i.e., the interconnections between B.H., myself, and the topic) and B.H.'s traditional understanding that everyone is both male and female (i.e., her interconnections with her cultural epistemology).

Self-definitions such as these confound many assumptions about the "berdache" category. If those who perceive "berdache" to be a gender-mixer (Callender and Kochems 1983; Williams 1986) or a gender-crosser (Forgey 1974; Whitehead 1981) were relying on such personal descriptors, they would be forced to exclude *nádleehí* individuals who, such as P.K., define themselves as "a man attracted to men." Such a definition indicates neither mixing nor crossing. Furthermore, P.K.'s personal identity is not easily rectified with B.H.'s self-definition as a "complete woman"—at least it is not if we assume *nádleehí* (and possibly similar others) to be a fixed, static concept.

The variability of what or who is *nádleehí* is no less problematic when we consider *nádleehí* on an individual basis. As B.H. demonstrates, self-perceptions can vary according to the interconnections within a conversation. Given that we cannot easily characterize an individual, let alone a group of people with similar backgrounds such as Navajo *nádleehí,* categorical identifications across disparate cultures become tenuous. Understanding *nádleehí* requires shifting epistemologies from the categorical to the dynamic. In so doing, we can begin to know *nádleehí* as process, a nonstatic identity that changes in response to her interconnections.

Ubiquity of Male and Female

D.B. describes the third aspect important to understanding *nádleehí:* the ubiquity of male and female, as in, "This order already exists. *Sa'ąh naagháí* is male and *bik'eh hózhǫ* is female. That is what everything is, and that is what leads to variation." All things, then, are of *sa'ąh naagháí bik'eh hózhǫ,* as is any seeming variation or "alternate." *Nádleehí* as male and female or masculine and feminine is not a point of uniqueness but of similarity.[12] For example, H.A. describes the bi-gender capabilities in all humans: "We all possess both masculine and feminine characteristics in our body. For example, in a tragic situation, being a man, the female characteristics are elicited. The same is true for the woman. Some situation happens and it elicits the male, and she acts like a man. For that reason, because you need both, you have male and female characteristics."

Nádleehí specific expression of male and female is distinctive, but *nádleehí* and possibly similar persons are not the only expression of both male and female.[13] Thus *nádleehí* and possibly similar others are not *uniquely* "gender-mixers." Everyone is of *sa'ąh naagháí* and *bik'eh hózhǫ́;* everyone is a "man-woman."

Finally, the ubiquity of male and female challenges the notion of "alternate gender" as a descriptor for *nádleehí*. Martin and Voorhies (1975, 84–107), who were among the first to suggest the existence of more than the usual two genders (man and woman), noted that such persons were distinguished, in part, by their mixing of gender traits, unique social roles, and specific linguistic markers, such as the term *nádleehí* for Navajo "supernumerary genders." Jacobs (1983:460) added to the concept in a brief discussion on Tewa *kwidó* and raised an intriguing question: "Is it not possible that we are still asking the wrong questions because in Euro-American culture we have a difficult time accepting that there can be genuinely conceptualized a third gender that has nothing to do with transvestism or homosexuality?" Although several scholars would seem to have responded with a resounding yes to Jacobs (see, for example, Lang [1993 and in this volume] and Thomas [1993 and in this volume]), D.B. suggests such may not be the case, particularly to many Navajos: "Where is there anything that is not both male and female? Everything is two, so how can you have this as a third? You don't have man, woman, and another."

Consistent with D.B.'s understanding, another *hataałii* (often glossed as medicine person) explains that a hermaphrodite, that from which the nonhermaphroditic *nádleehí* are generalized, is also understood in terms of femaleness or maleness and not necessarily as a third sex.[14] "If I draw a line with male at one end and female at the other, is there any such person right in the center? No there couldn't be. You can't both have a breast and not have a breast. Even if one side of the body only had a breast, then you still have a breast. So to have both [sexes' complete anatomical features], that just won't be. There has never been one right here at the very center—there can't be."

Although *nádleehí* are linguistically designated; possess traits of both men, women, and those specific to *nádleehí;* and meet other criteria characteristic of alternate genders, they are not perceived as such by many Navajos.[15] "There are two—male and female—no others" (D.B.; cf. Walters in Jacobs in this volume). Furthermore, assuming that the hermaphrodite is simply a third sex, separate from male or female, may not be accurate. Hermaphroditic individuals possess "more" male or female anatomical features and are understood simultaneously as a hermaphrodite, male or female, male and female, and as a unique configuration of the maleness and femaleness (*sa'ąh naagháí bik'eh hózhǫ́*) of which everyone is composed.[16] Given the difficulty in understanding a hermaphroditic *nádleehí,* the basis for nonhermaphroditic *nádleehí,* we clearly face a challenge in understanding each. It is little wonder that although D.B., H.A., and *nádleehí* teachers noted that while *nádleehí,* as an identity, was acknowledged, the particulars of the identity remain variable.

How then to define *nádleehí?* Presently, it would appear to be a nearly impossible task. Western epistemologies do not accommodate persons who are both herself and himself as well as everything else. Instead, we must adopt a different way of perceiving the universe, one that is processual, interconnected, and dynamic. As D.B. said at the outset of our interviews: *"Sa'ąh naagháí bik'eh hózhǫ́* is everywhere, meaning it is male and female everywhere. It is a natural understanding of the natural order, and understanding how you fit in the natural cycle is key to understanding yourself." If it is key to understanding ourselves, it is essential to understanding *nádleehí.*

Conclusions

That which underlies the difficulty in classifying *nádleehí,* that is, the epistemological differences between Navajo and Euro-Americans, is also that by which we can understand them. I suggest we heed P.K.'s insight and see *nádleehí* "as humans responding to situations," that is, in terms of their interconnectedness. We cannot understand *nádleehí* traits, or the meanings of male and female, without this perspective. In its absence, we are attempting to hold dynamic processes in rigid, bounded categories, which does little more than frustrate our classification schemes.

Although our ease of communication would be interrupted by the loss of the category "berdache," our understanding could be greatly enhanced. Attempts at a synthesis, such as "berdache," have overlooked the cultural strata from which the individuals and their behaviors derive meaning. Shifting back to cultural context, however, would make available specific meanings as well as gain insight into cultural constructions of sex, gender, and other domains relevant to *nádleehí* and possibly similar others. Furthermore, a worldview-based analysis would enhance cross-cultural research. A comparison of a Lakota *winkte* and Navajo *nádleehí* would be far more accurate if it was first ascertained that such a comparison was valid. But more important, a deemphasis on categories would enable an appreciation of *nádleehí* in terms of their interconnectedness, variability, distinctness, and expression of that by which, and as which, we all exist. In so doing, *nádleehí* could be seen as people and known first as colleagues and friends.

Notes

Research for this chapter was funded in part by Sigma Xi, National Science Foundation, a Northwestern University Alumni Women's Fellowship, the Eleanor Foundation for Women, and a Northwestern University Dissertation Year Grant.

1. To avoid confusion with Euro-American terms, I have continued to use *nádleehí*. In this chapter, to maintain consistency with *nádleehí* use of the female pronoun for each other and themselves, I refer to male *nádleehí* with female pronouns. The term *nádleehí* refers to one who is *nádleeh,* which means becoming (the verb *-leeh*) by returning to a previous condition or state (prefix *ná-*), with the *-í* suffix meaning one who is (Young and Morgan 1987, 1992). Thus, *nádleehí* can be literally defined as one who becomes by cycling back to a previous condition or state. According to Leer (1994), *nádleehí* is a cognate with the Dene Tha term *ndadlinhi,* as in the phrase *Aa, tsido ndadlinhi* (Aa, the child who is made again); that is, a child who is a reincarnated relative (Goulet 1994:7, and in this volume).

2. My primary teachers were traditional Diné (Navajo) scholars, D.B. and H.A. While I had the privilege to learn from those involved in this work, my explanations can offer only a small and dim glimpse of the Navajo understandings. Responsibility for inaccuracies and misinterpretations rests with me. I deliberately avoid the use of the term *religion* to describe Navajo understandings. I present this particular Navajo worldview as a system of knowing, one which does not need to be compared to Western models to determine its reliability. As such, I use Navajo knowledge as the standard by which the success of Western models is measured (Faris 1990:240–41, n2).

3. An understanding of *sa'ah naagháí bik'eh hózhǫ́* in terms of the cycle by which and as which everything exists is only one way to discuss it. It has been a subject of intense research by students of Navajo culture for many years, such as Farella (1984), Reichard (1983), and Wyman (1970). In contrast to House (1993, and in this volume), my teachers did not restrict the usage of *sa'ah naagháí bik'eh hózhǫ́* to ceremonials but talked about it at length during our discussions. I implicitly trust their respectfulness of Navajo teachings and judgment in the teachings used; thus, I have retained the phrase.

4. I use the phrase traditional "Diné scholar" to maintain consistency with D.B.'s, H.A.'s, and others' titles at Navajo Community College and other organizations.

5. D.B. used Western scientific terminology throughout our discussions to illustrate *sa'ah naagháí bik'eh hózhǫ́* in terms familiar to me. I do likewise and with several cautions and rationales. First, the use of examples is not an application of one system to another. As one teacher states, *"Sa'ah naagháí bik'eh hózhǫ́* is a living system. All the natural processes are this living system, regardless of who is describing them." Second, my or D.B.'s use of examples from Western knowledge systems should not be construed as suggesting Navajo knowledge systems somehow require validation from the West. Finally, the use of examples from Western knowledge systems, in addition to discussions of Navajo teachings and approximate translation of Navajo concepts into English, permits examination of a concept from many different perspectives.

6. In Navajo, male is associated with protection and aggression and female is associated with the creativity, fruitfulness, harmony, and balance of *hózhǫ́* (D.B.). It also refers to the sexes. Because Navajo usage of male and female can include both sex and gender, what we distinguish as a gender trait (as opposed to a sex-related trait) may be characterized as "male" or "female" by Navajos.

7. "Drag queen," "gay," and "queen" appear in quotation marks when I employ the terms to indicate the different Navajo meaning for each. When *nádleehí* use the terms, it is assumed that they, as Navajo, are using them with the Navajo meaning; thus, the terms in *nádleehí* quotations do not appear in quotation marks.

8. I am uncertain how comparable persons of other Native people are to *nádleehí*. Rather than imply there is similarity by using the term "berdache," I have opted for a slightly more cumbersome descriptor: "other possibly similar" people.

The issue of sexual practice is one of the more contentious points in "berdache" studies. Katz (1976) does not hesitate to include numerous descriptions of Native Americans possibly similar to *nádleehí*. Williams and Roscoe are skeptical of those who suggest same-sex sexuality is not a primary factor in "berdache" status. Williams (1986:122–24) attributes the deemphasis to possible homophobia, and Roscoe (1987:171n8) describes accounts of *nádleehí* (and possibly similar others') heterosexuality as "unconfirmed reports." Jacobs and Cromwell (1992), Thomas (1993), Weston (1993), myself (Epple 1994), and others have challenged this conflation of "berdache" with Western gay constructs.

9. To his credit, Roscoe (1987:169) notes the importance of cultures' meanings, stating, "A grasp of the particular cultural context will enable scholars to more objectively evaluate and more effectively use reports on berdache roles."

10. For example, see Burns (1993); Little Thunder (1993, and in this volume); and Red Earth (1993, and this volume).

11. "Straights" are men who may be involved in a stable heterosexual relationship as well as with a *nádleehí*. In sexual practices, "straights" are the inserter, and *nádleehí* the insertee. P.A. notes that although there are Navajo "drag queens," there are no "drag queens" in Navajo culture. Many *nádleehí* teachers described "drag queens" as being more "flamboyant," "doing things [consuming alcohol, other-gender dressing, and flirting] to the extreme," and "insecure." They differ from drag queens in Western settings in cultural background, sexual practices, and other practices.

12. The ubiquity of male and female is relevant to the latest term, *two-spirit*, which originated from Native Americans. As Tafoya explains this, "Many Native people have difficulty in being comfortable with identifying themselves as Gay, Lesbian, or Bisexual, feeling as though they are 'being herded' into such categories by the power of English . . . 'Two-Spirited' indicates that someone possesses both a male and female spirit" (1992:256). Although self-designation is highly preferred to the imposition of Western categories, "two-spirit" is nonetheless problematic. The term/category continues to gloss cross-cultural differences, includes the Western-derived concept of "alternate gender," and lacks relevance to specific cultures. For example, in Navajo understandings everyone and everything is male and female; thus, the term *two-spirit* applies as accurately to a tree as it does to a *nádleehí*. As Thomas (1993, and in this volume) states, meaning arises out of situation, and, I add, not well-intentioned conference mandates (cf. Jacobs and Thomas 1994). Finally, when I asked my *nádleehí* teachers if the concept of "two-spirit," as Tafoya explains it, was relevant to them, they stated it was not. Instead, they have adopted the Western term *gay* to their own meanings and experiences.

13. In a longer version of this chapter (Epple 1993) and in my dissertation (Epple 1994) I describe *nádleehí* special status among the Navajo as her distinctive expression of the male and female ordering of the universe. In her gender mediation, socialization, and performance of tasks (and, for hermaphrodites, anatomy) *nádleehí* is clearly the inseparability of male and female.

14. H.A. explains this as, "The story of *nádleehí* rests on if that person has the sex [organs] of both. In real life, though, it's any person who has opposite behavior traits, and this response is based on actual *nádleehí*. People's approach to them is usually a generalizing that's going on."

15. Murray (1994) contends that linguistic markers are not necessarily indicative of alternate gender status. Clearly, we need to reevaluate the assumption that a unique term (such as *nádleehí, łhamana,* or *kwidó*) for a specific social role (such as "berdache") is proof positive of alternate gender status. My initial work with *nádleehí,* which includes the question, Are *nádleehí* a third gender? indicates that, in the explanations of my teachers, they are not an alternate gender status.

Although one can discuss seemingly *nádleehí*-specific traits, such as their association with wealth, respect, and gender mediation, these traits vary by context. For example, some clans did not hold *nádleehí* in high regard and allowed infant hermaphrodites to die (H.A.). The matter of alternative gender is also variable. For example, Thomas incorporates *nádleehí* into an alternate gender schemata (1993 and in this volume). Most of my *nádleehí* teachers did not agree with the alternate gender status and as in the earlier quotations from P.A. and B.H. provided other markers by which they identified themselves.

The male and female anatomical features are themselves male and female. As one traditional Diné scholar states, "Even the organs are male and female, inseparable and distinct. At the tip of the penis is a little vagina, while on the vulva is a little penis. That is how it is said in Navajo. So you see both penis and vagina, but only one functions [on a nonhermaphrodite]. It is like that in the hermaphrodite, too—you see both but only one functions."

16. In addition to understanding *nádleehí* as "sort of" having "more" male or female genitalia, *nádleehí* are recognized as the genders associated with male or female. For example, Hill notes that "[*nádleehí*] legal status is also that of a woman. The blood payment for the murder of a nadle is the same as that for a woman, which is higher than that required when a man is killed. . . . When [male non-hermaphroditic *nádleehí*] marry, they take the garb of a man and do man's work. If they marry men, it is just like two men working together" (1935:275, 276).

References Cited

Burns, Randy. 1993. Untitled commentary presented at "Revisiting the 'North American Berdache' Empirically and Theoretically." 92 Annual Meeting of the American Anthropological Association, Washington, D.C.

Callender, Charles, and Lee M. Kochems. 1983. "The North American 'Berdache.'" *Current Anthropology* 14(4): 443–56.

Epple, Carolyn. 1993. "Another 'Berdache' Headache; or, *Nádleehí* in Nava-jo Worldview: Implications for Western Constructs." Paper presented at "Revisiting the 'North American Berdache' Empirically and Theoretical-ly." 92d annual meeting of the American Anthropological Association, Washington, D.C.

———. 1994. "Inseparable and Distinct: An Understanding of Navajo *Nádleehí* in a Traditional Navajo Worldview." Ph.D. diss., Northwestern University.

Farella, John R. 1984. *The Main Stalk: A Synthesis of Navajo Philosophy.* Tuc-son: University of Arizona Press.

Faris, James C. 1990. *The Nightway: A History and a History of Documentation of a Navajo Ceremonial.* Albuquerque: University of New Mexico Press.

Forgey, Donald G. 1975. "The Institution of Berdache among the North American Plains Indians." *Journal of Sex Research* 11(1): 1–15.

Goulet, Jean-Guy. 1994. "Being Male and Female in the Context of Cross-Sex Reincarnation among Contemporary Dene Tha." Paper presented at "Revisiting the 'North American Berdache' Empirically and Theoretical-ly." 92d annual meeting of the American Anthropological Association, Washington, D.C.

Gunn, John M. 1917. *Schat-Chen: History, Traditions, and Narratives of the Queres Indians of Laguna and Acoma.* Albuquerque: Albright and Ander-son.

Hill, W. W. 1935. "The Status of the Hermaphrodite and Transvestite in Navajo Culture." *American Anthropologist* 37(n.s.): 273–79.

House, Carrie. 1993. Comments on papers presented at "Revisiting the 'North American Berdache' Empirically and Theoretically." 92d annual meeting of the American Anthropological Association, Washington, D.C.

Jacobs, Sue-Ellen. 1968. "Berdache: A Brief Review of the Literature." *Colo-rado Anthropologist* 1(2): 25–40. Reprint. Wayne R. Dynes and Stephen Donaldson, eds. 1992. *Studies in Homosexuality.* Volume 2: *Ethnographic Studies of Homosexuality.* New York: Garland.

———. 1983. Reply to "The North American 'Berdache.'" *Current Anthropol-ogy* 24(4): 459–60.

Jacobs, Sue-Ellen, and Jason Cromwell. 1992. "Visions and Revisions of Reality: Reflections on Sex, Sexuality, and Gender Variance." *Journal of Homosexuality* 22(4): 43–69.

Jacobs, Sue-Ellen, and Wesley Thomas. 1994. "Native American Two-Spir-its." *Anthropology Newsletter* 35(8): 7.

Katz, Jonathan. 1976. *Gay American History: Lesbians and Gay Men in the U.S.A.* New York: Thomas Y. Crowell.

Lang, Sabine. 1993. "Masculine Women, Feminine Men: Gender Variance and the Creation of Gay Identities among Contemporary North American Indians." Paper presented at "Revisiting the 'North American Berdache' Empirically and Theoretically." 92d annual meeting of the American Anthropological Association, Washington, D.C.

Leer, Jeffrey. 1994. Personal communication with the author.

Little Thunder, Beverly. 1993. "I Am a Lakota Womyn." Paper presented at "Revisiting the 'North American Berdache' Empirically and Theoretically." 92d annual meeting of the American Anthropological Association, Washington, D.C.

Martin, M. Kay, and Barbara Voorhies. 1975. *Female of the Species.* New York: Columbia University Press.

Murray, Stephen. 1994. "Subordinating Native American Cosmologies to the Empire of Gender." *Current Anthropology* 35(1): 59–61.

Parsons, Elsie Clews. 1920. "Notes on Ceremonialism at Laguna." *Anthropological Papers of the American Museum of Natural History* 19(4): 83–131.

———. 1939. "The Last Zuni Transvestite." *American Anthropologist* 41(n.s.): 338–40.

Red Earth, Michael. 1993. "Traditional Influences on a Contemporary Gay Identified Sisseton Dakota." Paper presented at "Revisiting the 'North American Berdache' Empirically and Theoretically." 92d annual meeting of the American Anthropological Association, Washington, D.C.

Reichard, Gladys. 1944. *Prayer: The Compulsive Word.* Monographs of the American Ethnological Society 7. Seattle: University of Washington Press.

———. 1983. *Navajo Religion: A Study of Symbolism.* Tucson: University of Arizona Press.

Robertson, Doyle. 1993. "I Ask You to Listen to Who I Am." Paper presented at "Revisiting the 'North American Berdache' Empirically and Theoretically." 92d annual meeting of the American Anthropological Association, Washington, D.C.

Roscoe, Will. 1987. "Bibliography of Berdache and Alternative Gender Roles among North American Indians." *Journal of Homosexuality* 14(3–4): 81–171.

Tafoya, Terry. 1992. "Native Gay and Lesbian Issues: The Two-Spirited." In *Positively Gay: New Approaches to Gay and Lesbian Life.* ed. Betty Berzon, 253–59. Berkeley: Celestial Arts Publishing.

———. 1993. "M. Dragonfly: Two-Spirit/Berdache and the Tafoya Principle of Uncertainty." Paper presented at "Revisiting the 'North American Berdache' Empirically and Theoretically." 92d annual meeting of the American Anthropological Association, Washington, D.C.

Thomas, Wesley. 1993. "A Traditional Navajo's Perspective on the Navajo Cultural Construction of Gender." Paper presented at "Revisiting the 'North American Berdache' Empirically and Theoretically." 92d annual meeting of the American Anthropological Association, Washington, D.C.

Weston, Kath. 1993. "Lesbian/Gay Studies in the House of Anthropology."
    Annual Reviews of Anthropology 22: 339–67.
White, Leslie. 1943. *New Material from Acoma.* Bureau of American Ethnol-
    ogy, Bulletin 136. Washington: U.S. Government Printing Office.
Whitehead, Harriet. 1981. "The Bow and the Burden Strap: A New Look at
    Institutionalized Homosexuality in Native North America." In *Sexual
    Meanings: The Cultural Construction of Gender and Sexuality,* ed. Sherry B.
    Ortner and Harriet Whitehead, 80–115. New York: Cambridge Universi-
    ty Press.
Williams, Walter L. 1986. *The Spirit and the Flesh: Sexual Diversity in Ameri-
    can Indian Culture.* Boston: Beacon Press. Reprint, 1991, with a new pref-
    ace.
Wyman, Leland. 1970. *Blessingway.* Tucson: University of Arizona Press.
Young, Robert, and William Morgan. 1987. *The Navajo Language: A Gram-
    mar and Colloquial Dictionary.* Albuquerque: University of New Mexico
    Press.
———. 1992. *Analytical Lexicon of Navajo.* Albuquerque: University of New
    Mexico Press.

★ ★ **9**

M. Dragonfly:

Two-Spirit and the Tafoya Principle of Uncertainty

Terry Tafoya (Taos/Warm Springs)

Long ago, a young boy fashioned a toy for his sister, to amuse her
and to distract her from her hunger, as they had no food. He wove
together corn-husk for wings, and assembled other things of his
world, creating something no one had ever quite seen before. That
night, as he and his sister slept with their hunger, the toy began to
move and fly about his home. This dragonfly, for such it was,
assisted the boy, his sister, and his people, providing them food.
Even today, the symbol of the dragonfly, its meaning of water and
life, is used in pottery and weaving.
traditional Pueblo story, as retold by Tony Hillerman (1986)

Ana kush iwasha (I am speaking to you).

Never before, in two decades of university teaching or presentations,
have I used a first-person voice in an academic setting. To a great extent
this was because of my early negative experiences while working in the
(then) emerging field of antiracism and antidiscrimination as a consultant for the Seattle public school system, where personal statements I
made were often discounted by antagonistic audience members as
"overly sensitive" or only reflecting my individual experience and not
Native American experiences as a whole.

But I am choosing, somewhat reluctantly, to speak because the concept of using one's own voice is a critical issue in understanding two-
spirit concerns. I am aware of the irony in the fact that I am not using
my first language to speak and must use English for the benefit of my
audience. But this illustrates the interactive nature of speaking in one's
voice. To be from a culture of oral tradition means that every time one
speaks in a public setting the event is a kind of ceremony. This ceremo-

ny involves spectators no less than actors, no differently than those who stand on Pueblo rooftops to watch ceremonies give something of themselves to what they see.

In this chapter I will play with the concept of M. Dragonfly, with its pun on the play *M. Butterfly,* because I think both this chapter and the play speak to much the same issues: presentation of self, perception of self and others, implications for cross-cultural communications, and, perhaps most important of all, the political and socioeconomic power involved in who defines whom with regard to gender and sexuality.[1] *M. Butterfly* is based on a historical event involving a French ambassador who maintained a long-term relationship with a biological Chinese male whom he believed to be a female Chinese Opera star. The play moves from a journalistic recounting of the event to a fictional exploration of how the ambassador made sense of his experience, concluding that "only a man can truly know how a woman is supposed to act" (Hwang 1989:63).

The statement crystallizes not only the message of the play but also the focus of this effort of creating a working model of conceptualizing what two-spirit means. The ambassador's premise is that those in a dominant position of power and authority are the only ones who "truly know" how those in lesser positions of power and authority "are supposed to act." I suspect those who define themselves as two-spirit are also examining how they "are supposed to act," having been historically instructed by non-Native "experts" about the nature of their role.

The story of the Dragonfly also offers a metaphor of the two-spirit. Not born but created and, once created for a specific purpose, gaining a life of its own, surpassing the intentions of its creator, and eventually providing something life-affirming and nurturing. The creation of the Dragonfly speaks also to the independence of its actions and behaviors from its creator and its power to instruct its creator. I believe that is also what we are witnessing at this historic moment. Native people are choosing the name *two-spirit* to represent an aspect of themselves. They are also empowering themselves to act independently from the anthropologists who have worked hard to define them (an act of creation in itself) and to take the opportunity to instruct the anthropologists and each other in a manner that may prove to be as life-affirming and nurturing as the work of the Dragonfly.

To choose the name *two-spirit* for oneself, as opposed to "berdache" [*sic*] from the history of non-Native people, is to speak in what Cindy

Patton has termed "dissident vernaculars," terms that move "away from the model of pristine scientific ideas which need 'translation' for people lacking in the dominant culture's language skills or concepts. 'Dissident vernaculars' also suggests that meanings created by and in communities are upsetting to the dominant culture precisely because speaking in one's own fashion is a means of resistance, a strengthening of the subculture that has created the new meaning" (1990:148).

I have always been a rim-walker, neither one thing or another, in much that I do and am. Let me therefore take privilege and say that I am not speaking as an anthropologist, although I completed all the coursework for a doctorate in anthropology. As one whose paternal relatives reside in a pueblo that banned all anthropologists in the 1920s after Elsie Clews Parsons published unauthorized ethnographic materials of our village, I know all too well that research does not exist in a political vacuum.

Were I speaking as an anthropologist, I might point out that the symbol of the Dragonfly reflects an entity that begins its life in one form, an aquatic larval stage, and then transforms into something completely different. Were I an anthropologist, I would explore this in remarkable detail and draw parallels of how a two-spirit may begin as a biological male or female but transform into someone quite different. But, not being an anthropologist, I will not mention any of this. Besides, I know of no formal traditional association of the Dragonfly with the two-spirit. Such is the power of words, however, that for all I know the Dragonfly will become a new symbol for "The Movement." According to a personal communication from Will Roscoe, Winfield Coleman, a Cheyenne scholar, has stated that there is a possible connection with the "Dragonfly Lodge" of the Cheyenne to the "berdache." In this connection, the Dragonfly is a symbol of the whirlwind, that which connects Mother Earth and Father Sky, the bridge between female and male principles.

Were I a political writer rather than a simple storyteller, I might also point out the exciting evolution and empowerment of the transgendered community as its members struggle to wrest the control of gender definitions from the hands of the medical establishment, insurance companies, and politicians—not to mention the manufacturers of restroom signs. The discovery that there are lesbians, bisexuals, or gays emphasizes the fact that gender orientation and sexual orientation are two separate categories. As Weeks points out, "Despite the lack of any scientific basis for such a view, many authors have either treated sexual orientation as a facet of gender, or have confounded gender role behavior and sexual orientation" (1988:42).

Many voices and many audiences work together to understand an event. These voices are also internal as I debate with myself about how to phrase something, how much detail to use, or how to frame it through an amusing analogy or snappy symbol. As a trained storyteller, I am constantly evaluating the knowledge base and reaction of my audience. Indeed, although the inherent message may be intended to be the same, the methodology of delivery to various audiences may be quite different, and the results are also different because the action of accommodating to the audience will frequently mean reenforcing its existing schema or worldview. This is why automatically translating "two-spirit" as a "gay role," or "what we call our homosexuals," makes speaking much easier but may not contribute to the exchange of accurate meaning. Winfield Coleman, in presenting his research on Cheyenne androgynous priests, remarked that when he was last on the Cheyenne reservation, a tribal member said something about, "those . . . what do you call 'em—lesbians?" to which Coleman replied, *"Heemaneh.* The term historically used for the two-spirit by the Cheyenne" (Roscoe 1994:570).

But is this really the term used for Cheyenne two-spirits historically, or is it possibly something else? And was the tribal member really forgetful of his language's term for such an individual to the point where he had to be reminded by the anthropological Keeper of Knowledge, or was the tribal member attempting to communicate in a manner he believed Coleman would understand? Or was he, as I feel many members of various tribes are doing, attempting to understand a difference in the traditional role of the *heemaneh* and contemporary individuals who may indeed be lesbian?

Often, for the sake of expediency and other reasons, Native American people may translate something that does not reflect how we perceive something but that works within a specific context. For example, my administrative assistant tried to call one of my relatives, Sobiyax, on the Skokomish Reservation to see if he would be willing to substitute for me at a speaking engagement. Several months earlier, my assistant had asked how I was related to Sobiyax and, not wanting to go into detail, I said, "Oh, he's a cousin," because I knew that would satisfy my non-Indian assistant's curiosity and was minimally accurate. My assistant stated his request to the switchboard operator on the reservation and emphasized that my message was important and that I was "a relative." When the operator paused before replying, he elaborated and told her I was Sobiyax's "cousin." She laughed and said, "That Terry Tafoya, he's no relative, he's just relative."

Within many Native communities and languages there are a variety of identities. For example, in my mother's language, there are twenty-eight specific identity terms for oneself. In the context of my family, the most distant English term of relationship on a personal level is *cousin*. Because of the historical and personal involvement I have with Sobiyax and his family, a more appropriate and respectful term in English would be "my brother," reflecting not only my emotional relationship with him but also our similarity in age. Were he much older, I might call him "Dad" or "Uncle." This is, of course, speaking abstractly. In reality, I would call him by his spiritual name, Sobiyax, and he, as a sign of endearment and intimacy, would call me by one of my spiritual names. And in both cases we would use the spiritual names we had "witnessed" in our respective Naming Ceremonies. The switchboard operator was Sobiyax's eldest sister. Inadvertently, my assistant managed to insult two of my relatives on my behalf without having a clue about what he was doing.

Just so. Names themselves are not the only issue, but the context of their use is an essential consideration. Hayles (1993) suggests that many people with a scientific bias hold what she calls the "gift-wrap idea of language." They see language as a gift wrapping that I use to hand you an idea. You receive the package, unwrap it, and take out the idea. In this view, the wrapping is purely instrumental, a way of getting an idea from me to you. The idea is what counts, not the wrapping. People trained in literature tend to think this view of language is completely wrong. They deeply believe that the language constitutes an idea rather than expresses it. Because no two verbal formulations can ever be identical, to say something in other words is to say something different (Hayles 1993:48).

Considering that "berdache" is frequently glossed in the literature with such English classifications as hermaphrodite, transvestite, or homosexual, we might do well to question the context in which these terms are used. DeCecco and Elia remind us that the "labels of bisexual, heterosexual, and homosexual suggest an isomorphism to a person's sexual behavior, sexual fantasies, erotic arousal, and affectional relationships that are not consistent with research evidence" (1993:45; cf. Blumstein and Schwartz, 1977; Masters and Johnson, 1979). In addition, such categories emphasize discontinuities rather than consistencies along the full range of variations in erotic and affectional preferences. Even Freud seemed aware of the complexity of this construction when he wrote: "What is for practical reasons called homosexuality may arise from a whole variety of psychosexual inhibitory processes; the particular process we have singled out is perhaps only one among many, and is perhaps related to only one type of homosexuality" (1914:101).

Only one type of homosexuality indeed! What is the sexuality of the one who partners a two-spirit? If one accepts the concept of more than two genders, then such a "man" or "woman" is not having a homosexual relationship but is fundamentally engaged in a heterosexual encounter by being involved with a third or fourth (or fifth or sixth) gender. And were I an activist, I might remind the reader of Foucault's suggestion that the so-called scientific categories of gender and sexuality are medical and therefore pathologically focused and "constitute a sexuality that is economically useful and politically conservative" (1978:36). As Janice Irvine, a sexology critic, points out, the underlying theories of only two genders, or heterosexuality versus homosexuality, inform sexological practices in important ways: "Sexology contributes to the collective sexual discourse of the medical and psychiatric professions, a discourse that is itself a means of social control. Categories of 'natural' and 'deviant' not only operate on the personal level to shape individual experience, but underpin the legal system as well. Whenever a personal preference/orientation becomes a 'sexual dysfunction,' a 'sexual deviancy,' or a crime is a political decision often related to its status in the psychiatric community" (1990:104).

Weeks states that standard sexual classifications are "not inborn, pregiven, or 'natural' . . . these classifications are striven for, contested, negotiated, and achieved often in the struggles of the subordinate to the dominate" (1988:207). Were I a historian, I might remind the audience that the hatred and oppression against Native Americans by European invaders and colonialists might have had some influence on what so-called informants would discuss, considering that the interviewer might classify community-sanctioned behavior as a "sexual dysfunction, a sexual deviancy, or a crime." I might point out that the 1513 event of Balboa's executing forty Native people he labeled "sodomites" might instruct the subjects of anthropologists to be somewhat hesitant in their discussions of gender and sexuality in general (Goldberg 1992:180). Greg Sarris, a Pomo scholar and speaking as both a Pomo and an academic, reminds us that "representatives from the dominant culture exploring the resistance of a subjugated people are likely to see little more than what those people choose or can afford to show them" (1993:68). Sarris might suggest that even such "gay-positive" works as those of Walter Williams, which attempt to "give voice" to the Native two-spirit, are typical ethnographic reports that provide a "story of a story." "The reality of the situation is that the self which is identifiable as Indian, and has come to signify Indian in the text, is Indian in contact with non-Indian" (89).

Ultimately, it is probably impossible ever to recapture objectively accurate information on Native concepts of sexuality. Written historic records are likely to tell more about European observers' sexuality than that of those observed. Historically, ethnic animosity against Native people was usually so intense that "rationality [was] usually the first sacrifice, where those one opposes are automatically called perverted, cannibals, thieves, and degenerates" (Tannahill 1980:168). It may be difficult to know when one is reporting and when one is propagandizing. Thus, it is possible that the Spanish used such accusations as "they are all sodomites and practice that abominable vice" (Salmoral 1990:76) to justify their conquering efforts, much in the manner of contemporary anti-gay efforts by Christian extremists. Who knows how many of those accused or noted as hermaphrodite, transvestite, or homosexual were what are now labeled as two-spirit?

Sarris is a powerful advocate for our awareness of not only acknowledging what the experience of the observed and observer may be, as well as their interaction, but also for the interaction of the reader of texts that report these interactions and intersections, moving far afield from the gift-wrap theory of ideas.

In 1985, at the International Academy of Sex Research, I suggested the Tafoya Principle of Uncertainty. I called it that because I discovered that you get tenure faster if you name something after yourself. In physics, the Heisenberg Principle of Uncertainty states that one can know the speed of an electron or its location, but one cannot know both simultaneously. In other words, to know its location, the electron needs to be in a fixed place and not moving; to measure its velocity, the electron must be moving and not in a fixed place.

The Tafoya Principle of Uncertainty states that in cross-cultural research one can have context or definition but not both at the same time. The more one attempts to establish a context for a situation or process, the more one will blur a clean, simple definition for a situation or process and the more one will lose a sense of context. Attempting to define two-spirit will cause a loss of context. Attempting to provide a context for the two-spirit will blur any simple and specific definition of the experience. This is not to say that any labels dealing with sexuality and gender are hopeless or self-defeating. As DeCecco and Elia suggest, "Such labels may have great utility in studies that treat them as loosely descriptive social constructs rather than as intrinsic traits that are predictive of the sum of an individual's erotic and affectional desires" (1993:45). Problems arise in the Godel-esque attempt to describe what ultimately lies outside of one's ability to define.

Before I let the Dragonfly go free, I suggest that I have always found that Native American traditions provide a floor rather than a ceiling; one is provided a foundation of understanding rather than a limitation. Perhaps the truth of the two-spirit is best understood by Foster's definition: "A truth, they might say, that could be approached only along a ladder of parables and enigmas and silent little explosions of enlightenments" (1975:207).

Ana kush nai (it is finished).

Note

1. *M. Butterfly* is not to be confused with *Madame Butterfly*, Giacomo Puccini's operetta about the relationship between a Japanese woman and an American army lieutenant, later rewritten as *Miss Saigon*, the story of a Vietnamese woman and American serviceman.

References Cited

Blumstein, Phillip, and Pepper Swartz. 1977. *American Couples: Money, Work, Sex.* New York: Pocket Books.

DeCecco, John P., and John P. Elia. 1993. "A Critique and Synthesis of Biological Essentialism and Social Constructionist Views of Sexuality and Gender." In *If You Seduce a Straight Person, Can You Make Them Gay? Issues in Biological Essentialism vs. Social Constructionism in Gay and Lesbian Identities*, ed. John P. DeCecco and John P. Elia, 1–26. New York: Harrington Park Press.

Foster, M. A. 1975. *The Gameplayers of Zan.* New York: DAW Books.

Foucault, Michel. 1978. *The History of Sexuality.* Volume 1: *An Introduction.* New York: Pantheon.

Freud, Sigmund. 1914. In *The Standard Edition of the Complete Psychological Works of Sigmund Freud*, Volume 2 (1953–74), ed. James Strachey. London: Hogarth Press.

Goldberg, Johnathan. 1992. *Sodometries: Renaissnance Texts and Modern Sexualities.* Stanford: Stanford University Press.

Hayles, Katherine. 1993. Quoted in Janet Stites, "Bordercrossings: A Conversation in Cyberspace." *OMNI* 16(2): 38–48, 105–13.

Hillerman, Tony. 1986. *The Boy Who Made Dragonfly: A Zuni Myth.* Albuquerque: University of Mexico Press.

Hwang, David Henry. 1989. *M. Butterfly.* New York: New American Library.

Irvine, Janice M. 1990. *Disorders of Desire: Sex and Gender in Modern American Sexology.* Philadelphia: Temple University Press.

Masters, William, and Virginia Johnson. 1979. *Homosexuality in Perspective.* Boston: Little, Brown.

Patton, Cindy. 1990. *Inventing AIDS.* New York: Routledge.

Roscoe, Will. 1994. "How to Become a 'Berdache': Toward a Unified Analysis of Gender Diversity." In *Third Sex, Third Gender: Beyond Sexual Dimorphism in Culture and History,* ed. Gilbert Herdt, 329–72. New York: Books.

Salmoral, Manuel Lucena. 1990. *America 1492: Portrait of a Continent Five Hundred Years Ago.* New York: Facts on File.

Sarris, Greg. 1993. *Keeping Slug Woman Alive: A Holistic Approach to American Indian Texts.* Berkeley: University of California Press.

Tannahill, Reay. 1980. *Sex in History.* New York: Stein and Day

Weeks, Jeffrey. 1989. "Against Nature." In *Homosexuality, Which Homosexuality?* ed. Dennis Altman et al., 199–214. Amsterdam: Schorer Press.

Part 3: Two-Spirit as a Lived Experience:
        Life Stories

★ ★ 10

I Am a Lakota Womyn

Beverly Little Thunder (Standing Rock Lakota)

The very mention of "Washington, D.C.," is enough to trigger insecurities that I hold inside over my lack of formal academic education.[1] As I put my thoughts into writing for this work I can only pray that the words that come from my heart will be heard and understood.

I am glad that I was able to hear the words of all those who spoke during our meeting in 1993 in Washington, D.C. It was good to hear where those who have written about my people are taking their studies these days. As I heard the word "berdache" [*sic*] used, I found myself wondering, "Where am I as a womyn in this word?" Its meaning had no place in the description of my life. The word is meant to describe males, not me. I am a Lakota womyn, and I know that my own people have a name for me.

Most tribes that I have had the honor of knowing have specific names for men who love men and for wimmin who love wimmin. I have personally spent much of my life being placed in the "other" category in the Western world. The suggested label of "designated other" (when referring to me in my relationship with a womyn partner) did not appeal to me. Because I had no role model to look toward for guidance, I found myself learning and adopting the terms used by the mainstream feminist community I became involved in. Although I did not totally fit in with the beliefs of some of these wimmin, I was able to learn from them and empower myself to follow the path that I needed to.

I can understand that there may be a need by some to find a pan-Native term that can be used as a marker for the general population of

Native lesbians and gays. We are all so different in so many ways, however. Culturally and physically, we are all different. Each tribe has its own name, its own structure. How can we all even be called "Natives"?

Whether we are talking about the past or the present, in terms of tribal identity or sexuality, the tendency to lump us all under one label is still true. We may all be men who love men or wimmin who love wimmin, but we have all come to this place in a different manner.

I had read accounts of one or two people who lived in the past. The studies seem to focus on one or two individuals who lived their lives in a different time, under different social circumstances and with varied influences. Frequently, these accounts were obtained from someone who knew someone who knew someone (in other words, gossip). The stories were often written as if those in the past were the only true two-spirit people to have lived.

The words I would like to see written about me and read fifty years from now should be words that reflect who I am as an individual. I am a female, and I have no desire to be a male. I am able to perform many tasks that are considered male jobs. Yet, I am also able to do and enjoy doing many things that are considered female. I am also able to bear children and have done so.

Being a womyn who loves another womyn does not mean that I reject being a mother. I am, in fact, a mother to five children: two daughters and three sons. Having children helped me to look closer at the world into which I had brought them. It was important for me to, at least, get them to the doorway of their ancestors and teach them the basic values of the Lakota people and culture.

Many two-spirit wimmin I meet are very involved with children. Sometimes the children are their own, other times the children in their lives are nieces or nephews. Like myself, these wimmin share an interest in providing guidance to young people that will enable them to live their lives in a good way. There is a concern that the young ones need to have encouragement to feel good about who they are and the decisions they make.

My experience has been that one of my daughters has many aunts and uncles in the two-spirit community. They are there for her. She is a beautiful and well-centered young womyn today as a result of the help and guidance she received growing up in the two-spirit community. In the recent past, our people raised their children with the collective support of all the tribal members. What we are doing in the two-spirit community is no different from that old way.

It can be hard for those who have unsupportive families. Once I heard a young two-spirit man cry because his sister would not allow him to hold his newborn nephew. She had told him that she did not want her son to be gay. Another two-spirit couple were parenting the natural son of one of the wimmin. The natural mother became ill and died. Her brother then used the tribal courts to have the child taken from the remaining parent and have her forbidden from seeing the child again. No one seemed to be concerned with how the child may have felt being taken from both of the only parents he had known.

Two-spirit womyn and men are concerned for the future of their people. Children are a respected part of that circle of human life. All adults are role models and teachers for the next generation. This gives adults the responsibility of showing the young ones how to honor themselves and respect their choices as well as their place on this earth.

My experience began in Los Angeles, California, where I was born to a mother who was not expecting me to arrive so soon. I was born in the county hospital. Mother told me that this was because she was not able to get home to North Dakota. She also told me that we did go home when I was older and spent some time there in a small town called Kenel, in North Dakota.

My mother and father were alcoholics. There were many quite remarkable things about my mother, however her alcoholism drove her to send me to live with my relatives for much of my early life. Sometimes people tell me that I was lucky. My relatives assume that somehow these experiences formed my spiritual nature. They want to believe that I was taught all there is to know about Lakota spirituality when I was a child. They are incorrect. I am spiritual because it is what I have chosen to be. It is a part of who I am as a person.

I grew up in foster homes, boarding schools, and detention centers. I even spent some time in two convents. During this period I even thought it would be fun to be a nun.

I was not overly fond of boys. I was molested frequently as a child and as a result was fearful of males. I did not want to get married and have children. Out of fear and to prove to myself that I was not "queer," I did get married, and I did have children. I do not regret this. I do, however, feel just a little bit sorry for those men whom I must have made unhappy.

I felt torn between Christianity, which was part of my life, and the traditions in which I was raised. I did not seem to fit into the Christian world, yet I was also aware of the homophobia in the world of my people. I could not find peace in being who I was.

In my early twenties I became active in the American Indian Movement. It was very frightening. I attended the Sweat Lodge Ceremonies and in doing so became aware of my responsibility to teach my children and guide them in the ways of their ancestors. I felt that if this were a path that they chose to follow when they were adults at least they would know how to access it. Of course, this meant that I had to learn it in order to teach them. It was certainly a crash course in spirituality. There I was, a young mother in her twenties trying to learn and teach my children Lakota in a small town where no one else spoke the language. The sweat lodge I was able to take my children to was being led by men who were just learning themselves. It was not easy.

As I became more deeply involved in the ceremonies of my people and began to participate in the Sun Dance Ceremony, I became more and more terrified of being "found out." I feared that if anyone knew of my desire to be with another womyn I would be stricken from the ceremonies that were now such an important part of my life. My fears turned out to be real, but I never expected that the same people who taught me so much about the Lakota ways would be some of those who would later reject me so completely.

This rejection came in 1985 when I attended the Sun Dance Ceremony in South Dakota. I went there and told the community that I could no longer pretend to be someone I was not. I could no longer sit quietly while cruel jokes were made about lesbians and gays. The word *lesbian* was at the time the only way I knew how to identify the feelings I felt. European influences had almost eradicated the recognition and role of people like myself among my own people.[2] The rejection hurt. It hurt a lot.

My involvement in the Lakota spiritual community was a large part my life and who I am. Being turned away by the Lakota wimmin and men with whom I had prayed and danced was devastating. Before I left the community, two older wimmin came to see me. I was told that there was no need for me to be there and be the subject of this anger. I was told that our people have trouble remembering the place of honor that my kind once held. I was told to go and have a ceremony for others like myself. I was told to listen to Spirit.

After a year I was directed by Spirit to have a ceremony for my own kind—a Sun Dance ceremony that was different from those that I had learned. And so it began. The first three years were hard. I had to separate myself from the first group I had led in the ceremony. I left because of the direction I saw them going. It was not the way I had been taught to honor my people. No matter what, I was determined to do what I had to do in an honorable way for the sake of my ancestors. Now, as part of my continued determination to hold wimmin-only Sun Dances, we have our ceremony each full moon of July in the hills of California. There are few dancers. Each is a two-spirit womyn willing to prepare and honor the ceremony.

I am sure that there are some of my own people who feel that what I do is wrong. I have been forced to find in my own way a means of continuing with the expressions of my spiritual beliefs. I have done the best I can. Sometimes I have made mistakes, and at other times I may have appeared rebellious. I may have even appeared to be disrespectful of my own people. To maintain my center I have needed to do the things I have done in my life.

In the non-Native community of lesbians and gay people I have been told that being two-spirited means that I am a special being. It seems that they felt that my spirituality was the mystical answer to my sexuality. I do not believe this to be so. My spirituality would have been with me, regardless of my sexuality. This attitude often creates a feeling of isolation. I live in a white society that finds me exotic. At the same time, I can be ignored by people I love, respect, and sometimes work with.

I have had to learn that sometimes I am on the cutting edge when I do what is best for myself. To protect myself I have learned to keep a lot of "band-aids" handy—especially those nurturing and caring friends I call on when things get rough. Doing so has been helpful for the times when not just strangers but people I love and care about attack and judge my actions. There are so many of us who have been involved in a struggle for dignity for such a long time. Often we have struggled on our own without the support of our people. Every now and then we come across someone who will listen to us and offer moral and emotional support. When this happens, as it did during the second Wenner-Gren Foundation Conference meetings in Chicago in 1994, I feel the struggle is worth it.

I hear the stories that my brothers and sisters tell, and I find that I feel a deep love for these human beings who have endured so much pain in their lives. Yet they were willing to take the risk of sharing some of their most hurtful moments with a room full of anthropologists in Washington, D.C., Chicago, and now with the world by publishing their feelings and ideas in this book.

It is time that anthropologists write about those of us who are alive now. And they must *listen* to us, hear us, and use our own words, not just their special anthropological language. The combined words are the ones people will read fifty (and more) years from now. There are not just two or three of us; there are not just those of us who have contributed to this volume. There are hundreds, even thousands, of us, and we all struggle to live our lives with dignity and pride.

Just as my Lakota ancestors continue to struggle, I have come before you and tried to use your language to help you understand that "berdache" is not who I am. I have tried to understand the scope and purpose of those who continue to work in the field of anthropology. I have read paper after paper written by anthropologists and historians, some of which are in this volume, and I continue to see this same inappropriate word used for us. In spite of the fact that the Native people in this volume have clearly expressed that the term is not acceptable, it is still being used by some who insist that our request that they stop doing so impinges on their "academic freedom" or their "right to free speech." When I read or hear such statements, I feel invisible. I hear and read about men who lived before us and again I feel invisible. There is so little written about the role of wimmin loving wimmin in the various tribes. I can not help but wonder how the young wimmin of future generations will feel. Will they feel invisible too?

During our discussions in Washington, D.C., I heard someone make the comment that two-spirit people must be innovative. I have found this to be true. In order to survive the attacks and the fear of others, I have had to be innovative. I have needed to find ways to validate myself, ways to maintain my integrity and pride. There may be some people who chose to see me as a spiritual leader. I want to be clear that I do not see myself in this way. When others ask me why I have chosen the path that I follow, I tell them that it is the path I have been directed to follow. Only the Creator can know why and what my purpose is.

The world of the academy seeks to find and provide answers to questions, such as why are some people lesbian or gay and others are not. There are those who swear "it must have been the water in a town" or "the way a person was brought up." We have all heard the various theories, yet none of us knows the answer.

The next seven generations are going to be affected by the work that has begun by the contributors to this book. If I, as a Native womyn, sound angry and arrogant, then it may be because our voices have never been heard before without a non-Native person first editing our thoughts into something that they deem more "suitable" and "appropriate." The unique experience of each person who has been a part of this long process is important. Whether we are a manly womyn, a womynly man, transgendered, heterosexual, asexual, or otherwise, we are all one with creation.

No one person can speak for so many Native two-spirit people, no single term can apply to all of us at any time. Instead of focusing on one or two people who lived in the past it is now time to begin to write about those of us who live today. Anthropologists of today have the opportunity to record the contemporary life of our people, not just our history, for future generations.

These days I no longer ask for respect, and I do not ask for sensitivity. I will not bend over backward to be seen or heard. These days I demand respect and sensitivity, and I demand to be seen and to be heard. I demand all of these because they are my right as a human being.

I hope these words provide another step toward what is going to happen in the next few years to change how people write about us and record our lives. I pray Native people can reach understanding and clarity among themselves so that the voices of all my people can and will be heard. I pray that all humans can honor and respect the individuality of everyone who lives on Mother Earth.

Notes

1. As indicated in the "Introduction," the first Wenner-Gren Foundation Conference and the American Anthropological Association session on "Revisiting the 'North American Berdache' Empirically and Theoretically" were held in Washington, D.C., in November 1993. I had considerable anxiety about being in that city for several reasons, only one of which was speaking to a group of academics.

2. It is ironic that while my people so strongly rejected me and others like me, certain white male academics had "rediscovered" Lakota *winkte* and were making references to the "privileged" and "honored" status of the ancient ones found in old anthropological and historical writings. Some even went so far as to argue that modern *winkte* still had status in our communities (Williams 1986), when my experience showed otherwise.

Reference Cited

Williams, Walter. 1986. *The Spirit and the Flesh: Sexual Diversity in American Indian Culture.* Boston: Beacon Press. Reprint 1991, with a new preface.

★ ★ **11**

Traditional Influences on a Contemporary Gay-Identified Sisseton Dakota

Michael Red Earth (Sisseton Dakota)

Growing up as an urban Native, I was not exposed to a traditional Dakota upbringing, although I believe my culture expressed itself to me in a variety of ways. As a gay man, I was treated with a combination of traditional and assimilated beliefs regarding my sexuality. Although some of these beliefs contradicted each other, they dictated how I was treated by my immediate family and the larger Dakota community.

My name is Michael Red Earth. I am queer. I am in my early thirties. I am an artist and an activist. I am Sisseton Dakota and Polish American. I grew up in Minneapolis, Minnesota. I have lived in the Seattle, Washington, area for more than ten years. My partner Lee, who is white, and I have been together for more than ten years.

I am half Polish. My father's father was a first-generation Polish American. Knowing I am half Polish is the extent my father's ethnic heritage has had on me. My father's relationship with my mother was not accepted by his family.

My mother is the oldest of four daughters. My grandmother died when my mother was about fourteen. After this happened, my mother and her sisters were forced to leave the reservation and attend the Indian Boarding School in Flandreau, South Dakota.

The policy at the Indian boarding schools was to reeducate and assimilate Indians into white culture. Expressions of Indian heritage were suppressed and punished. I believe this is important because it affected my mother's worldview as it related to me and my sexuality.

My mother and father met in the city of Minneapolis, Minnesota. My relationship with my mother and father was good. Honesty and telling the truth were their guiding principles as they reared me.

Our extended family could be broken down into two groups. The first group, the urban Indians, consisted of my mother's sisters, their partners and children, and quite a few cousins. The cousins were not all biological relatives but also relatives by tribal affiliation. I was encouraged to think of these tribal kinspeople as cousins.

The urban Indians all lived within walking distance of each other, with a few living in the same apartment building as we did. Even though I was an only child, it seemed that I had sisters because of the proximity of my "cousins."

The "Reservation Indians," the second group, were family members who decided to stay on our reservation, the Lake Traverse Reservation of the Sisseton-Wapheton Dakota Tribe. Our reservation is located in the northeast area of the state of South Dakota, approximately four hours by car from the twin cities of Minneapolis-Saint Paul.

Even though the "Reservation Indians" were closer to the traditional ways of our people geographically, our relatives on the reservation were fairly assimilated. I believe this was because of the boarding school curriculum, the Episcopal church, and exposure to Western culture via television and "big city" relatives.

Let me try to explain some of the contradictions of this "assimilation." Although both groups of family had bought into the idea that Western culture was "better" and could offer more opportunities than the "traditional" life-style, both groups of family still observed traditional events and were subtly influenced by traditional ways.

For example, every year the city Indians would "go home" for the pow-wow. Most funerals incorporated memorial giveaways a year after the burial. Animals and natural elements were acknowledged as having spirits that could be offended. There was an awareness of the traditional ways, just not an obvious observance of them on a daily basis.

At a very early age I was aware—like many other gay youths—that I was different. This difference did not escape the attention of family members, either.

I remember myself being a quiet, serious child. Kids my own age would comment that I walked and talked "like a girl." A difference was also noted by some elders. Recently, my mother told me that when I was still a toddler some of the elders on the reservation had told her I was *"winkte."* Because of her assimilation, my mother translated this into "homosexual."[1] When I pressed her on this subject, she remembered that the elders said this with no apparent judgment. They said it as if they were simply stating a fact. She chose to take comfort from the lack of judgment and hoped they were wrong.

Every summer during the school vacation I would be sent to the reservation to stay with my grandfather and his second wife and their teenage children. Being a city Indian, I was not much help with the farming chores. Being a boy, I was not expected to be interested in cooking and cleaning. Being who I am, I was not. I would have been bored except for one thing: my step-grandmother's beadwork. She supplemented the family income by doing beadwork. She would make beaded belts and medallions to sell through an Indian women's craft cooperative. I was fascinated by her beadwork, and at an early age I was learning various beadwork techniques.

The ramifications of this may be obvious to some people. Among our tribe, beadwork is considered to be women's work. By expressing an interest in beadwork, I was making a declaration to my family that I was more interested in women's work. I was choosing to be *winkte* even though I did not realize I was making a declaration, but thereafter people treated me differently.

I was allowed to become my step-grandmother's companion. I was not pressured to go play with the boys but was allowed to accompany her to quilting bees and beadwork sales and on shopping trips. I was allowed into areas that other boys would not be allowed, specifically restrooms to escort younger female cousins and rooms where women were undressing and changing. The only people who would object to this behavior were women who did not know me. My behavior was allowed to continue unquestioned and unchallenged until I became a teenager. As I entered puberty, and at the time I should have started to show an interest in girls but did not, my differences started to become a problem.

Because of the Stonewall Riots, "Gay Liberation" was now part of the American cultural vocabulary. The words that were part of the assimilationist Indian vocabulary were *faggot, pervert,* and *homo.* The people who knew and sometimes used these words were my urban assimilated aunts and their white male partners. The people on the reservation may have known those words but chose not to use them. They would continue to refer to me using terms that expressed my good nature, willingness to help, and respect for my elders. I was still the exemplary young adult in their eyes.

I became a source of conflict, an example of the contradictions between the assimilationist and traditional views. The assimilationist view would believe that because I was gay I was bad, but the traditional views of the importance of family and respect for a person's spirit helped them see that "Michael is good." The assimilationist would feel that effeminacy is "bad" for a boy, whereas the traditional way allowed my interest in beadwork and feminine behaviors to be nurtured. One of the feminine behaviors that was nurtured was taking care of children, which conflicted with the assimilationist belief that it is bad to have gays around kids. One of the most interesting manifestations of this contradiction between the assimilationist and traditional views was the way my family peers (my cousins) could denigrate gays and lesbians but be the first to come to my defense when I was threatened because I was gay.

Honesty and telling the truth is important in my family. So when I was fifteen I officially "came out." When I did, I did so in a big way. I came out to my mother and other members of my family. I came out at school by volunteering at a gay service organization for a social studies project. I totally immersed myself in the gay culture of the late 1970s.

The reaction among my family was predictably along assimilationist and traditional lines. The assimilationists, including my mother, were upset for the obvious reasons. The traditionalists were confused—they didn't know what this meant.

After coming out at my high school, my school experience became intolerable because of the hassles related to my sexuality and so I quit school. Unfortunately, my elders, without knowing all my reasons for dropping, came to see "being gay" as being bad because they felt it was the reason I quit school. I think the elders imagined that I chose to do "this gay thing" and deliberately stop being a "good son and family member." And in a sense I did—but not out of disrespect for them. Harassment at school had led me to make this hard decision, so I went where it seemed that nurturance and support were forthcoming.

Immersing myself in gay culture of the late 1970s could more accurately be described as immersing myself in white gay culture. Up to that point in my life, even though I knew I was sexually and affectionately attracted to men, I thought I was the only Native gay there was. Among my family, until I quit school, there seemed to be acknowledgment that I was different from the other heterosexuals, and they allowed me to be different although no one ever talked about the matter with me. I believe this was due to assimilation and the fear of anything sexual.

Because no one talked to me, I learned to define myself as a gay man by my exposure to white American culture. To be a successful gay man, I had to become a white gay man. To the confusion and disappointment of my family, both urban and reservation, I removed myself from my Native heritage.

One of the first things that I did, as I bought into the ready-made white gay culture, was convince myself that my family had rejected me because (according to white gay culture) all gay people are oppressed by their families. I looked back at every harsh word and every hurt I received from my relatives and attributed the reasons for those behaviors to me being gay. Now I realize that they didn't reject me (I'm not implying some didn't have strong feelings), but they needed time to figure out their feelings.

The other things I did to immerse myself in white gay culture were to go to marches and demonstrations, involve myself in gay organizations, and socialize in exclusively gay and lesbian circles. As I developed self-confidence in the gay community and learned to raise my voice for gay and lesbian rights, I learned more about myself. I learned to be proud of who I was, and I learned to speak out for myself, but I realized that a part of me was missing: my Native heritage. I would remember and miss my family and wonder how I could bridge the two worlds in which I wanted to live—the white gay world and my Native world.

When I was twenty-seven I learned about the Second Annual Native Gay and Lesbian Gathering. I immediately saw an opportunity to reconnect with the Native part of my heritage because I was the only Native queer that I knew of. Even though I had lived in two major cities, both with sizable Native populations, no Native gays or lesbians were in my circle of friends.

I recently told my twenty-year-old cousin about this experience. I got to the gathering and felt as if I were home. It seemed just like the gatherings I remembered on the reservation. People had traveled great distances to be together, to laugh, to joke, to eat, and to pow-wow. I instantly felt comfortable, and for the first time in my life I felt whole and complete. I was not suppressing or ignoring any part of myself. I saw all my relations in the other people gathered there. By this, I mean that I saw uncles and cousins and elders from our tribe, not literally but figuratively in the sense that I realized that for the first time in my life I was not the only one. I hadn't been seeing the others because you don't see "white queers" in Indian Country. My cousin asked what I meant by "white queers in Indian country." I said, "I thought to be queer you had to be concerned with a certain type of style, a certain type of look and a certain type of philosophy to live your life by, all defined by rich white gays. Being Indian didn't fit in with that look. I realized that I was seeing queer Indians all along, but I was not seeing the queerness because it didn't fit in the parameters I had set. When I saw queer Indians, I didn't see the queer, I saw the Indian." My cousin was confused and asked me to clarify what I saw when I saw Indian. I responded, "When I finally looked, I didn't see a queen screaming, 'MARY!,' I saw a queen saying, 'Eh-h-h-h.'"[2]

After my first Native Gay and Lesbian Gathering I tried to learn all I could about *winkte,* "berdaches" [*sic*], *nádleeh,* and two-spirited people. This process helped reacquaint me with the elements of my personal heritage that I had suppressed. I found that many were still there besides the behavior related to my sexuality, but, again, I wasn't used to seeing such elements in the white cultural context.

As I learned more about what was written about *winkte* and their historical roles, I realized that the description did not fit me. According to the information to which I had access, if I was *winkte* I was submissive in sex, cross-dressing, and had responsibilities defined by female gender roles.

Even though I had manifested all of these qualities at some time, they were not true of me all the time and subsequently were not an accurate description of my personality or behavior. What I did find that matched my personal experience was the expectation that I would be "in service" to my community. Because I would not be directly responsible for rearing children, I was expected to have more time and energy to give to my family and community. I believe this is the reason the disappointment was so great when I did not finish high school and I withdrew from my family. I was not participating in my culturally prescribed role.

There has been some discussion that the *winkte* role may be overly positive and not accurate in its acceptance of an alternative gender or sexuality. From my experience, I reject this. That my family treated me with respect and expected excellence was not an accident nor an isolated phenomena. The fact that my family has been assaulted by assimilationist policies for four generations and is still capable of progressive thinking toward someone of an alternative sexuality is not happenstance.

The difficulty for my family came when they tried to incorporate their indoctrinated feelings from assimilation with our cultural legacy. It is as if I am a painful reminder of how things used to be. If people are supposed to be ashamed of me, then I am a painful vision of the way the future can be. It is not a simple matter of accepting my gayness because of the old ways. My Native culture must sort through many complex feelings. I, too, had the same problem when I tried to reconcile being gay with a traditional point of view.

In today's world, it is easy to become confused by titles: gay, straight, bi, *winkte,* or queer. For me, once I realized that my family was responding to me and interacting with me with respect and acceptance, and once I realized that this respect and acceptance was a legacy of our traditional Native past, I was empowered to present my whole self to the world and reassume the responsibilities of being a two-spirited person.

Notes

1. The tendency to let words define people and their characters was pointed out to me recently. A young man from my tribe came to me for help. I assumed he came to me because I am an "out" queer in my tribe, and I thought he was having difficulties because of the assimilated views about homosexuals in our tribe. I took on the task of educating him about our cultural legacy and the historic acceptance of people who are now being called "homosexual" instead of *winkte.* Although some of what I told him was in accord with his life experience, I soon realized that I was not touching upon the areas that were troubling him. I was at a loss about what to do. It was not until I had a conversation with Jason Cromwell that I realized that I was putting him into a category and what was probably causing the young man from my tribe so much confusion was his realization that he may be transgender not homosexual (see Cromwell in this volume for further information about the differences between homosexual and transgender people). Even I need to be periodically reminded that it is easy to confound diverse cultural and individual sexuality categories.

2. "Eh-h-h-h" is pronounced "a" as in "day." It is an exclamation to let the listener know that the speaker has said something humorous.

12

A Postcolonial Colonial Perspective on Western [Mis]Conceptions of the Cosmos and the Restoration of Indigenous Taxonomies

Anguksuar [Richard LaFortune] (Yup'ik)

My name is Anguksuar, that is my use-name. I am a citizen of Yupiit Nation, of the Kuskokvagmiut, which translated into English means the People from the Great River. I am mixed blood and have been raised with the influences of both my blood family and adoptive white missionary family.

I was raised speaking Yupik until the age of four; thereafter I was raised speaking English. Even after we had relocated away from my homeland I was encouraged in my pursuit of activities that are usually identified with feminine interests. It makes me wonder if the beliefs and attitudes of my progressive, midwestern, white, middle-class family may have been significantly influenced by the cultural practices of my Yupik relatives. According to traditional teachings, Yupik culture—like many other Aboriginal cultures—embraces a social structure that provides a spectrum of genders and promotes respect for the varieties of human gender expression.

As an eight- or nine-year-old child, I distinctly remember playing with children from a nearby neighborhood one summer where I grew up in Calgary, Alberta. We were running among the prairie grass, up and down a hill in Bridgeland, our neighborhood. A boy, whose name I did not know and still do not know, stopped in his tracks as we were running along the trails and turned, looked at me, and said, "Are you a boy—or a girl?" I also stopped, looked at him, and offered the most honest answer I could: I was a boy. He considered that for a moment and said, "Are you sure?" To which I said, "Yes." That answer apparently satisfied him, because he turned around and we continued running down the hill.

A few years earlier, the children in my school would play schoolyard games based on comic-strip characters. Sometimes I would be "Batgirl," for example, either by my own choice or the designation of classmates. My identity did not fit into a usual category of Western society; if it did, these young children were of an age that did not yet allow them to internalize the intellectually and spiritually backward view that only two genders exist.

When I reached early adolescence my family moved to the United States. I lived in rural Michigan, in urban Pennsylvania, and in Minnesota, where as a young adult I was welcomed into the cultural and ceremonial life of the Ojibways and Dakotas, on whose land Minnesota is becoming established (Colonization is a continuing process, not simply a historical event.)

Around the same time that my learning process began in the cultural universe of my Native neighbors, I was slowly becoming enmeshed in the often exciting, frequently frustrating, and usually bewildering flow of American gay society. It was also at this time that I embarked on my first long-term relationship: Alcohol became my frequent companion for almost eight years. Fortunately, Aboriginal identity, spirituality, and sexuality began coalescing into something familiar and consistent with my psyche and spirit. In fact, the teachings I was receiving from my Ojibwe, Dakota, Lakota, and HoChak (Winnebago) neighbors in the early 1980s included information about *winkte.*

In 1986 and 1987 our community in Minneapolis began organizing toward the reemergence of lesbian, gay, and transgendered people who had often been relegated to family and cultural obscurity. I hesitate to characterize this organizing as being part of a "movement," although it has come to share some of the trademarks that we commonly recognize with civil and human rights movements. By this time Gay American Indians (GAI) in San Francisco had been long-established; Nichiwakan, a lesbian-gay Native society in Winnipeg was also forming, but few people in the United States were aware of it.

There is a tremendous history that Native people could share about culture, identity, and sexuality. We have so many stories to tell, some of which can serve as excellent primary-source material and some of which is highly entertaining but may have more limited academic usefulness. Some stories share the best of both distinctions. I would like to share a brief story, but I would also like to open a door and provide a glimpse of the spiritual and intellectual traditions that have defined the dimensions of the universe for many Natives. The thoughts are my recollections, and sometimes interpretations, of oral and contemporary teachings. My words cannot represent any monolithic Native culture.

With respect to the past few decades' discourse on human sexuality I recall a few powerful thoughts that impressed me some years ago while reading a work of Vine Deloria, Jr. Deloria, a contemporary Native scholar, noted that Western Rational tradition has been very good at "analyzing," whereas many Native traditions have been good at what might be called "imagining." As Albert Einstein declared (an observation frequently seen on a popular tee-shirt), "Imagination is more important than knowledge."

Western thinking switched priorities at some point for a number of reasons to follow what is known as linear thought away from medieval European attempts to "know the mind of God" via philosophy. Modern science emerged, and a giant clockwork was hopefully set into motion. Chaos—the unknown and imagination—was being deconstructed and reassembled, and a mechanistic model of the universe became the fixing point for scholarly (and eventually popular) consciousness. Linear flight from disorder led directly to quantum theory. This scrambling toward something orderly and manageable has landed right back of the lap of the Great Mystery: chaos, the unknown, and imagination. Einstein, Werner Karl Heisenberg, and many others were forming unheard-of ideas, to the despair of the scientific community.

This is the world, as Fritjof Capra (1982) has noted, where "there is activity, but there are no actors. There are no dancers, there is only the dance" (92). "This is the world where things don't actually exist but have a tendency to exist" (80). This is the world where answers to questions become increasingly tentative as the questions become infinitely more subtle. This is a region of the cosmos familiar to many indigenous taxonomies and to which the Western mind is finally returning, although not without some degree of fear, confusion, and, very rightly, fascination. When I read Capra's description of the "Crisis of Perception" that appears to be afflicting Western societies, it seemed to make perfect sense that culture, identity, gender, and human sexuality would figure prominently in such a crisis.

Where do painful questions of such gravity begin? In considering Western interpretations of the situation, I began by thinking of Newton, Descartes, and Bacon and stopped at the present intersection of time and space, where transplanted societies are given to cooking in microwaves, traveling by the Concord, and communicating by FAX. To me, it seems perfectly understandable that a general sense of proportion—human perception in particular—has been lost in the shuffle as a result of these and other developments in recent Western technology.

Reductionist thinking may serve many purposes, but I'd like to employ the results of this reduction as a contrast to the story that I promised: There was a family in Minneapolis, a Lakota/Ojibway woman (and her mother), her Ojibway husband, and their three children. Beginning in 1986 they often had me over at their house, inviting me to feasts and ceremonies and generally involving me in their family's life. After awhile, it became apparent that one of the reasons they liked having me around was because they were a young couple, my age.

One day, the two women and I were out playing Bingo and winning. The young mother mentioned to me that they liked having me around because they knew that I brought good luck. And this kind of shocked me because I had only recently started to learn this sort of information in bits and pieces. I knew that many Native people had become homophobic and acquired other forms of intolerance in recent generations, but I did not know that more than a few contemporary people still knew and practiced these traditional teachings. The young mother further told me about a prophesy she had learned from some of her elders. I have since found that there are other highly specific prophesies connected to this topic that don't seem to be evident in the scholarly literature but are still rehearsed among Native communities.

The teaching shared with me stated that "at a time directly preceding a great cleansing in society, the *winkte* and *koshkalaka* would reappear, as out of the grass. Not just a few, but in great numbers." Regardless of the kinds of oppressions and sufferings that have faced Native communities, Aboriginal people are seeing this prediction borne out and have taken great care to work cooperatively with it. We have not been trying to force the issue because there is a time and a schedule of events that we might not be able to understand and with which we must cooperate. Trying to force the issue, or being militant, is not only out of keeping with the teachings we have been given but it could also be considered disrespectful. In addition, we may upset the balance of something that is supposed to progress of its own accord.

I do not want to descend into a Neptunian miasma (as my friend Hortense would say) and enter the realm of unordinary reality, paranormal psychology, or indiscriminate mineral worship, but because I briefly raised the subject of quantum theory I might as well risk examining the subject of the irrational. Absent from much of the general dialogue about contemporary two-spirit people, in contrast to the historical record of the "berdache," is the topic of spiritual experience and understanding, which continues to be relevant.

The dissonant paradigms with which we deal can be painful and difficult. The fact is that little discussion has been devoted to spiritual experiences, as a number of people have noted, and we need to look at these ideas as they pertain to the lives of contemporary people. An academician may wish to assert that there are no more classic "berdaches," that there are simple remnants of Native cultures, and that Native people, in large part, no longer know who they are nor know their traditions. These rather narrow Western parameters and definitions mark a startling contrast to the ways that many Natives regard their lives and origins. Our methods of measuring may not exactly mesh with what academia regards as acceptable or empirical knowledge, but we do continue with our dreams, prophesies, and other esoteric knowledge.

Many of us two-spirit people continue to talk about our experiences among ourselves, although it is certainly not an everyday activity. To this day, unordinary reality is not an unordinary part of our existence. For many of us, it remains a meaningful part of our lives; we pay close attention to events, and they do not derive from drug-induced states or as results of alcoholic hazes. It is beyond the ability of acceptable scientific practice to fit these ideas within existing constructs.

The term *two-spirit,* which has come into recent popular usage, originated in Northern Algonquin dialect and gained first currency at the third annual spiritual gathering of gay and lesbian Native people that took place near Winnipeg in 1990. What we who chose this designation understood is that *niizh manitoag* (two-spirits) indicates the presence of both a feminine and a masculine spirit in one person.

More essentially, it may refer to the fact that each human is born because a man and a woman have joined in creating each new life; all humans bear imprints of both, although some individuals may manifest both qualities more completely than others. In no way does the term determine genital activity. It does determine the qualities that define a person's social role and spiritual gifts. Some traditional teachers have expressed pointed concern that the term is being grossly equated with the concept of "homosexual." These teachers rigorously remind us that there is no resemblance between the two concepts.

Thus, the sudden appearance of Native people claiming two-spirit identity should not be interpreted as a strategy for acquiring political power (if it were a strategy, it would be a silly one). Likewise, it would be a mistake to think that this is a recently developed fiction used to resituate individuals into tribal communities that sometimes reject them on the grounds that homosexuality is a malady "brought by the white man." What is happening, actually, is that we are remembering again who we are and that our identities can no longer be used as a weapon against us. It is once again a source of our healing.

Reference Cited

Capra, Fritjof. 1982. *The Turning Point: Science, Society, and the Rising Culture.* New York: Bantam.

13

Navajo Warrior Women:

An Ancient Tradition in a Modern World

Carrie H. House (Navajo/Oneida)

I was born in the spring, when baby eaglets make their first cry. My parents named me after my mom's side of the family. Carrying her mother, father, sister, and brothers' names, I am of Navajo/Oneida descent. Fortunately, Navajo (Diné) and Oneida are matriarchal. I am born of the Kiyaá'aanii (Towering Rock House Clan), born for the Turtle Clan (Oneida). My maternal grandfather's clan is Tsenjikini (Honey-combed Rock People); my paternal grandfather's clan is Tl'izi lani' (Many Goats). My ancestral homeland is called T'eel Ch'init'ii (The Area Where Marsh Cattails Are Coming Out in Rows). I explain these things because they give my indigenous identity, who I am and where I come from. I am proud and happy to be who I am. My life is blessed.

I have incorporated the dualities of my grandparents, parents, and eight siblings and also grasped, admired, and shared qualities of our holy Diné deities. It is a joy that my family is very accepting of me, my partner, friends, and relatives.

I will share some parts of my life because I feel it is valid to do so in a world of shiny objects and change. Some people study things of the past and think that cultural traditions and ecosystems are lost or preserved at museums (as if lost). But I hope my constant evolutions of past, present, and futuristic ways can show an understanding of balance, no matter how chaotic or beautiful my life is.

As a child, my little natural self took me to the top of a pickup truck and broke my arm (at age two), almost burned a house (at age six), retreated to the mountains for almost a full day (at age five), and played football, which resulted in broken or dislocated bones. After high school I decided to attend a university in Montana, about a thousand miles from home. I went from being part of a majority to being part of a minority in an unaccustomed environment—an educational institution. After five years I dropped out as an undergraduate student in natural resources conservation and involved myself in making nature and wildlife films and videos, fighting forest and range fires, and writing poetry. Another factor in leaving school was my homesickness. It took me about seven years of fighting fires, freelancing film and video production, participating in various biological studies and experiments, and sporadically visiting home before I settled in my own home among relatives. The forces of nature and dreams made me realize the true importance of home. While I was away from home I shared with friends a reverence of family and homeland. It was not until I met Deban, my former partner, that I felt capable of establishing a home, however.

Now I am back in school, studying construction technology and electronic publishing. It is a perfect time in my life to prosper in an emotional, spiritual, physical, environmental, and creative way. It was a unique acculturation experience for Deban (a non-Native) and me. The community gradually gathered and accepted the fact that we renovated and built a house, garden, and studio for ourselves and our extended family. Patience will determine our outcome in terms of the community's acceptability, but whether they liked doing so or not, people had to deal with our presence.

For many years, research had been conducted among and about my people by non-Indian people and, for the most part, they lacked the context for proper interpretation. They have misunderstood or failed to grasp many meanings in our lives. For example, although some people function according to restrictive Western notions of gender and sexuality, not all do. Outsiders not understanding the differences have led to misrepresentations in writings about us. At this time, American Indians are making important and positive gains in the recovery of their voices, lands, artifacts, and traditions once thought to be lost. Young Indian people who find themselves outside the gender roles proscribed by an alien Western culture have begun to seek the new-old paths provided by the ways of their people. Perhaps it may some day prove valuable to them, as well as to the world at large, to have access to alternative ways of seeing themselves in other than the persuasive Western perspectives surrounding so-called gender roles and sexuality.

The entities of the universe and family are my life. Of extreme importance are my parents because their life experience provided happiness, strength, love, knowledge, and generosity. These are true gifts of our ancestors and creator. My mother inherited land, objects, language, and respect. She was raised in the transitional era of automobiles, wagons, cameras, tribal politics (her father was the Navajo president and councilman), cultural activities, and Catholicism. My father inherited gifts similar to my mother's. He was also raised in that transitional era but had a nomadic ability to experience his Navajo and Oneida cultures. Both parents worked most of their lives for their families. My mother had various jobs with the tribe, and one of them was working with the *Navajo Times,* my inspiration for travel adventures and the source of my interest in media, photography, people, and land issues. My father served in the Korean conflict as a U.S. Marine and in the Army National Guard. His occupations varied, but for the most part he worked at a natural gas compressor station, the source of my interest in machinery, natural fuels, welding, heavy equipment, and two-way radios. Contributions from my parents' family and relatives are enormous, resulting in my duality, spirituality, and balance.

Our oral traditions acknowledge that the he-shes and she-hes (those who hold in balance the male and female, female and male aspects of themselves and the universe) were among the greatest contributors to the well-being and advancement of their communities. They were (and we are) the greatest probers into the ways of the future, and they quickly assimilated the lessons of changing times and people. Recent studies into the lives of contemporary she-hes and he-shes have recovered models or near models of this rich, inventive, reverential, and highly productive approach to keeping balance within a society viewed as an extension of nature.

Many non-Native outsiders, and unfortunately indigenous Native insiders are desecrating our artifacts, our children, and our way of life. I feel offended when people think of the term *tribal* as having to do with horrible, disgusting warfare or scalping activities. Many of these attributes were introduced, in magnitude, to North American tribes by Euro-Americans. For example, it is considered a battle when the U.S. Cavalry obliterates millions of indigenous Native children, women, and men, yet it is considered a massacre when a couple of hundred soldiers die at the hands of a few "guerrilla" indigenous Native warriors (composed of women and men). If I were to defend our ancestral land from encroaching settlers and other government agencies I, too, would possess many technical devices: cameras, assault weapons, computers, and, most important, spirituality.

My female relations (in the past and present) have feminine war names that translate to "warrior-girl" (*baa'* or *dlininh*). "Girl" can be applied to an elder woman. There are occasions in our clan system where a younger person would call a seventy-year-old man "grandson." This fluidity in the use of gender-marking terms demonstrates how our society accommodates the shifts in a person's social status over time (whether within a single day or over the course of a lifetime).

I was pained by Epple's discussion of *sa'ąh naagháí bik'eh hózhǫ́* in Washington, D.C., and her inappropriate separation of elements of *sa'ąh naagháí bik'eh hózhǫ́* (1993). Use of the words for this sacred entity should not be heard or seen in an analytical academic context, yet it occurs again in her chapter in this book. It is disrespectful, especially without an offering, and I wonder about the intention of her informants. It is not appropriate to have our creation stories and mythology challenged with Western scientific theories.

As for science, nature, and *nádleeh,* as presented here it is all too simple. Humans are on the brink of extinction. Without our indicator species and/or balancing factors we will either be nonexistent or we will transform (if we have not done so already). No one sex or gender is elite, but they are equal, just as First Woman and First Man. Should there be another conflict or separation of the sexes, then possibly the *nádleeh* (male-female or female-male) will pursue the Creator's divine powers of balance.[1]

There are taboos associated with almost anything in the cosmos. The roles of *nádleeh* are special. I feel and instinctively know in my heart that it is not strictly forbidden for different genders to be partners with different genders—our oral traditions play these roles out—if one can see beyond superstitions and Western perspectives.

I would like to thank all of the people I have met on this sanctified journey. I hope my thoughts will aid other endeavors. Before the first Wenner-Gren Conference in Washington, D.C., I had never shared information pertaining to Navajo *nádleeh.* I have now shared some information and grown to understand that doing so takes great offerings, otherwise mentioning the sacred beings and concepts of *nádleeh* could be a blasphemy. I cannot analyze, interrogate, or decipher these aspects of my culture when the true understanding is kept sacred and sanctified among my people. How else would our culture persevere? What can I share and expect to be returned to the vast population of Native people whose lives, land, and language are severely endangered? I hope those who read this will also understand, respect, and appreciate the private lives that encompass our community.

Hagoonee' (we are parting in a mutual agreement that the dialogue will continue).[2] Thank you.

Notes

1. This is in reference to the Navajo origin story that explains how the *nádleeh* were able to resolve the conflict between women and men that had led to their moving to separate sides of a river (Haile 1981). The first lesson learned from the separation, according to the *nádleeh,* was that men and women should not live in separate worlds but rather together, cooperatively. Another lesson pertinent to this book is that the *nádleeh* are available to Navajo women and men in times of intersexual discord, as well as on other occasions. When there is chaos or confusion, the *nádleeh* (as cultural entities) come into the community to bring order and clarity.

2. Coeditor Wesley Thomas's note on *hagoonee': Hagoonee'* has generally been translated into English as "goodbye." In practical, traditional, everyday Navajo use and understanding of the word, however, it conveys a mutual agreement that the dialogue will be continuing.

References Cited

Epple, Carolyn. 1993. "Another 'Berdache' Headache; or, *Nádleehí* in Navajo Worldview: Implications for Western Constructs." Paper presented at "Revisiting the 'North American Berdache' Empirically and Theoretically." 92d annual meeting of the American Anthropological Association, Washington, D.C.

Haile, Berard. 1981. *Women versus Men: A Conflict of Navajo Emergence.* Lincoln: University of Nebraska Press.

★ ★ 14

I Ask You to Listen to Who I Am

Doyle V. Robertson (Sisseton/Wahpeton Dakota)

Each morning I open my door and survive in a world of ignorance and bigotry that attempts to deny me the right to be who I am. But you will find little self-pity in me. I am learning the advantages of attempting to become the best of both cultures I claim as a part of me while grounding myself without the false securities sometimes found when one is surrounded by others who seem to be the same.

I am a modern-day *winkte* and possess a singular voice that needs to be heard.[1] You may be asking yourself, "How does he arrive at claiming to be a *winkte?*" My only reply is, "I know it is so."

I am Dakota. Sisseton/Whapeton is the band of my father and where my enrollment lies.

I am Scottish. Both my mother and father carry the blood of these Celtic people.

I am loved. My partner since 1981, Greg Jeresek, is a gay-identified Caucasian of Slavic descent. It is important to bring this up because being loved has had a way of liberating me to explore these previously undefined areas of sexuality and culture. The path of discovering my role in the circle has been less lonely with Greg walking at my side. The insights and support he has provided have been important in giving voice to my own thoughts.

Most of my experience of being Native in America is not being Native. I am not unique in that experience, but I am clear in how it has impacted me. My parents worked overtime (both literally and figuratively) to ensure that I and my siblings were fully assimilated into the dominant culture. As a product of the "boarding school system," my father convinced my mother that the racism that shaped his life would not be passed down into another generation. Their job of separating us from our Native heritage was made easier by the tragic auto-accident death of my full-blood Grandma Jane when I was a little over ten. Before that time, there were trips on a regular basis to the reservation at Sisseton and the hills of Veblen, South Dakota, where what seemed to me in my child's mind countless Natives were introduced as my relatives. At an early age I was already so assimilated that I had no context in which to place these people, and in fact I was already so far removed from a Native experience that my earliest recollections of my interactions with my Dakota relations was of *not* interacting.

My first *wacipi* (pow-wow) memory is one of being frightened, in tears, locking myself in the family car—terrified of the colorful people in full regalia who in movies killed people like me. What a horrible image I now think that is and proof of how powerful internalized racism can be. Of course, I now can also laugh at the fun my relatives must have had scaring me through the car window when they realized how frightened I was of them. I'm sure to this day my father is teased "about the time Doyle locked himself in the car to get away from the bad Indians."

And then there is my gay Uncle Ole.[2] His being different was never talked about, just accepted. He played an important but unacknowledged role in my life; but as a child he was relegated to the eccentric but lovable person who single-handedly kept the household together whenever my mother had a child. And another. He stayed right in our home and cooked, cleaned, disciplined, and taught us so my mom could rest and spend quality time with the new infant. He stayed as long as he was needed or until he was needed more somewhere else. It was one of his definitions of the *winkte* tradition acted out in his place and time. So what role was it that I now know he played in my life? That of giving me the courage to blaze my own trail, redefining the *winkte* of today without the active support of the tribal community. He represented his generation's manifestation of cultural continuity within that period of change, just as I am attempting to do today.

Cultural change is and always has been reflected in many ways, and one clue of that is found in the language of the Dakota people. In my late-life attempts to learn my Native tongue, Brent Derowitsch, a language advisor, relates one breakdown of the word *winkte* as *wi*(n) (woman) and *kte* (to kill). *Kte* has little significance to the meaning of the word when it stands alone, but it is thought to relate to a ritual dance in which the *winkte* played an important role. In conversations that Brent had with my Uncle Ole, he noticed my uncle referred to himself as a *winkta—kta* being a verb auxiliary meaning "will" or "shall" or the old verb (currently unused) translated as to "wait for." When Brent went to his Dakota language instructor at the University of Minnesota to further his research on the usage of the word *winkte,* this elderly Dakota woman related, with much discomfort, the verb *iwinkta.* In the Dakota language, *i* is often added to a verb to make a noun; but in this case, *i* was added to the noun *winkta* to form the verb *iwinkta* (to glory in or be proud of). She then abruptly closed the discussion by stating that the verb was not in use anymore. It is easy for me to speculate on and conclude why that is so.

I grew up always feeling different but working very hard to pretend that I was not. I worked hard to achieve good grades (I graduated from high school with high honors and went on to a private college); to make money (I learned early in life that money was given for hard work, and it also was a necessary evil to survive in our dominant culture); to get attention (I was a middle child and found my attention requirements fulfilled due to a gift of music that led me, at sixteen, to tour Europe, singing classical Western music while Lakota relations were dying to keep their traditions alive at Wounded Knee); and to fit in (I found that being gay in America was better if you pretended you were not).

In my attempt to stop pretending and try to fit in, I left all that I knew—my family, friends, the changing seasons, and the places where I spent my formative years—and found myself in California, working once again to not be different. But the Grandfathers had yet to teach me that being different was my gift. One of those teachings turned out to be Greg. It was in the gay subculture of Los Angeles that I met the person with whom I would share my life. And what attracted Greg to me? He said I was different.

It is at this point the path I was walking became familiar, yet unknown, like a forgotten past. I don't mean to imply that I immersed myself in my Dakota culture, but I did start to seek and achieve balance in my life. I no longer feared the Native side of my makeup and began to see the power and beauty of the ceremonies and medicines. Another of the many steps I took was to return to Minnesota. Greg and I spent three years negotiating the logistics of our relationship, and by 1984 I was living on our farm in a rural area of central Minnesota. It was there that I began to reestablish an appreciation of nature that I had experienced as a child. I gardened, canned, and roamed the farm, where we still live. I opened a small pizza business on Main Street in a community of six hundred people. Retired farmers and other locals bet their pocket change that "the faggot wouldn't last six months." Six months have passed twenty-two times over, and I have owned and operated the pizza shop for more than ten years. As the day-to-day details of running a business have changed, so, too, has my perception of my role in being there.

It was early in this period I read Walter Williams's *The Spirit and the Flesh*, which offered validation of many of my inner feelings and a vehicle for reconnecting with the traditions of sexual acceptance in my Native cultural history. I began to believe I am special—not because some anthropologist I did not know (at that time) told me in a book I had read that I was historically a "healer" or a "medicine man," but special because forces outside of me and within this human realm I inhabit tell me that it is so. And I believe it is so.

One beautiful summer day in the recent past, for example, I was feeling a little down and blue. Mice were plentiful in the fields that year, and I was often visited by my winged brother, a hawk. Because I was a bit depressed that day, I decided that I needed to soar with my brother who seemed to always come when I called for him. So I called. And called again. No hawk. What I didn't need was to drag my spirit further down by dwelling on the fact my brother wasn't hungry, so I determined to take delight in the environment that surrounded me. As I walked the yard, I was struck by how the plants, shrubs, and trees Greg and I had planted reminded me of my maternal grandparents' farmstead in South Dakota. Because they were the non-Native side of the family, it brought to my mind the Scottish blood previously mentioned and what totems may have been important to the tribal people of Scotland. The "good luck" that Anglo culture assigns to four-leaf clovers stems (I assume) from an old tradition of possibly viewing the plant as a totem, much as I viewed my brother hawk. So I inwardly claimed that ancient Celtic tradition in the only way I knew, by softly humming, and then beginning to sing, "I'm looking over a four-leaf clover." Before the first line of the song was completed, I spotted a four-leaf clover at my feet. The Grandfathers taught me a valuable lesson that day about claiming my whole being, the mixture of Native and Anglo influences, in creating my special path to being a *winkte* (*iwinkta*) in the late twentieth century.

I am a digger of the sacred stone of my people. It has become a solitary quest to remove the stone needed to make the pipes that my two-spirit sisters and brothers will one day be shown in their dreams to carry. I entered into this personal pact in a convoluted fashion. Being the consummate caretaker that I can sometimes be, when a two-spirit brother from the North was told he was last in line for the making of his pipe unless he could provide his own stone for the maker I immediately agreed to get the stone for him because "I live in Minnesota and it is not that far away to Pipestone." Had I been raised with any information on the traditions, I would have offered my condolences and kept my head bowed and my mouth shut. When I followed through on my promise and went to Pipestone, I had been briefed on the difficulty of my task but not the enormity. Twelve feet of granitelike quartzite covered by four feet of topsoil was the frosting that covered the prize of the pipestone beneath. Only hand tools are allowed for the removal of the sacred stone.

I was able to retrieve a quality piece of stone for my friend, but more important I received my own gift of a place that has become my prayer lodge and honor site. My pit has become a refuge and another sign that the path that I am walking is uniquely my own. To dig the stone one must show proof of one's Native heritage, yet the first question asked by tourists and scholars alike is, "Are you Indian?" To justify my place in any setting seems to be a constant in my life, yet every time I'm confronted with that reality, it doesn't get any easier. The oral traditions state pipestone represents the blood of the People. I know this also to be a truth. Much like a woman in her cycle went away to her menstrual hut to bleed on the earth and so renew each, so, too, do I find it necessary for the earth to renew herself with my blood. There has not been a time that I have not bled as a payment for the work I do. I am extremely thankful that the Ancestors, unlike humans, do not require proof of my heritage to accept the gifts that I give and receive from that special place.

I am telling my story as an alternative to the limited definition of who I am that was placed upon me by the dominant culture. The Dakota are a people who rely on an individual's vision as a foundation for the manifestations of their life. One follows the path that is shown to them. As such, the vision is the path and the path becomes you on your given vision or quest. It is as my uncle, now more than seventy, says about the reservation community's reaction to him as being, "Oh, that's just Ole." An acknowledgment of their awareness regarding his difference and an expression of their acceptance of him are rolled into that one simple phrase.

My uncle's given name is not Ole, nor is mine "the pizza man." But I am proud to wear that label when I see how owning a restaurant is an adaptation of the *winkte* tradition. The stories of the Dakota tell of how one of the *winkte*'s role was to feed the people. My uncle fulfills that role in his way by cooking the community meals for the annual *wacipi* and bringing soup to the shut-in elderly on the reservation at Sisseton. Those are manifestations of the *winkte* role in appropriate places and times. I live in a non-reservation, predominantly Caucasian community and still feed the people, but I receive payment for the work that I do in my place and time. I am proud to be "the pizza man" when I see the goodwill that has been cultivated in my community because of the work I do.

Every time that homophobia, racism, and ignorance are confronted head-on, there is a battle, and I am in the trenches of that war by standing up on the Main Street of a small town as an openly "queer Indian." But those words are only an identifier others place on me, they are not the essence of who I am. The hostility and hatred that was displayed toward me has waned, but there is always a strong and silent undercurrent that every once in awhile will strike out and catch me by surprise. My response to those attacks is to stand firm in my beliefs, express my opinion, and then trust the relationships I have established with others who have more "validity" that can help in allowing them to speak out. In spite of it all, after more than ten years of attempting to live my life in an open and out fashion with all the integrity I can muster, the simple phrase, "Oh, that's just the pizza man" is my current community's adaptation of the reaction the reservation gives to my uncle.

I find it a bit problematic that there seems to be an insistence in defining two-spirit people in terms of the past. Two-spirit is a term contemporary Natives, myself included, have chosen for ourselves as an identifier. I do hold a fear that we may be resolving the elimination of one definition—"berdache" [sic]—but walking a similar path of misunderstandings in our approach to defining the term *two-spirit*. I would caution both my Native brothers and sisters and those in the dominant culture to avoid having to have this same discussion at some point in the future. We are not always surrounded by tribal communities that accept us as an intrinsic part of the whole. Many of us find ourselves alone in a hostile world. I am thankful that on my walk I have found Greg as a partner, friend, and guide in creating our own understandings of old traditions. This allows me to walk my path with pride and courage. He has helped show me the truth of the spirit being found in the souls of all individuals is not limited to those with a darker skin color, nor is it limited by happenstance of birth.

As thankful as I am for those who have walked before me, I wonder why their path is more important than those my two-spirit relations walk today. The opportunity to speak out as a *winkte* in the late twentieth century is an honor, and I trust that my words will bring courage to a future seeker. I thank those teachers who have prepared me to believe that the thoughts I have and the words I speak are valid. It will become more important to open the dialogue of spirit within the bodies of all races as we attempt to heal the world, and I am proud to be taking part in that discussion. And to my ancestors, who have placed me here as a mixed-blood two-spirit, may my life bring honor to their choice.

I am proud to be a first-generation, off-the-reservation, mixed-blood *winkte*. I am attempting to discover how all the aforementioned influences (and more) play out in my life. I am growing weary of never being "Native enough" or "gay enough" or "white enough." What I do not need added to the mix is being limited by what, in my life experience, is the meaningless word "berdache."

I am not, nor do I want to be, the stereotype of a cross-dressing, man/woman, sexually anal-passive individual best suited to sewing, beading, and carrying in wood for the fire on which to cook supper.

I am Dakota.
I am Scottish.
I am loved.
I am different.
I am a pizza man.
I am a digger of the sacred stone.
I am a faggot.
I am special.
I am *winkte.*
I am two-spirit.
I am Doyle.

Notes

1. I would like to respond to remarks by a reviewer of an earlier version of this chapter who felt that it should be deleted from this collection be-

cause of my "cultural location." There are, and will be, many people of both races and various backgrounds who may question my validity to make a contribution. How is it that a mixed-blood (who "does not live in the context of a traditional society"), nonactivist (isolated from the gay community that many alternative-sex and gendered people take for granted) "gay Indian" (as opposed to "berdache") is given the voice to speak? My reply is that I represent only one of the hundreds of two-spirits who are never allowed the opportunity to speak because we do not fit into the neat little compartments that make it easier to be "objects of study" rather than the complex and varied individuals that we are. I wonder whether a self- and/ or tribal-identified *winkte* removed from his "traditional community" in, say, 1834 would be any less of a *winkte*. The same question applies to me today as a first-generation, off-the-reservation, mixed-blood *winkte,* and I should not be written off as invalid. I hope that I can open this debate into uncomfortable areas so I know that I have spoken well.

2. I recently had my uncle read this chapter to receive his permission to describe him in the manner I had already committed to paper. When asked what he thought regarding my identification of him as "gay," he responded, "Oh, that's okay." Knowing him well enough to understand he needed to be pressed to give a complete answer, I asked again if it was acceptable. His second response was that he found the word *gay* to be "neither descriptive nor offensive."

Reference Cited

Williams, Walter. 1986. *The Spirit and the Flesh: Sexual Diversity in American Indian Culture.* Boston: Beacon Press. Reprint 1991, with a new preface.

★ ★ 15

A "Berdache" by any Other Name . . .
Is a Brother, Friend, Lover, Spouse:

Reflections on a Mescalero Apache Singer of Ceremonies*

Claire R. Farrer

To Begin

The business of names is a complex one. Bernard Second, the "ber-dache" [*sic*] of my title, was a Mescalero Apache man who was also a holy man, a ritual specialist, a religious leader, and a healer for his peo-ple—those who live on the Mescalero Apache Indian Reservation in south central New Mexico. Some also called him a shaman and a med-icine man, terms he despised as much as he despised "berdache." Off the reservation, he was often referred to as a philosopher or an ecumen-ical priest. He was a man who rejected all titles, save two: *gutą́ą́ł* (sing-er [of ceremonies]) and *hastíín* (adult male person).

Similarly, Bernard's sexuality defied categorization. He was an uncle to scores, brother to several, friend to many, social or religious father to tens (and perhaps biological father to one, although he is not so named on the birth certificate), lover to some (males and females), and spouse to one. Once (in 1991), when walking along the Sacramento River in northern California with Terry Tafoya, the eminent Taos/Warm

---

Editors' note: Unlike the previous chapters, this story is told as a combination biog-raphy of Bernard Second and autobiography of Farrer's relationship with Second. She makes no effort to speak for Second and says so. She speaks about him from her point of view and the multifaceted, long-term relationship they had. In this regard her essay pulls together our interest in recovering anthropological narratives on two-spirits (Part 1), our concerns with terminology (Part 2), and our concern with "voice" as reflected in the other essays in Part 3. Farrer brings these ideas together and pro-vides a good transition to the next section.

Springs psychologist, I said Bernard was a member of the Apachean third gender, *ndéʔisdzan* (man-woman). But the more we talked the more we realized the idea of a third gender was too impoverished. We experimented, unsatisfactorily in my mind, with ideas of a fourth and even a fifth gender. Now I believe it is more accurate to state that Bernard was a multigendered person, a felicitous term I borrow from Sue-Ellen Jacobs (1993).

Bernard knew much more than did any regular man or woman as a consequence of being a multigendered person. He was identified as being special from the age of seven, when he began his training to be a singer and linguist.[1] Only as he aged did he realize he was super-gendered. He was consciously taught men's things and knew them impeccably: how to hunt, skin, and butcher animals; how to protect his family—especially his sisters in his matrilineage; how to do morning prayers; and how to read the sky. He also was taught, and was expert in, women's things: how to weave a basket, how to make a cradle for a newly born baby and how properly to place the infant in that cradle, how to do fine stitchery, and how to prepare food and clothing. He never offered an explanation of why he was multigendered, saying only that he did men's and women's work because "the Vision [that he had as a seven-year-old boy] told me my people would come to me one day and say, 'O! My Brother! Show me how to do the old things.' And they *do!*" (Friday, February 7, 1975).

He also learned how to do the things associated with Power, whether it was to sing a ceremony, heal a broken bone, and see over a long-distance or tell time, season, and place from close observations of the night sky.[2] It is a positive gift to be multigendered but also it is a burden for—at least at Mescalero—it means being several different people confined in one body.

Sometimes there were conflicting demands placed upon him, such as when he was expected to be present and act in specific—but changing—roles within a given event. Although he was a master of shifting genders and roles in accordance with the demands of context and situation, it was like trying to accomplish everyday living in a foreign language: it required conscious effort and thought. That concentration, in turn, taxed both his body and mind. After such episodes he usually tried to leave the reservation for a time: a time of being, a time without demands made upon him. When he could not escape the reservation per se, he often escaped into alcohol to flood out the conflict and allow himself simply to be.[3] Other times he would escape mentally, visiting those he loved and cared about; while his physical body remained at Mescalero, his essential self traveled and communicated.[4]

Bernard died, a young man in his early forties, in November 1988. The family refused to allow an autopsy, so no one knows precisely why—in Anglo terms—he died except that he willed himself to do so. He had seriously prepared to die for a year before breathing his last, using the time to tie up as many loose ends as he could and give that counsel he felt was incumbent upon him to give. He was a man of power who had, he knew, flown in the face of Power too many times. The motivations for so doing were inconsequential, he believed, although I thought them very high-minded indeed. As Bernard said once, "You don't fuck with Power with impunity." When, time and again, he answered yet another call in an area for which he had been trained but in which he had exceeded the performance-time given him by Power, he did so knowing he was tempting Power's retaliation and that such retribution was sure to cause him pain and grief. Those of us in his family (I am but a fictive, adoptive member) were convinced our illnesses, tragedies, sorrows, or bad luck were just that—luck. Bernard, however, knew them to be Power's way of getting back at him for his disobedience. So he decided to cease endangering his family and to assume all responsibilities himself—and he began his dying process, including meeting with each of us in the family individually to give us instructions for our continuing lives and for his funeral (and, to his biological brother and sister, instructions for my funeral as well, as I learned only after his death).

It is not upon death and dying that I wish to concentrate, however.[5] Here I empirically explore one instance that involved both of us. This one instance does not always paint me in a good light, but so be it—it was accurately recorded. The instance does shed light on Bernard's life, the life of a man who qualified as a "berdache" in many ways. Yet, in many other ways, the term does not describe the range and depth that was the person, Bernard Second. Here I briefly comment on those aspects of the man that confound the term as it is generally understood and has been used in anthropological literature.

Bernard did not cross-dress. He always self-identified as male in sexuality, even when enacting various gender roles or activities associated with those roles. He spoke cryptically sometimes but never "backward"; rather, he was eloquent in several languages. He did not enact a woman's role as would a woman even when doing—"women's things." Although he lived sometimes in what Anglo-America terms homosexual relationships, he never automatically assumed the woman's role; who did what in his relationships was always a matter of mutual negotiation. Although he lived sometimes in what Anglo-America terms heterosexual relationships, he never automatically assumed the man's role; who did what in his relationships was always a matter of mutual negotiation. Whatever he did in any facet of his life, he did as a man (*hastíín*); but he was not limited by male genitalia. He neither celebrated nor denied his multigendered and multisexual life—rather, it was simply his life.[6]

One further caveat is in order: I am not an expert on the people referenced by the infelicitous term "berdache," nor do I consider myself expert on much of anything else. As Bernard used to tell me, "Power has given you insight." I have learned a great deal through trying to turn insight into understanding, but in the end it is only *my* understanding.[7] I do not presume to speak, in general or in particular, for the Mescalero/Chiricahua/Lipan Apache people with whom I have lived and worked since 1964. I relate here only what, through Bernard, I experienced and how I have come to interpret that experience. This caveat is necessary, I believe, for I put little stock into what non-Indian, so-called experts have to say about being Native American or even the Native American experience (if, indeed, there can be a common experience from such a large and diverse population).

From February 1975 until November 1988 I worked—and sometimes lived—with Bernard Second. He was my teacher, brother, friend, and advocate. What little I know I learned primarily from him. Most of the insights bestowed were through him. Because the understanding and discussion are mine alone, they are certainly open to other interpretations.

Our relationship began in 1975 after I had been living at Mescalero for four months. Everyone, from Wendell Chino, the tribal president then and now, to the Mescalero equivalent of the man-on-the-street maintained I should work with Bernard Second. The difficulty was finding him. Only later did I learn that he had been "hiding" from me, several times—to my chagrin—in plain sight. While trying to make contact with him I became acquainted with his wife; she and I remained friends even after their subsequent divorce.

In early February 1975, when my day's agenda had been irrevocably altered without my consent, I stopped by the museum where Mrs. Second worked to have a cup of coffee with her before returning to my house to work on fieldnotes and bake cookies for my daughter and her friends, who usually came to our house after school. It was then that I met Bernard. He was, according to his wife, waiting for me in her office. And so he was.

He indicated that he had called me. I, in the first of what was to become an embarrassingly high number of pig-headed, insight*less* occasions, insisted that my telephone had not rung. We laughed at my literal-mindedness in later years after I had learned to attend to his calls—and even to place a few myself.

I also learned that wintery morning that Bernard had dreamed me, not specifically the physical me but rather that someone was coming with whom he was to work for the rest of his life and who would "carry" certain things for him after his death until the time when they are to be returned to the proper person in the tribe. As a matter of fact, he was upset initially that I am a woman because his sacred knowledge was male knowledge and his dream had included sharing much of that knowledge with the One-Who-Was-Coming, as he thought of me before learning my name. He had assumed he was looking for a man.

I had been introduced at a tribal meeting that occurred while I was still unpacking after my arrival on the reservation and before I thought I had started fieldwork. A summons from Wendell Chino to attend an event, however, was as much a demand then as it is now, and so the boxes were put aside for a time while I attended my first tribal meeting. Bernard and his wife were present at that meeting. He told me, that first day I met him, that he had realized instantly when Wendell Chino introduced me to the assembled people of the tribe four months earlier that I was the one he had dreamed and had been expecting. He also admitted that he could not accept the realization because he was so convinced he was awaiting a man. Therefore, as he put it, he "flew straight into the face of Power" and looked for "signs" before he would allow himself even to speak to me. He was never specific about what those signs were; he told me only that I had said and done things that convinced him that I was indeed the One-Who-Was-Coming. When he was finally convinced, he stopped hiding and called me to him. We began working that very day and continued to work together for almost fifteen years, until his death in November 1988.

I felt as though I was in something like the Twilight Zone early in 1975 at that initial point in our very new relationship. *I* liked to think that my being at Mescalero was the result of very tough negotiations that Wendell Chino, acting on behalf of tribe and council, and I had conducted for eighteen months. I liked to think that *I* had chosen to work there for both intellectual and personal reasons. It was disconcerting to learn I was merely the enlivened pawn in someone's dream. I also liked to think that I was at Mescalero to attend to children's free play as an entrée into culture-specific communication patterns that could then be used in classroom interactions to facilitate learning. I most specifically was *not* at Mescalero to probe esoterica or carry anything for anyone. And I certainly was not prepared to cope with the revelations that were made that first day. Nonetheless, following training at the University of Texas-Austin, I, like any good and proper anthropologist/folklorist, noted our conversation in my field notebook and later transferred the notes to my permanent record-keeping system. And I marveled at Bernard's insistence that I always have my tape recorder with me, for the things he was to tell me were important to remember, and "white people have terrible memories."

Thanks to primary enculturation, my memory is trained. Bernard facilitated that training when he took me to a then-remote part of the reservation and told me that I could keep anything I could remember—the telling of this incident constitutes the burden of this chapter. After that outdoor session, I wrote the notes that I quote here. He later checked those notes and admitted that my mother had indeed done a good job in training my memory. He, however, continued to hone it through the years.

The Data: On Winds and Beliefs (or Lack of the Latter)

Taken from fieldnotes of Saturday, June 28, 1975:

> Bernard led me to a sloping area off the road, but almost in view of it, where we could see . . . [local landmarks]. We sat in a little clearing that was free of debris—no dried leaves, no fresh leaves, no pine needles, no sticks, no stones. It was almost as though it had been swept clean but there were no broom marks on the beige, packed sandy earth. All around us were piles of dead vegetation or newly emerging plants, pebbles, rocks, sticks, evergreen needles. He said we were going to talk—no tape recorder, no pen, no notebook. I am to remember and whatever I remember I may have. White people, he says, rely too much on tools and have forgotten how to use their minds and memories.
>
> He began by telling me he is a homosexual, *ńdéʔisdzan* (man, woman). The term *homosexual* was not used by Bernard; it was my translation of *ńdéʔisdzan*. I would not translate it so now. The term should be spelled

ńdé?isdzan, with the *n* being pronounced with a high tone and a semi-glottal preceding the *i*. The connotations are different for Apaches than for Anglos. For Apaches it is a viable life-style, he says. In the old days there was institutionalized homosexuality. The men were gone for long periods of time, either hunting or warring/raiding. Young boys/men of fourteen to sixteen to mid-twenties who were being taught how to be proper male adults did "women's work," such as getting water, wood, cooking, etc. They also provided sexual services for their "brother-friends" if they so chose. This did not mean either or both were homo-sexual; it was, rather, situational homosexuality. The older man was most likely married, and happily so, while the younger man was expect-ed to marry after having proved himself as a hunter of animals and men. They did not maintain their sexual relationship in camp at home; it was for warpath and hunting. (Some few were true homosexuals, though, just as today.) No older man ever forced himself on a younger one just as no proper Apache raped a woman. [The Spanish and later Anglo records support this assertion.] An Apache man suffers enormous status loss by forcing himself sexually on anyone: "He does not even deserve to be called a man, a human being." [I added in the margins: Brother-friends were partners on hunt/raid, etc.; expected to go to each other's aid; some brother-friends age mates.]

While he was speaking a gentle, warm breeze seemed to be swirling around us, yet the leaves were not moving nor tree branches swaying. I really hadn't noticed it until I felt it change: it got cold and I shivered. I was also bursting with questions, but it certainly wasn't the time to in-terrupt him. He stopped himself and asked me why I didn't believe him. His tone was accusatory. I said, truthfully, I believed him but I had a lot of questions. He said that the questions had taken over my mind so I was no longer paying proper attention. When I was paying attention and while he was speaking the truth, the wind agreed. When I introduced conflicting thoughts, the wind registered the conflict and got cold. So, he said, I'd better ask my questions so I could concentrate again.

Why, I wanted to know, did he ask me to marry him when he's gay? He said it was man-woman talk. But also we were spending a lot of time together and people would talk about that. So I had to be incorporated somehow. If not wife, then sister. It would have been easier for . . . [his wife] whom, I learned, was jealous of me and trying very hard not to be. She knew Bernard was a homosexual when they married; but it was a status marriage for her because of Bernard's position in the religion and because of his "pitiful bit of power." Also, marrying her gained political advantage for . . . [one of Bernard's relatives] who was getting more heavily into tribal politics at the time. As I began thinking that it sound-ed like European royal marriage families, the wind abruptly changed again. B. told me to "Stop that!" I quickly said I believed him, that it sounded like European history and while I was trying to justify myself he told me that a mere person could not fool Power and that I must concentrate on what was being said. It is so rare for him to interrupt me that he really did startle me back to concentration, while I determined to open my mouth when I couldn't keep the thoughts or questions down.

[His wife] is free to take lovers as long as she is discreet. And, he says, she is not jealous of his male lovers—only of me. But co-wives are a fine Apache tradition, even quietly practiced today. He can talk to me, which he needs. But he hopes someday to have children—when he stops singing—and he feels he needs an Apache wife for that.

Now I, too, was very much aware of the wind. I think I knew for the first time what a soft wind meant. Yet I was half unbelieving and kept pushing down the wonder of how we could be rustled by wind when everything around us was still. I remembered reading Casteñada and thinking what a fool he was for not believing his own senses and here I was in the very same kind of situation. Part of me totally accepted the wind phenomenon: after all I'm on an Indian reservation with a powerful man and different rules obtain. But a larger part of me was saying it's crazy and wind doesn't blow just in one tiny spot, let alone change according to belief or lack of it. And it got cold again. Before B. could chastise me, I said I *was* trying very hard but all this was very new to me and extremely difficult to comprehend. He said, almost gently, that I should *believe*, not try to understand. Understanding may come later.

. . . Being homosexual doesn't automatically mean you should be a singer or shaman or holy man or medicine man. He named several singers who were/are married and who have children. It is wrong, he says, for . . . [a young boy's] mother to push him into being a singer just because he's effeminate and probably will be gay.

Bernard began talking about the time when he was seven years old and saw his life spread before him in dreams. He saw two paths: one led to being married and having children, living to a ripe age, and being respected but unimportant. The other path was a path of lonesomeness; he would die young, never have children of his own but all his people would call him father, and he would be a man of power. There were things for the tribe someone had to do. He felt compelled to follow the second path eve[n] though it saddened him even as a child.

His words were so powerful and evocative that I seemed to feel the anguish he faced; I felt sorry for the little boy he'd been for such a short time. It was as though I was seeing through his little boy eyes into a log hut with old people and parents and siblings and knowing, feeling, I was going to surpass even my singer-grandfathers and experiencing the overwhelming loneliness. I was almost crying when I was shocked to discover the wind, feeling like a warm feather, was stroking my cheeks *from different directions*. Bernard said, "Now you are paying attention!"

. . . Bernard has a hard time calling me Ginger [my nickname], he said, because the male Ginger who died young was Bernard's love and lover. His voice catches just talking about him. He feels it is ironic that I, who am close to him in many ways, am also Ginger. It is also ironic because I'm white. He mused more to himself than me I thought, that maybe that was a reason why he thought of marrying me.

. . . [He related another incident from his past I do not discuss here.] And the wind threatened to be a little tornado or cyclone as it blew up dust devils that danced around us, this time swirling in several directions through the leaves on the ground around us. When he calmed down, so did the wind. It stopped entirely when I asked why Power was letting me understand; I was no longer not believing the wind's behavior but I, to be truthful, wasn't really believing it either. Bernard got almost indignant when he said that I didn't understand *anything;* Power has simply given me insight—and only a little of that. I seemed then to see me, again through Bernard's eyes, and sensed his disappointment last Fall when he realized the one he'd expected and with whom he was to work was not only white but also a woman and further a woman with a child and no brothers or husband. More work for him. It was uncanny, but I believed I felt the wind caressing a validation to my thoughts and "vision."

. . . I seemed to feel the wind change and thought I'd better say what was on my mind before I was told to pay attention again. So I asked how come he was drinking when he had to sing. He said beer is not really drinking and that his people used to make *tiswin* [mild, corn beer] when they could *"get"* corn (meaning raid or maybe trade) and that the old singers drank *tiswin* so he could drink beer. . . .

Then he began talking of the book he wants us to do "the Foreword" and he seems to be in a hurry to do the taping for it. He says he will die young and he "doesn't have much time." . . .

. . . A light rain began to fall and Bernard interpreted it as being a blessing . . .

. . . Lightning struck nearby and Bernard rose to pray. His power is from lightning.

The Discussion

Gender and sex are so deeply embedded in English behavior and language that those of us who are native speakers of the language have a difficult time with languages where such considerations are irrelevant. The Athapaskan languages, in which the Apachean languages and

Navajo fall, are languages where there are no gender-specific pronouns and where gender is not coded in nouns either. For instance, in the fieldnotes material just quoted, I had no way to translate ńdéʔisdzan other than as homosexual—a totally inappropriate designation. Now I would translate it literally as man-woman, or metaphorically as two-spirit, or use Jacobs's term, multigendered. In Mescalero, such verbal gymnastics are unnecessary because there is neither gender nor sex attributed to any pronoun or noun. When it is important to know the gender or sex of an individual, that information is made available from context or through additional words or phrases. These linguistic differences mean that gender, an emotionally charged issue in mainstream America, takes on very different coloration in the Native American communities with which I am familiar.

Gender is an issue where there is cross-cultural difficulty; yet, it is much easier to discuss gender than it is to say meaningful things about terminology for societal roles, such as that of "berdache." I have often wondered about the utility of using an Anglicized pronunciation of a French word—borrowed from North Africans who took it from Persians—to describe a Native American phenomenon and have wondered whether it even adequately described the Northern Plains and Great Lakes people to whom the word was first applied. As the term has been used and misused in English in both scholarly and popular literature, it seems to have lost all luster and become almost a synonym for "different," with little, if any, understanding of the role(s) of a person so characterized in any given culture, let alone the rarity of the phenomenon.

I do not now (and did not ever) think of Bernard Second as a "berdache," although he did many things that are included in the repertoire of what it has said people so termed do. But he also did *not* do many things people so termed are supposed to do. At the same time, there is no doubt that he was a very special man indeed and that he had abilities far different from those encountered among most people—whether or not they are Mescalero Apache Reservation residents.

The adult residents (and even many of the children) of Mescalero all acknowledged that Bernard Second was a man of power, but many were unaware of his enacted sexual expressions even while knowing that he was a repository of information about both men's and women's things, especially as they had been done in the past. This knowledge did not lead to a need to characterize him or to apply any special term to him, other than that of a Man of Power. The love affair with labeling and classification seems to me to be a peculiarly Western one that has no particular appeal for Native Americans, at least not for the Mescalero.

Nonetheless, rejecting titles and classifications, as Bernard did during his lifetime, still leaves me, the anthropologist/folklorist, with a problem of how to communicate the specialness of an extraordinary person. It was Bernard's stated intent that such communication was necessary; in fact, it accounted in large measure for my association with him and for his insistence that I record almost everything he told me. Bernard was a man with charisma, and those who knew him realized his specialness even when they did not fully comprehend what he did. I have published a solution to this cross-cultural problem of understanding that is working—at least for me for the present (Farrer 1991). The solution involves a theoretical construct that I call "chiasm."

Chiasm is a complex phenomena (plural intended). It can be a person, place, event (including speech and music events), or performative (Austin 1975), as well as be performed or enacted, or it can simply exist in situ. For example, powerful singers of ceremonies and powerful medicine people can be, and are, chiasms at Mescalero. Similarly, caves, owls, visions, and the girls' puberty ceremonial are also chiasms, as are a host of other things.

When a chiasm is perceived, people are able to see simultaneously that which is before them, its structure, alternatives to it, and what it potentiates. People see this present lived reality (what we usually call the everyday), the special event or person before them, the relationship of lived reality to That Which Is and That Who Sustains All, as well as potential reorderings or rearrangements of the present lived reality. A chiasm is a moment or an eternity of seeing through and beyond the lived present. It is through the opening of a chiasm that people understand the mythic present: understand, for example, that the Warrior Twins truly are not dead nor gone beyond reach, but that they exist here, now, within, without, next to, behind, in front of, above, and below.[8] People understand why one does not say their real names unless one is calling them into immediate presence. Chiasms are powerful. And, usually, only the powerful dare enter them, have the courage to experience them on an equal footing, for one risks obliteration from too much knowledge, too much power, too much seeing, too much knowing, just as one risks obliteration from the seduction of having the ability to know beyond and to see into and around with a measure of understanding. People's proper place is in this present lived reality, existing with the mythic present in the lived present; people's proper place is not forever in a chiasm. All singers know this; they know the risks involved in probing chiasms. But not all singers of ceremonies are equally gifted. Only some singers also know how to create chiasms for their people and how to lead their conjoint visions and how to conduct the group and individual journeys to and from chiasms.

I believe that people in all cultures experience chiasms, although not all cultures validate chiastic experiences. Regardless of cultural validation or the lack of it, it is helpful in understanding when I consider the "berdache" phenomenon in conjunction with the theoretical construct of chiasm. The one who opens and closes chiasms, the one who presents alternatives and potentialities to others, the one who sees both as it is and as it can be, the one who enters and leaves alternative reality at will, the one who understands how the mythic present and lived present are truly the same; that one is a person of enormous power. That is one who can instruct another—even a white woman—how to attend properly to the messages of the wind. Such a person can create the stage on which another is both audience and actor while also knowing what was in the head of the playwright and the motivations leading to the play—not only in the drama of the lived present but also in the construction of the drama and its relationship with the mythic present and with all that is, was, will be, or may be. The multigendered person, at least at Mescalero, is living a chiasm permanently in that such a person is said to "see two ways," meaning to be able to comprehend and structure the world in both male and female ways simultaneously.

To be quite clear and straightforward: it is irrelevant whether or not gender issues or sexuality are parts of the idea of a "berdache." It is irrelevant whether or not certain speech forms are used while others are rejected. It is irrelevant whether the person so termed accepts the term or eschews all labels. It is irrelevant whether or not anyone believes they exist or ever existed. It is even irrelevant, although unfortunate, that an inappropriate term has been applied for so long to First Nations people of the North American continent.

None of the irrelevancies change the basic fact that those who have the power to open, close, explain, and live in chiasms are persons of power who tread the often hidden line between myth-time and our-time. They *do* know much more than ordinary people. They *can* control weather. They *are* seen in two or more places simultaneously. And, much to the awe and joy of plain people like me, they *enable* others to glimpse what their lives of power are like—lives lived in glory and lives lived in lonesomeness. What they can never be is plain, everyday people: that is both their comedy and tragedy. They *are* different, so profoundly different that I wonder if those of us not so gifted—or cursed—will ever understand what it is like to be husband-wife to a lover, to be son-daughter to That Which Is and Who Sustains All, to be father-mother to a people, to be brother-sister to the wind.

To End

The conferences for which this chapter was originally prepared and later modified have resulted in several issues that need to be confronted openly. At the request of the people so termed, the old term will no longer be used in favor of two-spirit, a term that is to be used in English and not translated into other languages, for it then assumes connotations, in some Native languages, that are far from its meaning in English. Although it is the current term preferred by many contemporary First Nations people, it does not convey the complexity of the real person who was Bernard Second. And, as Wesley Thomas pointed out in one of our discussion sessions, in Athapaskan languages "two-spirit" carries unpleasant connotations of the living and the ghosts. The business of names is a tricky one indeed, and it is not yet settled to everyone's satisfaction.

It also became clear, during our meetings, that some First Nations people believe my characterization of Bernard Second to be a romantic one. Some who knew Bernard in off-reservation contexts noted that he did not always have an easy time by being a multigendered person. They are right, I am sure. I have also reported accurately, however. Sometimes life is romantic. And, at least when I was with him off-reservation, there was no difficulty with his sexuality or enacted gender role(s). There were times when I wondered, however, such as the time he was living with my daughter and me in Washington, D.C., and returned from a weekend away in an oddly subdued mood, or the time we were together in Santa Fe and he was jailed for fighting downtown after having gone to a club to dance and drink. But I have no direct knowledge that these times were because of his multigendered or sexual life.

Nonetheless, the noting of the romantic nature of my presentation does raise another issue that must be addressed: the ease of Bernard's adjustment at Mescalero. Multigendered adult people at Mescalero are usually presumed to be people of power. Because they have both maleness and femaleness totally entwined in one body, they are known to be able to "see" with the eyes of both proper men and proper women.

They are often called upon to be healers or mediators or interpreters of dreams or expected to become singers or others whose lives are devoted to the welfare of the group. If they do extraordinary things in any aspect of life, it is assumed that they have the license and power to do so and, therefore, they are not questioned. Whether people are heterosexual, homosexual, bisexual, (culturally appropriate) female gender, (culturally appropriate) male gender, or multigendered, they are accepted as they are—for each of us must be true to our own pathway.

When a person violates the pathway given, Power first attacks those who are loved. Next Power will attack the person not following her or his pathway. The person may well go crazy or die in mysterious circumstances or suffer other catastrophes. Therefore, a proper Mescalero adult must be whatever one is in terms of gender, sexuality, social roles, and otherwise. A proper adult person would not dream of mounting a challenge to Creator nor to the pathway set for that person by Creator or through understandings with Power.

I have carefully specified "proper adult person" in the immediately foregoing discussion, because the reality of Mescalero reservation life is not so simple, or romantic, for young people. Here I would like to engage in a full discussion of the now adult man who was the boy—described in the quoted fieldnotes—whose mother was pushing him to become a singer because he was effeminate as a child, by both Apache and Anglo standards. I do not have his permission to do so, however, and will have to defer the discussion or perhaps never engage it. Those who are still in their teens and early twenties, or sometimes even younger, as with the boy in my fieldnotes, do not have such an easy time. They are subject to enormous amounts of teasing, and sometimes even physical violence, when they are seen to be different from the expected norms.

When one is young, the pathway to follow is still unfolding. It is at this time that the community seems to believe that it has license to try to shape the decisions being made. Often, the shaping is done in ways that are abusive and even physically or psychologically threatening to a young person. I have heard terrible "jokes" about those young people who are not fulfilling expected sex and gender roles at Mescalero. The jokes stop, however, along with the teasing and other abuses, when the person has reached a certain age and sense of self, when the person is able to communicate that the life-style is not chosen but rather is given and the individual is following his or her appropriate pathway.

One such person at Mescalero I have known since she/he was quite young, in contrast to only having met Bernard after he was an adult.

The young person to whom I have reference is now the age Bernard was when I first met him, that is in his/her early thirties, an age when she/he is able to follow one's own pathway with impunity and relative freedom from community comment. Leslie—a pseudonym chosen because in English it is a name used for both men and women—has an occupation/career that is not gender specific in either English or Mescalero life. That career allows a steady income that is spent on behalf of those in Leslie's matrilineage or often on behalf of others who are unrelated but who need assistance. Leslie is very generous. Leslie is also recognized as a person with power, a person who knows some ceremonies and can do some healing; there is a presumption that she/he will learn more as aging occurs. And it is Leslie who is first on scene when there is a new baby and people need help with errands, housework, cooking, and baby or older child care. Leslie sometimes lives with families for weeks or months after life crises. And sometimes Leslie lives with a lover with the same genital equipment as that with which Leslie was born. Although I watched, and heard, abuse heaped on Leslie in younger life, that is no longer the case, at least not at home at Mescalero.

For the past four hundred years there have been enormous pressures for First Nations people to assimilate and acculturate to European and Euro-American norms. That there are still multigendered—two-spirit—people with viable places and roles in their reservation communities speaks to the persistence of underlying cultural values and wisdom embodied in First Nations cultures. These are values, with associated wisdom, that I believe could well be adopted by mainstream Euro-Americans. We are far too poor in human resources to waste any talents, especially the talents of those who can see two ways, who are endowed with more than most, who know what it is like to be different but valued, and who can also speak to the nasty underside of contemporary cultures, whether those are mainstream or First Nation. We are each relatives to those to whom we were born; we are each embraced by friends to whom we are not related; we are, as well, each in relationships, regardless of our sex or gender or our partners; we are all human beings. Truly, we are all in this together.

Notes

1. The identification came through dreams whose meaning, although clear to him, were also interpreted by his grandfathers, both of whom were also singers. He spoke several languages: Mescalero Apache, Chiricahua

Apache, Lipan Apache, the Western Apache languages (White River, Cibicue, etc.), Jicarilla Apache, Navajo, English, Spanish, and German— learned in the order listed.

2. The word *Power* is capitalized to reflect something like an entity; the word in lower case refers to using the gifts of Power.

3. This was an area that sometimes caused conflict between us. I used to say that he and his people were doing to themselves what my people had been unable to do for more than four hundred years: defeat Apaches. Self-administered alcohol was causing the ruination of what constant warfare and decimation, whether through killing or governmental rules, had not been able to do. Bernard never fought me on this issue; he would simply state, "Sis, it is my life. I just need to stop thinking for a while." And I would cry.

4. For more on this phenomenon, see the chapter, "When Prophecy Succeeds," in my forthcoming *Kaleidoscopic Vision and the Rope of Experience*.

5. For a discussion of those issues, see the chapter "A Death Well-Lived," in Farrer (in preparation).

6. Within a couple of months of our working together, when Bernard was still married to a woman, he told me he was also gay and had a male lover. I had supposed that because I, an outsider, was informed of his sexuality it was common knowledge. Several times I was surprised to find that it was not commonly known on the reservation; indeed, some of Bernard's siblings were unaware of his multigendered sexual life-style until they were well into their twenties and, in one case, into her thirties.

7. B.S.: "The ability to understand is the ability to perceive and appreciate" (from tape made in July 1975).

8. For an extended discussion of the concept of the mythic present, see Farrer (1994).

References Cited

Austin, J. L. 1975. *How to Do Things with Words.* 2d ed. Cambridge: Harvard University Press.

Farrer, Claire R. 1991. *Living Life's Circle: Mescalero Apache Cosmovision.* Albuquerque: University of New Mexico Press.

———. 1994. *Thunder Rides a Black Horse: Mescalero Apache and the Mythic Present.* Prospect Heights: Waveland Press.

———. In preparation. *Kaleidoscopic Vision and the Rope of Experience.*

Jacobs, Sue-Ellen. 1993. Personal correspondence with author.

Part 4: Comments, Reflections, and Generalizations

★ ★ **16**

Gender Statuses, Gender Features, and Gender/Sex Categories:

New Perspectives on an Old Paradigm

Lee M. Kochems and Sue-Ellen Jacobs

At the time of the first Wenner-Gren Foundation Conference on "Revisiting the 'North American Berdache' Empirically and Theoretically" in 1993 it had been twenty-five years since the publication of Jacobs's article on the "berdache" [sic] and ten years since Callender and Kochems's "The North American 'Berdache.'" Who would have thought that someday a group would spend two full days discussing the subject with Native Americans, especially with Native American lesbians, gays, two-spirits, and their positive supporters.[1]

First Nations people (including Native American Indians and Eskimos) and non-Native American anthropologists from the United States, Canada, and Germany have continued to engage in discussions of changes in perceptions of, and the living of, Native American cultures, and that is significant. As Native Americans take on a greater role in what was formerly "berdache" studies, Western cultures again and again benefit.[2]

Comments on Selected Essays

One of the main lessons from the work presented in this volume is that "berdache studies," like all studies of Native Americans, is complicated by wide ranges of diversity; drawing cross-culturally generalizable conclusions is difficult, if not impossible, concerning the creation and maintenance of social persona (and other aspects of culture). For example, we can thank Arnold Pilling (in this volume) for uncovering more diversity in the details and individual expressions of cross-dressing among Native Americans. Studies of Native American gender diversity and sexuality will forever benefit from the examples of his meticulous research and documentation of specific Californian and Zuni male-bodied persons. Claire R. Farrer's essay (in this volume) on what Kochems (1993) has called "the beingness" of Bernard Second provides an equally important example of clarity of research. Providing a lucid account of conversations with Second, she reveals that even within a single individual, working assiduously within his cultural traditions (Mescalero Apache), life-course issues arise that may affect self-identification and self-expression so that the individual is not necessarily always of a particular gender and/or sexuality.

Anguksuar [Richard LaFortune] (1993 and in this volume) and Lee Kochems (1993) bemoan the fact that descriptions (and by that we mean more than just lists) of performances, experiences, events of power and spirituality—what might be called "mysticism"—have been sorely lacking in the work on "berdache"/two-spirit American Indians and Eskimos, with the exception of the work by Goulet (1982; 1988; and in this volume) and Bernard Saladin d'Anglure (1986).[3] Anguksuar addresses issues of spirituality in his essay in this volume.

Wesley Thomas's delineation of the traditional, transitional, contemporary, and assimilated *nádleeh* helps provide a model for addressing the *nádleeh* and other genders in a context that accounts for change (from traditional to modern roles and across cultures from Navajo to and through mainstream American culture). Yet this raises other questions in exploring the identity of assimilated and contemporary *nádleeh* in cultural context. Once again, the terms and contexts are as difficult to sort out as "berdache" was. Stating that two Navajo identities are "similar to Western gays and lesbians" (Thomas 1993 and in this volume), for example, neglects the subtle influence of mainstream American culture—or its not-so-subtle influence, as Michael Red Earth's personal story highlights (1993 and in this volume). Even more so, the complex discourse on identity that is part and parcel of gay and lesbian American culture involves the meaning and significance of concepts and identities: "gay" and "homosexual," "lesbian" or "gay woman," "queer," "closeted," "coming out," "discreet," "gay-identified," "outing," "men who have sex with men," "gay black men," and "black gay men," to name just a few. Some concepts are no more or less complex than "third gender," "berdache," or "two-spirit," so we must wonder about the terms that conflate cultural diversity and sexual or gender identity.

Jason Cromwell's discussion (in this volume) of female-to-male transgender persons examines how androcentrism, phallocentrism, heterosexism, and homocentrism have rendered, and continue to render, female gender variance invisible. What can be done to change this situation? What about sensitivity training entitled the "cultural diversity of sex and gender"? But how many people in the anthropological profession would participate in such training? *umm... the choir...*

Those who do this work keep relearning that as members of an investigative social science discipline they are not beyond the need of such consciousness-raising experiences. They echo Evelyn Blackwood's *Noone is!!* insistence (in this volume) on the importance of intensive, detailed contextual studies of gender-variant people. Jean-Guy Goulet, Carolyn Epple, Wesley Thomas, and Sabine Lang have all demonstrated the value of contextual studies in their contributions to this volume. The issue of gender is still haunting, however. Blackwood suggests that the focus of work must shift to an examination of gender ideologies. Sue-Ellen Jacobs (1993 and in this volume) asks, "How, when we return from the field, do we make sense of the data, make it accessible to our colleagues, engage in comparative studies of gender ideologies until those gender ideologies themselves become the focus of our inquiry?" To do so means more than just examining social relations and cultural features in context. Kochems posits further that it requires unpacking the system of gender-related categories, statuses, roles, and features and then examining how they relate to each another.

Unpacking Gender Systems

What follows are a few suggestions intended to facilitate unpacking gender systems in order to gain insight into and refine theoretical approaches to studies of gender ideologies.

The Mainstream American Gender System

Mainstream American heterosexual culture has established the parameters for the racial, gender, and sexual oppression that most contributors to this volume have experienced. Table 16-1 represents a model of gender ideology in mainstream American culture.

At the foot of the table is the label "gender/sex category"; there are two, "male" and "female." There are also two under "gender status": "man" and "woman." When a child is born into this system, the first thing said is not, "It's a male," or, "It's a female"; what it said is, "It's a

Table 16-1. Mainstream American Culture Gender System

Gender status	man	woman
Gender features		
dress	pants	dress
occupation	breadwinner	caretaker
demeanor	aggressive	passive
sexual object choice	women	men
Gender/sex category	male	female

boy," or, "It's a girl." "Boy" equates with "young man," and "girl" with "young woman." It is already assumed that the child will grow to be a man or woman. In other words, the gender category determined by the recognition of biological, physiological features of morphological sex is the basis of the mainstream American culture system of gender.

Immediately linked to gender category in this system is a compulsory gender status. Individuals born male are expected to become men; those born female are expected to become women. In this system there are no other gender statuses or gender/sex categories acceptable. What mediates the system are gender features. Their importance is ordered inversely in Table 16-1 (and subsequent tables). The most important feature is at the bottom and the least important is at the top. The examples used in Table 16-1 are the same that have been used in many articles about the "North American 'Berdache'" (Callender and Kochems 1983; Whitehead 1981): dress, occupation, demeanor, and sexual object choice.

"Sexual object choice" is at the foot of Table 16-1 because it is the primary gender feature, the foundation of mainstream American culture's system of gender ideology and the basis for the rest of the system. For example, if a male-bodied person's sexual object choice is considered to be inappropriate for his gender category, then he no longer can claim to be an appropriate (or true) man, nor can he claim privileges associated with that gender status. It is probably acceptable, however, if he wears the "wrong" clothes one day. As long as he sleeps with the right person and the sex in which he engages—and this is important— is male-to-female, reproductive penile-vaginal intercourse, then his gender status is that of man.

There is no other gender/sex category, nor any other gender status, for those who do not fit into this system. Such individuals are consid-

Table 16-2. Deviants

Male	Female
fag	dyke
hermaphrodite	
gay	lesbian
bisexual	
transexual	
transvestite	
transgender	

ered to be deviants: fags, dykes, lesbians, gay people, bisexuals, transsexuals, and transgenders (Table 16-2). Hermaphrodites are interesting in that the usual solution is to operate and "fix" them (as, at least, pseudo-females) so they too conform to the dual gender/sex system.

The example of "deviants" gives a sense of how a culturally constructed gender ideology operates in a uniform way. It involves statuses, features, and categories that are completely relevant to the culture. These are the terms used for relationships and associations. Any other person discussed in this culture should fit into the model.

Native American Gender Systems

Callender and Kochems (1983) made an effort to locate an overarching way of examining gender ideology. Two gender/sex categories, male and female, are presented in Table 16-3; there are three gender statuses, however: "man," "two-spirit," and "woman."

The two-spirit status was formerly called "gender-mixing" (Callender and Kochems 1986). Any one of the terms could be substituted for Native terms, such as, in Lakota, *wičaša* (man), *winkte* (two-spirit), and

Table 16-3. Native American Gender Systems

Gender status	man	two-spirit	woman
Gender features			
sexual object choice	women	?	men
demeanor	masculine	mixes gender	feminine
dress	male	statuses and	female
occupation	hunter	gender features	weaver
Gender/sex category	male	male and female	female

Source: Cf. Callender and Kochems (1983).

winyan (woman); in Tewa, *sedó* (old man, husband), *kwidó* or *kweedó* (two-spirit), *kwiyó* (old woman, wife), or *kwee* (woman, wife); and, in Navajo, *hastiin* (man), *nádleeh* (two-spirit), and *'asdzą́ą́n* (woman). The features that link male to man and female to woman, that is, category to status, are ordered differently than those found in Table 16-1. There, "sexual object choice" is fourth, the most important. "Demeanor," then "occupation," and then "dress" constitute the descending order of importance (Callender and Kochems 1986). In Table 16-3 "sexual object choice" is at the top, indicating least importance, whereas "occupation at the bottom is most important. If we would settle for a descriptive term it might be "gender-mixer" for what is now "two-spirit." Gender-mixer, however, is not a label for the status; it is a description of behaviors and other activities associated with the status. Two-spirit is a self-proclaimed Native American/First Nations gender/sex status and category, and the term is not intended to be descriptive by some who call themselves two-spirit.

Across Native North America, male and female are recognized features. Gender status terms are related to that recognition, but so are other features of being a person (demeanor, dress, occupation, sexual object choice, talent, dreams, callings, expectations, and needs). And so there are three-gender systems based on ideologies that recognize (at minimum) two phenotypic sex (or genital) categories (male and female) and multiple-gender categories. To skeptics who have not learned to think in terms of multiple-gender categories (e.g., Epple in this volume; Murray 1994; Roscoe 1987; Williams 1986), we point out that such categories are not Euro-American-centric (Table 16-1), wherein two clearly defined things are referred to as sexes or genders and everything else is "deviant."

In addition to gender categories, we also need to understand culturally specific gender ideologies that are made up of status features, categories, and roles. Roles are associated with statuses. The fulfillment of roles (or lack thereof) is how people move through their lives, meeting the obligations socially ascribed to their statuses.

In the Navajo situation, as defined by Wesley Thomas, there are five genders (Table 16-4). There are three gender/sex categories because each of the statuses (female *nádleeh* and male *nádleeh*) in traditional Navajo terms, as translated in Thomas's work, relies on the notion of *nádleeh* associated with female- or male-bodied persons. Thomas refers to the body as one of the significant features in the traditional Navajo perspective, thus "body" is included in the gender/sex category. Thomas provides Native terms in all of these places and cautions that the system

Table 16-4. The Basic Navajo Gender System

Gender status	woman 'asdzáán	female nádleeh	hermaphrodite nádleeh	male nádleeh	man hastiin
Gender features					
sexual object choice	men and nádleeh	women	?	men	women and nádleeh
demeanor	feminine	masculine	androgynous	feminine	masculine
dress	female	male	androgynous	female	male
occupation	weaver	hunter	varies	weaver	hunter
Gender/sex category	female body		mixed genitalia	male body	

Source: Thomas, Table 7-2 in this volume.

only represents traditional, not contemporary, Navajo characterizations. The order of the features in Table 16-4 is based on a combination of Thomas's work and the general conception of the four gender features Callender and Kochems used in 1983 and understood to be significant among what has been called "berdache." It is unclear how those features would be used by the *nádleeh* with whom Carolyn Epple has worked (Epple in this volume).

The Balkans Gender System

The Balkans gender system, as described by Grémaux (1989; Grémaux 1994) and interpreted by Dickemann (1993) and Cromwell (this volume), is based on two gender/sex categories (Table 16-5). One is associated with two gender statuses; the other category, male, is only associated with one.

Table 16-5. The Gender System in the Balkans

Gender status	woman	verginésha (sworn virgin)	man
Gender features			
natal residence	leaves	stays	stays
dress	female	male	male
demeanor	feminine	masculine	masculine
sexual object choice	men	celibate (?)	women
occupation	weaving	farming	farming
	cooking	hunting	hunting
Gender/sex category	female	female	male

Sources: Cf. Dickemann (1993), Grémaux (1994), and Cromwell (in this volume).

Conclusion

Those categories and statuses of gender ideology that represent people should be accompanied by materials obtained through in-depth ethnographic investigations in context, including contexts when two cultures come in contact. With that we walk the fine line between context and definition (LaFortune [Anguksuar] 1993; Anguksuar in this volume) and the "Tafoya Principle of Uncertainty" (Tafoya 1993 and in this volume).

Notes

Special thanks to Wesley Thomas for assistance in revising earlier versions of this paper.

1. Lee Kochems said at the American Anthropological Association session in Washington, D.C., in 1993, "I wish Charlie [Callender] were here. Let it be known at the outset that any incisive thought that I might present during these comments could only be so by virtue of my professional and personal association with Charlie." Any imprecision or errors in this chapter are solely the responsibility of Kochems and Jacobs.

2. At the risk of "making the 'berdache' an icon of the other" (Jacobs 1993 and in this volume), Kochems feels that he has gained personally through his involvement in the examination of two-spirit people. It is one important aspect of what helped him begin to understand what a "positive other" he could be as a gay man.

3. The early works by these two Canadian scholars are conspicuously absent in Herdt (ed. 1994), Roscoe (1986), and Williams (1986).

References Cited

Callender, Charles, and Lee M. Kochems. 1983. "The North American 'Berdache.'" *Current Anthropology* 24(4): 443–70.

———. 1986. "Men and Not-Men: Male Gender-Mixing Statuses and Homosexuality." In *Anthropology and Homosexual Behavior,* ed. Evelyn Blackwood, 165–78. New York: Harrington Park Press.

Dickemann, Mildred. 1993. "Balkan Sworn Virgins: A European Cross-Gendered Female Role." Paper presented at "Revisiting the 'North American Berdache' Empirically and Theoretically." 92d annual meeting of the American Anthropological Association, Washington, D.C.

Goulet, Jean-Guy A. 1982. "Religious Dualism among Athapaskan Catholics." *Canadian Journal of Anthropology/Revue Canadienne d'Anthropologie* 3(1): 1–18.

————. 1988. "Representation of Self and Reincarnation among the Dene Tha." *Culture* 8(2): 3–18.

Grémaux, René. 1989. "Mannish Women of the Balkan Mountains: Preliminary Notes on the 'Sworn Virgins' in Male Disguise, with Special Reference to their Sexuality and Gender-Identity." In *From Sappho to De Sade: Moments in the History of Sexuality,* ed. Jan Bremmer, 143–72. London: Routledge.

————. 1994. "Woman Becomes Man in the Balkans." In *Third Sex, Third Gender: Beyond Sexual Dimorphism in Culture and History,* ed. Gilbert Herdt, 241–81. New York: Zone Books.

Herdt, Gilbert, ed. 1994. *Third Sex, Third Gender: Beyond Sexual Dimorphism in Culture and History.* New York: Zone Books.

Jacobs, Sue-Ellen. 1968. "Berdache: A Brief Review of the Literature." *Colorado Anthropologist* 1(2): 25–40. Reprint. Wayne R. Dynes and Stephen Donaldson, eds. 1992. *Studies in Homosexuality.* Volume 2: *Ethnographic Studies of Homosexuality.* New York: Garland.

————. 1993. "Introduction: Is the 'North American Berdache' Merely a Phantom in the Imagination of Western Anthropologists?" Paper presented at "Revisiting the 'North American Berdache' Empirically and Theoretically." 92d annual meeting of the American Anthropological Association, Washington, D.C.

Kochems, Lee M. 1993. Comments on papers presented at "Revisiting the 'North American Berdache' Empirically and Theoretically." 92d annual meeting of the American Anthropological Association, Washington, D.C.

LaFortune, Richard [Anguksuar]. 1993. Comments on papers presented at "Revisiting the 'North American Berdache' Empirically and Theoretically." 92d annual meeting of the American Anthropological Association, Washington, D.C.

Murray, Stephen B. 1994. "Subordinating Native American Cosmologies to the Empire of Gender." *Current Anthropology* 35(1): 59–61.

Red Earth, Michael. 1993. "Traditional Influences on a Contemporary Gay Identified Sisseton Dakota." Paper presented at "Revisiting the 'North American Berdache' Empirically and Theoretically." 92d annual meeting of the American Anthropological Association, Washington, D.C.

Roscoe, Will. 1987. "Bibliography of Berdache and Alternative Gender Roles among North American Indians." *Journal of Homosexuality* 14(3–4): 81–171.

Saladin d'Anglure, Bernard. 1986. "From Foetus to Shaman: The Construction of an Inuit 'Third Sex.'" *Inuit Studies* 10(1–2): 25–113.

Tafoya, Terry. 1993. "M. Dragonfly: Two-Spirit/Berdache and the Tafoya Principle of Uncertainty." Paper presented at "Revisiting the 'North American Berdache' Empirically and Theoretically." 92d annual meeting of the American Anthropological Association, Washington, D.C.

Thomas, Wesley. 1993. "A Traditional Navajo's Perspective on Navajo Cultural Construction of Gender." Paper presented at "Revisiting the 'North American Berdache' Empirically and Theoretically." 92d annual meeting of the American Anthropological Association, Washington, D.C.

Whitehead, Harriet. 1981. "The Bow and the Burden Strap: A New look at Institutionalized Homosexuality in Native North America." In *Sexual Meanings: The Cultural Construction of Gender and Sexuality,* ed. Sherry B. Ortner and Harriet Whitehead, 80–115. New York: Cambridge University Press.

Williams, Walter L. 1986. *The Spirit and the Flesh: Sexual Diversity in American Indian Culture.* Boston: Beacon Press. Reprint 1991, with a new preface.

On the Incommensurability
of Gender Categories*

Alice B. Kehoe

That the term "berdache" [*sic*] is unfortunate as well as generally unsuited to North American Indian cultures is all too clear. The question is not what other term should be substituted but whether there is a phenomenon to be surveyed and discussed. The Wenner-Gren conferences demonstrated the existence of many concepts of the nature of humans among the disparate indigenous nations. Arnold Pilling, for example, deconstructed the standard anthropological literature and showed how ill-supported are many alleged reports of "berdaches." Other chapters in this volume, such as Wesley Thomas's on Navajo concepts, build data within a cultural context. From these bases cross-cultural inquiries into the premises and realities of human existences may be reconfigured.

Western culture premises that phenomena can and should be bounded and that the boundaries should be explicit and unambiguous (Hudson 1975). Anthropology is a Western science, and as such it is inevitably an ethnoscience, no more to be privileged than any other. In regard to "sex" categories, Irene Elia (1986) has shown that many animals, for example, many fish, shift from "male" to "female" capac-

why must brd everything?

Editors' note: Kehoe's essay queries aspects of "social persona" expected in mainstream American culture (cf. Kochems and Jacobs in this volume) and introduces aspects of the important work of Bernard Saladin d'Anglure. By doing this, Kehoe critically situates the diversity of two-spirit manifestations within gender studies. Further, her references to aspects of religion and spirituality not mentioned elsewhere in discussions of the lives of two-spirit people expand the essays by Goulet, Anguksuar, and Little Thunder.

ity, or vice versa, and sometimes back again. Such shifting is common among animals, yet when Ursula Le Guin wrote about it her book (1969) was classed as fantasy science fiction.

In contrast to Western culture, many other cultures value dynamic shifting, transformations, and existence in more than two dimensions (Irwin 1994). Bernard Saladin d'Anglure (1994) has documented human gender-shifting in the Canadian Inuit cultural universe in great detail. There, it is averred, an infant's genitals may be changed at birth, and individuals may be transvestite for years in fulfillment of reincarnated forebears' genders.

A second characteristic of Western culture is its projection of oppositional dualism as paradigmatic structure. There is no particular reason that humans must fall into a bimodal set, that is, male and female. Genetically and morphologically, millions of members of the species are more than simple XX or XY, or the shape of their genitalia seem inconclusive compared with ideal male and female. The Western paradigm exacts a cruel toll upon hundreds of American babies whose healthy little bodies are surgically mutilated so that their "ambiguous" or "ill-formed" genitalia will appear "close to normal," although not necessarily close to normal for their genetic sex (Fausto-Sterling 1993).[1]

Another feature of standard Western thinking is that survival of the species is entirely dependent upon the oppositional pair of "father" and "mother." The species reproduces, it is true, only by the joining of sperm with ova, but anthropologists have long pointed out that pater and mater are not necessarily genitor and genitrix. Nurturers and teachers are at least as necessary to a human's growth and successful adulthood as are sperm-producer and ovum-producer. Rather than follow Western culture's relatively recent (according to Foucault [1978]) insistence on male plus female equals sex, it is more useful for anthropologists to document and discuss the species' many cultural plans for successful reproduction of fully human persons. Many of the essays in this volume develop the theme of nurturer and teacher roles, especially in the context of persons whose intellectual and emotional capacities lead them to seek a life more intense or challenging than the ordinary adult's.

Social Personae

In probably any society, social persona may override sexual categorization. Behavior considered appropriate for persons of one gender may be demanded of individuals initially assigned to the other sex when a family or community lacks a physically appropriate person to fill the role. Societal structure can call forth what appears to be cross-dressing or occupational crossing when a household needs but lacks a person of a certain social category (e.g., "eldest sister" in Zuni households, "inheriting son" in Albanian households, and "hunter" or "woman" in Iglulik Inuit households [Saladin d'Anglure 1994:98]). Cross-dressing may be required in the performance of ritual acts, for example by the Blackfoot holy man Four Bears (NisoXkyaio) who died about 1889 (Kehoe 1995). Four Bears was pitied by the Moon (for the Blackfoot, a feminine aspect of the holy). When calling upon this power to aid those who appealed for his help, Four Bears would put on a woman's dress and might require a supplicant to suckle at his nipple. This ritual enactment of nurturing overrode his everyday masculine persona.

Focusing on social personae permits a latitude of discussion more fruitful than reiterating the Indo-European male/female/neuter. (I use the term *social persona* rather than *role* to emphasize identity and sense of self as well as behavior.) Gender, in the narrower, linguistic usage, can be other than male/female/neuter. In his textbook on gender in language, Corbett (1991:20–24) cites Algonquian to illuminate gender that does not refer to sex. Three generations of ethnographers—A. I. Hallowell, Mary Black-Rogers, and Robert Brightman—have studied with Ojibwe, Cree, and Northern Cheyenne collaborators to discover how nouns are assigned gender in these related Algonquian languages. "Animate" and "inanimate" are the names given to the two Algonquian genders by English-speakers. Animate nouns designate beings perceived as imbued with power; inanimate nouns designate objects devoid of power. It is human perception rather than physics and chemistry that assigns gender.

Because humans may be gifted with revelations that transcend everyday experience, the animate gender incorporates a number of nouns that scientifically educated Westerners, lacking social knowledge of such revelations, would assume to be inanimate. This observation of the social foundation of gender in Algonquian points to the social foundation of gender in Indo-European (Corbett 1991:12, 23) as well and to the probability that social factors may similarly overwhelm physical attributes in the formation of social personae.

Transvestism is another obfuscating common term rooted in Western dichotomies. Comparing clothing cross-culturally and historically amply illustrates the arbitrariness of how clothing style is assigned to men and women. Only brassieres and jock straps are unequivocally sex-specific. The flowing toga of a classical Mediterranean or contemporary African gentleman is virtually identical to the flowing sari of a Hindu lady. Pantaloons have been proper for women in much of Western Asia for centuries, and kilts were manly attire in Scotland and in southwestern U.S. pueblos. In Europe, celibate male priests may still wear long skirts—cassocks—covertly signaling their abjuration of manhood (although not of masculine gender).

Clothing is remarkably multifarious, simultaneously signaling reproductive category, class, occupation, age, ethnic affiliation, and political philosophy. I recall a young woman professor I met at a university in India. She considered herself a disciple of the Mahatma Gandhi, proud to be a citizen of India and committed to rejecting harmful social practices such as untouchable caste status. An older woman professor at the university wore beautiful saris and jewels to signal her Indian citizenship and refusal to ape Westerners even though she had obtained her doctorate at Oxford. The younger woman understood her colleague's strategy but felt it alienated her from Gandhi's principle of simplicity. The younger professor decided to wear homespun *khadi* tunics and trousers, investing herself with clothing the Mahatma would have worn, but she worried that others would misperceive her as a transvestite wishing to be masculine. A somewhat analogous example would be that of Katharine Hepburn and Marlene Dietrich, who during the 1930s wore trousers to signal their demand to enjoy the social privileges of upper-class men rather than the restrictions (especially the double standard for sexual activities) placed upon upper-class women. Hepburn and Dietrich could fine-tune their clothing, makeup, hairstyles, and gestures to convey, simultaneously, high-class status, professionalism, and feminine sexuality. Like the Gandhian professor in India, the actresses needed to reject skirts in order to communicate their refusal to follow oppressive convention blindly. Many American Indians, in the past as today, have chosen clothing to signal an unconventional social persona. Correctly reading the signal often requires thick description.

Dress must be chosen; one's body is a given. That genes make human bodies immutable follows from the worldview orientation toward objects—nouns—as discrete, bounded entities. Corbett remarks, "Gender in Algonquian is semantically based, but the semantics are rooted in a culture [in which] . . . fluidity is an essential part of the world view, with the result that gender assignment too can vary" (1991:24). Robert

: very varied

Brightman (1993) describes this Algonquian worldview of manifestations, of transforming beings, rather than discrete objects. Saladin d'Anglure, in a detailed discussion of Inuit belief in the mutability of biological sex, reminds us that this belief is not fantastic but "fed by the frequent genital anomalies in nature and inherent in sexual reproduction" (1994:89).

The Inuit with whom Saladin d'Anglure studied, and many other northern First Nations (Mills and Slobodin, eds. 1994), see infants as reincarnations of other people and sometimes of spirit beings. The incarnated soul must be recognized by giving an infant its name, and an infant might be thought to incarnate several souls, requiring the child to carry several names. Rasmussen mentions a woman with sixteen names, "as a bag round her" (quoted by Saladin d'Anglure 1994:90). To accommodate the incarnated souls an Inuit child might be raised as the gender of the principal incarnation, regardless of the child's physical sex. The child might also alternate—day by day in one example (Saladin d'Anglure 1994:94)—or change gender at puberty. Inuit midwives or mothers might hold a newborn's penis in the belief that doing so will prevent it from shrinking and the child's groin "cracking open" into a vulva. A girl who had initially been born with boy's genitals but had "cracked open" was likely to be a dominating woman (Saladin d'Anglure 1994:84–87). Saladin d'Anglure's vivid details from firsthand fieldwork cogently express the worldview of mutability, a worldview as well grounded in realistic observation as the Western worldview emphasizing dichotomy and boundedness.

From a perspective of mutability, fixed identities are unnatural. A person may be inclined, or may chose, to emphasize qualities tending to be characteristic of men or of women or qualities believed to be characteristic of spirit beings in the sense of a "third gender" (Saladin d'Anglure 1994:98–105, quotation marks in original). In that the person gifted with power to transcend ordinary human limitations transcends ordinary gender behavior correlations, there is warrant to use the term *third gender* for circumboreal-circumarctic societies' shamans. Nevertheless, as Saladin d'Anglure indicates by consistently using quotation marks around the term, it is not really appropriate nor particularly illuminating. "Gender" is a limiting, constraining concept. From the point of view of these northern societies, it is these gifted persons' larger range of capacities that must be noted. From this position, the recently popular term *two-spirit* is inadequate and overly Westernized in its implication of dichotomy. Someone should remark, "Two-spirit?

Who's counting?" Rasmussen's woman with sixteen names illustrates the infelicity of two-spirit.

European observers usually spent little time living within Indian communities and so were unable to know what behavior was appropriate only to a ritual condition or particular life stage. Did some untrained European observers mistake contraries—persons so imbued with holy power that they could neither dress nor act as ordinary people—for "berdaches"? The application of terms must be traced carefully to their first use in print. What may have actually been observed, its context then, and its context in its descendants' present culture must be evaluated using both other written sources and direct discussion with members of the Indian nation.

Much classic ethnographic literature is worse than casual notes in that it transcribes memory rather than observed behavior. It is understandable that unsophisticated European soldiers, priests, or entrepreneurs might facilely label an Indian person with a term, for example, "berdache," that some aspect of the Indian's dress or stance connoted. The anthropological literature unfortunately tended to compound the confusion by treating the untrained observer's term as God's Truth. There may be incongruence between Western categories of being and gender and the concepts of other cultural traditions. To say that their worldviews are antithetical to that of Western societies is to fall into the trap of oppositional dualism characteristic of the Western tradition. Some contemporary members of the First Nations are comfortable with behavior and gender status incommensurable with dominant American role assignments, whether "straight" or "gay." This volume explores the incommensurabilities between First Nations and dominant Western categories.

These First Nations of America are reasserting themselves. Repatriating their patrimonies from sterile collections and restoring their languages to their children, First Nations communities can reopen the varieties of roles and social personae conceptualized in their heritages. Among the hundreds of First Nations people who find that the labels "gay," "lesbian," and "bisexual" miss the point of their expression of a variant life outlook, someone came up with the term *two-spirit,* and it quickly caught on. Two-spirit is not a "traditional" term, and if it were it could be traditional only for one or a few nations. It is an example of the vitality of contemporary First Nations cultures, expressing for these persons a mode shared across the diversity of their native nations.

Note

1. Inuit claim the genitals change spontaneously (the penis shrinks or the clitoris grows) as the baby emerges, and the birth attendant may grab at the organ to prevent a child of the desired sex from changing. We would not accept this as actually happening. Fausto-Sterling refers to actual surgery in the United States.

References Cited

Brightman, Robert. 1993. *Grateful Prey.* Berkeley: University of California Press.

Corbett, Greville. 1991. *Gender.* Cambridge: Cambridge University Press.

Elia, Irene. 1986. *The Female Animal.* New York: Henry Holt.

Fausto-Sterling, Anne. 1993. "How Many Sexes Are There?" Paper presented at the annual meeting of the History of Science Society, Santa Fe.

Foucault, Michel. 1978 [1976]. *The History of Sexuality.* Translated by Robert Hurley. New York: Random House.

Hudson, Liam. 1975. *Cult of the Fact.* London: Jonathan Cape.

Irwin, Lee. 1994. *The Dream Seekers.* Norman: University of Oklahoma Press.

Kehoe, Alice B. 1995. "Blackfoot Persons." In *Native American Women and Power,* ed. Laura Klein and Lillian Ackerman, 113–25. Norman: University of Oklahoma Press.

Le Guin, Ursula K. 1969. *Left Hand of Darkness.* New York: Walker.

Mills, Antonia, and Richard Slobodin, eds. 1994. *Amerindian Rebirth: Reincarnation Belief among North American Indians and Inuit.* Toronto: University of Toronto Press.

Saladin d'Anglure, Bernard. 1994. "From Foetus to Shaman: The Construction of an Inuit Third Sex." In *Amerindian Rebirth: Reincarnation Belief among North American Indians and Inuit,* ed. Antonia Mills and Richard Slobodin, 82–106. Toronto: University of Toronto Press.

★ ★ 18

You Anthropologists Make Sure
You Get Your Words Right*

Clyde M. Hall (Lemhi Shoshoni)

You know, twenty years ago I would never have thought that I would be in front of all these anthropologists, talking about such a personal subject as my own people and friends. In fact, if you had come to the reservation, I probably would have chased you off with a gun. I am serious. I was that kind of person back then. But that is water under the bridge. Here I am with all you fine folks, and not only that but I have a lover of seven years who I've pushed through school to become an anthropologist. My! How times have changed.

For a long time I had been wondering if maybe something like this [conference] could happen. I can tell you all that it should not be regarded as something that has come full circle, not even partially, not even a quarter of the way or an eighth of the way. It is just the beginning—it is just the first step. It should be continued, the discussion between Native American two-spirit people and anthropologists, some of them who are two-spirited themselves and others that are just around for curiosity or to write a good paper. We should keep the dialogue going.

Yesterday, at our Wenner-Gren Conference, I was waiting for things to get really hairy and for people to start jumping on chairs and jumping up and down in our discussion. I was disappointed. I guess it is the old radical in me coming out. It was a nice discussion, but it could have

Editors' note: What follows is a transcription of a speech that Clyde Hall gave at the first Wenner-Gren Conference in Washington, D.C., in 1993.

gone further. That word "berdache" [*sic*].

Incidentally, I am not going to tell my life story like some of my brothers and sisters have, and that is not to say anything bad against them because I enjoy hearing their stories. It helps me to think that I am not the only one to have gone through this kind of a thing. But my story is for sale in *Living the Spirit* (M. Owlfeather in Gay American Indians comps., ed. Roscoe 1988). I am probably one of the most public individuals around—true story.

Anyway, I also sell these kinds of things, "genuine 'berdache' crafts."* I get these little knives up in Yellowstone Park for a little bit, and then I fix them up just like the old-time knives. I brought this knife up as an example of words; I want to tell you a little bit about Shoshone words.

I am a fluent speaker of Shoshone. There are a lot of words in Shoshone and I am sure in other languages, Sioux and what have you, that you cannot really put a definition on in English. It takes a lot of talking to describe these words in English, but when you are talking with your fellow tribespeople, they get it. You do not have to explain it. That is what I feel like we've been doing. We have gotten a kind of dialogue going, but we're using too many words about the word "berdache." Take, for instance, this knife, in Shoshone if you have a knife like this it is called a *wihi*. This is a *wihi mokottsih* [sheathed knife]. But if you put it like this, then it becomes a *tosa wihi* [unsheathed horizontal knife]. And if you put it like this, it becomes a *wean wanton* [knife pointed upward], which is also the Shoshone word for an excited male sexual organ. But it all means "knife," just the way you use those words. That is the way with the word that has been tossed around—maybe I started it, I do not know—the word *tainna wa'ippe* or "tannowaip" as someone put in there. I wish you people would get your spelling right! You know, there is a Shoshone-English dictionary called *Newe Natewinappeh: Shoshoni Stories and Dictionary* (Miller 1972).

Make sure that you get your words right and your words defined right. That word *tainna wa'ippe*—there are other words in Shoshone that mean the same thing and are being used on different occasions. For the women, there is *taikwahni wa'ippena'*, for men there is *taikwahni tainnapa'* or sometimes *taikwahni*, depending on which you use and the way you use it. So you are making the same mistake in Shoshone and in Navajo and a lot of other situations here: many times assigning

---

Editors' note: Here, Hall used a small knife and a decorated scabbard to illustrate various Shoshone words for "knife."

a label to a thing that cannot be labeled, other times assigning the wrong label to something.

Back home, when Sabine Lang came to do her fieldwork, she said she wanted to meet some "warrior women," so I told her, "O.K., come to the reservation, I'll introduce you to some warrior women." But Sabine came back one time from interviewing one of these individuals, and she said, "You know, they're just the kind of women I am looking for but they do not know who they are." Well, it is not that they do not know who they are, just because they do not know the label anthropologists have put on them—because they are just who they are. They are just beings, that is the way the Great Mystery made them. They come out into this world like that. And they are just living their lives, of who they are and what they are interested in. And who they are interested in. And how they want to dress. And how they want to act. Do you think that the old-time people who are now referred to by anthropologists as "berdache" for the most part used that word as part of their vocabulary? I do not think so, because they were just manifesting who they were. And how they lived. It was something that was given to them by Spirit—this way of living.

My people have a little story, and I'll share this. Before you are born, we have in Shoshone what is called *kammut*. And it is a rabbit. Before you're born when your mother spreads her legs to have you come into this world, there is a rabbit that runs out first. This rabbit goes everywhere, runs all around, sometimes all around the world. But sometimes you try to be smarter than the rabbit. You say, "Oh, that rabbit went that way, I can see his tracks, so I am going to go this way." But you know, that damn rabbit has already been there! And you are following the path that rabbit ran anyway. Now think about that. That is the way we think about our lives and our way of being and living. Because it is a life given by Spirit for us to live in this world at this time. And we have no choice in it. We have no choice in going with it and living it as best as we can. That is the way we always pray.

We always say, *"Dammen Appe,"* "Holy Spirit," or "Sacred Spirit," or "Great Mystery" (or whatever you want to say) "I put my life into your hands." This is the way we say it. Because we live with Spirit everyday. It is not something that we try out on Sundays and forget about the rest of the time. Our lives are two-spiritedness. What we do, how we live, the way we live, the songs we sing, the children we have are all interconnected with this Spirit. Like this [interlocks fingers of both hands]. There is no putting it into little boxes like we are trying to do here with the word "berdache," because it is all part of this circle and it is all interrelated. I think that is what each one of my brothers and sisters has been trying to tell you.

Something that has been left out of this whole conference is that element of spirituality, and that is the glue that makes it all stick together. That is the glue that makes us two-spirit people go with it and live our lives the way we do. If you leave that out then it is not going to make any sense. It has to be addressed, and it has to be thought about. And then it makes perfect sense, the way we live our lives.

I thought I would share a few of these thoughts, random thoughts, and I hope they have made sense because a lot of times what I do is I just open my mouth and I let Spirit talk. That is the way I do things.

I will leave you with something. And it is something we Indian people back home do. At one time Indian people would talk sign language, faster than Natives speak the spoken word. It is like this [makes hand signs]. That means, may the Great Mystery make sunrise in all your hearts forever.

References Cited

Miller, Wick R. 1972. *Newe Natewinappeh: Shoshoni Stories And Dictionary.* Salt Lake City: University of Utah Anthropological Papers 94.

Roscoe, Will, ed. 1988. *Living the Spirit: A Gay American Indian Anthology.* Compiled by Gay American Indians. New York: St. Martin's Press.

★ ★ 19

The Dilemmas of Desire:

From "Berdache" to Two-Spirit*

Gilbert Herdt

Over the past century it has become increasingly apparent from anthropological reports and more recently from the voices of cultural actors themselves that "sexuality" in the Western meanings of the word does not apply in every respect to the phenomena surrounding sexuality in non-Western worlds. This is because Western sexuality in the modern period has come to exclude areas of ontology so critical and pervasive elsewhere across time and space: concepts of the whole person that incorporate spirit, mind, and social relations (rather than the more restrictive idea of "sexual actor" common in the United States); the sensibilities of the body, whose essences and practices, the inscriptions of the social into the surface of the body, make sexuality into a matter of cultural reasoning and sociality; well-being, the emotions, and their manifestations in notions of health maturities and healing concepts; and the passions, or eros, of being with others sexually or playfully but without necessarily romance or procreation in the modernist sense of these ideals.

Editors' note: Herdt articulates an important theme touched on by some explicitly (Anguksuar, Farrer, Jacobs, Little Thunder, Robertson) and implicitly by all contributors: the desire and longing to be accepted as a self-named person. Herdt gives a clear overview of the power of language to subjugate, denigrate, and demonize individuals and notes how reductionist approaches to gender issues that rely solely upon "sexual behavior" obscure other aspects of gender identity and social persona (cf. Kehoe in this volume). He also describes changes in the way anthropologists and Natives are coming to terms with their long-held disagreements over the use of language markers.

Given such historical and cultural prejudices in the reduction of the whole person to the categorical sex act, we begin to understand the magnitude of the physical and epistemic violence propagated by early modern white settlers in North America upon the "berdache" [*sic*] (Williams 1986). The whites imposed the "berdache" notion upon individuals of divergent sexual and gendered natures, resident and proud members in the villages of their tribal groups. Where before, in precolonial times, these individuals belonged to their own ontological cultural categories and had their own lifeways, desires, and plans, thereafter they were made the objects of reaction and ridicule because the outsiders resorted to the crudest of exotic reductions and seized upon "berdache" as an imported grab-bag category that condensed meanings of "invert," "slaveboy," "cross-dresser," and who knows what else in the later-nineteenth-century oppression of such people (Williams 1986).

Thus, the deconstruction of the colonial category "berdache" and the establishment of meanings emerging from this volume are the most powerful examples I have witnessed of how social change alters the categories of understanding with which we measure the individual and culture. This constitutes a profound example of how a new anthropology of sexuality can be constructed to open the discourse on cultural diversity rather than compare cultures against a limiting norm that takes Western culture as the ideal model. In rethinking these issues we realize, therefore, that Western notions of cultural agency, individual development, and desire must give us pause, for they are not only essential to the act of comparing necessary to anthropological science but also too limiting for such comparisons.

Some of the most important words and concepts used in the chapters of this book are either generally unconnected to sexuality or only vaguely related to it in the Western model. These include "spirituality," "medicine," "identity," "identities," "ritual," "mythic practice," "gender," and "power" as sometimes used in the sense of spiritual or metaphysical agency. The word "sexuality," sometimes used reluctantly and at other times used forcefully, hinges upon a Western ideal. "Berdache" belongs, of course, to the colonial discourse of the nineteenth century; even earlier, it was inscribed in encounters with North American Indians and later in histories and ethnographies written by WASP Americans. How old-fashioned and even racist the word sounds now. By contrast, many North American Indians prefer to call themselves "two-spirit" or use that term in reference to others. As a result, I now use two-spirit instead of "berdache" in my work and teaching, not because the term is "politically correct" but because it is culturally accurate and meaningful. It is also in keeping with what personhood means to North American Indians themselves, which for an anthropologist is always of great import.

Let me mark off the "spiritual" aspect of the two-spirit nature in these cultures. In papers delivered at the American Anthropological Association session in Washington, D.C., in 1993, the spiritual seemed to me to underlie much of what I heard people tell about their lives in general and their sexuality in particular, although that is not always apparent in the published accounts. This is a bit hard for the average person in the United States to grasp, although with the advent of new discussions of faith and fundamentalism in many quarters throughout the world (Gellner 1992) we can begin to see the complexities of how the spiritual and the sexual may be laced into or suppressed by religious traditions. In general, this kind of emphasis upon the spiritual dimension of sexuality is missing or largely outside of the Western discourse on the sexual, at least since the rise of the bourgeois in the period following the French revolution in Western Europe and the United States (D'Emilio and Freedman 1988; Foucault 1980; Herdt, ed. 1994; Williams 1986).

Another concept, although not mentioned at the conference, was in my mind during some of the discussions: desire. I do not mean sexual desire in the narrow sense, for this would undermine my critique of the narrowness of Western sexuality. In Western discourse it has long been common to think of the sexual as restricted to genital pleasure or pertaining only to genital relations, which is obviously too narrow to capture the meanings of the erotic in many times and places. Indeed, the category of eros is more certainly a point of contrast between the Ancient Greeks and ourselves, and the erotic is more in keeping with the notions of the sexual and the whole person as found in Native North America (Herdt 1989; Williams 1986).

By desire, then, I mean a set of intentional states of the agent that not only reflect closely felt interests and needs of the developmental life course of the whole person/body/spirit but also are contained within and imagined by the cultural reality of their times (Herdt 1989; Herdt 1991). The anthropologist A. I. Hallowell (1955) defined this area of ontology and culture better than any other scholar, and although he typically ignored sexuality in the narrow sense his fine and sensitive ethnographies of the Ojibwa and other American Indian people were instrumental in showing how their cultural being could become infused with many of the meanings of the erotic we would identify with desires. The idea of an ontological or cultural reality must entail all the necessary constituents that create the desire for a genuine and satisfying life: concepts of the whole person, time, space, and social and physical action and a vision of having a certain social and spiritual being and locating this ontological being in a body like those represented in the symbolic media of ritual, myth, and drama that occupy social space. For the individual actor this means occupying a certain role, such as the two-spirit person, with all the full meanings of being, eros, and happy sociality in the particular and lived traditions of a community.

I will use the multidimensional idea of desire as a way of rethinking the work on sexuality and gender with which I am associated and which is inextricably linked with the delicate historical burden of an anthropology that has represented the other as the multigendered, sexual, and spiritual natures of persons from Native American cultures even as it has ignored, suppressed, or misunderstood the meanings of same-gendered desires and relationships within its own culture (Herdt 1987; Herdt and Boxer 1992). The dilemma in thinking of these desires resides in a simple Western prejudice: to express a certain sexuality is to preclude all other desires, including a yearning for the spiritual.

In the last century it was common in anthropology, medicine, and sexology to reduce the whole person to something smaller, typically a type or even a subtype, such as a "homosexual" or "invert," or to place some such stigma on society (Robinson 1976). What Freud advanced of this sexological tradition was eventually to find its way into anthropological studies of the "berdache," as exemplified, for instance, by Devereux's (1937) classic essay on the Mojave. This model suggested that the "raw" potential of "berdache" individuals must be biologically "deviant" or "abnormal," with the "biological inversion" of the "berdache" lumped into a vague category of "congenital homosexuality" (Mead 1935:283). Now we recognize that these ideas echoed the nineteenth-century sexology assumptions that human nature is dimorphic and the teleological purpose of sexuality is always restricted to heterosexual reproduction (critiqued in Herdt, ed. 1994).

But even Devereux's account of the Mojave was far too rich to fit into this meager mold. For instance, Mojave recognized a distinctive ontology of two-spirit persons, expressed in heartfelt desires, task preferences, and cultural transformation with respect to the genitals and to person pronouns. The social role was sanctified by spiritual power—an attribute lacking in the Western conception of these variations of sex/

gender. Furthermore, the Mojave did not stigmatize the role, nor even the partners or lovers of the two-spirited. The spiritual aspects are especially significant because the Mojave two-spirit person was sanctified by two symbolic institutions: an origin myth, widespread, and a dream theory suggesting that Mojave women's dreams would influence fetuses (reviewed in Herdt 1991).

How different is our tradition, which labors under the reductionism of the whole person to the sexual. Even now it is common for television or the newspapers to reduce the whole person to one-dimensional social roles (husband and wife), or modes of production (lawyer, teacher, or farmer), or sexual relations (e.g., the homosexual). Such reductionisms are informed by the concepts of man and woman, or contractual relations (to practice law), or sexual practice (e.g., homosexuality) harbored in society. In the sexuality study it is still common practice to reduce the whole person to category terms such as *heterosexual* or *homosexual*. This biased baggage of meanings, a burden from the past, is further exaggerated by characterizations of the "berdache" in the ethnographic texts of the later nineteenth and early twentieth centuries (Herdt 1991). In these texts, "berdache" is regarded as a creature of failed biology, for example, hermaphrodism (Hammond 1882; Hill 1935), or failed morals (Bancroft 1874; Lafitau 1724:603-4, 608; Lumholtz 1912:252-53), or as someone not able to live up to an expected norm (Erickson 1949:183f; Hassrick 1982:135f; Hoebel 1958:589; Linton 1936:480; Mead 1935:260f; Opler 1965:111). In the functionalist theories and ideas of anthropological forerunners, such as Devereux (1937), Kroeber (1940:209-10), and Seligmann (1902), among others, a "deviant" category was created for the purpose of allowing this person to adapt or live in a given culture. Now, anthropologists have come to the problem of how to label, classify, and otherwise think of those people referred to, historically, as "berdache." I am immediately thrown back to the practice of never reducing the whole to the singular. Spirituality, power, sexuality, gender, identities, and desires are what constitute an individual who otherwise is classified by only one of these—if by spirituality only, then as a shaman; if by power only, then as tribal president, judge, or shaman; if by sexuality, then as only a homosexual; and so on.

But in this book many other categories and terms have been added and offered to represent the lives of various kinds of persons, because we are dealing with real people and whole lives that go far beyond the sexual. I think Jason Cromwell has it right in saying, "Let's not call these persons this, let's not call them that, there are all kinds of things we should not call them. What do we call them? Or how do we represent them or ourselves?" Immediately the problem of dualistic thinking occurs, thinking that tries to represent the multiplicity of categories of actual experience. Wesley Thomas refers to this in his contribution on Navajo gender categories, and Sue-Ellen Jacobs reminds us that we must not reduce "berdache," or all of the other various series and sequences of personhood, to the problem of gender and sexuality. But at the same time we would bring other things to the fore in attempting to understand and think about people's lives, traditions, and cultural realities because that is what we are dealing with—the cultural and social realities, and the inner worlds, of people. In their "Introduction" to this volume, Jacobs, Thomas, and Lang remind us that HIV/AIDS are relevant to the concerns of understanding and sensitively intervening in real-life situations that place people at risk of infection. Here, as elsewhere, the lessons to be learned are the precise meanings of local culture and the ontological system of sexual conduct in order to stage an effective effort on behalf of disease prevention (Herdt 1992).

During discussions at the first Wenner-Gren Foundation Conference, I heard several distinctions made about how and where contemporary "berdache" or two-spirit people locate themselves, their identities, and their traditions. First, they locate themselves within a friendship circle, a very small, intimate circle of people known to each other in face-to-face relations. Second, some locate within a particular community, bounded by time and space, but not part of a larger tribal tradition. Third, others locate within a tribal culture, which is a bounded, historical tradition that spans diverse communities.

We might think of these three distinctions as meaningful within a certain territory—to insiders within a common field of social and sexual conduct. But these are different domains and cultural spaces of meanings from those of outsiders—such as anthropologists and other social scientists—who have sought to understand them. We see now the importance of regarding these insider and outsider categories and spatial meanings as separate and inviolable in order to preserve the full dignity of two-spirit people and their sense of spirituality. The latter do not necessarily experience any dilemma of desires within themselves regarding their two-spirit nature. When they opt to place themselves in the larger socio-sexual field, however, they are taking on a role and the responsibilities and burden of such a role that has gender, sexuality, and power connotations, and the latter may impose unexpected dilemmas of being and action.

In a collection on third sexes and third genders I grappled with these issues in a broader context of questioning the assumption of Western culture that all people and all communities divide the world into pairs, the dyad of male and female (Herdt, ed. 1994). If we examine concepts of third sex or third gender, across history and cultures, the variations on the Western model are so impressive that they cannot help but persuade us of an ethnocentrism in the core, emic concept of sexuality as defined in the West.

Nearly a century has passed since the accounts of the two-spirited became a matter of scientific concern to Western life, and we still understand little of this complex divergence between the Western and non-Western areas of meaning. At least we have come to a new historical era when the kinds of descriptions and comparisons necessary to understand and inform can occur, and we can begin to make sense of the much larger and more interesting sexual world beyond that of the West. That is why the conferences were so historically significant and that is why they and this volume mark not the end but rather the beginning of something new.

Note

My thanks to Sue-Ellen Jacobs for her kindness and patience during my completion of the manuscript for this chapter and for her critical and helpful comments on its first draft. I also thank all of the participants in the Wenner-Gren Conference for their gifts of teaching, the greatest gifts there are.

References Cited

Bancroft, Hubert Howe. 1874. *Native Races of the Pacific States of North America*. Volume 1. New York: D. Appleton.

D'Emilio, John, and Estelle Freedman. 1988. *Intimate Matters: A History of Sexuality in America*. New York: Harper and Row.

Devereux, George. 1937. "Homosexuality among the Mohave Indians." *Human Biology* 9(7): 498–527.

Erickson, Eric H. 1949. "Childhood and Tradition in Two American Indian Tribes." In *Personality in Nature, Society, and Culture*, ed. Clyde Kluckhohn and H. A. Murray, 176–203. New York: Knopf.

Foucault, Michel. 1980. *The History of Sexuality*. Translated by Richard Hurley. New York: Viking.

Gellner, Ernest. 1992. *Postmodernism, Reason, and Religion*. New York: Routledge.

Hallowell, A. I. 1955. *Culture and Experience*. New York: Schocken Books.

Hammond, William A. 1882. "The Disease of the Scythians (Morbus Feminarum) and Certain Analogous Conditions." *American Journal of Neurology and Psychiatry* 1(3): 339–55.

Hassrick, Royal. 1982. *Das Buch der Sioux*. Cologne: Diederich.

Herdt, Gilbert. 1987. *The Sambia: Ritual and Gender in New Guinea*. New York: Holt, Rinehart and Winston.

———. 1989. "Self and Culture: Contexts of Religious Experience in Melanesia." In *Religious Imagination in New Guinea,* ed. Gilbert Herdt and Michele Stephen, 15–40. New Brunswick: Rutgers University Press.

———. 1991. "Representations of Homosexuality in Traditional Societies: An Essay on Cultural Ontology and Historical Comparison, Part I." *Journal of the History of Sexuality* 2(n.s.): 602–32.

———. 1992. "Introduction". In *The Time of AIDS,* ed. Gilbert Herdt and Shirley Lindenbaum, 3–26. Newbury Park: Sage Publications.

———, ed. 1994. *Third Sex, Third Gender: Beyond Sexual Dimorphism in Culture and History*. New York: Zone Books.

Herdt, Gilbert, and Andrew Boxer. 1992. "Introduction: Culture, History, and Life Course of Gay Men." In *Gay Culture in America,* ed. Gilbert Herdt. 1–28. Boston: Beacon Press.

———. 1993. *Children of Horizons*. Boston: Beacon Press.

Hill, W. W. 1935. "The Status of the Hermaphrodite and Transvestite in Navajo Culture." *American Anthropologist* 37(2): 273–79.

Hoebel, E. Adamson. 1958. *Man in the Primitive World: An Introduction*. 2d ed. New York: McGraw Hill.

Kroeber, Alfred L. 1940. "Psychosis or Social Sanction." *Character and Personality* 8(3): 204–15.

Lafitau, Joseph Francois. 1724. *Moeurs des Sauvages Americquains*. Volume 1. Paris: Saugrain.

Linton, Ralph. 1936. *The Study of Man*. New York: Appleton-Century.

Lumholtz, Carl. 1912. *New Trails in Mexico*. New York: Charles Schribner's Sons.

Mead, Margaret. 1935. *Sex and Temperament in Three Primitive Societies*. New York: Morrow.

Opler, Marvin K. 1965. "Anthropological and Cross-cultural Aspects of Homosexuality." In *Sexual Inversion,* ed. Judd Mormor, 108–23. New York: Basic Books.

Robinson, Paul. 1976. *The Modernization of Sex*. New York: Harper and Row.

Seligmann, C. G. 1902. "Sexual Inversion among Primitive Races." *Alienist and Neurologist* 23(1): 11–15.

Williams, Walter L. 1986. *The Spirit and the Flesh: Sexual Diversity in American Indian Culture*. Boston: Beacon Press. Reprint 1991, with a new preface.

Native American Genders and Sexualities:

Beyond Anthropological Models and Misrepresentations

Evelyn Blackwood

The study of two-spirit people (which used to be called "berdache" [*sic*] studies) continues to be an intriguing, thought-provoking, and critical area of research for Native Americans, gays and lesbians, and anthropologists. It was originally dominated by the questions and perceptions that European-American anthropologists brought to the material and as a result tended to reflect Euro-American conceptions of gender. This volume brings to the forefront both the diversity of two-spirit people and the inadequacies of anthropological theories used to account for them in Native American cultures.

Several essays discuss earlier interpretations of historical data on Native American two-spirit people. Early in the twentieth century, the central question was, Why does someone become a two-spirit? Scholars of that generation provided various explanations, from the biological to the functional to the psychological. The explanations primarily depended on how one defined a two-spirit person. Turn-of-the-century scholars thought two-spirits were "failed" men and women, individuals who had odd desires or could not live according to the norms for their gender and thus chose to switch genders.

By the early 1970s a new surge of interest resulted in a range of articles dedicated to understanding what constitutes a two-spirit person and seeking greater information and detail on their incidence among Native American nations. Focusing on individual attributes and occupational choices, the articles advanced the idea that two-spirit people could be defined by their occupation, dress, and sexual preference.

Such role-based analysis—two-spirits are recognizable because they do things typically associated with opposite-sexed bodies—provided a handy checklist of attributes. For instance, if a male-bodied person washes dishes, handles finances, wears women's dress, weaves, and gathers, then that person must be two-spirit.[1] Or, if an individual is a mediator, ritual specialist, or healer of special diseases, and these tasks are not associated closely with either gender, then that person must be "mixed" or third gender. Or, if an individual has sex with another of the same type of body, that person must be homosexual and two-spirit. This perspective focused solely on characteristics that distinguished a two-spirit category from other social categories.

The problems these scholars faced in understanding two-spirit people came from several directions. Dominant gender ideology in America equates one's sex with one's gender. Most non-Native Americans have difficulty perceiving a physical male as a woman or a physical female as a man. The critical importance of biology to Western constructs of gender meant that white scholars were rarely able to separate biology from gender successfully when talking about two-spirit people. Most non-Native scholars referred to two-spirits by the pronoun appropriate to physical sex, not gender. Roscoe (1991) calls We'wha "he" despite the fact that We'wha lived as a woman and was perceived as a woman by contemporary anthropologists. Williams (1986) describes two categories of Native American "males": two-spirit and normal. I used the female pronoun when I wrote about Sahaykwisa, the Mojave *hwame* who was female-bodied (Blackwood 1984). These terms give undue emphasis to the biological aspect of a two-spirit person and tend to overshadow the importance of their social being.

In the rush to categorize two-spirit people, scholars were guilty of generalizing about the "North American two-spirit," placing all two-spirit people in a single category. The "berdache" were broadly defined as persons who take up the role of the opposite sex and share certain features, such as cross-dressing and homosexuality. Williams's (1986) description of two-spirit people extends beyond North America to include Central American cases as well. He also draws close parallels between two-spirit people and the *mahu* of the Pacific. This overgeneralization can be remedied by attention to local meanings and gender systems that lump together divergent practices.

Another problem in the literature on two-spirit people is the tendency to apply American gender markers to them. In their earlier works Williams (1986) and Lang (1991) use the terms *effeminate* and *housewife* for male two-spirits or *manly* and *independent* for female two-spirits. The problem with these terms is that they universalize American notions of gender identity. What does "effeminate" mean in a social context in which women control household affairs and hunt small game? What does "independent" mean for a female two-spirit who is part of the kinship and social network of the community? Such an individual may do things differently than women, but she does not do them alone. Without an adequate understanding of gender relations in particular Native American groups, such terms provide little insight into two-spirit gender.

Following the line of Jacobs (1983) and Martin and Voorhies (1975), I decided to define two-spirit "status" as a separate gender (Blackwood 1988). Recognizing the two-spirit category as a gender moved that category beyond binary gender systems and made it equivalent to the genders "man" and "woman." It also fit the data in certain instances and was particularly compelling as an explanation for why two-spirit people in many nations are identified by different terms than those for woman or man (for example, the Mojave call a female two-spirit *hwame,* which is different than the term for woman). This formulation highlighted the way two-spirit gender is not binary, oppositional, or derived from biology (see also Jacobs 1983; Roscoe 1994). But as the essays in this volume show, even that definition may be true only in some instances.

Labels and More Labels

Since the early 1970s certain terms used to label two-spirit people, such as *hermaphrodite* or *transvestite,* were dropped in favor of a new set of terms, including *cross* or *mixed gender, not-man/not-woman, man-woman,* and *third (fourth, fifth,* and so on) *gender.* This volume takes issue with many of these terms and rightly so. None apply to all cases, and some are not useful at all. Farrer states that the designation "third gender" is impoverished because her experience with a two-spirit person led her to believe he was multigendered. I used "cross gender" as a way to signify that two-spirit people shift from one category of sex/gender into another, but I later abandoned that term, concluding that two-spirit gender does not necessarily mean "jumping from one gender to its opposite" (Blackwood 1988:171). Cromwell makes a similar argument in his discussion of transgender people. One does not "cross" if one has always believed oneself to be a particular gender.

The term *mixed gender,* as used by Callender and Kochems (1986), is problematic because it implies that persons of one sex cannot successfully become the gender of the other sex. Callender and Kochems argued that a male-bodied two-spirit person cannot fully be a woman because of the inability to replicate a woman's physiological functions. According to this perspective, a two-spirit person mixes genders because they are physiologically one sex but the other gender. This reasoning is mistaken, however, because it confuses sex with gender. Although the dominant American notion of gender assumes that gender derives from sex (i.e., one's sex determines one's gender), physiological function is not part of gender because gender refers to social characteristics and patterns of behavior. "Mixed gender" may be appropriate in cases where a person mixes both masculine and feminine but not in cases where gender conforms to the dominant cultural category.

As noted throughout this volume, the term "berdache" is no longer acceptable in referring to Native American genders. I am happy to discard it for all the reasons mentioned in other essays: because of its problematic origins; because it is a reminder of the imposition of colonial categories, morality, and values on Native ways; and because many Native American two-spirits reject the term and choose to define themselves by their own term. Future work on particular Native American nations should use the terms of the group or the pan-Indian *two-spirit* when speaking about two-spirit people.

In attempting to find a "scientific" signifier for two-spirit practices, several contributors have come up with new designations, such as *gender variance* and *alternative gender.* These terms pose another set of problems. "Gender variance" is confusing because the word *variance* can be taken to refer to the range of expressions within one gender. Gender in any culture is not a rigid category or set of rules to which all men and women conform precisely (there may not even be boundaries). Using "gender variance" assumes the presence of an identifiable category from which some deviate. As used in this volume, it refers only to two-spirits and transgenders (or other genders in addition to masculine and feminine), but it could also include a whole range of other "variations," such as female-bodied women who are not stereotypically feminine but are still considered women. Consequently, "gender variance" as an appellation for two-spirit people is imprecise.

The term *alternative gender* is unsatisfactory because it implies the existence of a standard system (of two genders) plus "alternatives," marking two-spirit as different than a standard gender. The term implicitly evokes the dual gender Euro-American system that recognizes only two valid genders; anything else is a deviation (alternative). But the lesson to be learned from groups that have multiple genders is that, for them, gender ideology does not make sense without the two-spirit gender (for instance, the *lhamana* or *nádleehi*). It is a unified multiple-gender system, not a two-gender system plus one or two derivations. Epple underscores this point, arguing that the concept of alternative gender is a Euro-American construct of a-situational traits and non-dynamic genders that does not necessarily reflect gender in other cultures. Given these considerations, it seems inappropriate to refer to two-spirit gender as a variant or alternative gender.

Some authors in this volume, intending to identify both the subject's body and gender, use the terms *manly females* and *womanly males* to describe two-spirit people. As with earlier terms, however, these give undue emphasis to the biological aspect of the individual while downplaying the social. Here the use of "manly" or "womanly" implies an ability to be manlike or womanlike but not quite men or women. If we are to be consistent in seeing two-spirits as social men or women, we should call them "female men" and "male women." But even these terms tend to replicate our folk bias concerning the inability to separate sex from gender. To the extent that two-spirit people are different from each other because of their female or male bodies, it is important to distinguish between the two, but the labels so far proposed may not be the answer.

Diversity, Not Definition

Scholars continue to seek definitions for two-spirit people despite the fact that, as Tafoya (in this volume) states, they may be able to get either the context or the definition but not both. The quest for definition remains unresolved and problematic in studies of Native American sexuality and gender because every attempt at definition creates a reductive category within which to slot the experiences of two-spirit people. Anthropologists need to do less defining and universalizing or they will be guilty, as Tafoya reminds them, of playing a role similar to scientists and sexologists of the late nineteenth century. By codifying, normalizing, and medicalizing hetero- and homosexuality into existence, they created a means of social control through sexual classification that shapes and limits individual experience. By attempting to define two-spirit gender, scholars wittingly or unwittingly codify categories that are always contested and achieved rather than natural and unchanging. As is clear from the Native authors in this book, anthropologists need to do less defining and universalizing and pay attention to what two-spirit people say about their lives.

The many problems of definition and labeling are clear from these essays. Any label, any definition, excludes some two-spirit people. The Native writers in this volume recognize the many conflicting identities and genders they manage, from lesbian and gay to white, Native, pan-Indian, urban, rural, traditionalist, and assimilationist. Neat definitions and categories cannot account for the range of identities. Instead, they force two-spirit people to justify who they are if they are different than the categories anthropologists have created for them. Little Thunder states that she is a Lakota womyn, a female who has no desire to be a male and who can perform many tasks that are considered male jobs. She is a mother who has strong spiritual beliefs, and she loves women. But lest her description of herself become a definition, she adds that she is different than other two-spirit women. Robertson argues for validity as a *winkte,* an identity he, as a gay man, a Scot, and a Lakota, is redefining. What he is not is a cross-dressing, bead-sewing, sexually anal-passive man/woman. On the other hand, Red Earth explains that although he sometimes takes the submissive role in sex, cross-dresses, and has responsibilities that are defined by female gender roles, that is not the case all the time and thus would not accurately define who he is. All three identify as two-spirit; their personal journeys point to the complexity of identities in a contemporary world. Such identities cannot be encapsulated in any of the anthropological terms for two-spirit people. As Little Thunder states, "No single term can apply to all of us at any time."

Contributors to this volume move beyond the "labeling and mounting" phase to consider two-spirits as part of lived human culture (rather than relics of the past) situated within social relations and formed through negotiation and contestation. Red Earth writes that claiming the *winkte* title has been a continual process of reconciling and negotiating (white) gay and traditional identities. In seeking to remember "who we are," Anguksuar shows that being two-spirit is not simply remembering a traditional identity but creatively constructing an identity that speaks to both the past and the present. Anthropologists need to follow the lead of the Native scholars and activists in this volume and realize that, as with other cultures and identities, two-spirit identities shift constantly; they are never definitive or static.

The essays in this volume show that by contextualizing the lives of two-spirit people within their own cultures and gender systems and within larger sociocultural and historical contexts the diversity in what was and is two-spirit begins to appear (see also, arguing for gender variability among the Navajo, Lorrie 1993; Roscoe 1991). Epple states that contemporary Navajo *nádleehí* feel that their gender identities change in response to their interconnections with others. One of Epple's consultants states that no one can say what constitutes a *nádleehí*. Each individual Epple interviewed (who were all male) uses different terms to talk about herself, leading Epple to conclude, among other things, that dress, occupation, and sexual practice are not adequate markers of the contemporary *nádleehí*. Robertson distinguishes between his identity as *winkte* with that of his uncle, who was also *winkte* and represented a different generation and way of accommodating to social processes on and off the reservation. In each case the importance of context is emphasized.

Thomas and Epple (both in this volume) compare Navajo genders. Epple refuses to define *nádleehí* because of the variability of gender among the *nádleehí* to whom she talked. Further, because all Navajo contain within themselves both masculine and feminine, she argues against the use of concepts such as "gender mixing," "third sex," or "third gender." She calls for a shift from a categorical to a dynamic analysis of two-spirit. From his position as a Navajo and anthropologist, Thomas (who uses a different spelling of the Navajo term than Epple) reemphasizes gender categories in his analysis of *nádleehi*, stressing the differences between two-spirit people who are traditional and assimilated Navajo as well as those who consider themselves lesbians and gays. Despite the large number of categories that Thomas uses for two-spirit people, he ultimately concludes that gender possesses a negotiated quality, depending to a large extent on context. Epple and Thomas provide important evidence for the need to understand categorization as well as negotiation in two-spirit identity.

Several essays provide an important critique of over-reliance on rigid definitions of occupational role or sexual object choice to identify two-spirit people. In reviewing earlier colonial and ethnographic texts, some scholars incorrectly identified certain Native American individuals and practices as two-spirit. Beatrice Medicine (1983), a Lakota anthropologist, was the first to point out the problem. She noted that the manly-hearted women and warrior women of the Plains nations were alternative roles for women, not two-spirit genders. Several authors in this volume (Pilling, Goulet, Epple, and Kehoe) show that certain individuals previously identified as two-spirit were in reality shamans or temporary or situational cross-dressers. Although some of these mistakes arose from an over-eagerness to make visible a once despised and neglected identity, they highlight the necessity of attention to the historical and cultural context within which two-spirit people live and the relation of two-spirit people to other people and genders.

Previous scholarly writing on two-spirit people tended to focus on the sexual or the gender component of their lives because sexuality and gender were thought to be the key areas of difference. As this volume shows, however, many other aspects of social life and culture also bear on two-spirit identity. Some two-spirit people follow a spiritual calling, such as shamans. Jacobs (1983) describes the *kwidó* (also spelled *kweedo*) having a "special relationship to supernatural forces." Goulet shows the importance of Northern Athapaskan reincarnation beliefs in the formation of individual identities. People whose genders in a previous incarnation were different than their present gender come to understand themselves as combining both the masculine and feminine. Farrer suggests that possession of ritual knowledge and power may be an important factor in the development of two-spirit identity. Her description of Bernard Second, a Mescalero Apache she identifies as two-spirit, shows a strong link between his complex personality and the force of his spiritual power. The importance of a spiritual calling is highlighted by several Native authors (Hall, Anguksuar, Little Thunder, and Red Earth), who find being two-spirit as simple and difficult as "following the path" (becoming who they were meant to be).

Another important question concerns the place of the body in constructions of gender. Both Epple and Thomas suggest that bodies as well as identities must be considered in an analysis of two-spirit categories. Thomas assigns individuals to different gender categories, depending on their physical bodies. He distinguishes among hermaphrodites, male-bodied, and female-bodied two-spirits to arrive at eight sex/gender categories. Cromwell (in this volume) also argues that transgenders in the United States occupy a different gender than either masculine or feminine because their bodies are not appropriate to their gender. He suggests that two genders have always been present in the United States although the medico-psychiatric establishment has suppressed that fact by forcing transgenders and hermaphrodites to choose between masculine or feminine. He argues that in a system in which gender is rigidly attached to sex, someone whose gender is different than that assigned on the basis of physiology becomes an individual of interme-diate gender. Cromwell thus equates transgenders with two-spirit be-cause they occupy an intermediate gender, mixing bodies and genders (a view similar to Epple's and Thomas's findings).

Although this argument may be appropriate to Euro-American and Navajo genders, it raises the question of whether biology has some-thing to do with gender outside of particular cultural interpretations. Leaving aside the difference in bodies, a masculine or feminine trans-gender reflects the norm in the United States. Transgenders do not change the gender system unless their identity is different than either masculine or feminine. Men without penises or women without vagi-nas are still men or women. On the other hand, if transgenders are neither masculine nor feminine, then American society could be said to have a multiple-gender system. Aside from these questions, the im-portance of the transgender and two-spirit critique is that bodies have no relation to gender.

Conclusion

These essays provide a complex vision of two-spirit identity that di-rects attention to new questions and possibilities. Weston (1993) in her review of lesbian and gay studies in anthropology, advocates a focus on two-spirit subjectivity, not on constructing bounded catego-ries. How do two-spirit people position themselves in relation to male and female? What kinds of power are they negotiating through their claim to two-spirit identity? In what way are they building symbolic capital? Her questions are a good corrective to previous studies that imposed a static conception of gender on two-spirit people in "tradi-tional" cultures. On the other hand, her questions also suggest that there are only two gender categories, masculine and feminine, against which the two-spirit person must somehow situate her- or himself. The implicit privileging of two genders that Weston suggests leaves the binary in place and places the two-spirit person on the outside of a coherent gender system.

Other questions that writers might consider in analyzing two-spirit identity include: Is two-spirit gender a rejection of an assigned gender? Is it a resistance to rigid gender categories? Or is it a significant, endur-ing social relationship?

These essays suggest the importance of pushing the analysis of two-spirit gender toward the question of social relations. How do two-spirit people position themselves in relation to other Natives as well as white gays and lesbians? What relationships do they maintain with the larger communities around them? How do they fit into the social system at the institutional level? What power relations are expressed through the two-spirit gender? In describing how he came to know himself as two-spirit, Red Earth illustrates the complexity of relations he developed with his reservation and urban relatives and friends in the white gay community. All have bearing on who he is as a *winkte,* an identity not easily encapsulated in any one form. But we should expect no less. Gay and lesbian identities and genders have shifted and multiplied, fractured and reformed many times since the early 1970s. The inability of scholars to define "a lesbian" adequately should be clear indication that no identity will be defined in simple terms.

Recognizing two-spirit as an identity rather than an immutable gender may be the most fruitful direction to take. Both Thomas and Lang suggest that two-spirit can be compared to an ethnic identity. Lang suggests that we should not prioritize gender or sexual preference in a study of two-spirit but rather view it as an ethnic identity. That suggestion draws an important connection with ethnic and gay studies by emphasizing the way in which identities are constantly changing and transforming in relation to other cultural, political, and economic processes.

This book is eloquent testimony to the fact that the study of two-spirit people has moved beyond the limitations of anthropological models and representations. In so doing, anthropologists will hopefully abandon the distorted perceptions of those colonizers, conquerors, missionaries, and ethnographers who have written about two-spirit people. Anthropologists may also have to abandon their search for the "traditional" or "classic" two-spirit person. Reconsiderations of past work are still important and useful correctives to earlier misperceptions, as Pilling, Goulet, and others have shown. But as this book attests, the greatest potential for two-spirit studies comes from culturally based, contemporary research. This book is a testament to diversity and to the potentialities of two-spirit identity. As Herdt suggests, the study of two-spirits includes spirituality, power, sexuality, gender, identities, and desires. The new work will help to foreground the contextualized and contested nature of two-spirit gender identities, as well as the way contemporary two-spirit Native Americans negotiate the plurality of identities with which they are faced.

Note

1. I follow Cromwell's usage (in this volume) of the terms *male-bodied* or *female-bodied* to identify physiological sex.

References Cited

Blackwood, Evelyn. 1984. "Sexuality and Gender in Certain Native American Tribes: The Case of Cross-Gender Females." *Signs: Journal of Women in Culture and Society* 10(1): 27–42.
———. 1988. Review of *The Spirit and the Flesh: Sexual Diversity in American Indian Culture*, by Walter L. Williams. *Journal of Homosexuality* 15(3–4): 165–76.
Callender, Charles, and Lee M. Kochems. 1986. "Men and Not-Men: Male Gender-Mixing Statuses and Homosexuality." In *The Many Faces of Homosexuality: Anthropological Approaches to Homosexual Behavior*, ed. Evelyn Blackwood, 165–78. New York: Harrington Park Press.
Jacobs, Sue-Ellen. 1983. Comments on "The North American 'Berdache,'" by Charles Callender and Lee M. Kochems. *Current Anthropology* 24(4): 459–60.
Lang, Sabine. 1991. "Female Gender Variance among North American Indians: A Cross-Cultural Perspective." Unpublished ms. University of Hamburg.
Lorrie, Annie. 1993. "Gender, Kinship and the Modern Sexual Identity: An Ethnographic Look at Negotiating Contemporary Sexual Meanings According to Traditional Navajo Values." Honors thesis, Stanford University.
Martin, M. Kay, and Barbara Voorhies. 1975. *Female of the Species*. New York: Columbia University Press.
Medicine, Beatrice. 1983. "'Warrior Women': Sex Role Alternatives for Plains Indian Women." In *The Hidden Half: Studies of Plains Indian Women*, ed. Patricia Albers and Beatrice Medicine, 143–73. Lanham: University Press of America.
Roscoe, Will. 1991. *The Zuni Man-Woman*. Albuquerque: University of New Mexico Press.
———. 1994. "How to Become a Berdache: Toward a Unified Analysis of Gender Diversity." In *Third Sex, Third Gender: Beyond Sexual Dimorphism in Culture and History*, ed. Gilbert Herdt, 329–72. New York: Zone Books.
Weston, Kath. 1993. "Lesbian/Gay Studies in the House of Anthropology." *Annual Review of Anthropology* 22: 339–67.
Williams, Walter. 1986. *The Spirit and the Flesh: Sexual Diversity in American Indian Culture*. Boston: Beacon Press. Reprint 1991, with a new preface.

Part 5: Dealing with Homophobia

★ ★ 21

Dealing with Homophobia in Everyday Life*

Introduction: Words, Ceremonies, and Everyday Lives

Claire R. Farrer

In the following transcript, our everyday words appear almost exactly as spoken. We purposely left them largely unedited in an effort to share some of the emotions—fear, anger, love, and acceptance—expressed on that May 1994 morning in one of the windowless conference rooms of the Field Museum of Natural History in Chicago. This was the third in our study group's meetings; many of us were perplexed that still there was so little understanding and that such wide gulfs separated some of us. We did not agree. We did not agree even within categories, such as Native to Native, anthropologist to anthropologist, two-spirit to two-spirit, male to male, or female to female.

A few had already left the conference to catch airplanes, but most of us remained, our suitcases standing as silent sentinels along the walls. We were not quite finished, but none seemed to know how to begin to breach the walls erected by acrimonious words that threatened to entomb each of us in a personal cell. Spontaneously, the bridges appeared as both Beverly Little Thunder and Clyde Hall began ceremonies of healing that gathered us in a circle, facing each other. Those bridges allowed us to climb out of our individual cells, leave behind our acri-

---

Editors' note: Participants who took part in the talking circle convened at Chicago's Field Museum, where the second conference funded by the Wenner-Gren Foundation for Anthropological Research was held. They included those who have contributed to this volume, as well as others (Native Americans and non-Natives) who had asked to join the study group after the 1993 meetings in Washington, D.C. The "new" members of the group are not listed out of respect for their anonymity. We have chosen to use first names for participants.

mony, and begin again to address each other as community members.

The ceremonies segued into a talking circle. We turned to Bea Medicine, the senior First Nations person present, to be our moderator. We did not consciously set out to deconstruct the walls of acrimony, but that is what happened in most instances. Rather, we set out to do a simple thing: reflect and talk about homophobia in our lives—not as scholars, not as two-spirit people, not as anthropologists or psychologists, not as gay or lesbian or bisexual or transsexual or heterosexual persons, not as any category of being other than human being. There was no agenda, no topic other than reflection on homophobia.

It was a powerful time. Some of us cried. Some of us hugged each other. Some of us cried for each other. Some of us embraced what previously was impossible for us to confront, let alone embrace. And, sadly, some of us were unmoved—isolated in a cell of our own making and turning away from the keys of freedom leading to understanding and acceptance. But most of us were grateful for the place we reached, led by Beverly Little Thunder and Clyde Hall and mothered by Bea Medicine.

Although not in the transcript, our talking circle ended with each, in turn, walking within the circle and greeting each other person. Some of us could only shake hands and speak the most perfunctory of words, but most of us hugged, often kissed, and offered words of apology and support to each other. Bitterness and misunderstanding formed a rivulet and flowed out of that room. I shall do whatever is in my power to turn that rivulet into a flowing, joyous cascade until we can appreciate each other for what we are and how we can better the world around us rather than focus on what divides us. I am not so naive as to suppose that our rivulet cum cascade will not encounter rocks—even gigantic boulders. Each of us in the flow, with the conjoined support of the others, can slide around such obstacles and, in time, even tumble the rocks and boulders into a part of the greater whole that is humanity, unencumbered by labels.

In the following, the first names of all individuals who participated in the second Wenner-Gren Conference are used; some did not contribute to this collection, others did. Only those included in the volume are listed as contributors; the others remain nominally anonymous.

The Transcript

Arnold: I am slowly overcoming the homophobia I have absorbed from my surrounding environment. I find that it is important that I attempt to solve that issue before I try to do much of anything else. It has been a slow process of some years at this point, and starting when I was pretty old, too.

Carrie: As for homophobia: It exists just about everywhere. I find myself in circles listening to people talk about the matter in a negative way, sometimes I do not say anything and other times I will interrupt the conversation and briefly highlight the importance of Native gays/lesbians. I will participate in various awarenesses, but I am not the town-crier—speaking (loud) to the masses. I see, feel, and know the Native population in my community (a sixty-to-one-hundred-mile radius) is subtle in their acceptance. I've shown my video to some of my family, [a] Native film/video festival, and to some educators, but I do not quite feel I have the product that I want to be shown in my community. With practice I sense society is able to bend and accept Creator's gifts.

Deban: It has never been particularly important for me to be out or whatever. I have seen a lot of discrimination around gay and lesbian issues, but I am just who I am. Where we live now I take into consideration the cultural perspectives and being sensitive about that too, but I am still just how I am, and it seems to be pretty well accepted. I know that people are not ignorant or stupid or anything like that, they know what is going on around them. There is definitely uncomfortableness in some situations, but primarily I think we are fortunate in our situation. I am very close with Carrie [House]'s family, and that is nice. They seem accepting. I think education of the youth is really important, but it has never been a big thing to me. I do not need to be very vocal about who I am or how I am. I just live my life and allow that to be whatever it is.

Bea: I have a question. In many of the Native American communities that I know there are questions raised about interracial alliances. I was just wondering how you dealt with that in the community.

Deban: Well I have not really noticed that it has been that difficult. I can definitely tell when people do not think that maybe Indian people should be with anybody from even another tribe perhaps. But a lot of times, too, we are in situations where people do not necessarily recognize that we are together as a couple. It is just— I am her friend or something. I know that they have a lot of incorrect assumptions. We will go to a chapter meeting or something, and I do not really understand Navajo (but I am learning a little bit), and maybe I will catch some things. And so I think, "Wow, they think that," but I understand that it is going to be some time coming. And I think it is just going to take time. It takes time. And I have that time. I do not expect to be accepted just like that. Over time, over years, or whatever, as people see who I am and how I am, that is what it takes.

Paul: The way I deal with homophobia, whether it is very blatant and obvious, I confront it, and I do not let it pass without my saying something. That comes from my activist background. Being one of the organizers of ACT UP Chicago, I had to be out in front. I was a press spokesperson for several years so I have dealt with verbal abuse, physical abuse, with homophobia right in my face. My immediate reaction is to come on as strong as they do and try to confront it. And if you can get to the stage where you can talk a little bit, maybe try to explain why it is we are being out there, why it is we are being open. We are not trying to put our sexuality in their face, but we have other issues that deal with our lifestyle. One of the things I am noticing about being an employee of an institution like the Field Museum is that there is homophobia but it is very subtle and underlying. And one of the issues we are working on here—a lesbian and gay museum workers' group—is we are trying to get insurance benefits for same-sex domestic partners. We have been working for two years. We finally got Blue Cross/Blue Shield of Illinois, our insurer, to agree to cover us, and the board of directors said no. They would not do it. I think we are dealing with homophobia with some of the people on the board. Our next plan of action is to confront the board of directors individually and then have time with them as a whole and present our issues. My personal view of dealing with homophobia is that you have to confront it. You cannot let it pass.

Achiel: On a personal level, I felt it important not to consider myself the victim of society. Because I found that as long as I was in that kind of victimization pattern, I found it very self-destructive. You cannot fight a big society, but by building a positive image of myself it was the very starting point of fighting negative attitudes. On the level of my community, I am teaching at the Roman Catholic Faculty of Theology, where we have openly supported, or more, our theologians in order to build a new understanding of sexuality in general. Unfortunately, several months ago we had to bury one of our best theologians who died of a heart attack. He was also my closest friend. After seven or eight years of harassment the Roman authorities forced his abdication, but we created a foundation in his name to allow graduate students to continue that type of work, which is very important in the Catholic church and other Christian denominations too. Not just homophobia or homosexuality or things like that, but a different vision of sexuality in general, human sexuality. We try to do that notwithstanding all the pressures we feel from conservative trends and Christianity.

Jason: I have to deal with two issues, not only homophobia but transgenderphobia as well. For my community itself, homophobia among many people is pretty much there. But at least in many of the states right now, because of various initiatives that are trying to outlaw homosexuality and transsexuality and all of that, a lot of people are coming together and working together and trying to bridge the two communities. I think the greatest concern for my community is internalized transgenderphobia. There is a great deal of fear, and because of the way the discourses are constructed there is a great deal of internalized shame around being a transgender person. Being as out as I am in the various venues of my life I still face this sometimes when I am coming out or know that is going to happen. I feel this fear. One of the things I try to do is get across the message that we do not have to be ashamed, that we have not done something wrong, that we are not some pariah of society. In fact, we should have [a] tremendous amount of pride in what our lives have accomplished. It is more a one-on-one kind of thing with people in trying to educate and to make clear that homophobia reflects on our own internalized transgenderphobia.

Jean-Guy: Homophobia exists first in myself; that is where I experienced it first. It was in my reaction, for instance, when many years ago I saw two men kissing each other on a street corner as they were parting. I was shocked. When we talk about challenging homophobia I think it is a very personal thing to do. It operates at very unconscious levels at times, and I surprise myself, thinking, "I have these thoughts." In my view the most powerful way to change is through real friendships with individuals who are gay and lesbian. To me, that is the most profound way to change. Because when I integrate these friends in my life, something changes for good. When we first met as a group in Washington, D.C., I remember Sabine [Lang] receiving a beaded collar and tie, given to her with humor and love by Native American Indian gay men. When they gave her this gift they said they had felt deeply respected by her when she approached them for her Ph.D. research, and they addressed her as a "two-legged creature." This is a very important concept, for it recognizes in each individual something other than what one has between one's legs and what one may happen to do with it. We are two-legged creatures among many other creatures. And we relate to each other in many ways. Participating in this group is important for me to undo some of my homophobia and whatever other prejudices I may have. Change occurs through many ways, it is incremental. I do not know all the steps, but it is possible to change. The potential is there in all of us to treasure and to nurture diverse friends and fellow human beings.

Walter: Yesterday I made the statement that coming out of the research for the class I am teaching called "Overcoming Prejudice" there are two areas that research tends to show have had a dramatic impact on reducing different forms of prejudice: one was an ongoing one-to-one dialogue with people you are having a continuous relationship with. It is impossible to do that if you are in the closet. What that would imply is that people would have to be open about themselves and not be hiding things, especially to those people who are close to us in our lives—and quite often they may be the last people that we are open to. We may go out, march in a parade or something like that, but then we are not open to our family, our extended relatives, our long-term friends, our co-workers. I think the implication is that—and again drawing on those traditions of different tribes—that was the message: it was those family relationships that really provided the basis for that strong position within the community.

The other thing that I mentioned yesterday was the impact of the mass media. In a way this is kind of humbling to scholars who write scholarly books. The mass media are actually the things that are really more important: film, television, popular literature and places like this, which is why I think Paul's idea of the museum exhibit is so important. This is something that is going to reach a lot of people. Let us face it, most people are not going to pick up and read a scholarly book, are not going to read articles in scholarly journals. I think it is important for us, as scholars, to keep our sense of perspective in mind that it is not just our writing of scholarly works but also what we can do to assist other people who are going to have much more of an impact on society than we can. I think it is important for us to offer ourselves to be there to assist people who are going to get that message out. It is important that the work that Doyle [Robertson] and Carrie have been doing on the video productions be continued. That is how you reach people.

Another thing that the research tends to show that I did not mention yesterday is that one way that you convince people to change their attitude is to point out to them in ongoing discussions that there is an inconsistency between this particular prejudice and their larger value system. And if you can figure out some way to do that, then that has a big impact. I have had Native people come up to me and tell me they have had relatives or co-workers or close friends who are very strong about their value system of protecting their tribal heritage , and then they point out, "Well, in our tribal heritage, this two-spirited idea was very respected." And it kind of throws a lot of people into a little crisis of reexamination. And it is that crisis of reexamination combined with that ongoing one-to-one relationship with the person that is really what leads people to reexamine their prejudices and change their minds. But I think some of these ideas that are coming out of the research are just scratching the surface of what we need to be learning about how to best go about doing this. And that is why I think it is important to get everybody's perspective and go around and see what are the different ideas that emerge.

Brenda: I think that heterosexism, like racism, is a learned behavior, and it can be unlearned. When people confront difference or otherness there is a fear that goes up, and there are a lot of misconceptions and erroneous assumptions that people have whether they get it from the media, or whether they get it from church or other friends or something like that. In order to deal with it, I think it is going to take a lot of education. I know that on the Navajo reservation—you had asked the question of interrelationships—I see that as following a similar pattern. When I am working with couples that are intermarried back home, couples who have been married for thirty years, when they first got together there was a lot of resentment towards them. I imagine there is a lot of resentment towards same-sex (mixed) couples who try to live back home. For Indian peoples it is really hard to remove yourself from your family, like so many I cannot make a qualification like that—but there are many gays and lesbians who move to another side of the continent and cut ties with their families. As Indian people, it is very hard to do that. Carrie makes choices to live back home, and I think with that it is just going to take a lot of patience . . . you really have to be steadfast in who you really are in going back home.

I think of the couples, the intermarried couples, I work with back home. There were people so resentful against them and saying, "This is not a traditional way of being married." And there are people who will say that about same-sex couples, "That is not being traditional." Then there are other people who will say, "It is okay because you are my granddaughter, you are my daughter, you are my son or my grandson," and they have an understanding about that. One woman asked, "What ingredient does it take for you and your husband to maintain the relationship after all that has been said about marrying outside the Navajo tribe?" She says, "Well, it takes a lot of patience. You have to be willing to just be who you are and be patient and, in time, these people will see what kind of person you are, and it is just a part of who you are and that everything else is just the same. But maybe they just learn something about you that they did not know about. But everything else about you, all the other values that you have."

In terms of dealing with heterosexism, I think it is like racism too. When we as Indian peoples confront racism, it can be so tiring that sometimes we have to pick our own battles. Sometimes heterosexism can be blatant, sometimes it can be really covered over—just like racism. And so when you feel it you go through all those emotions that you do when someone is being heterosexist. I think you have to pick your own battles on that because you can just wear yourself out trying to educate people about what a Navajo person is or what a gay person is. I think it takes a lot of patience on your part and on the other part to get through this educational process. And it is a process. Maybe a lifetime process. I think these patterns of behavior can be unlearned, just like racism. That is it.

Wesley: I have dealt with homophobia on three levels. On the first level in Western culture, if someone makes some derogatory remark I usually tell them, "I am sorry you have a problem with that, but I do not." That is how I usually deal with it. And it just depends on what takes place after that. I have dealt with that on an individual basis. When dealing with other Native people, I usually tell them that maybe they should look more into their culture to find out who they are before they make a remark like that. The most important area, and where I really put my feet down, or my pumps down, if it is somebody who is Navajo who makes a remark, usually I respond to them in Navajo to find out if they speak the language. If they speak the language I usually tell them, in Navajo, that they are not responsible for me, and I am not responsible for them. They have to know who they are to make a statement because they have to have some sort of power to be judgmental on other people from traditional Navajo views. And you cannot do that if you do not have that power. You cannot pass judgment on somebody else without having a stable ground yourself. Usually that is my confrontation with other Navajos. If they do not speak Navajo, I usually just respond that they should learn more of their culture before they make a statement like that. Because making a statement like that is telling me they are unsure of who they are. When it gets into somebody from the Navajo Nation I do not let them get away with it.

Sabine: I am what my culture defines as a lesbian. I do not think I ever had to cope with a lot of internalized homophobia; growing up as a child who was different from other kids in a number of respects. When I was ten, I read scientific books on human evolution and dinosaurs long before dinosaurs became popular; I was the worst tomboy in the village; when all the other teenagers were having wild parties, I devoted my evenings to the creation of watercolors and oil paintings and my weekends to the composition of short stories. The discovery that I was a lesbian did not really come as a shock to me. It was just another aspect of being myself, and, as it turned out, it also was no surprise to those close to me.

As far as homophobia in German society is concerned, I used to march in the German equivalent to Gay Pride parades a lot in the early 1980s; however, I do not think anymore that parades are the best way to help people overcome their prejudice against gay, lesbian, and transgendered people. They are a wonderful way to celebrate ourselves and our diversity, yet the average straight German bystander seemed amused, or, in a number of instances, even frightened or appalled, at the sight of screaming drag queens on roller skates or dykes wearing fedoras and neckties or crew cuts and black leather clothing—a bizarre crowd reaffirming their worst prejudices about lesbians and queers. Thus, personally, I have decided that the most promising way to help people to overcome any prejudice they may have is to interact with them on a personal level. Of course, I also hope that publications as well as writings by others and myself will aid people to rethink homophobia.

I see myself as a human being who happens to prefer sexual and social relationships with women but who has many other personality traits, interests, and gifts that to me are much more important and interesting than my sexual orientation. If someone dislikes me just because of my sexual orientation, well, it is *their* loss. Thus, I try to get people to see me and other gay people as complete persons not defined by or limited to sexual preferences. I have been out to my family and friends and also to students and staff at the anthropology department at [the] University of Hamburg for many years, and I have been very lucky—almost everyone has reacted in a very positive manner to my being Sabine, alias "Turtle," anthropologist, typist, cartoonist, and human being who also happens to be a lesbian.

Ginger: I am Claire, but more comfortably, Ginger. I grew up in a two-toned family. Half of them look like me—that is my father's half. The other half are southern Italians who are really Sefardic Jews. They are very dark people. And there was always prejudice on the part of my father's family against my mother's family, including—to the point when we lived in the far south during World War II, the Ku Klux Klan visited us, not only because of what they assumed to be a biracial marriage but also because of a woman who is a friend of ours who is black and who sometimes stayed in the house, and in Tennessee that was not allowed in those times. Early on, I decided there are a lot of crazy adult people, and I was not going to be one of them. I managed to construct a birthday cake kind of facade around me, filled with some frills and flowers and icings. I thought I was one of the least prejudiced people in the world. My first book was on women's issues attacking patriarchy. I began teaching courses in women's studies, gender things, in the 1970s. And then I phoned my physician, and a male answered, and I said, "I want to speak to the secretary," and he said, "I am the secretary." And I thought . . . there goes a slice of my carefully constructed cake! It was really embarrassing. Well, there have been several more incidents similar to that where I like to think I am at one place and something in life teaches me that I am really not there yet. The most recent one was at a salmon feed that the Native American students on my campus do every year. I had gone to this with one of my friends who is in a long-term lesbian relationship. A really attractive Indian man came by, and she said, fork coming to the mouth with salmon, "I could have his babies." And I said, "Hey, wait a minute, you are a lesbian. You cannot have it both ways." She said, "Oh yes I can." There went another piece of the cake!

I do not know how I can educate anyone else when I am still in the process of being educated myself. But I am a teacher, and I try to teach not just in the classroom but through my life. This last year has been a very fine year for me. I have had many honors on my campus, including several receptions and fairly uninteresting command performances, some of which I have asked biological family members to attend with me, others of which I have asked people in the community who have been important to me. We have a huge lesbian community where I live. And some of those women have been extremely important in my life. I have invited them as my surrogate family despite their protests that it would label me as lesbian to part of this community, which I figure is their problem not mine. I know what I do and with whom I do it, and I do not know that [what I do] is anybody else's business.

Terry: [Opens with a brief blessing in Native language.] My dear people. I actually started doing homophobia workshops probably ten years or more ago for Lincoln, Nebraska's school district, which struck me as odd as to why they wanted me there and why they wanted me. But it was because I had worked for about fifteen years in terms of anti-racism issues in public schools. It was just a natural progression to do those sorts of things as well. I periodically do very formal presentations on homophobia issues. But I think that really has less impact because you preach to the choir. The people who come are the people who really do not need to hear most of what you are saying other than to get the acknowledgment or the reassurance about what they are doing is important. But I speak an average of about three times a week somewhere in terms of a conference, or a keynote, or doing something in bilingual education, or in mental health, or in alcohol/substance abuse prevention, or in AIDS. I use that as an opportunity to pull in homophobia issues. I think of it in the way that you give a dog a pill in terms of wrapping hamburger meat around it.

If I am speaking to church ladies, I will somewhere along the line bring in homophobia issues. But I do it always having prepared them around the idea. I will start out with a traditional Native American legend. Maybe about Coyote's eyes. In terms of how Coyote lost his eyes, and he then has to try to see through the eyes of other animal people. The Warm Springs version of the legend is similar to a lot of other traditions, other cultures that will tell a similar legend. At Warm Springs it will end with the idea that the very last set of eyes he gets he trades with a woman, he gets flower eyes, kind of a daisy. And he trades those flower eyes for regular eyes, he tricks her in the sense of saying, "These are magic flower eyes. I can see everything. I can see further than anyone else. I can even see what your husband is doing while you are working so hard over here." And she takes the basket that she has on her back that is full of berries that she had been picking, and she said, "Gee I wish I had a set of eyes like that." And Coyote said, "You do. I tell you what. I will trade you straight across. You give me your ordinary, everyday eyes, and I will give you my magic flower eyes." And she agrees to this.

Now Coyote has normal eyes again and she has the flower eyes. She is looking around, and this kind of flower closes when the sun goes down. Her eyes close up because it is late afternoon, and she is blind. And she yells at Coyote and says, "Now I know you are the trickster, that stinky trickster." And she throws the flower eyes on the ground and says, "Give me my own eyes back." And Coyote says, "You did not want these eyes, you will have no eyes at all. You will spend all of eternity having to feel your way the way I had to feel my way around when I was blind." And as he spoke, he used his *tamanawit* on her, his spirit power. She started shrinking. She became smaller and smaller and smaller until she became the person we call "Shukshya." And Shukshya in English means snail. And that is why, today, when you see the snail, it still has to feel its way around just like Coyote had to feel his way around. And the basket she carried on her back became a shell the snail still carries.

Then from there I will talk about the idea of the reason why the snail woman is punished. The other animal people in the story who share their eyes with Coyote give up one of their eyes, keep the other one, but they refuse to give up their sacredness, their uniqueness. And the reason why she is punished is because she accepts the idea that one way of seeing is inherently superior to any other way of seeing or being. That sets the stage for me to talk about differences and respect and the idea of being created the way that you are in a sacred manner. And it allows me to talk about gender. It allows me to talk about ethnicity and language and spirituality and sexual orientation or sexuality.

It all becomes part of one package, and psychologically this is related to what we call the "yes set effect." The "yes set" is the idea that, psychologically, if I can get you to agree with me four times, you will tend to agree with me on my fifth statement if I have set the stage around the idea that these are appropriate ways to respond. This is our traditional way within our culture and our community, then it is logical when I finally get around to including the sexuality aspect of it, that is accepted too. But when we started doing racism workshops we discovered that it was real hard to get people to respect other people's culture unless you understood what your own was. You start from understanding your own to be able to respect others. And that way I feel, too, that when I am talking about sexuality I really do not focus only on gay and lesbian or transgender. I try to talk across the board in terms of sexuality so that everybody hears something that may relate to them.

And, finally, because I am on the faculty of the Kinsey Institute, when I talk about sexuality it is from the point of view of, "Here is the best scientific knowledge we know. I am not offering you my opinions, I am not offering you my values, but I am speaking to you as a social scientist who has been trained in a certain way. And when we get more information, we change because that is what science is all about. But for right now, here is the best scientific knowledge I know how to share with you." And then that way it is not people challenging me about my trying to push my agenda but it is rather that they would have to respond to the empirical data, which certainly can be done a few times. But it sets it in a very different tone because then I am not attacked.

And when I have been on "Talk Live" on CNBC, that was something that got the most response I have ever experienced because the show got good ratings so they repeated it at least nine different times. And so people on reservations would come up to me, saying they videotaped my telling Coyote's sex stories and talking about homosexuality in China as well as in Native American community because people would call in from South Dakota and Georgia and other places wanting this kind of information. And one of the things we find, particularly in the Kinsey Institute, is that people are so hungry for information on sexuality because there is no adequate source of it for so many different people. And so it was a chance to speak again, not as Terry Tafoya but as someone who is considered an authority on certain levels within this field. I guess the most important thing for me is that I do not always talk about me. I try to stay in terms of a presenter because that is usually why I am asked to be there.

Doug: I guess if you will listen fast than I will talk fast. Just in terms of following up with some of Terry's thoughts that he shared is that in taking one step back before we even discuss strategies to deal with homophobia I think we also need a parallel track to talk about racism and sexism within the gay/lesbian/bisexual/transgender community. Because if we really are going to have an opportunity to speak [with] one voice in trying to deal with homophobia, then we have to make sure that all our voices are a part of that message.

I think there is a real lie out there that the community has been a welcoming place for all peoples. Because it really has not. In terms of dealing with homophobia, I guess a lot of people say they never have known a gay/lesbian/bisexual/transgender person. One strategy we might use is to send a sign-up sheet around. We can sign our names and agree when we are going to come to each other's communities, peoples' homes, and be gay or lesbian or bisexual/transgendered for them.

I think in some ways it is knowing what set of eyes to see through in situations in terms of whether or not one sees through Eagle's eyes in terms of having a distance and being able to look at the whole picture. And understanding what might be an appropriate strategy for a situation. And I would suggest that some of what we would like to be about is sharing our strengths, our diversity, and the wonderful aspects that the Creator has given us. But sometimes it is also that one needs to step back and become almost seeing through mouse eyes in terms of the details and knowing when to go in and really to confront homophobia.

In a lot of the work that I do in terms of social work and mental health a lot of people experience that question of, "How do you know, when did you know that you were first gay or lesbian?" "Have you ever been with a person of the opposite sex?" "No." "Well, how do you know that you are gay or lesbian?" And, in fact, much of what I think we need to challenge is that each of us are given a spirit song. . . we would not ask someone who is straight, "When did you first know you were straight? Have you ever been with a person of the same gender? If you have not been with a person of the same gender, how do you know you are not gay? Bisexual? Transgender?"

I think that there are multiple ways of seeing and strategies that can be utilized and that there is no one right way to deal with homophobia, and I think we have to be respectful of the ways in which each of us chooses or is able to take on that challenge as it happens. And remembering our context of our membership in community, sometimes that membership in community is more important than our own individual need to necessarily confront or change someone else's way of seeing.

Beverly: As a Native womyn, encountering ignorance and bigotry has been an everyday event in my life—sometimes so much so that homophobia has been just another thing to deal with on an everyday basis. There are non-Natives who hurl hate-filled words and actions at me, but the ones that are the most painful are the ones that come from my own people. While it hurts no matter who does the attacking, the pain of being rejected by one's own people can be the most devastating. I have used various methods of protecting myself from homophobic behavior. One has been to isolate myself from my own people. I no longer go home to my reservation as often as I used to. I no longer attend social dances as regularly as I once did. While I continue to educate people about the issues that affect my people, I do not join organized groups of Native people who fight for Native rights. I was once very active in these groups. Among non-Native people I am very open about my sexuality. Once someone gets to know me they do not seem upset about my being lesbian. There are times that I feel like I am accepted as a lesbian simply because I am a Lakota womyn and being Native is an "in thing" right now. I have learned to accept myself and do find that homophobia directed at me is not as painful as it once was. In fact, I find that I feel bad for those who would shun me because I am a lesbian. They will never know what a valuable friend and ally they have passed by.

Michael: [Points to chart he has made showing relationships within and outside of his family of origin.] This is me, and this is what I see as the homophobic onslaught that I feel that comes from individuals, the culture, and institutions. Individuals, from people calling me faggot in a derogatory way on the street. Culture, just from the mass media that I have to deal with that glorifies heterosexual relationships and negates homosexual relationships. And the institutions, like the taxes, the marriage institutions that do not acknowledge who I am with my partner. I also experience racial onslaughts and also gender onslaughts when I express a feminine gender. The way I deal with all of this stuff, my support comes from first Spirit. And this is what I feel this whole conference is about. My support comes from all aspects of my life, and first of that is Spirit. What is in my heart that I know that I need in order to be able to say that I am a good person and a valuable person and I can contribute. That is one way that I deal with this. The other is family. My family supports me to deal with this. My partner, who is an amazing reserve of support. My friends. There are friends here in this room that I come to for support. And in my home community and communities—meaning work, where I live, the people that are my neighbors.

Now the only way that it is possible to get support from these people is for me to be open with all aspects of my life with them, to share every aspect. I cannot compartmentalize at all. I cannot be Michael the good son, or Michael the spiritual person, or Lee's partner, or just my friend's friend. I have to be all those things to all those people, and then they give me support. And what also happens, indirectly, with me being open with them, is that they also deal directly with a lot of these institutions for me. My mother is one of the persons who is the first to challenge anybody of our people who says anything negative about gay or lesbian or bi or transgender people, and that is very significant. The other thing I need to acknowledge is the support in this room and this conference. This supports me to go back to all these arenas. To be who I am and to deal with this, and also the racist and the sexist and the gender bashing and all those areas that are part of the big thing, which are all interrelated.

Sue-Ellen: No matter what courses I am teaching I always include some information, some topics, some reading on gender variance and sexuality. I do not come out in my classes in the first day or week. When I do come out, I do not come out with any kind of big deal about it. I use a simple little phrase such as, "We lesbians often find it difficult to understand," then I go right on. I look at the class, and invariably some heads come up suddenly; others just keep writing or nodding. I do not find comfort in confrontation and insisting that people hear my voice and see me as a particular type of person. That style is not comfortable for me. But if students (and others) can understand that this is just a matter of course, a matter of life, it is just the way the world is to me . . . I try to teach this image by the words and the readings that they use and then by my own behavior. It is a strategy that I developed over the past ten years because I still have a lot of internalized homophobia, which leads me to frequently feel not like "a good person" (responding to Michael's remark). Overcoming homophobia is a lifetime process for me and many others. One step at a time, one day at a time to deal with this issue. I cannot do it Walter's way, I have to do it my way.

Alice: I do not face overt homophobia in my daily life because I happen to be straight; in my immediate family, only a cousin is homosexual. But I do feel very strongly that our society has a powerful structure that can cruelly oppress everyone who is not a white, Anglo-Saxon, Protestant male of the middle or upper class. What I try to teach my students and anybody else I can reach is to recognize the power structure, to recognize the oppression and exploitation, and to struggle against it, realizing that all of us who are not in the privileged class are enmeshed in the same struggle. In the gender roles class I regularly teach, I reiterate again and again that racism, sexism, and classism (the oppression of the working classes by the monied classes) are aspects of the same phenomenon, the marginalization and exploitation of persons marked for the disadvantaged classes by socially defined characteristics.

In teaching, I seek out many examples from American history of persons with one or more of these characteristics who have struggled against the limitations assigned to them according to their class. My favorite example is Victoria Claflin Woodhull, born to servants in the early nineteenth century. Claflin ran for president, with Frederick Douglass as her vice-presidential candidate, and was arrested for attempting to vote; she and her sister were the first women stockbrokers on Wall Street; she published a weekly newspaper that was first in America to print an English translation of Marx's *Communist Manifesto;* she demanded that sex be consensual and [that] women have the right to refuse even their husbands; and she published the aggrieved husband's story of how his employer, the famous preacher Henry Ward Beecher, forced himself upon the man's wife.

That breach of respect for the dominant class brought persecution by Anthony Comstock, who claimed Claflin, her husband, and sister had sent obscenity—a description of Beecher's actions—through the mails. Comstock succeeded in jailing all three and bankrupting the paper. The woman's rights activist Elizabeth Cady Stanton admired Claflin and endeavored to work with her but was strongly discouraged by the other ladies in the woman's rights movement, who would not associate with a person of such lowly origin and radical views on human dignity.

My problem as a teacher is that the students who take my gender roles class are the exceptions to the usual run, students who are seeking an unusual perspective. What about the more ordinary students in the big introductory anthropology classes? That is the course where I may reach those who are not already "converted." In that course I try to combat prejudice in two ways, in class lectures and by involving them in reading ethnographies and ethnohistory written from the point of view of the marginalized groups. My supplementary textbook, *The Ghost Dance: Ethnohistory and Revitalization,* attacks racism by presenting in vivid detail the struggle of several First Nations to preserve their cultures and communities. The chapter on the second Wounded Knee battle, 1973—in the lifetime of the students themselves, not ancient history—hits especially hard, and in the final exam the students frequently mention that they had no understanding, before reading the book, of the conditions of their American Indian fellow citizens. That chapter of the 1973 event was written with the close cooperation of my colleague JoAllyn Archambault, an anthropologist who is Lakota.

A book combatting racism, and the ignorance of history that supports racism, may not seem relevant to homophobia, but I believe that prejudice is an edifice that can be weakened once any major part is pulled down. Directly relevant to homophobia is the material, in the introductory anthropology course, on evolution. It is a simple biological given that our species reproduces exclusively through the union of sperm and ovum, that is, the coming together of male and female gametes. We must assume that there has been natural selection for social behavior that contributes to this reproductive process, and cross-cultural comparisons do show that heterosexual copulation is openly valued, along with nurturance of the resulting new generation.

In my course, I explain that the biological given explains the recognition and privileging of parents with their offspring in every human society, but the necessity of heterosexual copulation for reproduction does not exhaust the roles available for humans, either in assigning occupations (i.e., by gender) or in participating in sensual pleasures. The rise of bureaucratic governance in our Western societies propels the strict categorization of persons according to single, unambiguous role-sets, for example, woman-wife/mother, homemaker/low-income job/purchaser (summed up in the 1920s as "Mrs. Consumer"). Other societies, and millions in our own nation who struggle against this bureaucratic dominance, make it clear that sexual behavior, family behavior, occupations, dress preference, [and] sensual enjoyments are separable and independent variables. Homophobia is one facet of the societal organization that relegates most people to subordinate positions in which any assertion of individual difference threatens the power structure and jeopardizes the individual's supposedly inalienable rights to life, liberty, and the pursuit of happiness—as seen in the remarkable history of Victoria Claflin Woodhull, who was called "Mrs. Satan" and has not yet been accorded the biography, or place in American history, she earned.

Richard: I do not believe in gay and lesbian and straight and bisexual and all the various kinds of labels that science and rational tradition have been trying to (unsuccessfully) construct over the last hundred or so years and create a measurable sort of set of units that we can apply uniformly to all human beings. And I try to communicate that in one way or another when I am in the community organizing or teaching, whether it is in Native or non-Native communities, whether it is in urban or reservation communities. I politely—and I usually try to employ implicit methods—try not to come right out and say it. But I make very clear that I do not believe in these. They are inappropriate certainly, but I also believe they are inaccurate. They are very short-sighted.

I also make clear, especially when I am talking with Native audiences, I say, "Look, this is our history, this is part of our history. This is something of which we should be very very proud because it is light years ahead of all the other things, all the other bullshit that we see going around us." And that this is the thing that they are looking for. It is one of the things that is being sought by societies that have large holes in the social fabric. Based on that, what I hope is implicit is the fact that because I have been taught who I am I fully expect the respect of the people who I am with because I am returning the expectation of being treated with dignity. And that is how I deal with homophobia.

Clyde: A lot of the way I deal with homophobia is explained in my chapter ["Children of Grandmother Moon"] in *Living the Spirit,* but I think that probably the main thing is by example, by setting [an] example of the kind of person you are and the way you live your life. Back home, living on the reservation, people are always watching you, looking at you, and scrutinizing you. Indians can be their own worst enemies by being racist among themselves and tearing each other up. It is an example of just being, living, by being that kind of person that you want people to honor and respect. Those people back home and other places that tear you up for who you are—well, that just shows insecurity on their part. You have to let it go and not really get angry with it.

One of the things that is going on back in Idaho that is very important is that we have a referendum that is going to effect all gay or two-spirited people in Idaho. If this passes, it is going to be terribly difficult to live there. About two months ago we had a debate between the American Civil Liberties Union representative and the coalition that is trying to put this referendum on the ballot. It never struck home exactly how racism and homophobia are related, how such referenda threaten all of us, not only me as an Indian person and as a two-spirited person. In the audience were a lot of gay people, a group of Indians, supporters for us, and also the neo-Nazis and white supremacists from up in northern Idaho and their supporters hanging on. It was kind of interesting to have us all in one room. It is a wonder something did not happen there. Until this one meeting it never hit home with me how important it is to hang in there. And in those states where these types of referenda are going on, everyone must do everything possible to see that they are defeated.

Evie: I have dealt with homophobia by writing about lesbians and gays in my field, by trying to be out in academia at the university, on the job . . . although I am not always. There is always a question of when to and how to. But it is not something that I deny either. For example, when I went on a job interview I was definitely out, and I feel like I am more consistently out now, and that is really important in academia because they just do not realize that we are there a lot of times. Also, teaching, which I think I need to develop more, to make homophobia more apparent in my teaching and writing. The other way is in my activism, such as my work in Hawaii on the same-sex marriage project. I think that is a really important way to fight homophobia also—to be active, fighting for civil rights for lesbians and gays. Those are some ways I try to deal with it, and it also helps me to feel better about who I am.

Doyle: It is repeating what everyone has said, and we talked about this the first night we were here. It's about all those things that have been mentioned. It's knowing who you are, your place in the community, knowing yourself. To me, it is continually reflected back that I am doing anti-homophobia work just by being who I am, including just coming to this conference. Before coming here, I was pitching manure on a farm, and I had to run into the hardware store for something. The owner of the hardware store is from a very conservative Catholic family. She said, "I thought you were leaving town." I said, "Well, I am." She said, "What is this for again?" And I basically said, "Well, it's a conference on Natives, sex, and spirituality." And everyone knows who I am and what I am, but to be confronted with that . . . I went on by saying, "You don't really think I could stay on Main Street of this town for ten years like I have if I was not aware of an alternative way of viewing myself. If I believed what the Catholic church taught me about who I was, I would be dead." And that is why it is important that we do those things.

Michael: May I say one last thing just for myself? It is in reference to what Alice said, and this is an example of where sometimes I feel I'm not listened to. Because, with your statements Alice, what I was hearing was that heterosexual couplings to produce children are privileged and always will be. And then you talked about compartmentalizing aspects of lives.

Alice: No, no.

Michael: Oh, okay. But that is what I was hearing, and that is part of the institutions of the cultures. But just the fact that heterosexual couplings are privileged: I do not think that is right at all, and I do not think it's a good thing. Yes, children are necessary for the species to survive. But that does not acknowledge the wealth of diversity of what creates families. You can have a man and woman create a baby, but that man and that woman may not be a good family. It may be better for that child to grow up with two women or two men or two women and a man, or two gender-identified men who are women.

Alice: Michael, that is exactly what I developed in the next half hour of that lecture topic, that the babies have to be produced biologically.

Walter: But it is not true that it has to be heterosexual.

Bea: It is not the privileging of everybody. It is a separate issue.

Alice: It may not be true among the richest classes of the first world nations, but it's basically true. It is built into all human societies that have survived. What I am trying to do in an introductory anthropology course, or do anywhere, is to get people to realize our biological nature as mammals sets patterns, constraints, and demands that must be recognized, then go on.

Sue-Ellen: There is no question about it, it is also the very argument that the fundamentalists use. While I would love for us, as a group, to be able to take on efforts to mediate disagreements about how we use evidence of cultural diversity in the face of biological imperatives, we have, unfortunately, run out of time.

Contributors

Anguksuar [Richard LaFortune] (Yup'ik) has published articles in community and mental health newsletters; he is also a mask carver, poet, storyteller, and advocate for HIV/AIDS programs.

Evelyn Blackwood, assistant professor of anthropology, Purdue University, in 1985 published the first refereed journal article on female "berdaches" ("Sexuality and Gender in Certain Native American Tribes: The Case of the Cross-Gender Females") in *Signs*. She has subsequently published numerous other articles and an edited volume on same-sex sexualities cross-culturally.

Jason Cromwell, Seattle, Washington, conducts research on transgendered people in the United States. Several of his articles have been published, and others are in press. His dissertation is entitled "Making the Visible Invisible: Constructions of Bodies, Genders, and Sexualities by and about Female-to-Male Transgendered People" (University of Washington, 1996).

Carolyn Epple, Navajo Community College, has written a dissertation entitled "Inseparable and Distinct: An Understanding of Navajo *Nádleehí* in a Traditional Navajo Worldview" (Northwestern University, 1995).

Claire R. Farrer, professor of anthropology, California State University, Chico, is author of *Living Life's Circle: Mescalero Apache Cosmovision* (1991), *Mescalero Apache Ethnoastronomy: Problems and Praxis* (in press), and numerous articles in journals and edited collections.

Jean-Guy A. Goulet, associate professor of anthropology, University of Calgary, has had work on the Dene Tha of northwestern Alberta published widely in refereed journals and edited collections. He (with David Young) is coeditor of and a contributor to *Being Changed by Cross-Cultural Encounters* (1994).

Clyde M. Hall (Lemhi Shoshoni), a former tribal judge and a practicing attorney, lectures widely on traditional Shoshoni and Bannock cultures. One of his articles appeared in the first anthology of Gay American Indian writings, *Living the Spirit* (1988).

Gilbert Herdt, professor of psychology and member of the Committee on Human Development at the University of Chicago, is known internationally for his work on human sexuality. His edited collection *Third Sex, Third Gender* appeared in 1994.

Carrie House (Navajo and Oneida, born of Towering Rock House Clan and born for Turtle Clan) freelances in film and video production. She is also a cultural and environmental conservator, a poet, and a "hotshot" firefighter.

Sue-Ellen Jacobs, professor of women studies and adjunct professor of anthropology and music, University of Washington, has published articles in journals and is coauthor of *Winds of Change: Women in Northwest Commercial Fishing* (1989) and other volumes.

Alice Kehoe, professor of anthropology, Marquette University, is author of *North American Indians: A Comprehensive Account* (1981, revised 1992), *The Ghost Dance Religion,* and numerous journal articles.

Lee M. Kochems, New York City Department of Mental Health, is coauthor (with Charles Callender) of a key *Current Anthropology* article on Native American gender variance: "The North American 'Berdache.'"

Sabine Lang, Hamburg, Germany, has written numerous articles in German and English on Native American gender variance and sexuality. Her dissertation, published in German as *Männer als frauen—Frauer als männer: Geschlechtsrollenwechsel bei den Indianern Nordamerikas* (1990), is to be published in English.

Beverly Little Thunder (Standing Rock Lakota), is a two-spirit womyn, public health worker, and advocate for Native women's issues. She is also a mother of five, a grandmother to four, an activist since birth, and dedicated to fight for social change.

Beatrice Medicine (Standing Rock Lakota), associate professor emeritus of anthropology, California State University, Northridge, is the author of numerous articles and coeditor of *The Hidden Half: The Lives of Plains Indian Women* (1983).

Arnold R. Pilling (1926-94), formerly a professor of anthropology, Wayne State University, is internationally known for his innovative research with the Tiwi of Australia and Indians of northern California. He cofounded the Society of Lesbian and Gay Anthropologists.

Michael Red Earth (Sisseton Dakota and Polish), writer, poet, graphic artist, playwright, and performer, is a frequent speaker at two-spirit gatherings and other settings in the United States.

Doyle V. Robertson (Sisseton/Wahpeton Dakota and Scot) has, with his partner Greg Jeresek, produced documentary videos on two-spirit lives; he is a frequent speaker at two-spirit gatherings in the United States and Canada.

Terry Tafoya (Taos/Warm Springs) is a mental health consultant and author of numerous articles concerned with Native American mental health, education, cultural studies, and storytelling. He provides AIDS information and support training to diverse groups in Native and non-Native communities.

Wesley Thomas (Navajo, born of Salt Clan and born for Edge of Water Clan), University of Washington, is a regular consultant on traditional Navajo cultural elements, a frequent guest lecturer in academic and nonacademic settings in the United States and abroad and in Native and non-Native communities, a consultant to the National Museum of the American Indian, and a poet and weaver.

Index